Foundations of Social Cognition

A Festschrift in Honor of Robert S. Wyer, Jr.

Foundations of Social Cognition

A Festschrift in Honor of Robert S. Wyer, Jr.

Edited by

Galen V. Bodenhausen
Northwestern University

Alan J. Lambert
Washington University

LAWRENCE ERLBAUM ASSOCIATES, PUBLISHERS
2003   Mahwah, New Jersey   London

Lawrence Erlbaum Associates, Inc., Publishers
10 Industrial Avenue
Mahwah, NJ 07430

Cover design by Kathryn Houghtaling Lacey

Library of Congress Cataloging-in-Publication Data

Foundations of social cognition : a festschrift in honor of Robert S.
Wyer, Jr. / edited by Galen V. Bodenhausen, Alan J. Lambert.
p. cm.
Includes bibliographical references and index.
ISBN 0-8058-4132-6 (alk. paper)
1. Social perception. I. Wyer, Robert S. II. Bodenhausen, Galen
V. (Galen Von), 1961– III. Lambert, Alan J.

BF323.S63F68 2003
302'.12—dc21   2003044837
                                                CIP

Books published by Lawrence Erlbaum Associates are printed on acid-
free paper, and their bindings are chosen for strength and durability.

Printed in the United States of America
10 9 8 7 6 5 4 3 2 1

CONTENTS

III   Motivational Contexts of Social Cognition

CONTRIBUTORS

Cameron Anderson
Dept. of Management and Organizations
Kellogg Graduate School of Management
Jacobs Center
Evanston, IL 60208

Herbert Bless
Sozialpsychologie
Fakultät für Sozialwissenschaften
Universität Mannheim
D-68131 Mannheim Germany

Galen V. Bodenhausen
Department of Psychology
Northwestern University
2029 Sheridan Road
Evanston, IL 60208-2710

Donal E. Carlson
Department of Psychological Sciences
Purdue University
West Lafayette, IN 47907-1364

Alison Chasteen
Department of Psychology
University of Toronto
100 St. George Street
Toronto, Ontario M5S 3G3 Canada

Deborah A. Greenspan
Graduate School of Business
Stanford University
518 Memorial Way
Stanford, CA 94304

David L. Hamilton
Department of Psychology
University of California at Santa Barbara
Santa Barbara, CA 93106-9660

E. Tory Higgins
Department of Psychology
Columbia University
1190 Amsterdam Avenue, MC 5501
New York, NY 10027-5501

Kurt Hugenberg
Department of Psychology
Northwestern University
2029 Sheridan Road
Evanston, IL 60208-2710

Amy L. Johnson
Department of Psychology
Indiana University
1101 E. 10th Street
Bloomington, IN 47405-7007

Leonel Garcia-Marques
Faculty of Psychology and Education Sciences
University of Lisbon
P-1600 Lisboa Portugal

Alan J. Lambert
Department of Psychology
Washington University
Campus Box 1125
St. Louis, MO 63130-4899

C. Neil Macrae
Department of Psychological
& Brain Sciences
Dartmouth College
Hanover, NH 03755

Lynda Mae
Department of Psychology
University of Southern Mississippi
Hattiesburg, MS 39406

William J. McGuire
Department of Psychology
Yale University
PO Box 208205
New Haven, CT 06520-8205

Daniel C. Molden
Department of Psychology
Columbia University
1190 Amsterdam Avenue, MC 5501
New York, NY 10027-5501

Thomas Mussweiler
Psychologie II
Universität Würzburg
Röntgenring 10
D-97070 Würzburg Germany

B. Keith Payne
Department of Psychology
Ohio State University
1885 Neil Avenue
Columbus, OH 43210-1222

Dacher Keltner
Department of Psychology
University of California
3210 Tolman Hall #1650
Berkeley, CA 94720-1650

Norbert Schwarz
Institute for Social Research
University of Michigan
PO Box 1248
Ann Arbor, MI 48106-1248

Steven J. Sherman
Department of Psychology
Indiana University
1101 E. 10th Street
Bloomington, IN47405-7007

Fritz Strack
Psychologie II
Universität Würzburg
Röntgenring 10
D-97070 Würzburg Germany

Michaela Wänke
Institut für Psychologie
Bernoullistraße 16
CH-4056 Basel Switzerland

Piotr Winkielman
Department of Psychology
University of Denver
2155 S. Race Street
Denver, CO 80208

Natalie Wyer
Social Psychology Department
Free University of Amsterdam
van der Boechorststraat 1
1081 BT Amsterdam, The Netherlands

1

Foundations of Social Cognition: An Introduction

Galen V. Bodenhausen
Northwestern University

Alan J. Lambert
Washington University

In their zeal to banish mentalistic theorizing from psychology, radical be-haviorists encountered considerable resistance from social psychologists. Although entirely sympathetic to the behaviorists' claim that external, situational forces exert powerful effects on behavior, social psychologists obstinately insisted that these effects are mediated by mental processes such as subjective construals arising in the mind of the actor. The funda-mental problem with this stance, as these behaviorists were quick to point out, is that it is all too easy to speculate about such processes, but a much

1

more difficult proposition to observe and document them with any kind of scientific rigor or precision. The field of social cognition arose in the 1970s as a response to the inadequacy of previous attempts to rise to this challenge in the domain of social psychological theory and research. Rather than concede that the mind must forever remain a murky and theoretically irrelevant black box, social cognition researchers sought to specify the cognitive structures and processes that putatively shape our understanding of social situations and that mediate our reactions to them. After 25 years of intensive scholarship, the fruitfulness of this endeavor is readily evident. And at the center of these accomplishments is the guiding influence of Robert S. Wyer, Jr. No one has done more to establish and popularize the social cognition perspective than Bob Wyer. This volume is a tribute to his remarkable contributions.

BOB WYER: A BRIEF BIOGRAPHY

It was a somewhat circuitous path that led Bob Wyer to the field of social psychology. Raised in upstate New York, he initially studied engineering at Rensselaer Polytechnic and after graduation, took a job at Bell Labs. Eventually, worried that he might have missed out on a classic liberal arts education, he decided to return to school (at the University of Colorado) for graduate study. He selected Psychology as his specialty field. Working with O. J. Harvey and William Scott, he began to investigate questions of cognitive organization and social information processing, establishing the themes that have guided his scholarship throughout his career. On completion of his doctoral studies, Wyer held academic appointments at the University of Iowa and the University of Illinois at Chicago Circle. In his earliest work, he investigated a range of fundamental questions about the nature of social beliefs, attitudes, and judgment. He developed a comprehensive view of the cognitive bases of judgment and inference in his first major book, *Cognitive Organization and Change: An Information Processing Approach* (published by Lawrence Erlbaum Associates in 1974). It was around this time that he moved to the University of Illinois at Urbana–Champaign, where he spent the next several decades of his research career. During that time, he began to develop a full-fledged social-cognitive perspective on topics such as attitudes, attribution, and impression formation, and he established himself as one of the most phenomenally prolific scholars in the history of social psychology. His rate of publication in the top journal of the field, the *Journal of Personality and Social Psychology*, is without peer, and his major theoretical contributions (in numerous *Psychological Review* papers as well as three major books) have provided conceptual syntheses of these extensive empirical investigations. These works identified and clarified most of the major issues facing social cognition research.

In addition to pursuing his own ambitious research agenda, Wyer devoted extensive amounts of time and energy in service to other scholars. As Editor of the *Journal of Experimental Social Psychology*, he was legendary for his rapid and painstakingly detailed feedback to the authors of submitted manuscripts. He also edited two of the most important scholarly outlets for integrative summaries of the progress made by social cognition researchers: the *Handbook of Social Cognition* (1984; 1994) and the ongoing *Advances in Social Cognition* series. To his dozens of graduate students, postdoctoral advisees, and faculty colleagues, Wyer is best known as an indefatigable source of feedback, advice, support, and encouragement.

Officially retired since 1995, Wyer continues to be more active than most scholars who are half his age. Since 1998, has been a Visiting Professor at the Hong Kong University of Science and Technology, and he has recently assumed the editorship of the *Journal of Consumer Psychology*. Largely because those who know Wyer can never think of him as retired, it was not until five years after his official retirement from the University of Illinois that a Festschrift Conference was held in Urbana honoring and celebrating his diverse contributions to the field of social cognition. This volume emerged from this joyous occasion.

ORGANIZATION OF THE BOOK

The topics covered in this volume address the gamut of theoretical concerns that have been central in social cognition research since the 1980s. In chapter 2, Bill McGuire provides an account of the initial emergence of the social cognition perspective from earlier research on attitude change. As he documents, Wyer played a key role in effecting this transition and thereby establishing what has become perhaps the most important and influential metatheoretical orientation of the field in the past 25 years. Each subsequent chapter covers a fundamental set of issues that has preoccupied the field's interest during this period.

The first section covers the fundamental elements of social-cognitive theorizing that have far-reaching implications for all aspects of social thought and action. Wyer's work strongly emphasized the central role played by expectancies in organizing judgment and memory processes. In chapter 3, Dave Hamilton and Leonel Garcia-Marques summarize and integrate the literature on expectancy effects, providing an elegant model to account for disparate findings emerging from prominent experimental paradigms. In chapter 4, Norbert Schwarz, Herbert Bless, Michaela Wänke, and Piotr Winkielman take up another fundamental topic that has long been associated with Bob Wyer: construct accessibility. In a well-known series of studies with Thom Srull, Wyer investigated how manipulating the accessibility of particular concepts might influence the impressions that people form of ostensibly unrelated stimuli. Schwarz and colleagues review the assumptions underlying this early work and show how subsequent research led to the development of a rich picture of how accessible concepts, and the subjective experience of conceptual fluency, influence judgment processes. Fritz Strack and Thomas Mussweiler, in chapter 5, next examine the role of selective accessibility of judgment-relevant information in the specific case of anchoring bias. Their impressive research program exemplifies the intellectual gains that can emerge when researchers seek out the psychological mechanisms underlying the mental biases long documented by judgment and decision-making researchers.

The second section of the book deals with the major substantive theme of Bob Wyer's research (and of social cognition research more generally); namely, the perception of persons and groups. In chapter 6, Donal Carlston and Lynda Mae examine the question of spontaneity in impression formation. Are there important differences in the impression formation process, depending upon whether perceivers are intentionally or only incidentally pursuing an impression formation goal? Carlston and Mae review prior work on incidental forms of impression formation, and they present an exciting new experimental technique for investigating spontaneous social impressions. Galen Bodenhausen, Neil Macrae, and Kurt Hugenberg then address the question of how impressions of the self and of other persons are influenced by stereotypes in chapter 7. Bodenhausen et al. argue that the stereotypes associated with various social identities can alternatively be activated or inhibited when we form impressions of individual group members, and they attempt to delineate the determinants and consequences of these differential reactions to possible bases for social stereotyping. The perception of groups per se is taken up by Jim Sherman and Amy Johnson in chapter 8. They review evidence suggesting that perceptions of groups vary as a function of structural properties of the relevant groups. Most notably, they examine how the concept of *entitativity* can account for differences in the way perceivers react to various kinds of aggregations of persons. In chapter 9, Alan Lambert, Alison Chasteen, and Keith Payne investigate the role of group-level prejudices in the impressions that are formed of individuals. Wyer has long been a strong advocate for the necessity of examining impression formation processes in contexts that permit the investigation of important naturalistic social factors (e.g., conversational pragmatics). Following this advice, Lambert and colleagues focus in particular on the role of the social context (specifically, private vs. public settings) in moderating the expression of prejudiced attitudes. Confirming the wisdom of Wyer's advice, they report some provocative and counterintuitive findings in this domain.

Another major theme of Bob Wyer's work has been the investigation of the affective and motivational context of social cognition. The contributors to the third section of the volume each examine how personal and social motives modulate fundamental aspects of social thought and conduct. In chapter 10, Tory Higgins and Dan Molden review the major themes of past research addressing the interface between cognition and motivation, and present a new approach to understanding how the perceiver's chronic or momentary motivational tendencies can influence their preferred strategies for making choices and their subsequent satisfaction. In chapter 11, Deb Gruenfeld, Dacher Keltner, and Cameron Anderson explore the linkages between social structure and motivation, specifically investigating how being in a position of power modulates the motivational and cognitive tendencies of the powerholder, thereby changing his or her behavior. The volume concludes with a contribution from the social psychologist who owes the most direct debt to Bob Wyer: his daughter Natalie Wyer. In chapter 12, she examines how the value orientations of perceivers define some of the most important parameters of social perception, and outlines how the value of egalitarianism is one motivational force that can and does exert considerable influence on intergroup perception. Each of these chapters confirms that the motivational context is an essential element of social cognition with far-ranging implications for how the social perceiver approaches the task of making judgments, forming impressions, or choosing behavioral responses.

Thus each contribution to this book addresses a major conceptual issue in the field of social cognition. Together, they present a state-of-the-art overview of the field as it currently stands. Our intellectual debts to Wyer are readily apparent as we reach an increasingly satisfying understanding of these concerns. Through his incredibly prolific research programs (yielding more than 140 publications), extensive editorial activities, and enormous impact on students, collaborators, and colleagues, Bob Wyer has truly established the foundations of social cognition.

2

The Morphing
of Attitude-Change
Into Social-Cognition
Research

William J. McGuire
Yale University

My being the oldest chapter writer in this book celebrating Robert S. Wyer's life and work so far gives me the inspiring opportunity of witnessing how social psychology progressed from here to there and of observing how much Bob's work contributed to that progress. His work is so high in quantity, quality, and variety that reviewing the long-term development of this one researcher reveals much of the evolution of the whole subdiscipline of cognitive social psychology. I describe how social psychology evolved from its mid-century focus on changing attitudes by persuasive communication to its end-of-century preoccupation with social cognition, including the content, structure, and functioning of thought systems.

Robert Wyer's contributions are so numerous and diverse that if I am to provide a broad perspective I must leave it for the contributors of other chapters to describe the context and evolution of specific lines of Bob's work. Diverse as they are, Bob's contributions exhibit the same strange neglect as do mine and as do the rest of this volume's contributors and indeed, most social psychologists; that is, we all study intrapersonal processes, and almost completely ignore interpersonal processes. Hence I shall devote most of this chapter to tracing what and how social psychologists have been studying about intrapersonal processes. This requires clarifying some complex processes involved in the morphing of earlier attitude-change into current social-cognition research. I shall begin tracing this background by concentrating on what I know best from having been in at its creation: particularly the Yale, Carl Hovland school of attitude change in fostering research on attitude change and social cognition. Two aspects of social psychological research that I particularly want to describe because they are so central to Wyer's work and my own are persuasion from within (as by Socratic questioning) and use of attitude change as a tool rather than as the topic for study in itself. To clarify how selective I am in focusing primarily on these two lines of work, I have listed in Table 2.1 several dozen additional rubrics under which Bob Wyer has made major research contributions.

SOCIAL PSYCHOLOGISTS' STRANGE NEGLECT OF INTERPERSONAL (GROUP) PROCESSES

I first locate Bob's contributions within social psychology by subtraction, pointing out the broad area neglected by Bob (and most of us), a neglect that ought to be corrected. A century-old mystery in experimental social psychology is why intrapersonal topics such as attitudes, stereotypes, and other cognitions have received so much more research attention than interpersonal and intergroup topics.

In sketching a history of social psychology in an article I wrote for the *European Journal of Social Psychology* (McGuire, 1986), I proposed that our subdiscipline was born around 1900, about a generation after the birth of psychology in general, the marker event for whose birth is often given as the 1879 founding of Wundt's Leipzig laboratory. The marker event for social psychology's birth can be given as the contemporaneous 1908 appearance of the first two English-language social-psychology textbooks (Ross, 1908; McDougall, 1908). Social emerged as a major subarea in psychology in the 1920s. Since then, social psychology has passed through five successive, overlapping hegemonies, as shown in Table 2.2. Of these five dominant eras from 1920 to 2000, only the 1935–1955 group-dynamics period was focused on interpersonal (group) topics. The other four eras were dominated by research on intrapersonal topics (attitude measurement, 1920–1940; attitude change, 1950–1970; social cognition, 1965–1985; and attitude systems, 1980 to 2000). This imbalance may be in the process of partial rectification: I conjectured (McGuire, 1986) that recent advances may indicate that in the 1995–2015 era social psychologists will refocus on interpersonal and intergroup processes for the first time since the 1935–1955 group-dynamics era.

That we social psychologists have concentrated on intrapersonal topics to the neglect of interpersonal and intergroup processes is paradoxical, con-

TABLE 2.1
Some Topics on Which Bob Wyer Has Made Major Research Contributions

Category Activation	Metacognition
Automaticity	Inhibition
Spontaneous vs. Deliberative Processing	Effects of Social Context
Pragmatics	Bin Models
Elaborative Processing	Implicational-Molecule Approaches
Entitivity	Subjective Experience
Humor Elicitation	Cognitive Organization
Semantics	Social Information
Comprehension and Verification	Attitude Change
Decision Making	Social Influence
Spontaneous Activation of Thoughts	Inference
Academic Achievement	Reasoning
Storage of Self-knowledge	Categorical Versus Conditional Beliefs
Goal Effects	Persuasion
Self-regulation	Person and Group Perception
Information Processing	Nonverbal Cues
Differentiation	Role Playing
Integration	Induction and Deduction
Subjective Expected Utility	Remote Cognitive Effects

sidering that our distinguishing "social" adjective connotes the interpersonal. A least-effort explanation for this paradoxical imbalance is that it is sufficiently hard to predict the thoughts, feelings, and actions of an individual; it becomes exponentially more difficult to predict what thoughts, feelings, and actions will emerge from these multiple individuals in an interacting group, as in Reid Hastie's (1993) demanding studies of jury deci-

Table 2.2
Successive Hegemoines in Social Psychology, 1920–2015

Years	Focus	Major Contributors
1920s and 1930s	Attitude-measurement era	L. L. Thurstone; R. Likert; E. S. Bogardus
1935–1955	Group-dynamics era	K. Lewin; T. M. Newcomb; M. Sherif
1950s and 1960s	Attitude-change era	C. I. Hovland; L. Festinger; W. J. McGuire
1965–1985	Social-cognition era	E. E. Jones; R. S. Wyer, Jr.; E.T. Higgins
1980s and 1990s	Attitude-systems era	A. H. Eagly; R. E. Nisbett; R. C. Petty
1995–2015	Interpersonal and intergroup era	M. Banaji; R. Hastie; D. M. Buss

sion making. For whatever reason, Bob Wyer, like the other chapter writers here, and most social psychologists since midcentury, have studied almost exclusively intrapersonal processes (attitudes, cognitions, memories, beliefs, etc.) and neglected interpersonal and intergroup processes.

INTRAPERSONAL PROCESSES: SOME CLARIFYING DISTINCTIONS REGARDING SOCIAL COGNITION

Adhering to this long tradition, this chapter concentrates on these intrapersonal processes on which social psychological research has usually focused. Among the successive hegemonies listed in Table 2.2, I do not insist upon the exact dates of the emergence and decline of the social cognition movement with which Bob Wyer is particularly identified as founding father and heroic contributor. However, I discuss two clarifying distinctions: (a) the difference between attitude change and social cognition topics and (b) the difference between social cognition and cognition without the "social" adjective.

Attitude Change Versus Social Cognition

In defining and distinguishing "attitudes" and similar constructs, Donald T. Campbell (1963) advocated employing the generic term of "(acquired) behavioral predisposition" that would characterize many response-directing processes distinctively labeled as attitude, motive, belief, value, drive, set, representations, Einstellung, determinierende Tendenz, etc. Such behavioral predispositions have a common function of channeling the person's responses into one versus other directions. Attitude change involves using some procedure (e.g., persuasive communications, modeling, etc.) to induce a change in the direction of a person's thought, feeling, or action responses, redirecting them at a new target or into a new path.

Attitudes function by directing responses but cognitions and related terms (beliefs, memories, etc.) function by selective perception, involving transformations of the known into knowledge, thus playing a stimulus function whereas attitudes play a response function. Both response-directing attitudes and stimulus-selecting cognitions help the person cope selectively with the overwhelmingly numerous options offered by the environment. Cognitions help coping with an overload of stimulus information; attitudes help select from among an excess of available response directions.

In regard to cognitions, I argued (McGuire, 1989) that knowledge representations are necessarily misrepresentations, triply distorting the known by under-, over-, and mal-representing it. Much cognition research is designed to identify these knowledge misrepresentations of the stimulus to facilitate understanding the misrepresentation and bringing the cognition into closer correspondence with the known. Bob Wyer and contributors of other chapters in this book have studied cognitions (i.e., transforming stimulus representations) more than attitudes (i.e., directive response predispositions) whereas I, because of my earlier start, have worked relatively more on attitude change than on cognitive representation.

Cognition Versus Social Cognition

A second ambiguity-reducing distinction involves the widespread use of the adjective "social." When social psychologists talk of social cognition, social inference, social representations, and so on, what does the "social" add to or subtract from the unmodified noun? Is Bob Wyer a cognitive psychologist or a cognitive social psychologist?

I argued (McGuire, 1986) that "social" is used ambiguously, going off in diverse directions to refer to at least a half-dozen distinguishing characteristics as sketched in Table 2.3, some of the distinctions being unrelated or even contradictory to others.

1.   The most obvious meaning is that processes such as cognitions, attitudes, decisions, and so forth are social to the extent that they focus on social content (e.g., cognitions of persons, of human institutions, of interpersonal relations, etc.).

TABLE 2.3
Variant Meanings of "Social" in "Social Cognition"

1. For cognitions representing social (human) realities

2. For cognitions shared (held in common) by members of the society

3. For cognitions acquired in interactions with other persons

4. For conscious, communicable cognitions

5. For cognitions upholding the Establishment status quo

6. For cognitions embodied in supra-individual aspects

2. Other theorists regard cognitions as "social" to the extent that they are shared by members of a society.

3. A third usage is to reserve "social" for cognitions that are acquired during interactions with other persons (rather than those derived from genes or personal experience).

4. Occasionally "social" is restricted to accessible cognitions, phenomenally retrievable by self and communicable to others, as distinct from "unconscious" cognitions.

5. A rarer usage is to limit "social" to conventional cognitions (e.g., stereotypes) that justify the Establishment status quo (as contrasted to antisocial, disruptive, or selfish cognitions).

6. Another usage is to call a cognition "social" to the extent it is embodied, not just in individual heads but also in transcendental aspects of the culture, such as language structures or human institutions.

Each of these meanings of "social" is reasonable in itself, but failure to make explicit which distinction one is making in a given usage can result in serious misunderstanding because some criteria are independent of and even antithetical to others. Content criteria (like 1) of what is "social" may be orthogonal to etiology criteria (like 3). Whether a cognition is "social" in being widely shared (like 2) may be negatively related to 3, its being "social" by having been acquired in interactions with other people (rather than deriving from species-wide genetic makeup). Furthermore, distinguishing some cognitions as "social" risks violating the parsimony principle, "No distinction unless it makes a difference." If one insists on speaking of "social" cognitions one must show that, however defined, they relate to interesting third variables differently from how "nonsocial" cognitions relate.

THE ATTITUDE-CHANGE RESEARCH
THAT EVOLVED INTO SOCIAL-COGNITION

Timing is everything. Bob Wyer is at least a half-generation younger than I am in both biological and PhD age, a time gap that made a substantial difference. Bob (and most other social cognition pioneers contributing chapters to this Festschrift) entered social psychology after 1970 without serving an appreciable attitude-change apprenticeship. In the first 10 years of Bob Wyer's intimidating volume of publishing, the word "attitude" appears in the title of only one or two of his articles, whereas among my contemporaries a dozen years earlier "attitudes" had been ubiquitous in our titles. It was a slightly different experience to enter the social-cognition era after having already been part of an attitude-change hegemony. That transitional experience gives me some insight about where Bob and other cognitive-social pioneers were coming from after the decline and fall of the attitude-change movement.

Attitude Change and Carl I. Hovland in War and Peace

The origins of the attitude-change flourishing in midcentury social psychology are remarkably focused and identifiable. Like many momentous innovations in science and society it was the fruit of war, the 1937–1945 global war. The U.S. Army published its World War II social-science research in the four "American Soldier" volumes, the third of which (Hovland, Lumsdaine, & Sheffield, 1949) reported the studies that inaugurated the attitude-change era.

Most social psychologists carried out or directed wartime research in the U.S. Army as commissioned officers (e.g., Stuart Cook, M. Brewster Smith) but others such as Hovland and his attitude-change colleagues (e.g., F. D. Sheffield, I. L. Janis), were civilians attached to the Army and given simulated ranks when needed for protocol or practical purposes. I too served in the U.S. Army during the Great Patriotic War but, being 15 years younger than these professionals, I volunteered for the Army as a 17-year-old high school graduate and served as a tank gunner. As a soldier I had a lot of attitudes but I never studied one.

Before The War. Hovland had done a human-learning dissertation at Yale for his 1936 PhD with the behaviorist Clark Hull. With a reverse symmetry, Hull's research switched from social influence (hypnosis) to learning theory and

Hovland's from learning theory to social influence (persuasive communication). Their common learning-theory background explains the oddity that Hull and Hovland each conceptualized social influence as a passive process. They depicted persuasion as teaching the person to carry out the hypnotist's suggestions or to use the source's persuasive arguments for guidance in how to adjust their attitudes. The layperson may regard social influence as a dynamic, motivated process but Hull, Hovland, and others in their behavioristic tradition regard it as a passive absorption of external information.

This is the Army, Mr. Hovland.   Hovland's sudden switch from being the world's greatest authority on human learning (Hovland, 1951) to being the world's premier attitude-change maven (Hovland, 1954) was a case of academics' felt obligation to play Dr. Win-the-War roles in the military in the 1940s. Hovland became director of the experimental unit (as distinct from the survey unit) of the Morale Division (also known as the Information and Education Division) of the U.S. Department of War (no euphemistic "Department of Defense" in those days). This Morale Division's mission was, with a minimum of equivocation and euphemism, to promote the soldier's desire to kill and be killed with zest. Grim words. They make one wince but should we have stayed home? In the historical process there may come moments when one must shout the big NO, and interpose oneself with deadly force between evil and its victims and say, "No! Not here. Not there. Not anywhere."

Hovland's unit worked under the major methodological handicap of not being able to make up its own persuasive communications; rather it had to use the propaganda "Why We Fight" films ("The Nazis Strike," "The Battle of Britain," etc.) already produced by Frank Capra for the Morale Division. Despite this limitation on how much independent-variable manipulation they were permitted, Hovland's unit did interesting work on such topics as temporal persistence of induced attitude change (the sleeper effect) and effects of one- versus two-sided presentation (Hovland, Lumsdaine, & Sheffield, 1949). They measured how these independent variables affected the films' success in changing attitudes on issues such as whether our British and Soviet allies were doing their share.

The Conquering Heroes Return to Yale.   Hovland returned to Yale at war's end as a recognized leader in psychology, bringing with him a group of his Army colleagues (e.g., F. D. Sheffield and I. L. Janis). At Yale they continued the persuasive communication, attitude-change research begun in the Army Morale Division, with the advantage that in civilian life they were able to construct their own communications, allowing manipulation in efficient experimental designs of theory-relevant independent variables. However, they lost the convenience of immense Army subject pools. They continued analyses of the Army data while collecting new data on emerging issues.

Show Me the Money

Hovland as Fund Raiser.   Hovland was still a young man of 34 when he returned to Yale from the War Department (though there remained scarcely 15 years before he died of leukemia). Government funding agencies for basic research, such as NSF, did not yet exist but Hovland had a rare talent for obtaining research funds from private foundations and corporations (e.g., the Rockefeller Foundation, Bell Labs, and General Electric). The amounts awarded were modest by present standards, but in those days researchers were good at making do with less. Hovland was generous in sharing the funds he raised with younger colleagues in the Yale Attitude Change project and elsewhere.

The Birth of Federal Government Funding For Behavioral Research. Until midcentury, research funding in the U.S. was pitifully meager, went hardly at all to the social and behavioral sciences, came largely from private rather than governmental sources, and went for applied mission-oriented rather than basic theory-oriented research. Lazarsfeld and his colleagues at Columbia University "moonlighted" by financing their study of the persuasiveness of the 1940 Roosevelt-vs-Wilkie presidential campaign by diverting research funds from a grant awarded to develop designed ads to sell refrigerators (Lazarsfeld, Berelson, & Gaudet, 1944). However, some influential U.S. civilian and military officials emerged from the 1941–45 war convinced that federal government financing of scientific research was needed and would be effective. Their evidence for efficacy was the obvious research-achieved advances during the war in military materiel and processes (radar, rocketry, DDT, antibiotics, and, most obviously, atom bombs). Motivations for continuing such advances were to win the Cold War with the Soviet Union and perhaps to avoid the economy's relapsing into a Depression such as that of the 1930s. At first, funding to support basic research in academia was hidden in the military budget, particularly through the Office of Naval Research, until the support moved above-board with the establishment around 1950 of the National Science Foundation.

All of the chapter writers in this volume have received research funds largely from federal government agencies, primarily NSF and NIH, and largely for basic research. The National Science Foundation funded basic research in the physical and biological sciences beginning about 1950, and in the social and behavioral sciences beginning about 1958. In the following year, 1959, I stood in the doorway of the modest NSF social science office, begging bowl in hand, and I came back for more support from NSF for the next 20 consecutive years, which I followed by another 20 uninterrupted years of eating, this time at the NIMH trough when the latter agency began, in about 1980, to allow one to present a larger begging bowl.

Funding From Private Foundations.

Nongovernmental funding sources might have developed had Hovland lived beyond the 1950s. From his 1934–1936 doctoral-student years at Yale until his death in 1961, Hovland had the Midas touch for getting research support. I doubt however, that he ever received appreciable governmental funding (except, of course, for the 1942–1945 war years when he was a Dr. Win-the-War civilian on the Army payroll). His human-learning research at the Yale Institute of Human Relations before the war and his Yale Program in Communication and Attitude Change after the war were funded mostly by the Rockefeller Foundation at levels rare in those years.

In-house Basic Research in Private Corporations: A Road Not Taken

Hovland pursued another opening to the private sector that involved a source of financial support for basic research that was even more novel than getting grants from private foundations such as Rockefeller, Ford, and Russell Sage (on whose boards Hovland served). He experimented in the 1950s with setting up basic behavioral research laboratories within U.S. corporations, particularly in Bell Labs and GE. Bell Labs had a long tradition of supporting in-house basic research in the physical sciences, taking in stride both successes (e.g., the transistor, cryptography) and failures (weather modification). Claude Shannon's (Shannon and Weaver, 1949) mathematical communication theory, developed at Bell Labs in the 1930s and popularized by Warren Weaver of the Rockefeller Foundation, had obvious behavioral science (including attitude change) relevance. In the 1950s Hovland guided Bell Lab's expansion into psychology. He also set up a smaller social science unit in General Electric, another corporation with a tradition of supporting in-house basic research. Later, Leon Festinger assumed the lead in staffing and guiding this GE unit. Getting the private sector to set up basic research laboratories alongside university and governmental laboratories, a process advanced by Hovland particularly at Bell Labs, was a success initially but ultimately lost momentum as an organizational model for several reasons, including Hovland's early death.

Where Hovland's funding efforts in the private sector did have a lasting effect pertinent to the social cognition movement was in the kind of work that he promoted at Bell Labs and Yale in his final 1950s decade. Hovland drifted away from attitude-change research in favor of work on topics such as concept attainment, positive and negative instances, assimilation and contrast in social perception, computer simulation, etc. This work led directly, independently of his attitude-change contributions, to the cognitive revolution. Three accounts have been written recently of Hovland's roles in shaping modern social and cognitive psychology (Rogers, 1994; McGuire, 1996; Shepard, 1997).

MCGUIRE'S AND WYER'S ROUTES FROM ATTITUDE CHANGE TO SOCIAL COGNITION

During the mid- and late–1950s Hovland, although dying of cancer, was engaged in encouraging private-sector laboratories to foster basic research (ultimately unsuccessful) and in doing research there on topics such as concept attainment and computer simulation of cognition (ultimately successful as an impetus to the cognitive social revolution). Where were I and Bob Wyer then? I was back at Yale, 1956–1959, serving the second of my three terms after having first obtained in 1954 a doctorate at Yale in human learning with Hovland as my mentor, after which I had gone to the University of Minnesota Laboratory for Research in Social Relations as Leon Festinger's first postdoc. Because of these personal ties, I was at least a peripheral player in these activities, interacting at Bell Labs and Yale with the Hovland group and at GE and Minnesota with the Festingerians during those late 1950s.

And where was Bob Wyer in those years? One might reasonably guess that Bob was still a youngster, riding a skateboard somewhere. How wrong this guess would be. Bob Wyer was then working at the same corporations: at GE in 1955–56 and at Bell Labs in 1957–1959. Both of these private-sector appointments were probably related to Bob's pre-psychology career in electrical engineering, and he was at GE and Bell Lab locations far removed from those where Hovland was promoting social psychology. Still, I am tempted to ask Bob if, back in those 1950s pocket-protector days, he ever noticed (say, in the Corporation dining room) groups of social psychologists wearing lampshades or other funny hats, loudly discussing the cognitive social revolution?

My Cognitive-Consistency Model and its Use of Attitude Change as a Tool

The main tradition of attitude-change research, from Hovland (1954) to the present (Petty & Wegener, 1998; Eagly & Chaiken, 1993, 1998), emphasizes a passive view of the person that is out of keeping with the more active, transformational view at the heart of the cognitive revolution. My own graduate student research (reported in Festinger, 1957 and McGuire, 1960a, 1960b, 1960c), based on an active concept of attitude change, used attitude change as a means rather than as an end; specifically, as a means for studying human cognition rather than for studying attitude change itself. The same can be said for Bob Wyer's early contributions (Wyer & Goldberg, 1970).

During my early years in psychology I was known, if at all, as an attitude-change researcher. This is misleading because I was interested in attitude change more as a means than as an end, mainly as it involved a peculiar persuasion-from-within kind of attitude change. My Jesuit college

(Fordham) Aristotelian-Thomistic philosophy courses had aroused my interest in how closely formal logics (such as Aristotelian syllogistic reasoning, symbolic logic, Boolean algebra, etc.) corresponded with actual human reasoning. Were these formal logics descriptive (and so of interest to psychologists) or merely prescriptive (and so interesting only to philosophers)? The 1930s Depression-years studies at Columbia University (Woodworth & Sells, 1935) of systematic reasoning errors (now "heuristics") in people's judgment of the validity of syllogistic arguments challenged me to "save" human rationality. For example, I hypothesized that logic-psychologic discrepancies might be due to flaws in formal logic rather than in faulty human reasoning. Following Aristotle, formal logicians typically use a two-value (true/false) judged truth scale; but I conjectured that people use a more empirically valid multivalued quasi-probability scale in judging the truth of propositions. If so, then syllogisms that are invalid when a two-valued truth scale is imposed for judging each proposition may often be valid when the thinker is using a probabilistic truth scale. Because of this probabilistic scaling refinement, my model of cognitive systems is often called "probabilogical theory." If it is implausible that human thinkers use a continuous probability scale for desirability, then they may use at least a multi(seven?)-level scale (e.g., with gradations of worst, worse, bad, neutral, good, better, best).

My model includes additional refinements such as postulating that people's cognitive systems are organized to maximize hedonic consistency (agreement between likelihood and desirability judgments on a given proposition) as well as logical consistency (consistency among the judged likelihoods or desirabilities of multiple logically related propositions). In the mid-twentieth-century behavioristic culture I was taking an aberrant position, especially at operationalist Yale, in theorizing that people have cognitions (conscious thoughts) and organize them into congruent (i.e., connected and consistent) systems.

In my first year in Yale's doctoral program in 1951 I took a physiological psychology course whose instructor, Frank Beach, described how organization of the central nervous system is studied by introducing an electrical stimulation or a lesion at a localized point in the spinal cord or brain and tracking how these induced disturbances spread to other cells in the neural system. This suggested to me the analogy that one could study the organization of thought systems by directly introducing a localized change on one judgment in a person's thought system and then tracking the remote ramifications of this induced change in the form of changes of likelihood or desirability judgments on other, unmentioned but psychologically related, propositions in the thought system. For the next two years as a psychology PhD candidate at Yale I assembled sets of psychologically related propositions, introduced a change in the person's likelihood or desirability judgment on one proposition in a set (e.g., by presenting discrepant expert norms on the propositional judgments), and then predicted and measured how this change had remote ramifications on the person's desirability and likelihood judgments on unmentioned but psychologically related propositions.

Four Lines of Empirical Implications of the Probabilogical Model

Table 2.4 shows four types of empirical predictions derived from the probabilogical cognitive-consistency theory.

1. A first type of predictions deals with how relations among one's desirability and likelihood judgments on a set of psychologically related cognitions (judgments) at a given point in time are in accord with one's theory of cognitive consistency, and especially when, how, and why this momentary internal structure of the cognitive system deviates from formal logic.

2. A second type of empirical implications deals with persuasion from within; that is, with how desirability or likelihood judgments on propositions can be changed without introducing any new information via a persuasive communication from an outside source, but simply by making more salient (available, retrievable) information already in the person's cognitive system. This salience can be manipulated by Socratic questioning or by directed-thinking tasks that make salient a biased sample of the person's cognitions. In contrast to the Yale school's passive conception of attitude change as the absorbing of new information in a message from an outside source, my more dynamic conception is of

TABLE 2.4

Four Lines of Empirical Research Emanating from My Probabilogical Cognitive-Consistency Model (See W. J. McGuire, 1981)

1. Consistency of likelihood and desirability judgments on related propositions at a given point in time

2. Persuasion from within by sensitizing the person (e.g., by Socratic questioning) to biased subsets of already-possessed information

3. Manipulating resistance to persuasion by sensitizing the person to selected cognitive linkages

4. Persuasive communications' remote ramifications on unmentioned but related beliefs

attitude change from within, by manipulating the salience of information already within the person's cognitive system.

3.   A third type of inference from my probabilogical theory predicts how the person's judgment can be made resistant to persuasion by prior sensitizing of the person to linked cognitions with which the person's judgment would become more inconsistent if he or she yielded to the persuasive communication. This line of work has been studied less than the other three. My well-known immunization research uses prior inoculation with a weakened form of the attacking material (McGuire, 1964) and so involves a resistence-conferring technique quite different from this probabilogics-linkage approach.

4.   A fourth, richest line of research provoked by my probabilogical theory deals with remote cognitive ramification of persuasive communications. The theory predicts that a persuasive communication from an external source will change the recipient's judgment, not only on propositions with which the communication explicitly deals, but also judgments on logically related propositions, even those not mentioned explicitly in the communication. By tracing the spread of changes to remote, linked propositions we can identify the organization of belief systems and their content, structure, and functioning. McGuire (1981, 1999) summarizes some of the work done in each of these four lines of research.

My calling this research "attitude change" stretches the term because it involves an unorthodox active persuasion from within and it uses attitude change, not as a topic for study in its own right but as a tool to study the content, structure, and functioning of cognitive systems. Nevertheless, my reputation for scholarship elicited numerous invitations to review the more orthodox attitude-change research for encyclopedia and handbook chapters (e.g., McGuire, 1966, 1968, 1969, 1973, 1974). In these reviews I dutifully described the field of attitude change as it existed, mainly involving passive attitude change by presenting new information from an outside source. This coverage of the field as it existed may understandably have produced the misperception that I was primarily interested in traditional attitude change per se.

Bob Wyer's Ascendance

Where does this leave us in the Hovland, McGuire, Wyer transition from attitude change to social cognition? Regarding Hovland's contribution, his wartime and 1940s Yale research on attitude change may have even slowed the cognitive revolution by his assumption that the person is a passive information-absorption target. In contrast, Hovland's 1950s Yale and Bell Labs cognitive studies (of concept attainment, computer simulation, etc.) did promote the cognitive revolution. My own attitude-change/cognitive-system research promoted the cognitive revolution by its more active thought-producing and organizing concept of the person. My approach used attitude change less as a topic of study in its own right than as a tool for studying cognitive systems: my agenda called for using attitude change as a way of inducing a localized belief change that could be tracked as it moved through the cognitive system. Our younger colleague, Bob Wyer, went directly into cognitive systems research in the 1970s using attitude change as a means rather than an end, both in the form of persuasion from within, as in the Socratic effect (Rosen & Wyer, 1972), and by presenting new information from an outside source and studying the remote ramifications on related but unmentioned segments of the cognitive system (Wyer & Goldberg, 1970). Both Bob Wyer and I were interested, not in how judgments (cognitions, attitudes) can be changed but in what their linked concurrent or sequential changes reveal about how these judgments are organized into functioning systems.

After my early 1950s work on this cognitive systems theory, mostly done as a graduate student, I put the topic on a back burner for three decades, from 1960 to 1990, when I focused instead on topics such as immunization against persuasion, personality and persuadability, anticipatory belief change, the self-concept, distinctiveness theory, and positivity asymmetries in thinking. I neglected the probabilistic cognitive systems model even though then and now I regard it as my most interesting contribution to the social cognition movement. My usual work style when I get interested in a topic is to do a half-dozen strategically organized (McGuire, 1989) empirical studies and one or two theoretical analyses and reviews, and then move on to other topics.

Also contributing to my switching my main research efforts away from this cognitive-systems theorizing was the publication from around 1970 of Bob Wyer's wonderful work using similar theorizing and methods. For example, Wyer and Goldberg (1970) developed a theory like mine and compared its predictive power to alternative cognitive-system theories such as Heider's (1958) and Abelson and Rosenberg's (1958). Another example is Rosen and Wyer's (1972) powerful studies on the Socratic-questioning effect. When I first reported the Socratic effect (McGuire, 1960c) I expected it to be a laboratory curiosity with small effect sizes but Wyer showed this effect to be robust. By the early 1970s it was evident to me that this work could be left in the powerful hands of Bob Wyer, who had already raised research in the area to a new level of sophistication as regards theoretical elegance, powerful methods, and efficiently designed programs of empirical studies. Many of the chapter authors in this book have had the similar experience of working on a topic only to find Bob Wyer doing work in advance of our own. How Bob has done so much, so well, on such a diversity of topics is a mystery to me. Perhaps other chapter writers here will let me in on Bob's secret of productivity while I am still young and can make good use of the information.

BOB WYER'S CONTRIBUTIONS BEYOND
HIS WELL-TEMPERED EXPERIMENTS

The Wyer basic-research productivity mystery (e.g., his publishing far more *Journal of Personality and Social Psychology* articles than any other researcher) deepens when we remember that Bob's achievements in raising the quality of published research have been manifested not only in his perfecting his own articles but also in his editorial work on other people's manuscripts. Again and again Bob has overpaid his dues by taking on formidable editorial tasks in books and journals. Many of us have received from Robert Wyer generous and valuable editorial critiques that deserved publication more than did our manuscripts that he was laboring to improve. Bob's term as editor of a journal is usually remembered as the journal's golden age. His sacrificing of his own work to help us with ours inspires and educates us to follow his example.

Bob's basic-research contributions in his own experiments and in editing ours, prodigious as they are, are not his only accomplishments that call for our admiration. Outside the scientific laboratory he put his efforts where his heart lay, striking blows for freedom in the civil rights movement, the anti-war movement, and the environmental movement. Even his recreations win our admiration, as typified in his months-long trek in remote jungles and rushing rivers in south Asia, living out of his 50-pound backpack. I raise my own worn walking stick to you, Bob Wyer, my walking stick that has recently held up my 75-year old body for 30 days across el Camino Francés de Santiago de Compostela, and which now I hold up in salute to you as you move ahead on less-traveled roads, where you dare to show us that we can trust the kindness of strangers.

Does this festive volume of tributes mark an end to the long era when we have counted on Bob Wyer's steady flow of innovative contributions? I do not believe it. John Wesley, after preaching 40,000 sermons, was chided when discovered working at his desk by the physician who had relegated him to his deathbed. Wesley asked, "Would you want the Lord to find me idle when He comes?" I keep the faith that this occasion marks a new beginning, a second spring, in which Bob Wyer will continue to work toward his 40,000th contribution, never idle as long as there are questions to answer or answers to question.

REFERENCES

Abelson, R. P., & Rosenberg, M. J. (1958). Symbolic psycho-logic: A model of attitude cognition. *Behavioral Science, 3,* 1–13.
Campbell, D. T. (1963). Social attitudes and other acquired behavioral dispositions. In S. Koch (Ed.), *Psychology: A study of a science* (Vol. 6, pp. 94–172). New York: McGraw-Hill.

Eagly, A. H., & Chaiken, S. (1993). *The psychology of attitudes.* Fort Worth, TX: Harcourt Brace Jovanovich.

Eagly, A. H., & Chaiken, S. (1998). Attitude structure and function. In D. T. Gilbert, S. T. Fiske, & G. Lindzey (Eds.), *Handbook of social psychology* (4th ed., Vol. 1, pp. 269–322). New York: McGraw-Hill.

Festinger, L. (1957). *A theory of cognitive dissonance.* Evanston, IL: Row, Peterson.

Hastie, R. (1993). (Ed.). *Inside the juror: The psychology of juror decision making.* NY: Cambridge University Press.

Heider, F. (1958). *The psychology of interpersonal relations.* New York: Wiley.

Hovland, C. I. (1951). Human learning and retention. In S. S. Stevens (Ed.), *Handbook of experimental psychology* (pp. 613–689). New York: Wiley.

Hovland, C. I. (1954). Effects of the mass media on communication. In G. Lindzey (Ed.), *Handbook of social psychology* (1st ed., Vol. 2, pp. 1062–1103). Cambridge, MA: Addison-Wesley.

Hovland, C. I., Lumsdaine, A. A., & Sheffield, F. D. (1949). *Experiments on mass communication.* Princeton, NJ: Princeton University Press.

Lazarsfeld, P. F., Berelson, B., & Gaudet, H. (1944). *The peoples' choice. How the voter makes up his mind in a presidential campaign.* New York: Duell, Sloan, and Pearce.

McDougall, W. (1908). *An introduction to social psychology.* London: Methuen.

McGuire, W. J. (1960a). Cognitive consistency and attitude change. *Journal of Abnormal and Social Psychology, 60,* 345–353.

McGuire, W. J. (1960b). Direct and indirect persuasive effects of dissonance-producing messages. *Journal of Abnormal and Social Psychology, 60,* 354–358.

McGuire, W. J. (1960c). A syllogistic analysis of cognitive relationships. In C. I. Hovland & M. J. Rosenberg (Eds.), *Attitude organization and change* (pp. 65–111). New Haven, CT: Yale University Press.

McGuire, W. J. (1964). Inducing resistance to persuasion: Some contemporary approaches. In L. Berkowitz (Ed.), *Advances in experimental social psychology* (Vol. 1, pp. 191–229). New York: Academic Press.

McGuire, W. J. (1966). Attitudes and opinions. In P. R. Farnsworth (Ed.), *Annual Review of Psychology,* (Vol. 17, pp. 475–514). Palo Alto, CA: Annual Reviews, Inc.

McGuire, W. J. (1968). Personality and susceptibility to social influence. In E. F. Borgatta & W. W. Lambert (Eds.), *Handbook of personality theory and research* (pp. 1130–1187). Chicago: Rand McNally.

McGuire, W. J. (1969). Attitude and attitude change. In G. Lindzey & E. Aronson (Eds.), *Handbook of social psychology* (Vol. 3, pp. 136–314). Reading, MA: Addison-Wesley.

McGuire, W. J. (1973). Persuasion, resistance and attitude change. In I. deSola Pool & W. Schramm (Eds.), *Handbook of communications* (pp. 216–252). Chicago: Rand McNally.

McGuire, W. J. (1974). Persuasion. *Encyclopaedia Britannica, 14* (15th ed., 122–127). Chicago: Encyclopedia Britannica.

McGuire, W. J. (1981). The probabilogical model of cognitive structure and attitude change. In R. Petty, T. Ostrom, & T. Brock (Eds.), *Cognitive responses in persuasion* (pp. 291–307). Hillsdale, NJ: Lawrence Erlbaum Associates.

McGuire, W. J. (1986). The vicissitudes of attitudes and similar representational constructs in twentieth century psychology. *European Journal of Social Psychology, 16,* 89–130.

McGuire, W. J. (1989). A perspectivist approach to the strategic planning of programmatic scientific research. In B. Gholson, W. R. Shadish, Jr., R. A. Neimeyer, & A. C. Houts (Eds.), *The psychology of science: Contributions to metascience* (pp. 214–245). New York: Cambridge University Press.

McGuire, W. J. (1996). The communication and attitude-change program in the 1950s at Yale. In E. E. Dennis & E. Wartella (Eds.), *American communication research: The remembered history* (pp. 39–59). Hillsdale, NJ: Erlbaum.

McGuire, W. J. (1999). *Constructing social psychology: Creative and critical processes.* New York: Cambridge University Press.

Petty, R. E., & Wegener, D. T. (1998). Attitude change: Multiple roles for persuasion variables. In D. T. Gilbert, S. T. Fiske, & G. Lindzey (Eds.), *Handbook of social psychology* (4th ed., Vol. 1, pp. 323–390). New York, McGraw-Hill.

Rogers, E. M. (1994). *A history of communication study.* New York: The Free Press.

Rosen, N. A., & Wyer, R. S., Jr. (1972). Some further evidence for the "Socratic effect" using a subjective probability model of cognitive organization. *Journal of Personality and Social Psychology, 24,* 420–424.

Rosen, N. A., & Wyer, R. S., Jr. Some further evident for the "Socratic effect" using a subjective probability model of cognitive organization. *Journal of Personality and Social Psychology; 24,* 420–424.

Ross, E. A. (1908). *Social psychology.* New York: Macmillan.

Shannon, C. E., & Weaver, W. (1949). *The mathematical theory of communication.* Urbana, IL: University of Illinois Press.

Shepard, R. N. (1997). Carl Iver Hovland. *Biographical Memories* (Vol. 73, pp. 3–32). Washington, DC: National Academy Press.

Woodworth, R. S., & Sells, S. B. (1935). An atmosphere effect in formal syllogistic reasoning. *Journal of Experimental Psychology, 18,* 451–460.

Wyer, R. S., Jr., & Goldberg, L. (1970). A probabilistic analysis of the relationships among beliefs and attitudes. *Psychological Review, 77,* 100–120.

3

Effects of Expectancies on the Representation, Retrieval and Use of Social Information

David L. Hamilton
University of California, Santa Barbara

Leonel Garcia-Marques
University of Lisbon

Without doubt, one of the most important developments in social psychology in the last 25 years has been social cognition, as both a conceptual and a methodological approach to social psychological topics. Also without doubt, one of the key figures in the emergence and development of that approach has been Bob Wyer. It is a privilege to be a part of this Festschrift honoring Bob and recognizing his important role in social psychology. Bob's significant and enduring contributions have been numerous and varied, a fact well reflected in the chapters in this volume. One topic in which he has played a central role in advancing our knowledge has been the cognitive representation of social information and its subsequent use. This chapter focuses on one subpart of that broader topic.

Until the mid-1970s, research on social perception had almost exclusively relied on judgments of one kind or another as a basis for inferring the nature of the underlying mental processes hypothesized to be important in our perceptions of others. For example, research on impression formation assessed people's trait inferences (Asch, 1946) and evaluative judgments (Anderson, 1981). Research on stereotypes had used checklists and trait ratings to assess people's beliefs about various groups (Brigham, 1971; Katz & Braly, 1933). Social cognition changed the nature of these research domains (Hamilton, Devine, & Ostrom, 1994). With the development of new techniques for more directly investigating cognitive processes, research began to focus on a variety of new questions. For example, researchers could explicitly study the acquisition of social information and the biases in its encoding and interpretation. They could study the inference processes by which the acquired information is transformed and expanded into mental representations stored in memory. And they could study the retrieval of information from those representations, both as a means of testing hypotheses about the nature of those representations and also for understanding how information is retrieved for various purposes and uses. These developments had an immediate impact on the nature of theory and research on both impression formation (Hastie et al., 1980) and stereotyping (Hamilton, 1981). Their more general impact on theorizing and research has been impressively developed in Wyer and Srull (1986, 1989).

EFFECTS OF EXPECTANCIES ON PROCESSING: CONGRUENCY EFFECTS

The great diversity and constant mutability of the social world ensure that there is never a dull cognitive moment for the social information processor. By contrast, our apparent cognitive stability may seem almost miraculous. One of the most popular social psychology brain-teasers has long been how it is that cognitive consistency prevails over and above social variability (e.g., Sherif, 1936). This tendency toward maintaining consistency is also evident in social information processing, in which our existing expectancies guide, and often bias, information processing in such a way that information that "fits" with our prior beliefs is given special status and has greater influence, compared to information that seems irrelevant to such expectancies.

Conceptual Framework

The most prominent solutions offered by early social cognition approaches for understanding this effect shared an important characteristic: the assumption that cognitive stability is achieved primarily through simplification of the input (i.e., the so-called "cognitive miser" metaphor, Taylor & Fiske, 1978). This view takes the bounded rationality hypothesis (Simon, 1957) as a starting point. Preservation of limited cognitive resources is viewed as one of the primary goals of social information processing. One way to preserve those resources is to reduce the demands on the processing system by limiting the amount of information one must contend with at any given moment. Simplification of information input can be a consequence either of the judicious neglect of the least relevant information or of the continual mental ability of going beyond the particulars, the ability to abstract (Bruner, 1957). These are but different means for the same end. In fact, both of them allow us to deal with the infinite social variety either by reducing the number of features to consider or by taking each social target as a token of a social type, with no further need to account for his or her uniqueness. Hence social categorization is one of the cognitive miser's best friends.

Evidence

Given this guiding metaphor, it comes as no surprise that early social cognition research concentrated on attention and encoding processes (Ebbesen, 1980; Crocker, Hannah, & Weber, 1983; Hamilton, 1979; Hastie, 1981, 1984; McArthur, 1982; Ostrom, Lingle, Pryor, & Geva, 1980; Taylor & Crocker, 1981; Taylor & Fiske, 1981; Wyer & Srull, 1980). This research showed the impact of prior learning and expectancies (impressions, stereotypes, and judgments) on the processing of new information from the social world. The variety of consequences that prior expectancies were shown to have on information processing was truly stunning. Expectancies can filter the information that is attended to and elaborated (Cohen, 1981; Darley & Gross, 1983; Ebbesen, 1981; Hamilton, 1979; Newston, 1976; Taylor & Fiske, 1981; White & Carlston, 1983; Zadny & Gerard, 1974). They can color the interpretation of observed behavior (Duncan, 1976; Sagar & Schofield, 1980). They can influence what information is stored and later available (Rothbart, 1981; Rothbart & John, 1985). They can shape the way our hypotheses are tested in social interaction (Snyder, 1981a). And they can affect the type of behavior elicited by the target of those expectancies (Jones, 1977; Snyder, 1981b). Thus new information is often interpreted in a biased, expectancy-congruent way.

All of these effects reflect expectancy-based biases that operate as information is encoded. A commonly-held view has been that expectancy-congruent information benefits from more attention and more elaboration, and therefore gets stored in memory better and is more easily accessible later on. Moreover, expectancy-congruent hypotheses stand a better chance of being tested and confirmed more often than they should, and expectancies can become self-fulfilling behavioral prophecies by guiding social interactions. These biasing effects all work toward the same end: they serve to maintain the prior expectancy that itself generated the expectancy-confirming outcome. The implication, as Hamilton (1981, p. 137) observed, is that "I wouldn't have seen it if I hadn't believed it."

In sum, the blossoming literature documenting these congruency effects in a variety of domains was crucially important in several ways. This work made important contributions not only toward understanding how prior beliefs can influence cognitive functioning but also contributed substantially toward laying the early building blocks of the newly-emerging emphasis known as social cognition. But it lacked one important ingredient: the emphasis on these congruency-biased encoding processes provided no means of accounting for some other findings, such as those results suggesting the opposite effect—namely, that information that contradicts a prior expectancy is given special processing.

EFFECTS OF EXPECTANCIES ON PROCESSING: INCONGRUENCY EFFECTS

At about the same time that much evidence was documenting that expectancies guide encoding in a confirmatory manner, Hastie and Kumar (1979) published their classic paper in which they demonstrated that expectancy-incongruent items of information are recalled with higher probability than expectancy-congruent items. Hastie (1980) introduced an associative network model to account for his findings, and that model stimulated an enormous amount of subsequent research.

Conceptual Framework

The associative network model introduced by Hastie (1980; Hastie & Kumar, 1979) and further developed by Srull and Wyer (Srull, 1981; Srull, Lichtenstein, & Rothbart, 1985; Wyer & Gordon, 1984; Wyer & Srull, 1980, 1986) provided an elegantly simple account of why incongruent items were better recalled. Unlike the conceptions underlying much of the other social cognition research at the time, this model was remarkably specific about underlying processes. In particular, the model specified effects that occur during information encoding, it detailed the consequences of those effects for how information is represented in memory, and it described the process by which stored items are retrieved from memory in a free recall task. In contrast to the very general "schema-like" ideas guiding much research at the time, including that which documented expectancy-consistent biases, this model made very specific statements about the cognitive processes that underlie social information processing. Consequently, in the hands of creative experimenters, the model became the basis for testing numerous hypotheses, many of which were either nonobvious or counterintuitive, and a great deal of research supported the basic tenets of the model.

In the developing field of social cognition, this model was perhaps the first to clearly distinguish between, on the one hand, processes that occur during encoding and representation of information and, on the other hand, the retrieval of information from memory. The essential elements of the model can be summarized briefly in terms of these two phases.

Encoding and Representation.   As each item of information is acquired, it is represented in memory as an attachment to a person node representing the target person. Information consistent with the prior expectancy is easily processed and represented in this network. In contrast, items that are inconsistent with that initial impression, being unexpected, are surprising and therefore are processed more extensively as the perceiver tries to incorporate them into the existing impression. In this process, the incongruent item spends more time in working memory, during which time the item is considered in relation to previously-acquired items that are retrieved from memory. Hence connections are formed between the inconsistent items and these other, previously-represented items. The important consequence of this encoding and representation process is that the encoding of expectancy-inconsistent items generates direct associative links between these items and (at least some of the) other items stored in memory.

Retrieval.   The model was developed as a conceptual framework for understanding memory for stored information in the impression formation process, and one of its important foci was the process by which this information is retrieved. Specifically, the model posits that retrieval begins by entering the person node and moving down one of the pathways associated with it. Once an item has been recalled, the preference is to traverse pathways directly connecting that item with another item, rather than returning to the person node. Because the inconsistent items are more densely interconnected with other items through such pathways, there are more "routes" to retrieval of an inconsistent item than of a consistent item. Therefore the probability of recalling expectancy-inconsistent items is higher than that for recalling expectancy-consistent items. This "incongruency effect" has been obtained in many studies (see Srull & Wyer, 1989).

Evidence

The fact that the model can account for the incongruency effect is not surprising in that it was developed for precisely that purpose (Hastie, 1980; Hastie & Kumar, 1979). The model does, however, make a number of other predictions, and studies have provided impressive support for them. For example, the model postulates that incongruent items become integrated into the emerging impression, an assumption implying that the perceiver seeks to achieve an integrated, organized representation of the target. If so, then the incongruency effect should be more prevalent when the perceiver assumes that the target is an organized entity, such as an individual person, than when that expectation is held less strongly, as for an unspecified group. Research has supported that prediction (Srull, 1981; see Sherman and Johnson chapter in this volume for discussion of related effects). The model also generates nonobvious predictions about the sequence of item recall, based on the postulated pattern of interitem associations. Specifically, whereas recall of a congruent item can, according to the model, be followed by recall of either an icongruent or incongruent item, recall of a congruent item should be much more likely to be followed by recall of an incongruent item. Studies have supported this prediction (Srull, 1981; Srull et al., 1985). Other new process measures such as interrecall times provided results that paralleled conditional probabilities of recall output (Srull et al., 1985). Similarly, the more extensive processing of incongruent items posited by the model should take more time, an effect that has been documented (Bargh & Thein, 1985; Stern, Marrs, Millar, & Cole, 1984). Presumably the more extended processing time for incongruent items is due (at least in part) to the retrieval of previously encoded items. If so, then those previously encoded items should be more available following an incongruent item than following a congruent item, a prediction that has been confirmed (Sherman & Hamilton, 1994). Also, given the unexpected nature of information that contradicts the emerging impression, incongruent items might trigger attributional processes aimed at explaining why the person performed this unexpected behavior. Studies have shown that such attributional thinking occurs following incongruent items, but not congruent items (Hastie, 1984; Susskind, Maurer, Thakkar, Hamilton, & Sherman, 1999).

   In sum, the associative network model guiding this research proved to be very useful, and the hypotheses derived from it generated an impressive body of research that garnered an array of supportive findings. It seems to provide an effective account of how and why incongruent items come to be recalled with higher probability than congruent items. However, the problem that remains is that, as we have seen, there is also evidence suggesting preferential treatment of expectancy congruent items during processing. This model would seem to have difficulty accounting for such effects.

TWO DIVERGING PATHS

Thus, we have seen that, after more than a decade of research investigating the effects of prior expectancies on social information processing, the result was two separate literatures, both of them sizeable, both of them including many ingenious experiments, but simultaneously supporting and maintaining two seemingly divergent principles. On the one hand, expectancies seemed to guide information processing in such a way as to maintain the status quo, to preserve the pre-existing belief system. On the other hand, information that clearly contradicts such expectancies is thoroughly processed, more densely integrated into the resulting cognitive representation, and therefore more available for retrieval at a later time for use on subsequent tasks.

By 1990, enough evidence on the general issue of how prior expectancies influence processing had accumulated that two independent meta-analyses were published at approximately the same time (Rojahn & Pettigrew, 1992; Stangor & McMillan, 1992). These two meta-analyses converge on one important conclusion: whereas expectancy-incongruent information is better recalled and discriminated than expectancy-congruent information, the reverse occurs for uncorrected recognition or response bias. In addition, the meta-analyses uncovered a host of moderators of the incongruency effect (e.g., individual vs. group nature of the target, number of trait dimensions to be considered, available cognitive resources, etc.).

Moreover, faced with these diverging patterns of findings, there was little effort, conceptually or empirically, to resolve this dilemma. The implicit, often unspoken, understanding among many researchers was that both outcomes—an advantage in processing for expectancy-congruent or for expectancy-incongruent information—can occur, but they presumably occur under different situational constraints (we are, after all, social psychologists!). Those conditions were not well specified, leaving a rather unsatisfactory state of affairs.

More recently there have been attempts to understand and account for both of these robust outcomes within a single conceptual framework. One such approach is represented in the Encoding Flexibility Model proposed by Sherman and his colleagues (Sherman, 2001; Sherman & Frost, 2000; Sherman, Lee, Bessenoff, & Frost, 1998), which posits differences in the encoding process for expectancy-congruent and incongruent information. The model is particularly focused on stereotype efficiency and the allocation of attentional resources. Sherman et al.'s (1998) analysis begins with the distinction between conceptual and perceptual encoding processes (Bobrow & Norman, 1975; Jacoby, 1983; Johnson & Hawley, 1994). Conceptual encoding processes are top-down, meaning-based processes whose goal is to extract the common gist of episodes or category instances. In contrast, perceptual encoding processes are bottom-up, data-driven processes whose goal is to encode the features of specific episodes. The model argues that stereotypes are eminently proficient cognitive structures because they allow for both the preservation and the effective allocation of cognitive resources. Stereotypes facilitate the extraction of the gist of stereotype-congruent information (i.e., congruent information benefits from heightened conceptual fluency). As a consequence, attentional resources can be devoted to encoding other stimuli, including stereotype-incongruent information. Thus as a rule, expectancy-incongruent information benefits from more extensive perceptual encoding (Johnson & Hawley, 1994; von Hippel, Jonides, Hilton, & Narayan, 1993). Moreover, the model posits that the proficient nature of stereotypes is particularly evident when cognitive resources are scarce. Under these conditions, the asymmetries between stereotype-congruent and -incongruent information, in terms of conceptual versus perceptual encoding processes, are dramatically accentuated.

Sherman et al. (1998) have reported impressive evidence in support of their proposals. For instance, Sherman et al. (1998, Experiment 1-2) showed that, especially under low resource (high cognitive load) conditions, participants took longer to process, and invested more attention in, stereotype-incongruent information relative to congruent information. Furthermore, also under low resource conditions, participants had better recognition performance for stereotype-incongruent information than for congruent information, because of the more accurate and detailed encoding that is characteristic of perceptual encoding (Sherman et al., 1998, Exp. 3-4). Under these same conditions, however, participants had better retention of the gist of stereotype-congruent information than of incongruent information, reflecting the greater conceptual fluency associated with encoding congruent information (Sherman et al., 1998, Experiment 5). In these ways, the encoding flexibility model elucidates some processes by which the processing of congruent and incongruent information may show differing outcomes within the same experimental context.

Whereas the research by Sherman and his colleagues has focused on differences in the way information is encoded, our recent work has emphasized differences in retrieval processes that can produce differing outcomes for congruent and incongruent information in the same experimental context.

THE TRAP MODEL

We have developed and tested a model aimed at addressing at least part of this dilemma posed by the divergent patterns of outcomes for expectancy-congruent and expectancy-incongruent information (Garcia-Marques & Hamilton, 1996; Garcia-Marques, Hamilton, & Maddox, 2002). The model begins with the basic elements of the associative network model that has proven so useful in this literature, and extends it in order to broaden the scope of phenomena that this approach can incorporate. Specifically, the model distinguishes between two different retrieval modes by which the perceiver might search the network representation, depending on immediate goals, tasks to be performed, and other factors. Given its emphasis on these two retrieval modes, we refer to it as the Twofold Retrieval by Associative Pathways (TRAP) Model. In this section we briefly summarize the core ideas underlying the model and guiding our research; more complete discussions of the model, its assumptions, and its implications are contained in the cited papers.

The TRAP Model adopts essentially the same assumptions regarding encoding and representation of expectancy-consistent and -inconsistent information that were specified in the associative network model summarized in the previous section. Items of information describing a target are encoded and stored in cognitive representation for that target. We assume that the associative pathways linking items to target node vary in strength as a positive function of the item's congruence with the preexisting impression of or expectancy about the target (Wyer & Martin, 1986). Therefore expectancy-congruent items are more strongly associated with the target node than are expectancy-incongruent items. Moreover, consistent with the reasoning described above, the expectancy-violating properties of incongruent items trigger more extended processing that generates a pattern of interitem associations, such that incongruent items become directly connected with other congruent and incongruent items already acquired and stored in memory. This increased processing, and consequent formation of interitem associations, is less likely to occur when expectancy-congruent items are encoded.

The key feature of the TRAP Model is its differentiation between two modes or strategies by which information can be retrieved from this representation. We call these strategies exhaustive and heuristic retrieval. *Exhaustive retrieval* involves a thorough search of memory, as typically seen in free recall. It is an effortful and resource-consuming retrieval process that involves systematically moving through the network of associative pathways to retrieve items. As such, the process uses each retrieved item as a cue for retrieval of subsequent items. Thus the exhaustive retrieval mode is unselective, attempting to recall as many items as possible, in any order ("Write down as many items as you can"), and its output is in the form of specific items retrieved from memory in this fashion.

In contrast, *heuristic retrieval* is a more selective search of memory, often focused on a particular type of information in memory, and does not involve thorough search and retrieval of specific items. Rather, heuristic retrieval uses the availability heuristic as a means of assessing the amount or frequency of information of a particular type that is represented in memory. That is, the degree of fit between retrieval cues and easily accessible memory traces is used as a cue to the prevalence of such information in memory. It is therefore a faster, more indirect way of assessing memory, and as such, is much less resource-demanding than the exhaustive mode. The result or output of heuristic retrieval is some summary statement, such as a frequency estimation ("How often did the target do X?") or trait judgment ("How Xish is the target?"), rather than a delineation of individual items of knowledge.

IMPLICATIONS FOR CONGRUENCY
VERSUS INCONGRUENCY EFFECTS

Let us now return to the lingering "tension" between the two bodies of find-ings that have accumulated: those suggesting favored treatment of expec-tancy-congruent information and those indicating special processing of expectancy-incongruent information. Does the TRAP Model offer a way of thinking about this seeming dilemma? The model does provide a framework for analyzing underlying processes that, at least theoretically, can produce both a congruency effect and an incongruency effect. Specifically, under many circumstances (including those represented in many of the experi-ments relevant to the preceding discussion), an exhaustive retrieval process would generate the advantaged recall of incongruent information, whereas a heuristic retrieval strategy would generate outcomes reflecting a congru-ency bias. Why is this so?

The goal of exhaustive retrieval is to generate as many of the stimulus items from memory as possible. To do so, one enters the network representa-tion at the target node, traverses down a pathway, and recalls the item en-countered. In moving to recall another item, the preference is to traverse pathways connecting the recalled item directly with other items, rather than returning to the target node and starting again. Because of the encod-ing processes described earlier, there are more pathways leading to incon-gruent items than to congruent items, and there is therefore a higher probability of recalling those incongruent items. This rationale simply reit-erates the process of recall delineated by Hastie (1980) and others (Srull, 1981; Wyer & Gordon, 1984).

In contrast, the goal of heuristic retrieval is to arrive at a quick and easy as-sessment of the relative prevalence of a certain type of information (e.g., intel-ligent behaviors performed by a target person). To make that assessment, the person again enters the network at the target node and then probes the stored information by exploring the associations that connect the target node with individual items. In contrast to exhaustive retrieval, the person does not move along pathways directly connecting stored items with each other, as this strategy could generate retrieval of numerous items that are irrelevant to the retrieval goal (i.e., how many intelligent behaviors?). Instead, the sense of how easily the relevant items are retrieved provides a basis for an overall judg-ment (e.g., frequency estimate, trait rating, etc.). Thus, this retrieval strategy arrives at its end product by use of the availability heuristic. How does that generate a congruency effect? The model assumes that pathways connecting expectancy-congruent items to the target node are stronger than items con-necting expectancy-incongruent items to the target node. That differential strength will make pathways leading to congruent items more easily accessible and will result in the sampling of more congruent than incongruent exemplars in this process. The apparent ease with which congruent items are retrieved will then result in overestimation of their prevalence in memory, thus producing congruency effects in judgments.

Thus the TRAP Model incorporates processing mechanisms for retrieval that would lead to either congruency effects or incongruency effects, depending on whether retrieval occurs via the exhaustive or heuristic route. Moreover, rather than simply accepting the assumption that one effect or the other will occur depending on the extant circumstances at the time, the model more precisely identifies an important factor guiding that outcome. Thus the model specifies a crucial condition that will determine which effect will occur—that is, the nature of the retrieval strategy that is employed. Can the model account for all of the differences in outcomes observed in this pervasive literature on congruency and incongruency effects? We make no claim that the model provides a complete accounting for all of the different patterns of results in the literature. We do know, however, that the model has received strong support in some of our initial experimental tests of its predictions, which have focused on specific comparisons under which congruency and incongruency effects have occurred. In the next section we review these studies and their findings.

EXHAUSTIVE AND HEURISTIC RETRIEVAL: RESEARCH ON THE TRAP MODEL

The Dissociation Effect

Our research began by testing these ideas in a context comparing two seemingly opposing outcomes that had been derived from very similar methods and procedures. Specifically, whereas Hastie and Kumar (1979) had found better recall for expectancy-incongruent items, Hamilton and Rose (1980) had shown that stereotypic expectancies generated higher frequency estimates for expectancy-congruent information. According to the TRAP Model, these two outcomes need not be viewed as conflicting, but could in fact even occur simultaneously.

To test this hypothesis, we (Garcia-Marques & Hamilton, 1996) combined the main features of the paradigms used by Hastie and Kumar (1979) and Hamilton and Rose (1980). Participants, who were given either impression formation or memory instructions, were presented a list of behaviors performed by two social targets. Expectancies were induced implicitly by providing the target's occupation, and the two targets had occupations that generated opposite trait expectancies (e.g., librarian—cultured; waitress—uncultured). One-third of the behaviors was expectancy-congruent, another third was expectancy-incongruent, and the final third was expectancy-neutral. Following a distracter task, participants were asked to free recall all the behaviors, to estimate the frequency of occurrence of behaviors illustrative of each trait, and to judge the target on several bipolar trait-rating scales.

The basic findings can be easily summarized. Incongruent behaviors were recalled better than congruent behaviors, but only under impression formation instructions. Frequency estimates, however, were higher for congruent behaviors than for incongruent behaviors, and trait judgments were biased toward the congruent pole of trait dimensions. Thus the results of the free recall task replicated the incongruency effect and the frequency estimation and trait judgment data replicated the expectancy-based illusory correlation effect. Hence the predicted dissociation occurred. In our view, these results are due to the distinction between the exhaustive search process engaged in free recall and the heuristic search process engaged in frequency estimation and trait judgment. What makes these findings impressive is that these seemingly incompatible effects were obtained on immediately successive tasks performed by the same participants.

Subsequent research has documented that this dissociative effect of expectancies is a robust finding. It has been replicated in several experiments with several different trait dimensions, using gender or occupation-based expectancies, with implicit or explicit trait expectancies, and with individual and group targets (Bardach & Park, 1996; Garcia-Marques, 1993; Garcia-Marques & Hamilton, 1996; Garcia-Marques et al., 2002).

Alternative Explanations

These findings provided strong support for our predicted dissociation. However, other possibilities remained. Thus two alternative accounts were tested in follow-up studies (see Garcia-Marques & Hamilton, 1996). We labeled the first alternative explanation the meaning-change account (Asch, 1946). According to this alternative, the obtained dissociation could simply be due to the re-interpretation of the presented incongruent behaviors. If incongruent behaviors are re-interpreted in an expectancy-congruent way, this elaborative activity could promote their better recall, but these reinterpreted behaviors would no longer be considered incongruent (Duncan, 1976; Sagar & Schofield, 1980; see also Crocker et al., 1983). Thus an apparent, but not actual, dissociation could follow. To test this alternative explanation, we modified the paradigm and had participants make ratings of the meaning of the behaviors presented. We found that the expectancies had only a slight effect on the interpretation of these behaviors (and only for expectancy-neutral behaviors). More importantly, there was never the case that an expectancy-incongruent behavior was rated as expectancy-congruent, as implied by this alternative interpretation. Thus the meaning-change explanation failed to account for the obtained dissociation.

The other alternative account was that frequency estimates and trait judgments could be directly derived from the previously held expectancies without reflecting learning or any probing of memory at all. To check whether frequency estimates and impression judgments reflected learning or simply reflected previously held expectancies, we manipulated the relative set size of congruent and incongruent behaviors presented. We found that both frequency estimates and trait judgments were indeed a function of relative set size. Therefore, these results could not simply reflect previously held expectancies.

Implications for Memory-Judgment Correlations

Further support for the distinction between heuristic and exhaustive search modes comes from correlational analyses of the data from our first study (Garcia-Marques & Hamilton, 1996). Previous research, beginning with Hastie and Park (1986) and Lichtenstein and Srull (1987), has shown that memory measures (specifically, recall) and impression judgments may or may not be highly correlated, depending on a variety of factors. According to the TRAP Model, frequency estimates and impression judgments are similar in that both involve cognitive tasks sharing a heuristic search component, and they are therefore likely to be influenced in similar ways by the external variables and constraints. Therefore the model assumes that these will generally be highly correlated. Free recall, in contrast, is the prototypical exhaustive search task and the model would not predict it to be generally well correlated with the other measures. Supporting this reasoning, Garcia-Marques and Hamilton (1996) found that frequency estimates and impression judgments were positively correlated with each other, whereas free recall was correlated with trait impressions only under very restricted conditions (i.e., under a memory-processing goal).

These results are important for several reasons. First, in differing ways and using different analyses, they further indicate the divergence between exhaustive and heuristic retrieval strategies. Second, they suggest caution in discussing the nature of memory-judgment correlations. That is, in our results, two different memory measures (free recall and frequency estimates), both of which are based on retrieval of previously-acquired information, had markedly different patterns of correlations with impression judgments.

Extending this analysis, it is important to note that, when interitem associations are *not* formed during encoding (e.g., under memory-processing goals), both heuristic and exhaustive retrieval are necessarily based on the same retrieval pathways (i.e., the associations between the target node and the stored items). In this case, the output of trait impressions and free recall can be correlated. However, in contrast with the framework developed by Hastie and Park (1986), we argue that, even in this case, the relation between the outputs of free recall and impression judgments is indirect. In our view, the correlation commonly obtained between free recall and impression judgments under memory conditions is due to their association with a third factor (i.e., the use of the same cues and pathways), and not to any direct causal relationship (i.e., calculating judgments on the basis of retrieved exemplars). Thus according to our reasoning, when the variability that trait impressions share with frequency estimates is partialled out, the correlation between free recall and impressions should disappear altogether. This is exactly what Garcia-Marques and Hamilton (1996) found.

Effects of Cognitive Load on Retrieval Strategies

Having established the basic dissociation between the two retrieval modes and having demonstrated both effects of expectancies simultaneously, our research then focused more specifically on testing some other assumptions essential to the TRAP Model (Garcia-Marques et al., 2002). As we explained earlier, the model assumes that the exhaustive mode is nonselective, is a cognitively demanding process, and that its output is elemental reproduction of previously learned items. In contrast, the heuristic mode is accessibility-based, is an efficient and resource-saving process, and its output is a composite memory judgment (cf. Hintzmann, 2001).

In one experiment (Garcia-Marques et al., 2002, Experiment 1), we tested the assumptions about the resource-dependent and nonselective nature of exhaustive retrieval. The experimental paradigm and procedure were similar to that used previously (Garcia-Marques & Hamilton, 1996, Experiment 1). To vary resource availability, we included a cognitive load manipulation, dividing participants' attention by use of a concurrent digit memory task (retaining a 9-digit number in memory). This cognitive load was introduced either at encoding or at retrieval. According to the TRAP Model, exhaustive retrieval is a highly demanding search process because traversing along inter-episodic retrieval pathways requires maintaining at least part of the episodic network in working memory, dealing with continually changing retrieval cues, and keeping track of previously used retrieval cues. Any or all of these aspects of the retrieval process could be easily disrupted by other demands on one's attention and resources. Therefore we predicted that a cognitive load introduced during either encoding or retrieval would undermine the incongruency effect in recall. Although earlier research has already shown that cognitive load at encoding removes the incongruency effect (Bargh & Thein, 1985; Macrae, Hewstone, & Griffiths, 1993; Srull, 1981; Srull et al., 1985; Stangor & Duan, 1991), we also predicted that the incongruency effect would emerge only when sufficient cognitive resources are available at the time retrieval takes place. In contrast, we expected no effect of the cognitive load manipulation on heuristic tasks (frequency estimates, impression judgments). In heuristic retrieval, memory is assessed by the ease of retrieval of a small subset of relevant episodes or by a global memory strength to a given retrieval cue or prompt. Therefore it is a less effortful and more efficient retrieval process, in the sense of being less resource-demanding and less prone to interference.

Cross cutting the cognitive load variables, we also manipulated the selectivity of the retrieval goal in this study. We instructed participants either to recall everything they could, in any order, or to first recall all instances of one type of behavior and then recall instances of the other type. Our reasoning was as follows: Even if integrative elaboration occurs (e.g., forming associations between items) and sufficient cognitive resources are available, the incongruency effect may not emerge if the retrieval goal operative at the moment induces a selective or ordered retrieval strategy. Suppose, for example, the recall instructions asked the participant to recall a certain type of item (e.g., intelligent behaviors), and then later asked for recall of another type of item (stupid behaviors). We refer to this as an *ordered recall* strategy, in contrast to the *unordered recall* strategy typically used in free recall tasks. In ordered recall, resorting to previously recalled behaviors as cues for the retrieval of the remaining items would be a rather cumbersome strategy, due to the number of associations (formed at encoding) that link a behavior to opposite types of behaviors. Thus if one were searching for intelligent behaviors, using specific intelligent behaviors as retrieval cues (and hence traversing interitem pathways) would probably result in retrieving a great number of goal-irrelevant behaviors (i.e., stupid behaviors). To prevent this outcome, it is likely that, in this more focused type of search, trait cues are used as guides to retrieval instead. As a consequence, inter-episodic retrieval pathways would not be explored and thus no incongruency effect would emerge. In fact, according to the present framework, only under unordered recall would the incongruency effect emerge.

The main findings of this experiment and their significance can be summarized as follows: First, cognitive load had a dramatic impact on the recall data. Having to perform a concurrent task—either at the time of information encoding or at the time of information retrieval—was sufficient to dissolve the incongruency effect. The results for the load at retrieval participants were particularly noteworthy because in this condition participants presumably were able to develop inter-episodic associations during encoding, yet the incongruency effect disappeared. Moreover, the analysis of conditional probabilities in recall showed that interitem associations were much less systematically explored when attention was divided at retrieval compared to impression formation baseline conditions. In contrast to these findings for free recall, cognitive load had no effect on tasks assumed to typically depend on a more efficient retrieval strategy, that is, the heuristic retrieval mode. Both frequency estimates and impression trait ratings were unaffected by the performance of a concurrent task.

Second, the manipulation of recall instructions also had strong effects. Asking participants to use an ordered recall strategy (first recalling all instances of one type of behavior and then recalling instances of the other type of behavior) made the incongruency effect disappear. By asking participants to retrieve a single type of item (i.e., the ordered recall goal conditions), free recall adopts the selective character of the heuristic retrieval process, and hence the inter item associations are not pursued during retrieval.

Memory Accessibility and Heuristic Retrieval

As we described earlier, the TRAP model contends that the output of heuristic retrieval is highly influenced by memory accessibility. Expectancy-based effects are obtained because expected information is inherently more accessible. A strict test of this contention can be achieved by the manipulation of retrieval fluency independently of expectancies (Gabrielcik & Fazio, 1984). We adopted exactly this strategy in a subsequent experiment (Garcia-Marques et al., 2002, Experiment 2). In this experiment, we used the same paradigm as in Garcia-Marques and Hamilton (1996) but we added a priming task to manipulate the differential accessibility of trait instances (expectancy-congruent, expectancy-incongruent, or neutral). This task involved presenting a subset of previously presented behaviors with the omission of group labels and asking participants to recall those behaviors. In the three priming conditions, the priming behaviors were stereotype-congruent, -incongruent, or neutral, respectively. This task was given immediately prior to the frequency estimation and impression judgment tasks. As we argued earlier, the heuristic search task uses the strength of association between target and item or the retrieval fluency of an item given a referent cue (e.g., a name or general characterization of the target) as a cue to memory content. Thus the TRAP Model makes the following predictions for these experimental conditions: Priming congruent instances should increase the magnitude of the usual illusory correlation effect in frequency judgments; priming incongruent instances should decrease it; and priming neutral instances should have little effect. Our results were consistent with these hypotheses. The illusory correlation effect was greatest after congruent priming, intermediate after neutral priming, and smallest after incongruent priming. This pattern also emerged in impression judgments.

These findings provide simultaneous support for a set of intertwined contentions derived from the TRAP Model. Specifically, they document that (a) frequency estimation and impression judgments are based on heuristic retrieval processes, (b) heuristic retrieval processes are highly dependent on memory-accessibility effects, and (c) expectancy-based illusory correlations are derived from the greater retrieval accessibility of stereotype-congruent information.

Elemental Versus Composite Retrieval Output

One of the important differences between exhaustive and heuristic retrieval is the nature of the output generated, which in turn reflects different underlying processes. To investigate this difference more specifically, we (Garcia-Marques et al., 2002, Experiment 3) employed a paradigm introduced in the cognitive literature some years ago, the part-list cues paradigm (Slamecka, 1968; see also Brown, 1968). In this research, the impact of presenting cues that in fact were a subset of the original stimulus list on a free recall memory test is assessed. The somewhat surprising but robust result in this literature is that the probability of recalling non-cued list items is decreased compared to non-cued conditions.

One prominent explanation for the part-list cue effect in recall emphasizes the role of associative interference and response competition (e.g., Rundus, 1973). This account rests on the assumptions that (a) the retrievability of a given stored item is a function of its degree of activation at the moment, (b) the total amount of item activation is fixed, and therefore relevant stored items must compete for retrieval, and (c) strongly activated items may therefore interfere with the retrieval from memory of less activated items. These assumptions are, in fact, incorporated in associative network models of person memory (Hastie, 1988; Srull & Wyer, 1989; Wyer & Srull, 1989). More recent approaches have attributed less importance to the associative strength component, and instead have emphasized the role of selective retrieval processes that inhibit non-target items in order to facilitate the retrieval of target items (Anderson, Bjork, & Bjork, 1994; Anderson & Neely, 1996; Anderson & Spellman, 1995). From either perspective, it follows that if a subset of the relevant stored items is made available at retrieval (e.g., priming or cueing), the consequence will be a decrease in the probability of non-cued items being retrieved.

In these theoretical interpretations, then, response competition is a crucial element underlying this effect. Response competition can only occur, however, when the target for retrieval consists of a set of individual items, as is the case in free recall. According to the TRAP Model, however, the output of heuristic retrieval can be a composite (i.e., the overall familiarity with the retrieval cue) because only a generic judgment is called for, not the retrieval of individual items. It follows, then, that whereas the elemental nature of exhaustive retrieval will often result in response competition, the composite nature of heuristic retrieval will often result in response integration. Based on this thinking, we hypothesized that part-list cueing would have a dissociative effect in exhaustive and heuristic retrieval tasks. Specifically, we predicted that presenting part-list cues at retrieval would inhibit retrieval of non-cued list items in free recall, but would increase the corresponding frequency estimates.

This experiment used a paradigm similar to the previous experiments (with the exception that we used only stereotype-congruent and neutral behaviors to minimize the formation of inter-episodic associations; such associations might undermine the inhibitory effects of part-list cueing; Anderson & McCulloch, 1999; Smith & Hunt, 2000). In addition, at recall, we either provided participants with a subset of previously presented behaviors to be used as cues or provided participants with no such cues.

The results showed that providing, at retrieval, a subset of behaviors included in the original stimulus list had the predicted dissociative impact on free recall versus frequency estimates. Whereas such cueing inhibited free recall, it increased the corresponding frequency estimates. As noted earlier, explanations of the part-list cue effect stress the role of item competition for retrieval. Response competition would be an important element characteristic of one of the retrieval processes highlighted by the TRAP Model: the exhaustive mode. On the other hand, in the other retrieval process identified in the TRAP Model, heuristic retrieval, such competition is unlikely because the output of retrieval is a generic judgment. In this case, therefore, the inhibition effect should not emerge. Instead, part-list cueing should produce an opposite effect in generic composite memory judgments because it will result in the increased accessibility of the target list as a whole and in a corresponding boost in frequency estimates. Thus the TRAP Model predicted this new dissociation of the effects of part-list cues in free recall (the prototypical exhaustive task) and frequency estimation (a task that depends on heuristic retrieval).

THE TRAP MODEL IN PERSPECTIVE

Our research on the TRAP Model began with a focused attempt to understand the seeming contradiction between two well-established findings: the incongruity effect in recall (Hastie & Kumar, 1979) and the expectancy-based illusory correlation effect in frequency estimation (Hamilton & Rose, 1980). Our model to account for these two effects posited that, instead of being due to differing representations (differentially formed under varying circumstances) of the same information, they reflect two different retrieval strategies, the exhaustive and heuristic retrieval modes, from the same cognitive representation. Our demonstration (Garcia-Marques & Hamilton, 1996) that both effects can be produced in the same experiment, by the same participants, on immediately successive tasks, provided strong evidence in support of the TRAP Model's analysis.

The goal of our subsequent research has been to extend the empirical base of support for the model and to shed new light on some long standing issues. In particular, our more recent studies (Garcia-Marques et al., 2002) have provided support for some key elements of the theoretical argument.

Specifically, we have shown that exhaustive retrieval, but not heuristic retrieval, is a cognitively demanding and resource-consuming process. It is therefore quite amenable to disruption from other, simultaneously performed tasks. In fact, our cognitive load manipulations had significant impact on exhaustive retrieval when imposed either during the encoding of stimulus information or while performing the recall task. The consequence was that the incongruity effect was effectively eliminated under these conditions. In contrast, these same cognitive load inductions did not have any noticeable impact on two heuristic retrieval tasks, frequency estimation and impression judgments, and consequently the overestimation of expectancy-congruent information was evident in all conditions.

Whereas the cognitive load manipulation was designed to undermine the incongruency effect through disruption of exhaustive retrieval, another study was focused on affecting heuristic retrieval by increasing the accessibility of a subset of items. This work varied the strength of the illusory correlation effect by priming a subset of items (e.g., expectancy-congruent or -incongruent items). Our results showed that this manipulation of accessibility had corresponding effects on the magnitude of resulting illusory correlations. Finally, in another study, we brought these two lines of work together. Using the part-list cueing paradigm, we were able to show that the same experimental induction (cueing) inhibited free recall of certain items, but increased frequency estimates for those items.

Implications for Impression Formation

Beyond providing evidence documenting the processes postulated in the TRAP Model, we believe our findings also have important implications for our more general thinking about the incongruency effect in the impression formation process. As we noted earlier, the incongruency effect has been replicated numerous times since Hastie and Kumar's (1979) original demonstration. And we have, of course, replicated this effect again in some of the studies we have summarized here (Garcia-Marques & Hamilton, 1996, Experiment 1; Garcia-Marques et al., 2002, Experiment 1). As a whole, however, our findings suggest that there may be serious constraints on the conditions under which the incongruency effect actually occurs. Specifically, we have found that the incongruency effect did not occur when participants were under cognitive load during encoding, when they were under cognitive load while engaging in the retrieval process, and when their task was to recall one type of item (e.g., congruent) and only subsequently to recall the other (incongruent) type of item. Moreover, past research has shown that the incongruency effect did not occur when the initial impression consisted of multiple trait expectancies rather than a single trait dimension (Driscoll & Gingrich, 1997; Hamilton, Driscoll, & Worth, 1989).

Thus there are a variety of conditions that constitute exceptions to the well-replicated effect.

These exceptions to one of social psychology's most replicable results become particularly interesting, and potentially quite important, when we consider the nature of the conditions under which the incongruency effect is and is not obtained. That is, the effect is quite replicable when (a) all information acquired pertains to only one trait dimension, (b) the information is processed with no distractions or demands on attentional and processing resources during either encoding or retrieval, and (c) the participant later tries to recall any and all information about the person, in any order, with no concern for content themes, and devotes himself or herself exclusively to this task. As social psychologists, we might legitimately wonder how often, in everyday life, these features characterize the conditions that exist as we form impressions of others. In contrast, it seems much more likely that impression formation typically occurs when (a) the perceiver learns an array of information pertaining to several facets of the person's life, (b) is simultaneously coping with multiple demands on cognitive resources, and (c) subsequent retrieval of specific information about the person will be for a given purpose that will guide the retrieval process to search for particular content. Yet based on the findings of our research and that of others (Bargh & Thein, 1985; Driscoll & Gingrich, 1997; Garcia-Marques & Hamilton, 1996; Garcia-Marques et al., 2002; Hamilton et al., 1989; Srull, 1981; Srull et al., 1985), it is precisely under those conditions that the incongruency effect is much less likely to occur. We believe that the pattern of findings that has emerged in this research literature seriously questions the extent to which, and how generally, the incongruency effect occurs in the impression formation process.

THE CONTINUING LEGACY OF BOB WYER

The specific theoretical ideas we have pursued in this research program, and the particular experiments we have developed to test them, were aimed at understanding the persisting evidence of what we earlier referred to as "two distinct paths" in the literature regarding the effect of prior expectancies on information processing. Although not conceived as tests of any of Bob Wyer's theories or hypotheses, we believe this program of research is noticeably "Wyeresque" in several important respects. Moreover, it is in those respects that we see evidence of Bob's pervasive and continuing influence—both direct and, as in this case, indirect—on the way researchers think about social information processing and the way they do research to study it. That is, we believe our work—as well as that of many other researchers—reflects some of the major themes of Bob's professional life.

First, our model derives very directly from the associative network model initially advanced by Hastie (1980; Hastie & Kumar, 1979) and further developed by Bob and his collaborators (Srull, 1981; Srull et al., 1985; Srull & Wyer, 1989). That theoretical development, and the research it inspired, was a major contribution to social cognition. Our work derived from that theoretical base, and this fact illustrates, in one small way, a larger, more general point: Bob's ideas and writings have had long-lasting influence on the subsequent work of others.

Second, our model attempts to recognize and understand processes that occur at different phases of information processing. That is, the TRAP Model recognizes (a) the nature of differential encoding processes for congruent and incongruent information, (b) the consequential differences in how that information is represented in memory, (c) different modes of retrieving information from that cognitive representation, and (d) the differential relations between the products of retrieval from those different modes (i.e., the broader issue of memory-judgment correlations). We believe that this inclusiveness reflects one of the hallmarks of Bob Wyer's work and approach to any topic he has pursued. Specifically, he has always tried to view any empirical finding, even the smallest results from a single experiment, in a broader perspective. There is always an emphasis on "the big picture."

And finally, a third feature of Bob's work, one that follows directly from the preceding point, is also evident in our approach. The TRAP Model is integrative, attempting to bring two seemingly contradictory empirical effects within one theoretical framework and to understand how they relate to each other. Bob's theorizing and research have always focused on integration of different processes and phenomena, often bringing together different, even disparate, processes and outcomes within a single theoretical structure.

Long-lasting theoretical developments, the big picture, and integration of different processes, phenomena, and even approaches—three hallmarks of Bob Wyer's thinking, of his theoretical and empirical work, and of his contributions to social psychology. We have presumptuously suggested that these virtues are, in some small way, also seen in our own work; we hope this is true. If so, then it serves as one example among many in which these themes of Bob's work are now evident in the work of others, not only among his remarkably talented cadre of former students but also in others who have had the privilege of knowing him and learning from him. The legacy of Bob Wyer continues.

ACKNOWLEDGMENTS

Preparation of this chapter was supported in part by National Institute of Mental Health Grant MH-40058 to the first author.

REFERENCES

Anderson, M. C., & McCulloch, K. C. (1999). Integration as a general boundary condition on retrieval-induced forgetting. *Journal of Experimental Psychology: Learning, Memory, and Cognition, 25*, 608–629.

Anderson, M. C., Bjork, R. A., & Bjork, E. L. (1994). Remembering can cause forgetting: Retrieval dynamics in long term memory. *Journal of Experimental Psychology: Learning, Memory, and Cognition, 20*, 1063–1087.

Anderson, M. C., & Neely, J. H. (1996). Interference and inhibition in memory retrieval. In E. L. Bjork & R. A. Bjork (Eds.), *Memory* (pp. 237–313). San Diego, CA: Academic Press.

Anderson, M. C., & Spellman, B. A. (1995). On the status of inhibitory mechanisms in cognition: Memory retrieval as a model case. *Psychological Review, 102*, 68–100.

Anderson, N. H. (1981). *Foundations of information integration theory.* New York: Academic Press.

Asch, S. E. (1946). Forming impressions of personality. *Journal of Abnormal and Social Psychology, 41*, 1230–1240.

Bardach, L., & Park, B. (1996). The effect of in-group/out-group status on memory for consistent and inconsistent behavior of an individual. *Personality & Social Psychology Bulletin, 22*, 169–178.

Bargh, J. A., & Thein, R. D. (1985). Individual construct accessibility, person memory, and the recall-judgment link: The case of information overload. *Journal of Personality and Social Psychology, 49*, 1129–1146.

Bobrow, D. G., & Norman, D. A. (1975). Some principles of memory schemata. In D. G. Bobrow & A. Collins (Eds.), *Representation and understanding: Studies in cognitive science* (pp. 131–149). New York: Academic Press.

Brigham, J. C. (1971). Ethnic stereotypes. *Psychological Bulletin, 76*, 15–33.

Brown, S. C. (1968). Role of stimulus-term and serial-position cues in constant-ordered paired-associates. *Journal of Experimental Psychology, 77*, 269–274.

Bruner, J. S. (1957). Going beyond the information given. In H. E. Gruber, K. R. Hammond, & R. Jessor (Eds.), *Contemporary approaches to cognition* (pp. 41–60). Cambridge, MA: Harvard University Press.

Cohen, C. E. (1981). Person categories and social perception: Testing some boundaries of the processing effects of prior knowledge. *Journal of Personality and Social Psychology, 40*, 441–452.

Crocker, J., Hannah, D. B., & Weber, R. (1983). Person memory and causal attribution. *Journal of Personality and Social Psychology, 44*, 55–66.

Darley J. M., & Gross, P. H. (1983). A hypothesis-confirming bias in labeling effects. *Journal of Personality and Social Psychology, 44*, 20–33.

Driscoll, D. M., & Gingrich, B. E. (1997). Effect of single-trait, social stereotype, and multi-trait expectancies on person impressions. *Journal of Social Behavior and Personality, 12*, 397–415.

Duncan, S. L. (1976). Differential social perception and attribution of intergroup violence: Testing the lower limits of stereotyping of blacks. *Journal of Personality and Social Psychology, 34*, 590–598.

Ebbesen, E. B. (1980). Cognitive processes in understanding ongoing behavior. In R. Hastie, T. M. Ostrom, E. B. Ebbesen, R. S. Wyer, Jr., D. L. Hamilton, & D. E. Carlston (Eds.), *Person memory: The cognitive basis of social perception.* Hillsdale, NJ: Lawrence Erlbaum Associates.

Ebbesen, E. B. (1981). Cognitive processes in inferences about a person's personality. In E. T. Higgins, C. P. Herman & M. P. Zanna (Eds.), *Social cognition: The Ontario symposium* (Vol. 1, pp. 247–276). Hillsdale, NJ: Lawrence Erlbaum Associates.

Gabrielcik, A., & Fazio, R. H. (1984). Priming and frequency estimation: A strict test of the availability heuristic. *Personality & Social Psychology Bulletin, 10,* 85–89.

Garcia-Marques, L. (1993). *The importance of being incongruent: How memorable would an uncultured librarian be? Towards a resolution of the apparent discrepancy between expectancy-based illusory correlations and incongruency effects.* Unpublished doctoral dissertation, Universidade de Lisboa, Lisboa.

Garcia-Marques, L., & Hamilton, D. L. (1996). Resolving the apparent discrepancy between the incongruency effect and the expectancy-based illusory correlation effect: The TRAP Model. *Journal of Personality and Social Psychology, 71,* 845–860.

Garcia-Marques, L., Hamilton, D. L., & Maddox, K. B. (2002). Exhaustive and heuristic retrieval processes in person cognition: Further tests of the TRAP Model. *Journal of Personality and Social Psychology, 82,* 193–207.

Hamilton, D. L. (1979). A cognitive-attributional analysis of stereotyping. In L. Berkowitz (Ed.), *Advances in Experimental Social Psychology* (Vol. 12, pp. 53–84). New York: Academic Press.

Hamilton, D. L. (1981). Illusory correlation as a basis for stereotyping. In D. L. Hamilton (Ed.), *Cognitive processes in stereotyping and intergroup behavior* (pp. 115–144). Hillsdale, NJ: Lawrence Erlbaum Associates.

Hamilton, D. L., Devine, P. G., & Ostrom, T. M. (1994). Social cognition and classic issues in social psychology. In P. G. Devine, D. L. Hamilton, & T. M. Ostrom, (Eds.), *Social cognition: Impact on social psychology* (pp. 1–13). San Diego, CA: Academic Press.

Hamilton, D. L., Driscoll, D. M., & Worth, L. T. (1989). Cognitive organization of impressions: Effects of incongruency in complex representations. *Journal of Personality and Social Psychology, 57,* 925–939.

Hamilton, D. L., & Rose, T. L. (1980). Illusory correlation and the maintenance of stereotypic beliefs. *Journal of Personality and Social Psychology, 39,* 832–845.

Hastie, R. (1980). Memory for behavioral information that confirms or contradicts a personality impression. In R. Hastie, T. M. Ostrom, E. B. Ebbesen, R. S. Wyer, Jr., D. L. Hamilton, & D. E. Carlston (Eds.), *Person memory: The cognitive basis of social perception* (pp. 155–177). Hillsdale, NJ: Lawrence Erlbaum Associates.

Hastie, R. (1981). Schematic principles in human memory. In E. T. Higgins, C. P. Herman, & M. P. Zanna (Eds.), *Social cognition: The Ontario symposium* (Vol. 1, pp. 39–88). Hillsdale, NJ: Lawrence Erlbaum Associates.

Hastie, R. (1984). Causes and effects of causal attribution. *Journal of Personality and Social Psychology, 46,* 44–56.

Hastie, R. (1988). A computer simulation model of person memory. *Journal of Experimental Social Psychology, 24,* 423–447.

Hastie R., & Kumar, P. A. (1979). Person memory: Personality traits as organizing principles in memory for behaviors. *Journal of Personality and Social Psychology, 37,* 25–38.

Hastie, R., Ostrom, T. M., Ebbesen, E. B., Wyer, R. S., Jr., Hamilton, D. L., & Carlston, D. E. (Eds.). (1980). *Person memory: The cognitive basis of social perception.* Hillsdale, NJ: Lawrence Erlbaum Associates.

Hastie R., & Park, B. (1986). The relationship between memory and judgment depends on whether the judgment task is memory-based or on-line. *Psychological Review, 93,* 258–268.

Hintzmann, D. L. (2001). Memory judgments. In E. Tulving & F. I. M. Craik (Eds.), *The Oxford handbook of memory* (pp. 165–178). New York: Oxford University Press.

Jacoby, L. L. (1983). Remembering the data: Analyzing processes in reading. *Journal of Verbal Learning and Verbal Behavior, 22,* 485–508.

Johnson, W. A., & Hawley, K. J. (1994). Perceptual inhibition of expected inputs: The key that opens closed minds. *Psychonomic Bulletin and Review, 1,* 56–72.

Jones, R. A. (1977). *Self-fulfilling prophecies: Social, psychological, and physiological effects of expectancies.* Hillsdale, NJ: Lawrence Erlbaum Associates.

Katz, D., & Braly, K. W. (1933). Racial stereotypes of 100 college students. *Journal of Abnormal and Social Psychology, 28,* 280–290.

Lichtenstein, M., & Srull, T. K. (1987). Processing objectives as a determinant of the relationship between recall and judgment. *Journal of Experimental Social Psychology, 23,* 93–118.

Macrae, C. N., Hewstone, M., & Griffiths, R. J. (1993). Processing load and memory for stereotype-based information. *European Journal of Social Psychology, 23,* 77–87.

McArthur, L. Z. (1982). Judging a book by its cover: A cognitive analysis of the relationship between physical appearance and stereotyping. In A. Hastorf & A. Isen (Eds.), *Cognitive social psychology.* New York: Elsevier North-Holland.

Newston, D. (1976). Foundations of attribution: The perception of ongoing behavior. In J. Harvey, W. Ickes, & R. Kidd (Eds.), *New directions in attribution research* (Vol. 1, pp. 223–248). Hillsdale, NJ: Lawrence Erlbaum Associates.

Ostrom, T. M., Lingle, J. H., Pryor, J. B., & Geva, N. (1980). Cognitive organization of person impressions. In R. Hastie, T. M. Ostrom, E. B. Ebbesen, R. S. Wyer, Jr., D. L. Hamilton, & D. E. Carlston (Eds.), *Person memory: The cognitive basis of social perception* (pp. 55–88). Hillsdale, NJ: Lawrence Erlbaum Associates.

Rojahn, K., & Pettigrew, T. F. (1992). Memory for schema-relevant information: A meta-analytic resolution. *British Journal of Social Psychology, 31,* 81–109.

Rothbart, M. (1981). Memory processes and social beliefs. In D. L. Hamilton (Ed.), *Cognitive processes in stereotyping and intergroup behavior.* (pp. 145–181) Hillsdale, NJ: Lawrence Erlbaum Associates.

Rothbart, M., & John, O. P. (1985). Social categorization and behavioral episodes: A cognitive analysis of the effects of intergroup contact. *Journal of Social Issues, 41*(3), 81–104.

Rundus, D. (1973). Negative effects of using list items as recall cues. *Journal of Verbal Learning & Verbal Behavior, 12*, 43–50.

Sagar, H. A., & Schofield, J. W. (1980). Racial and behavioral cues in black and white children's perceptions of ambiguously aggressive acts. *Journal of Personality and Social Psychology, 39*, 590–598.

Sherif, M. (1936). *The psychology of social norms*. New York: Harper's.

Sherman, J. W. (2001). The dynamic relationship between stereotype efficiency and mental representation. In G. B. Moskowitz (Ed.), *Cognitive social psychology: The Princeton symposium on the legacy and future of social cognition* (pp. 177–190). Mahwah, NJ: Lawrence Erlbaum Associates.

Sherman, J. W., & Frost, L. A. (2000). On the encoding of stereotype-relevant information under cognitive load. *Personality and Social Psychology Bulletin, 26*, 26–34.

Sherman, J. W., & Hamilton, D. L. (1994). On the formation of interitem associative links in person memory. *Journal of Experimental Social Psychology, 30*, 203–217.

Sherman, J. W., Lee, A. Y., Bessenoff, G. R., & Frost, L. A. (1998). Stereotype efficiency reconsidered: Encoding flexibility under cognitive load. *Journal of Personality and Social Psychology, 75*, 589–606.

Simon, H. A. (1957). *Models of man*. New York: Wiley.

Slamecka, N. J. (1968). An examination of trace storage in free recall. *Journal of Experimental Psychology, 76*, 504–513.

Smith, R. E., & Hunt, R. R. (2000). The influence of distinctive processing on retrieval-induced forgetting. *Memory and Cognition, 28*, 503–508.

Snyder, M. (1981a). Seek, and ye shall find: Testing hypotheses about other people. In E. T. Higgins, C. P. Herman, & M. P. Zanna (Eds.), *Social cognition: The Ontario Symposium in Personality and Social Psychology* (pp. 277–304). Hillsdale, NJ: Lawrence Erlbaum Associates.

Snyder, M. (1981b). On the self-perpetuating nature of social stereotypes. In D. L. Hamilton (Ed.), *Cognitive processes in stereotyping and intergroup behavior* (pp. 183–212). Hillsdale, NJ: Lawrence Erlbaum Associates.

Srull, T. K. (1981). Person memory: Some tests of associative storage and retrieval models. *Journal of Experimental Psychology: Human Learning and Memory, 7*, 440–463.

Srull, T. K., & Wyer, R. S., Jr. (1989). Person memory and judgment. *Psychological Review, 96*, 58–83.

Srull, T. K., Lichtenstein, M., & Rothbart, M. (1985). Associative storage and retrieval processes in person memory. *Journal of Experimental Psychology: Learning, Memory, and Cognition, 11*, 316–345.

Stangor, C., & Duan, C. (1991). Effects of multiple task demands upon memory for information about social groups. *Journal of Experimental Social Psychology, 27*, 357–378.

Stangor, C., & McMillan, D. (1992). Memory for expectancy-congruent and expectancy-incongruent information: A review of the social and social developmental literatures. *Psychological Bulletin, 111*, 42–61.

Stern, L., Marrs, S., Millar, M., & Cole, E. (1984). Processing time and the recall of inconsistent and consistent behaviors of individual and groups. *Journal of Personality and Social Psychology, 47,* 253–262.

Susskind, J., Maurer, K., Thakkar, V., Hamilton, D. L., & Sherman, J. W. (1999). Perceiving individuals and groups: Expectancies, dispositional inferences, and causal attributions. *Journal of Personality and Social Psychology, 76,* 181–191.

Taylor S. E., & Crocker, J. (1981). Schematic bases of social information processing. In E. T. Higgins, C. P. Herman, & M. P. Zanna (Eds.), *Social cognition: The Ontario Symposium* (Vol. 1, pp. 89–134). Hillsdale, NJ: Lawrence Erlbaum Associates.

Taylor, S. E., & Fiske, S. T. (1978). Salience, attention, and attribution: Top of the head phenomena. In L. Berkowitz (Ed.), *Advances in experimental social psychology* (Vol. 11, pp. 249–288). New York: Academic Press.

Taylor, S. E., & Fiske, S. T. (1981). Getting inside the head: Methodologies for process analysis in attribution and social cognition. In J. H. Harvey, W. Ickes, & R. F. Kidd (Eds.), *New directions in attribution research* (Vol. 3, pp. 459–524). Hillsdale, NJ: Lawrence Erlbaum Associates.

Von Hippel, W., Jonides, J., Hilton, J. L., & Narayan, S. (1993). Inhibitory effects of schematic processing on perceptual encoding. *Journal of Personality and Social Psychology, 64,* 921–935.

White, J. D., & Carlston, D. E. (1983). Consequences of schemata for attention, impressions, and recall in complex social interactions. *Journal of Personality and Social Psychology, 45,* 538–549.

Wyer, R. S., Jr., & Gordon, S. E. (1984). The cognitive representation of social information. In R. S. Wyer, Jr., & T. K. Srull (Eds.), *Handbook of social cognition* (Vol. 2, pp. 73–150). Hillsdale, NJ: Lawrence Erlbaum Associates..

Wyer, R. S., Jr., & Martin, L. L. (1986). Person memory: The role of traits, group stereotypes, and specific behaviors in the cognitive representation of persons. *Journal of Personality and Social Psychology, 50,* 661–675.

Wyer, R. S., Jr., & Srull, T. K. (1980). The processing of social stimulus information: A conceptual integration. In R. Hastie, T. M. Ostrom, E. B. Ebbesen, R. S. Wyer, Jr., D. L. Hamilton, & D. E. Carlston (Eds.), *Person memory: The cognitive basis of social perception* (pp. 55–88). Hillsdale, NJ: Lawrence Erlbaum Associates.

Wyer, R. S., Jr., & Srull, T. K. (1986). Human cognition in its social context. *Psychological Review, 93,* 322–359.

Wyer, R. S., Jr., & Srull, T. K. (1989). *Memory and cognition in its social context.* Hillsdale, NJ: Lawrence Erlbaum Associates.

Zadny, J., & Gerard, H. B. (1974). Attributed intentions and informational selectivity. *Journal of Experimental Social Psychology, 10,* 34–52.

4

Accessibility Revisited

Norbert Schwarz
University of Michigan

Herbert Bless
University of Mannheim, Germany

Michaela Wänke
University of Erfurt, Germany

Piotr Winkielman
University of Denver

Highlighting the role of information accessibility in human judgment has been one of the core contributions of social cognition research. Building on the path-breaking work of Higgins, Wyer, and colleagues (e.g., Higgins, Rholes, & Jones, 1977; Srull & Wyer, 1979), researchers documented the profound influence of "what happens to come to mind" across many content domains (for reviews see Bodenhausen & Wyer, 1987; Higgins, 1996; Wyer & Carlston, 1979; Wyer & Srull, 1989). As Wyer and Srull (1989, p. 103) put it in their integrative review, "the knowledge we have acquired and used most recently has a disproportionate influence on judgments and decisions to which it is relevant. These effects [...] appear to be evident at all stages of information processing." This insight has changed the field's perspective on human judgment and has become one of the most influential ideas that social psychology has contributed to the social sciences at large, as illustrated by its influence in public opinion research (Kinder, 1998), political science (Ottati, 2001), consumer research (Shavitt & Wänke, 2001) and survey methodology (Sudman, Bradburn, & Schwarz, 1996; Tourangeau, Rips, & Rasinski, 2000). Three related propositions have received particular attention, acquiring the status of truisms in social cognition research.

First, when forming a judgment, individuals rarely retrieve all information that may be relevant, truncating the search process as soon as "enough" information has come to mind to form a judgment with sufficient subjective certainty. Accordingly, the judgment is primarily based on the subset of information that is most accessible at the time. We refer to this assumption as *Proposition 1*.

Second, when individuals encounter new information, they usually do not entertain multiple possible interpretations. Instead, they interpret the information in terms of the most accessible concept that is applicable to the material at hand. Accordingly, accessible concepts of differential valence can give rise to differential interpretations, which result in differential evaluative judgments. We refer to this assumption as *Proposition 2*.

A third assumption holds that accessibility effects on overt behavior are mediated by differential interpretations of the situation. In the words of Wyer and Srull (1989, p. 147), "concepts that happen to be activated at the time […] events are experienced may influence the interpretation of the events and therefore may influence behavioral decisions." We refer to this assumption as *Proposition 3*.

These three propositions have received ample support across many content domains and are compatible with associative network models (e.g., Wyer & Carlston, 1979) as well as bin models (e.g., Wyer & Srull, 1989) of human memory. Nevertheless, they share the fate of many other exceptionally fruitful ideas in the history of science (see Root-Bernstein, 1989): By stimulating diverse novel lines of inquiry, they run the risk of eventually encountering data that are incompatible with the original formulation. In the present case, the accumulating body of research into knowledge accessibility increasingly indicates that the above truisms fail to capture the full complexity of accessibility phenomena in human judgment. In fact, we cannot predict how accessible information influences a judgment without taking additional variables into account. This chapter addresses these complexities.

We begin with a discussion of recall-based judgments. According to Proposition 1, we should be able to predict an individual's judgment solely by knowing what comes to mind. This, however, is not the case. First, the inferences that individuals draw from accessible content are qualified by subjective accessibility experiences that accompany the recall process (for

reviews, see Schwarz, 1998, and the contributions in Bless & Forgas, 2000).
In general, individuals' conclusions are consistent with the implications of
recalled content when recall is experienced as easy, but in opposition to the
implications of recalled content when recall is experienced as difficult. This
contingency is eliminated when the informational value of the subjective
accessibility experience is called into question. Moreover, it can be overridden by high processing motivation. We address the interplay of accessible
content, accessibility experiences, and processing motivation in the first
section. As will become apparent, our conceptualization of the informational value of accessibility experiences parallels the conceptualization of af-
fect-as-information, initially introduced by Wyer and Carlston (1979), who
were among the first to draw attention to the role of experiential information in social cognition (for a review, see Schwarz & Clore, 1996).

Second, when individuals draw on accessible content, its specific impact
depends on how it is used. Merely knowing that X is highly accessible is not
sufficient to predict how X will influence the judgment at hand. Instead, we
need to know if X is used in constructing a mental representation of the object of judgment, or of the standard against which the object is evaluated.
The former use results in assimilation effects, but the latter results in contrast effects (Schwarz & Bless, 1992a). This work into mental construal processes revisits topics of information organization and integration that
figured prominently in Wyer's (1974) *Information Organization and Change:
An Information Processing Approach*. We address these diverging influences
of the same accessible content in the second section.

Subsequently, we turn to a discussion of individuals' responses to new information. As is the case for recall-based judgments, trait priming procedures inherently confound what comes to mind with the ease with which it
comes to mind. We discuss possible implications of this confound and offer
some conjectures that qualify Proposition 2. Going beyond the encoding
principle of Proposition 2, a related body of research indicates that the influence of highly accessible concepts is not limited to the semantic interpretation of ambiguous information. Instead, highly accessible concepts also
influence the fluency with which new information can be processed. Fluency itself is hedonically marked, and high fluency results in more positive
evaluations, which are not mediated by semantic processes (Winkielman,
Schwarz, Reber, & Fazendeiro, in press), further highlighting the role of experiential information (Wyer & Carlston, 1979). We address these non-se-
mantic influences of concept accessibility in the third and fourth section.

Finally, Proposition 3 holds that accessible information influences behavior through its influence on the interpretation of the situation. Although
this possibility has received ample support (see Higgins, 1996; Wyer & Srull,
1989), recent research suggests that accessible concepts may also influence
behavior through direct links between the mental representation of concep-

tual knowledge and behavioral responses (Dijksterhuis & Bargh, 2001). We comment on this possibility in the final section and conclude with a discussion of open issues.

ACCESSIBLE CONTENT AND ACCESSIBILITY EXPERIENCES: BEYOND "WHAT" COMES TO MIND

Numerous studies are consistent with the assumption that judgments depend on the subset of potentially relevant information that is most accessible at the time (for reviews, see Bodenhausen & Wyer, 1987; Higgins, 1996; Wyer & Srull, 1989). For example, Strack, Martin, and Schwarz (1988) asked students to report on their dating frequency as well as their general life-satisfaction. When the satisfaction question preceded the dating frequency question, the two questions were uncorrelated, $r = -.12$. But when the dating question preceded the life-satisfaction question, the correlation jumped to $r = +.66$, presumably because the dating question rendered dating-related information highly accessible in memory. What has often been overlooked in studies of this type is that the priming manipulation (in this case, the preceding question) does not only influence what comes to mind, but also affects how easily it comes to mind. That is, priming manipulations inherently confound the increased accessibility of the primed content with the subjective experience of ease. When both components are separated, the emerging picture is more complex than Proposition 1 suggests.

If judgments were solely based on what comes to mind, we would then observe, for example, that a task that renders many of an individual's own assertive behaviors accessible in memory results in judgments of higher assertiveness than does a task that renders only a few assertive behaviors accessible. Empirically, this is not necessarily the case. Schwarz, Bless, Strack et al. (1991, Experiment 1) asked participants to recall either 6 or 12 examples of their own assertive or unassertive behavior. Subsequently, participants rated their own assertiveness. As predicted by the proposition that judgments depend on accessible content, participants rated themselves as more assertive after recalling 6 examples of assertive behavior than after recalling 6 examples of unassertive behavior (see Table 4.1). In contrast to this proposition, however, increasing the number of recalled examples reversed the observed pattern: Participants who successfully recalled 12 examples of assertive behavior rated themselves as less assertive than did participants who recalled 12 examples of unassertive behavior. Moreover, those who recalled 12 assertive (or unassertive, respectively) behaviors rated themselves as less (or more, respectively) assertive than those who recalled only 6 examples.

To reconcile these observations with Proposition 1, one may assume that the quality of the recalled examples decreased over the course of the recall task, leaving participants in the 12-example conditions with a poorer set of

TABLE 4.1

Self-reports of Assertiveness as a Function of Valence
and Number of Recalled Behaviors

	Type of Behavior	
	Assertive	Unassertive
Number of Recalled Examples		
Six	6.3	5.2
Twelve	5.2	6.2

Note. N is 9 or 10 per condition. Mean score of three questions is given; possible range is 1 to 10, with higher values reflecting higher assertiveness. Adapted from Schwarz, Bless, Strack, Klumpp, Rittenauer-Schatka, and Simons (1991, Experiment 1).

accessible examples. Content analyses indicated, however, that this was not the case. Instead, the observed reversal reflected participants' experience that it was easy to recall 6 examples, but difficult to recall 12. This difficulty, in turn, presumably suggested to participants that they could not be so (un)assertive after all, else it would not be so difficult to come up with 12 examples. Supporting this interpretation, the impact of participants' subjective accessibility experience was eliminated when they were led to attribute the experience to the influence of background music played to them (Schwarz, Bless, Strack et al., 1991, Experiment 3), reversing the otherwise obtained pattern. In this case, they drew on the recalled content and reported higher (or lower, respectively) assertiveness the more examples of assertive (or unassertive, respectively) behaviors they had recalled.

Further highlighting the role of subjective accessibility experiences, Wänke, Bless, and Biller (1996) controlled for accessible content by asking some participants to generate a few or many examples, and subsequently presented these examples to other, yoked participants. As expected, participants who actively generated examples drew on their accessibility experiences and were more influenced when the task requested few rather than many examples. In contrast, yoked participants, who merely read the examples generated by others, were more influenced the more examples they read.

Finally, Stepper and Strack (1993, Experiment 2) manipulated subjective accessibility experiences independent of the amount of recall. They asked all participants to recall six examples of assertive or unassertive behavior, thus holding actual recall demands constant. To manipulate the subjective recall experiences, they induced participants to contract either their corrugator muscle or their zygomaticus muscle during the recall task. Contraction of the corrugator muscle produces a furrowed brow, an expression commonly associated with a feeling of effort. Contraction of the zygomaticus muscle produces a light smile, an expression commonly associated with a feeling of ease. As expected, participants who recalled six examples of assertive behavior while adopting a light smile judged themselves as more assertive than participants who adopted a furrowed brow. Conversely, participants who recalled six examples of unassertive behavior while adopting a light smile judged themselves as less assertive than participants who adopted a furrowed brow.

In combination, these studies demonstrate that subjective accessibility experiences are informative in their own right. Moreover, their operation parallels the operation of other sources of experiential information, such as individuals' mood at the time of judgment (Schwarz & Clore, 1983; Wyer & Carlston, 1979). Finally, individuals do not draw on their accessibility experiences when their informational value is called into question.

Similar interaction effects of accessible content and subjective accessibility experiences have been observed across many content domains, ranging from judgments of risk (e.g., Raghubir & Menon, 1998; Rothman & Schwarz, 1998) and attitude strength (e.g., Haddock, Rothman, Reber, & Schwarz, 1999; Haddock, Rothman, & Schwarz, 1996) to evaluations of consumer products (e.g., Wänke, Bohner, & Jurkowitsch, 1997), assessments of one's own memory (e.g., Winkielman, Schwarz, & Belli, 1998) and estimates of frequency (e.g., Aarts & Dijksterhuis, 1999; Wänke, Schwarz, & Bless, 1995) and probability (e.g., Sanna, Schwarz, & Stocker, 2002). These studies illustrate throughout that any recall task provides two distinct sources of information: the content that is recalled and the subjective experience of the ease or difficulty with which it can be brought to mind. Which conclusions people draw from their accessibility experiences depends on their beliefs about memory (see Skurnik, Schwarz, & Winkielman, 2000, for a discussion).

Meta-Memory Beliefs

One meta-memory belief, which is at the heart of Tversky and Kahneman's (1973) availability heuristic, correctly holds that it is easier to recall examples of events that are frequent rather than rare in the world. Accordingly, individuals infer from ease of recall or generation that there are many relevant examples "out there," and that the recalled ones are relatively typical. Conversely, they infer from difficulty of recall or generation that relevant examples are infrequent and atypical. This results in judgments that are consistent with the implications of the content of the recalled examples when recall is easy, but in opposition to the implications of recalled content when recall is difficult (for reviews, see Schwarz, 1998; Schwarz & Vaughn, in 2002).

Another meta-memory belief correctly holds that it is easy to recall examples from categories that are well rather than poorly represented in memory. Accordingly, individuals use the ease or difficulty of recall to infer how much information about a category is stored in memory. For example, Winkielman, Schwarz, and Belli (1998) observed that participants who had to recall twelve childhood events subsequently rated their childhood memory as poorer than participants who had to recall only four events, despite the fact that they had just recalled three times as many events.

Importantly, these meta-memory beliefs can give rise to second-order inferences when an appropriate subjective theory is applied. For example, Winkielman and Schwarz (2001) suggested to some participants that unpleasant events might be poorly represented in memory because we avoid thinking about the "bad stuff," making it difficult to recall details of unpleasant periods of one's life. In contrast, they suggested to other participants that pleasant events might be poorly represented because we don't ruminate about the "good stuff," making it difficult to recall details of pleasant periods of one's life. As predicted, participants who had to recall 12 events, a difficult task, evaluated their childhood as less happy when the accessible meta-memory belief entailed that negative life-periods are difficult to remember than when it entailed that positive life-periods are difficult to remember. Similarly, Haddock et al. (1999) observed that participants who had to generate only a few arguments in favor of an attitude position held this position with greater confidence than did participants who had to generate many positions, presumably because ease of generation suggested that there are many supportive arguments "out there."

Finally, Wänke and Bless (2000) suggested that recipients of a persuasive message may assume that plausible and compelling arguments are easier to remember than specious ones. Consistent with this conjecture, they observed that the same argument, was more influential the more contextual cues facilitated its recall, thus inducing an experience of ease. We return to their study below, in our discussion of processing motivation.

Undermining the Informational Value of Accessibility Experiences

None of the discussed influences of accessibility experiences can be observed when the informational value of the experience is called into question. Variables that undermine the informational value of accessibility experiences include external factors that may influence recall or generation (e.g., Haddock et al., 1999; Schwarz, Bless, Strack et al., 1991), and attribution of the experience to task characteristics (e.g., "anybody would find this difficult," Winkielman et al., 1998). Moreover, individuals are unlikely to draw on experienced difficulty of recall when they assume that they are not particularly knowledgeable in the respective content domain (Sanna & Schwarz, in press). Not being able to name famous Spanish matadors, for example, doesn't imply there aren't any; it only implies one does not know them. Reliance on accessibility experiences therefore requires the tacit assumption that one is knowledgeable in the content domain. In apparent contrast to this generalization, Ofir (2000) observed that participants with low knowledge were likely to rely on their accessibility experiences, whereas participants with high knowledge were likely to draw on accessible content. This finding may reflect either that the low-knowledge participants were unaware of their lack of expertise or that the high-knowledge participants were not only more knowledgeable, but also more motivated to engage in systematic processing, an issue to which we return in the following section.

Processing Motivation

Complicating things further, individuals' reliance on accessible content versus accessibility experiences depends on the processing motivation they bring to the task. In most cases, judges are likely to rely on their accessibility experiences as a source of information when processing motivation is low, but to turn to accessible content when processing motivation is high, even when this content was difficult to recall. This observation is consistent with the assumption that reliance on accessibility experiences is part of a heuristic processing strategy, whereas reliance on accessible content is part of a systematic processing strategy (Schwarz, 1998).

Rothman and Schwarz (1998; for a conceptual replication, see Grayson & Schwarz, 1999) asked male participants to recall either a few or many behaviors that increase or decrease their risk for heart disease. To manipulate processing motivation, participants were first asked to report on their family history of heart disease. Presumably, this recall task has higher personal relevance for those with a family history of heart disease than for those without, once this history is rendered salient. As shown in Table 4.2, men with a family history of heart disease drew on the relevant behavioral information they recalled. They reported higher vulnerability after recalling eight rather than three risk-increasing behaviors, and lower vulnerability after recalling eight rather than three risk-decreasing behaviors. In contrast, men without a family history of heart disease drew on their accessibility experiences, resulting in the opposite pattern. They reported lower vulnerability after recalling eight (difficult) rather than three (easy) risk-increasing behaviors, and higher vulnerability after recalling eight rather than three risk-decreasing behaviors.

In addition, participants' perceived need for behavior change paralleled their vulnerability judgments, as shown in the bottom panel of Table 4.2. Note that participants with a family history of heart disease reported the highest need for behavior change after recalling eight risk-increasing behaviors,

TABLE 4.2
Vulnerability to Heart Disease as a Function of Type and Number
of Recalled Behaviors, and Family History

	Type of Behavior	
	Risk-increasing	Risk-decreasing
Vulnerability Judgments		
With family history		
3 examples	4.6	5.8
8 examples	5.4	3.8
Without family history		
3 examples	3.9	3.1
8 examples	3.2	4.3
Need for Behavior Change		
With family history		
3 examples	3.6	5.2
8 examples	6.3	4.7
Without family history		
3 examples	3.4	3.0
8 examples	2.8	5.6

Note. N is 8 to 12 per condition. Judgments of vulnerability and the need to change current behavior were made on 9-point scales, with higher values indicating greater vulnerability and need to change, respectively. Adapted from Rothman and Schwarz (1998).

whereas participants without that family history reported the lowest need for behavior change under this condition, again illustrating a reversal in the judgmental outcome. In combination, these findings (and their conceptual replication; Grayson & Schwarz, 1999) suggest that individuals are likely to draw on their subjective accessibility experiences under low processing motivation, but on accessible content under high processing motivation.

While this generalization is likely to hold for recall and generation tasks of the type discussed above, Wänke and Bless (2000) reported an interesting exception. As already noted, they assumed that individuals may hold the belief that it is easier to remember plausible and compelling arguments rather than specious ones. If so, they may consider a given argument more compelling when they find it easier to recall. To manipulate participants' accessibility experiences, Wänke and Bless provided participants with retrieval cues that made it either easy or difficult to recall a given argument from a previously presented message. As expected, participants were more persuaded by the same argument when this manipulation facilitated its recall. Consistent with the general observation that argument quality is more likely to influence attitude judgments under high processing motivation (for a review, see Eagly & Chaiken, 1993), this effect was more pronounced under high than under low processing motivation. As this example illustrates, the impact of processing motivation is likely to depend on the meta-memory belief that is brought to bear on the accessibility experience in the first place, adding an additional level of complexity to the interplay of accessible content, accessibility experiences, and processing motivation.

Conclusions

In combination, the reviewed research highlights that we cannot predict judgmental outcomes by merely knowing what comes to mind, in contrast to Proposition 1. Instead, we need to consider the accessible content, the accessibility experience and its perceived diagnosticity, and the person's processing motivation. When processing motivation is high, judgments are indeed based on accessible content, as predicted by Proposition 1, even when this content is difficult to bring to mind. When processing motivation is low, however, judgments are only consistent with accessible content only when recall is easy—not when it is difficult. This contingency is eliminated when the informational value of the accessibility experience is called into question, in which case judges draw on the only diagnostic source of information left: accessible content. Different meta-memory beliefs may add additional complexity to these contingencies for some tasks, as the results of Wänke and Bless (2000) illustrate.

While the above effects are reliably replicable (for a review, see Schwarz, 1998), we know little about how these contingencies play out under natural conditions. We surmise that Proposition 1 holds up very well under most natural conditions. Despite the fact that Proposition 1 does not capture the complexity of the underlying processes, its predictions will be right more often than wrong — although sometimes for the wrong reasons.

First, suppose that a person approaches the task with high processing motivation. In this case, the person is likely to rely on a systematic processing strategy that draws on accessible content rather than accessibility experiences (e.g., Grayson & Schwarz, 1999; Rothman & Schwarz, 1998). Accordingly, her judgments will be consistent with recalled content, as predicted by Proposition 1.

Second, suppose that a person approaches the judgment task with low processing motivation. In this case, we may expect that the person draws on her accessibility experiences instead of accessible content. But given that information search is truncated early under conditions of low processing motivation, the person is unlikely to encounter any recall difficulties to begin with. If so, the most likely accessibility experience is one of ease. Drawing on this experience, the person will arrive at a judgment that is consistent with the implications of recalled content, again in line with the predictions of Proposition 1.

Third, recall will be experienced as difficult under the limited information search that characterizes low processing motivation only when the person's knowledge in the content domain is extremely limited. In this case, the person's judgments are likely to be in opposition to the implications of recalled content, in contrast to the predictions of Proposition 1.

Finally, if the person is aware of her limited expertise, she may correctly attribute the experienced difficulty to her own lack of knowledge. This attribution, in turn, would undermine the informational value of the experienced difficulty of the task at hand (as shown by Sanna & Schwarz, in press). Hence the person would draw on recalled content despite the fact that it was difficult to bring to mind, as observed under (mis)attribution conditions (e.g., Sanna & Schwarz, in press; Schwarz et al., 1991).

As these conjectures indicate, the predictions of Proposition 1 would be violated only when recall is experienced as difficult, despite a limited recall effort, and when this difficulty is not attributed to one's own lack of knowledge. As a result, the predictions of Proposition 1 provide a good approximation under most natural conditions, although not always for the right reason. Next, we turn to another set of complications, namely the complications that arise from the use of accessible content.

INFORMATION ACCESSIBILITY AND USE: MENTAL CONSTRUAL PROCESSES

How a given piece of accessible information influences a judgment depends on how it is used. Evaluative judgments that are based on features of the target (rather than on the perceiver's affective response; see Schwarz & Clore, 1996) require two mental representations: a representation of the target and a representation of a standard against which the target is evaluated (Schwarz & Bless, 1992a). Both representations are formed on the spot, drawing on information that is chronically or temporarily accessible. Information that is used in forming a representation of the target results in assimilation effects; that is, the inclusion of positive (negative) information results in a more positive (negative) judgment. Conversely, information that is used in forming a representation results in a contrast effect; that is, more positive (negative) information results in a more positive (negative) standard, against which the target is evaluated less (more) favorably. Hence the same piece of accessible information can have opposite effects, depending on how it is used. The variables that influence information use can be organized by assuming that perceivers tacitly ask themselves three questions, which serve as filters that channel information use.

Why Does it Come to Mind?

The first filter is: "Am I only thinking of this information because it was brought to mind by some irrelevant influence?" If so, the accessible information is not used in forming a representation of the target. Accordingly, awareness of the priming episode, for example, undermines use of the primed information, resulting in contrast effects (e.g., Lombardi, Higgins, & Bargh, 1987; Martin, 1986; Strack, Schwarz, Bless, Kübler, & Wänke, 1993).

Does it Bear on the Target?

When the information passes this first test, the second filter is: "Does this information represent a feature of the target?" This decision is driven by the numerous variables known to influence the categorization of information, including the information's extremity and typicality, as well as the presentation format and related context variables (for reviews, see Schwarz & Bless, 1992a; Martin, Strack, & Stapel, 2001).

Although these variables are crucial under natural conditions, they are ambiguous with regard to the role of categorization processes per se. For example, the observation that a typical and an atypical exemplar have differential effects on the evaluation of a group may reflect (a) that the typical exemplar is included in the representation of the group, whereas the atypical exemplar is not, (b) that the two exemplars differ in the information they bring to mind, or (c) both. To isolate the role of categorization processes per se, we therefore need to rely on manipulations that elicit different categorizations of the same information, as a few examples may illustrate.

In a political judgment study, Bless and Schwarz (1998) took advantage of the ambiguous category membership of the highly popular Richard von Weizsäcker, who, at the time, was President of the Federal Republic of Germany. On the one hand, the President is a politician; on the other hand, his office as a formal figure head (similar to the Queen in the United Kingdom) commits him to refrain from party politics. This allowed us to ask some respondents if they happened to know of which party Richard von Weizsäcker was a member, but to ask other respondents if they happened to know which office prevents him from participating in party politics. Evaluations of his party served as the dependent variable. Relative to a condition in which Richard von Weizsäcker was never mentioned, participants evaluated his party more positively when the party membership question elicited his inclusion in the representation formed of his party. Conversely, they evaluated his party more negatively when the presidency question elicited his exclusion from this representation (see also Stapel & Schwarz, 1998).

Similarly, Bless and Wänke (2000) presented all participants with the same list of moderately typical television shows and asked them to select two shows they considered (a) typically favorable, (b) atypically favorable, (c) typically unfavorable, or (d) atypically unfavorable. Because all shows were similarly typical, participants' actual selection was driven by their favorability. Nevertheless, the typicality component of the categorization task influenced participants' overall evaluation of television programs in general, relative to a control condition (see Table 4.3). After selecting two favorably evaluated shows, they evaluated television programs in general more positively when the selection task entailed that they are typical rather than atypical. Conversely, after selecting two unfavorably evaluated shows, they evaluated television programs in general more negatively when the selection task entailed that they are typical rather than atypical. Thus the same exemplars (television shows) elicited assimilation or contrast effects on judgments of a superordinate category, depending on their categorization.

TABLE 4.3

Category Evaluations as a Function of Exemplar Valence and Exemplar Typicality

	Assigned Typicality		
	Typical	Atypical	Control group
Valence of exemplars			
Favorable	4.6	3.5	—
Unfavorable	3.3	4.6	—
Control group	—	—	4.1

Note. Evaluations ranged from 1 to 9, with higher scores indicating more positive evaluations. Adapted from Bless and Wänke (2000).

Extending this theme to issues of stereotype change, Bless, Schwarz, Bodenhausen, and Thiel (2001) provided all participants with the same description of a target person, whose features were partly consistent and partly inconsistent with the stereotype about a group. After participants read the description, they answered different knowledge questions that did or did not invite the inclusion of the exemplar in the representation formed of the group. As shown in Table 4.4, inclusion of the (somewhat) atypical exemplar in the representation formed of the group elicited less stereotypical judgments of the group, indicating stereotype change. Yet the desired stereotype change observed in judgments of the group came at a price for the atypical exemplar, who was now evaluated in more stereotypical terms. Conversely, excluding the exemplar from the representation of the group elicited less stereotypical judgments of the exemplar. Yet this beneficial effect for the exemplar came at a price for the group, which was now evaluated in more stereotypical terms. In short, inclusion resulted in assimilation effects, and exclusion resulted in contrast effects, on judgments of the exemplar as well as of the group.

On the theoretical side, these findings again highlight that the same information can affect judgments in opposite ways, depending on how it is used. On the applied side, these findings suggest that stereotype change involves an unfortunate trade-off between the group and its individuated members, in which beneficial changes for one come at a price for the other.

Finally, one of the most reliable determinants of assimilation and contrast is the categorical relationship between the primed information and the target itself. Suppose, for example, that a preceding question brings Richard Nixon to mind and participants are asked to judge the trustworthiness of "American politicians." Nixon is a member of the superordinate target category "American politicians," resulting in an assimilation effect in the form of

TABLE 4.4

Stereotypic Evaluations as a Function of Target and Categorization

	Inclusion	Control	Exclusion
Judgmental target			
Group	3.67	3.84	4.83
Exemplar	2.64	2.33	1.78

Note. Higher scores reflect more stereotypic evaluations. Adapted from Bless, Schwarz, Bodenhausen, and Thiel (2001).

lower trustworthiness. Yet ratings of other exemplars from this category (e.g., Newt Gingrich) show contrast effects, reflecting that lateral categories are mutually exclusive (e.g., Schwarz & Bless, 1992b; Stapel & Schwarz, 1998; Wänke, Bless, & Igou, 2001). This divergent effect of primed information on superordinate and lateral targets is at the heart of many asymmetries in public opinion; e.g., the observation that Americans distrust Congress but trust their own representative.

Conversational Norms

The third and final filter pertains to the norms of conversational conduct that govern information use in conversations: "Is it conversationally appropriate to use this information?" Conversational norms prohibit redundancy and invite speakers to provide information that is new to the recipient, rather than information that the recipient already has (for a review, see Schwarz, 1994; 1996). Hence highly accessible information is not used when it violates this conversational norm, again resulting in contrast effects (e.g., Schwarz, Strack, & Mai, 1991; Strack, Martin, & Schwarz, 1988).

Information that passes all three tests is included in the representation formed of the target and results in assimilation effects. Information that fails any one of these tests is excluded from the representation formed of the target, but may be used in forming a representation of the standard, resulting in contrast effects.

The Size of Assimilation and Contrast Effects

Theoretically, the impact of a given piece of information should decrease with the amount and extremity of other information used in forming the respective representation (see Wyer, 1974).

Supporting this set size principle, we observed attenuated assimilation as well as attenuated contrast effects the more other information is temporarily (e.g., Bless, Igou, Schwarz, & Wänke, 2000) or chronically (e.g. Wänke, Bless, & Schwarz, 1998) accessible and used in forming a representation of the target or of the standard, respectively.

Conclusions

As this selective review of mental construal processes indicates, Proposition 1 fails to capture the complexity of the processes underlying recall-based judgments. Even when people draw on accessible content rather than their accessibility experiences, we cannot predict the impact of a given piece of accessible information without taking its use into account. The same information can elicit assimilation as well as contrast effect, depending on whether it is used in forming a representation of the target or a representation of the standard against which the target is evaluated.

Subjective accessibility experiences are likely to add further complexity to the construal process. Theoretically, we may expect that information that is difficult to bring to mind seems less typical for the target category (see Tversky & Kahneman, 1973) and is thus less likely to be included in the representation formed of the target. The findings reviewed in the section on accessibility experiences are compatible with this conjecture, but do not allow us to separate the effects of perceived frequency ("How many exemplars are out there?") and perceived typicality ("How typical are the ones I retrieved?"). This issue awaits further research.

CONCEPT PRIMING AND ACCESSIBILITY EXPERIENCES

We now turn to a discussion of Proposition 2. This proposition holds that ambiguous information is interpreted in terms of the most accessible applicable concept. "When two or more concepts are potentially applicable for interpreting a behavior, the first concept that is identified [...] is the one that is typically used" (Wyer & Srull, 1989, p. 117). Hence, readers interpret a sentence such as, "Donald was well aware of his ability to do many things well" (taken from Higgins et al., 1977) either as indicating that Donald is "confident" or that he is "conceited," depending on which of these concepts was primed. We surmise that such encoding effects not only require that the respective concept comes to mind, but that it does so easily — which is virtually guaranteed by the priming manipulation. Although a direct test is not available, several observations are consistent with this conjecture.

Using a scrambled sentence task, Srull and Wyer (1979) observed that encoding effects "increased with the number of trait-relevant priming items" and "decreased with the time interval between the performance of the priming task and presentation of the stimulus information" (Wyer & Srull, 1989, p. 121). They interpreted these findings in the context of their bin model of memory. According to this model, "the more often a trait concept is primed, the more copies of it should be made and redeposited on top of the semantic bin"; conversely, the longer the time interval, the more likely it is that other applicable concepts are "activated in the interim, and copies of these concepts are redeposited in the semantic bin on top of the explicitly primed concept" (Wyer & Srull, 1989, p. 120). Hence the frequency of priming increases, and the length of the time interval decreases, the likelihood that the primed concept is retrieved later on.

This interpretation has two important implications. First, it assumes that the observed differences are solely due to differential likelihood of concept retrieval. That is, a larger number of participants is assumed to retrieve and apply the primed concept under conditions of frequent priming and short delays. Second, it locates the observed differences between, rather than within, participants: Once the concept is retrieved and applied, the judgment is the same, independent of frequency of priming and time interval. Relevant is solely if the concept is retrieved at the time of encoding. If true, this process should result in differential variance within the experimental conditions: The larger the proportion of participants who retrieve the concept, the smaller the variance in the respective condition of the experiment. Empirically, this was apparently not the case (see Srull & Wyer, 1979).

Alternatively, we may locate the observed differences within participants by assuming that time interval and frequency of priming influence the ease with which the primed concept comes to mind. From this perspective, participants interpret any thoughts that happen to come to mind while reading the target description as their response to the target (see Clore, 1992; Schwarz et al., 1991, for a discussion). The faster the respective trait concept "pops to mind," the more indicative it seems, resulting in a more extreme trait judgment. This process would result in the patterns observed by Srull and Wyer (1979), without entailing a prediction of differential variance within the respective experimental conditions. Of course, the viability of this ex post interpretation is an open issue. Nevertheless, several findings are compatible with the theoretical assumptions.

If encoding effects of concept priming are based on a metacognitive process by which individuals use their own apparent reactions to the target as input into the judgment, we should observe that priming effects are not obtained when perceivers are aware that the concept may come to mind for "the wrong reason" (see Clore, 1992; Schwarz & Bless, 1992a; Schwarz & Clore, 1996, for related discussions). Empirically, this is the case and primed concepts are not applied when perceivers are aware of a potential influence of the primes (e.g., Lombardi et al., 1987; Strack et al., 1993). In this case, perceivers discount the primed concept and turn to other applicable concepts instead, often resulting in a contrast effect.

These conjectures suggest that accessibility experiences may contribute to the encoding effects predicted by Proposition 2. As in the case of recall-based judgments, priming procedures inherently confound accessible content and subjective accessibility experiences. Unfortunately, the empirical exploration of this issue is hampered by a lack of suitable experimental procedures that go beyond the manipulation of participants' awareness of the priming episode, discussed above. Hence a core theoretical issue of social cognition research awaits experimental ingenuity: Is the mere accessibility of a trait concept sufficient for the commonly observed encoding effects, or does the application of the accessible concept require the subjective experience of ease, which is virtually guaranteed by the manipulations we use in priming experiments?

CONCEPT ACCESSIBILITY AND PROCESSING FLUENCY: NON-SEMANTIC EFFECTS OF PRIMING

Independent of the open issues addressed above, all researchers agree that concept priming influences subsequent evaluative judgments through differential semantic interpretation of ambiguous input information. This assumption is well supported by the available evidence (for reviews, see Higgins, 1996; Wyer & Srull, 1989). Recent findings suggest, however, that concept priming may also influence evaluative judgment in ways that are not mediated by differential semantic interpretation of the input. We now turn to this research.

As a growing body of work into perceptual fluency indicates, a given object is evaluated more positively the more easily it can be perceived (for a review, see Winkielman, Schwarz, Reber, & Fazendeiro, 2003). Hence any variable that facilitates fluent perception is likely to increase liking, from figure-ground contrast (e.g., Reber, Winkielman, & Schwarz, 1998) and presentation time (Reber et al., 1998) to previous exposure (as known since Zajonc's [1968] demonstration of the mere exposure effect). Extending this theme, Reber et al (1998) observed that participants liked a given picture more when it was preceded by a subliminally presented matching, rather than mismatching, contour. In none of these cases can the difference in evaluative judgment be traced to differences in the semantic interpretation of the targets. Instead, the available evidence suggests that fluency is hedonically marked and itself experienced as positive (Winkielman, et al., 2003).

Consistent with this hedonic marking assumption, the influence of fluency is not limited to explicit judgments, for it can also be captured with psychophysiological measures. Specifically, Winkielman and Cacioppo (2001) observed that high fluency is associated with increased activity over the region of the zygomaticus major ("smiling muscle"), which is indicative of a positive affective response.

These observations suggest the possibility that concept priming may influence judgment in ways that are not mediated by semantic interpretation. To the extent that concept priming facilitates fluent processing of subsequent associatively related stimuli, it may increase liking of these stimuli even under conditions in which differential interpretations of the stimuli are unlikely. Winkielman and Fazendeiro (2001) explored this possibility in a cross-modal priming task. Specifically, they showed participants a series of unambiguous pictures of common objects and animals. Each picture was preceded by a letter string consisting of either a word or a non-word. Participants first indicated, as fast as possible, whether the letter string was an actual English word. They subsequently reported their liking for the picture. The letter strings served as the fluency manipulation. Some pictures were preceded by matched words (e.g., picture of a dog preceded by the word "dog"), introducing the highest level of fluency. Other pictures were preceded by associatively related words (e.g., picture of a lock preceded by the word "key"), introducing a medium level of fluency. Yet other pictures were preceded by an unrelated word (e.g., picture of a desk preceded by the word "dog"), introducing the lowest level of fluency. The results showed a robust effect of concept priming on participants' evaluation of the target pictures. As expected, pictures preceded by matching words were liked significantly more than pictures preceded by related words; those, in turn, were liked significantly more than pictures preceded by unrelated words. Follow-up studies showed that these fluency effects do not require that the concept primes immediately precede the target pictures. Instead, the same pattern of effects was obtained when participants studied a list of concept primes before they were exposed to the pictures.

In combination, the Winkielman and Fazendeiro (2001) findings indicate that the influence of concept priming is not limited to the interpretation of ambiguous information. All of the pictures presented were unambiguous, and it is hard to see how exposure to the prime "key" would influence the semantic interpretation of an unambiguous picture of a "lock." But the concepts "key" and "lock" are closely associated in semantic memory, and priming "key" temporarily facilitates the processing of a picture that presents a "lock." This increased processing fluency is itself hedonically marked, resulting in more positive evaluations as well as more positive psychophysiological responses. Accordingly, fluency effects provide a further illustration of how priming procedures can influence evaluative judgment through individuals' reliance on experiential rather than semantic information, as already observed in our discussion of accessibility experiences.

Concept-Behavior Links

Much as the Winkielman and Fazendeiro (2001) studies suggest that priming effects on evaluative judgment are not necessarily mediated by differential interpretations of information about the target, priming effects on behavior are not necessarily mediated by differential interpretations of the behavioral situation. Although primed information can undoubtedly influence behavior through differential construal of the situation (for an early demonstration, see Schwarz & Strack, 1981), a growing body of research suggests a more direct link.

Bargh, Chen and Burrows (1996), for example, observed that priming the elderly stereotype with words such as "Florida" or "bingo" induced participants to walk more slowly to the elevator after completion of the experiment. Similarly, Dijksterhuis and van Knippenberg (1998) found that priming the professor stereotype increased, and priming the soccer hooligan stereotype decreased, individuals' performance on knowledge tests. The authors attribute these findings to a direct perception-behavior link (for reviews, see Bargh, 1997; Bargh & Chartrand, 1999; Dijksterhuis & Bargh, 2001). Consistent with this suggestion, neuropsychological research indicates that the same neurons are involved in perceiving an action and executing it (for a review, see Rizzolatti & Arbib, 1998). Similarly, semantic processing of action verbs is associated with increased brain activity in regions corresponding to the execution of the respective action (e.g., Pulvermüller, Härle, & Hummel, 2001). If so, semantic and perceptual processing may increase the activation of representations that are directly involved in acting, thus facilitating behavioral responses that are not mediated by differential interpretations of the meaning of the situation (for an extended discussion, see Dijksterhuis & Bargh, 2001).

In addition, a growing body of research shows that goals, like other mental representations, can be automatically activated by features of the environment, initiating processes of goal pursuit that parallel deliberate goal enactment (for reviews, see Bargh & Gollwitzer, 1994; Gollwitzer & Moskowitz, 1996). These automatic processes can be intentionally employed to facilitate goal attainment: By forming an implementation intention that links critical situations with goal-directed responses, individuals may delegate the initiation of goal-directed behavior to anticipated situational cues. This strategy can overcome limitations of prospective memory (e.g., Chasteen, Park, & Schwarz, 2001), and has been found to reliably facilitate goal-directed behavior (for a review, see Gollwitzer, 1999).

In combination, these lines of research demonstrate that highly accessible information can influence behavior in ways that do not reflect differential interpretations of the situation, in contrast to the commonly accepted Proposition 3.

Conclusions

As this selective review indicates, the accessibility of information plays a crucial role in human judgment and behavior, much as early social cognition theorizing predicted. A quarter century later, however, the accumulating evidence indicates that the underlying processes are more complex than has commonly been assumed. In retrospect, it becomes apparent that early social cognition theorizing overemphasized the role of semantic information at the expense of experiential information, and paid insufficient attention to a judge's active role in the use of a given piece of information (Schwarz, 2000). Notably, Bob Wyer has seen the potentially crucial role of these variables early on. For example, Wyer and Carlston (1979) suggested that affect may serve as a source of information in its own right. This conjecture was well supported by subsequent research (for reviews, see Schwarz & Clore, 1996; Wyer, Clore, & Isbell, 1999) and has paved the way for the later exploration of other sources of experiential information, such as accessibility (Schwarz, 1998) and fluency (Winkielman et al., 2003) experiences. Similarly, our treatment of inclusion/exclusion processes (Schwarz & Bless, 1992a) owes much to Wyer's (1974) early discussion of information organization and integration and his later exploration of conversational aspects of human judgment, which highlighted the individual's active role in information use (Wyer & Gruenfeld, 1995). As the reviewed research demonstrates, we cannot understand the role of information accessibility in human judgment without taking these variables into account.

First, consistent with a growing interest in metacognitive processes in social and cognitive psychology, the reviewed work highlights that the phenomenal experiences that accompany the thought process can themselves serve as an important source of information. The experience of a given piece of semantic information coming to mind not only renders this semantic information available for further use, as assumed in Proposition 1; it also provides experiential information that qualifies the implications of the semantic information. The underlying processes are reasonably well understood for recall-based judgments (Schwarz, 1998), but their implications for priming effects on the encoding of new information (Proposition 2) have hardly been addressed. Unfortunately, priming procedures necessarily confound changes in what comes to mind with how easily it comes to mind—a priming procedure that leaves us searching for the primed concept is a procedure that did not work. The observation that awareness of the priming episode undermines the otherwise observed encoding effects (e.g., Lombardi et al., 1987; Strack et al., 1993) parallels the observation that misattribution manipulations undermine the impact of accessibility experiences on recall-based judgments (e.g., Schwarz et al., 1991). We therefore conjecture that accessibility experiences play a crucial role in both phenomena, an issue that awaits further research.

Second, priming effects on the evaluation of new information are not necessarily mediated by differential semantic interpretations, in contrast to Proposition 2. Instead, highly accessible concepts can facilitate the fluent processing of new information. Fluency of processing, however, is itself hedonically marked and results in more favorable evaluations without changes in the semantic meaning of the stimulus (Winkielman et al., 2003).

Third, even within a purely semantic framework, we cannot predict the outcome of a judgment by merely knowing what comes to mind, in contrast to Proposition 1. Instead, we need to consider how accessible information is used in forming mental representations of the target of judgment and of a standard

(Schwarz & Bless, 1992a). Most important, the same accessible input can give rise to assimilation as well as contrast effects, depending on its use.

Finally, highly accessible information can influence behavior in ways that are not mediated by differential interpretations of the behavioral situation, in contrast to Proposition 3. This presumably reflects that the same mental representations are involved in perceiving and acting (Dijksterhuis & Bargh, 2001), resulting in activation effects that bypass the usually assumed interpretation stage.

In combination, these findings cast doubt on the viability of familiar truisms, which we all came to like. Hopefully, repeated exposure to the more complicated story will facilitate its fluent processing and easy recall in the future, lending it the ring of "truth" that the earlier propositions enjoyed—until we need to revise the present story as well.

ACKNOWLEDGMENTS

Foremost, we thank Bob Wyer for countless hours of discussion that profoundly influenced how we think about human judgment. Over the years, he served as post-doc advisor to two of us (Norbert Schwarz and Michaela Wänke) and was a frequent visiting professor at our current and former German institutions (University of Mannheim, University of Heidelberg, and ZUMA), an outstanding host during our various visits at the University of Illinois, and a valued friend and collaborator. We wouldn't do what we do had it not been for his influence, even where we disagree. Thank you, Bob!

Preparation of this chapter was supported through a fellowship from the Center for Advanced Study in the Behavioral Sciences to Norbert Schwarz. Parts of the reported research were supported through grants from the Deutsche Forschungsgemeinschaft to Herbert Bless, Norbert Schwarz, and Michaela Wänke and through funds from the University of Michigan to Norbert Schwarz and from the University of Denver to Piotr Winkielman.

REFERENCES

Aarts, H., & Dijksterhuis, A. (1999). How often did I do it? Experienced ease of retrieval and frequency estimates of past behavior. *Acta Psychologica, 103,* 77–89.

Bargh, J. A. (1997). The automaticity of everyday life. In R. S. Wyer (Ed.), *Advances in Social Cognition* (Vol. 10, pp. 1–61). Mahwah, NJ: Lawrence Erlbaum Associates.

Bargh, J. A., & Chartrand, T. L. (1999). The unbearable automaticity of being. *American Psychologist, 54,* 462–479.

Bargh, J. A., Chen, M., & Burrows, L. (1996). Automaticity of social behavior: Direct effects of trait construct and stereotype activation on action. *Journal of Personality and Social Psychology, 71,* 230–244.

Bargh, J. A., & Gollwitzer, P. M. (1994). Environmental control of goal directed action: Automatic and strategic contingencies between situations and behavior. *Nebraska Symposium on Motivation, 41,* 71–124.

Bless, H., & Forgas, J. P. (Eds.). (2000). *The message within: The role of subjective experience in social cognition and behavior.* Philadelphia: Psychology Press.

Bless, H., Igou, E., Schwarz, N., & Wänke, M. (2000). Reducing context effects by adding context information: The direction and size of context effects in political judgment. *Personality and Social Psychology Bulletin, 26,* 1036–1045.

Bless, H., & Schwarz, N. (1998). Context effects in political judgment: Assimilation and contrast as a function of categorization processes. *European Journal of Social Psychology, 28,* 159–172.

Bless, H., Schwarz, N., Bodenhausen, G. V., & Thiel, L. (2001). Personalized versus generalized benefits of stereotype disconfirmation: Tradeoffs in the evaluation of atypical exemplars and their social groups. *Journal of Experimental Social Psychology, 37,* 386–397.

Bless, H., & Wänke, M. (2000). Can the same information be typical and atypical? How perceived typicality moderates assimilation and contrast in evaluative judgments. *Personality and Social Psychology Bulletin, 26,* 306–314.

Bodenhausen, G. V., & Wyer, R. S. (1987). Social cognition and social reality: Information acquisition and use in the laboratory and the real world. In H. J. Hippler, N. Schwarz, & S. Sudman (Eds.), *Social information processing and survey methodology* (pp. 6–41). New York: Springer Verlag.

Chasteen, A., Park, D. C., & Schwarz, N. (2001). Implementation intentions and facilitation of prospective memory. *Psychological Science, 12,* 457–461.

Clore, G. L. (1992). Cognitive phenomenology: Feelings and the construction of judgment. In L. L. Martin & A. Tesser (Eds.), *The construction of social judgments* (pp. 133–164). Hillsdale, NJ: Lawrence Erlbaum Associates.

Dijksterhuis, A., & Bargh, J. A. (2001). The perception-behavior expressway: Automatic effects of social perception on social behavior. In M. Zanna (Ed.), *Advances in Experimental Social Psychology* (Vol. 33, pp. 1–40). San Diego, CA: Academic Press.

Dijksterhuis, A., & van Knippenberg, A. (1998). The relation between perception and behavior, or how to win a game of trivial pursuit. *Journal of Personality and Social Psychology, 74,* 865–877.

Eagly, A. H., & Chaiken, S. (1993). *The psychology of attitudes.* Fort Worth, TX: Harcourt Brace Jovanovich.

Gollwitzer, P. M. (1999). Implementation intentions: Strong effects of simple plans. *American Psychologist, 54,* 493–503.

Gollwitzer, P. M., & Moskowitz, G. B. (1996). Goal effects on cognition and action. In E. T. Higgins & A. Kruglanski (Eds.), *Social psychology: Handbook of basic principles* (pp. 361–399). New York: Guilford.

Grayson, C. E., & Schwarz, N. (1999). Beliefs influence information processing strategies: Declarative and experiential information in risk assessment. *Social Cognition, 17,* 1–18.

Haddock, G., Rothman, A. J., Reber, R., & Schwarz, N. (1999). Forming judgments of attitude certainty, importance, and intensity: The role of subjective experiences. *Personality and Social Psychology Bulletin, 25,* 771–782.

Haddock, G., Rothman, A., & Schwarz, N. (1996). Are (some) reports of attitude strength context dependent? *Canadian Journal of Behavioral Science, 24*, 313–317.

Higgins, E. T. (1996). Knowledge activation: Accessibility, applicability, and salience. In E. T. Higgins & A. Kruglanski (Eds.), *Social psychology: Handbook of basic principles* (pp. 133–168). New York: Guilford Press.

Higgins, E. T., Rholes, W. S., & Jones, C. R. (1977). Category accessibility and impression formation. *Journal of Experimental Social Psychology, 13*, 141–154.

Kinder, D. R. (1998). Opinion and action in the realm of politics. In D. T. Gilber, S. T. Fiske, & G. Lindzey (Eds.), *The handbook of social psychology* (Vol. 2, pp. 778–867).

Lombardi, W. J., Higgins, E. T., & Bargh, J. A. (1987). The role of consciousness in priming effects on categorization: Assimilation versus contrast as a function of awareness of the priming task. *Personality and Social Psychology Bulletin, 13*, 411–429.

Martin, L. L. (1986). Set/reset: Use and disuse of concepts in impression formation. *Journal of Personality and Social Psychology, 51*, 493–504.

Martin, L. L., Strack, F., & Stapel, D. A. (2001). How the mind moves: Knowledge accessibility and the fine-tuning of the cognitive system. In A. Tesser & N. Schwarz (Eds.), *Blackwell Handbook of Social Psychology: Intrapersonal processes* (pp. 236–256). Oxford, UK: Blackwell.

Ofir, C. (2000). Ease of recall vs. recalled evidence in judgment: Experts vs laymen. *Organizational Behavior and Human Decision Processes, 81*, 28–42.

Ottati, V. C. (2001). The psychological determinants of political judgment. In A. Tesser & N. Schwarz (Eds.), *Blackwell handbook of social psychology: Intra-individual processes* (pp. 615–633). Oxford, UK: Blackwell.

Pulvermüller, F., Härle, M., & Hummel, F. (2001). Walking or talking? Behavioral and neurophysiological correlates of action verb processing. *Brain and Language, 78*, 143–168.

Raghubir, P., & Menon, G. (1998). AIDS and me, never the twain shall meet: The effects of information accessibility on judgments of risk and advertising effectiveness. *Journal of Consumer Research, 25*, 52–63.

Reber, R., Winkielman P., & Schwarz, N. (1998). Effects of perceptual fluency on affective judgments. *Psychological Science, 9*, 45–48.

Rizzolatti, G., & Arbib, M. (1998). Language within our grasp. *Trends in Neuroscience, 21*, 188–194.

Root-Bernstein, R. S. (1989). *Discovering: Inventing and solving problems at the frontiers of scientific knowledge.* Cambridge, MA: Harvard University Press.

Rothman, A. J., & Schwarz, N. (1998). Constructing perceptions of vulnerability: Personal relevance and the use of experiential information in health judgments. *Personality and Social Psychology Bulletin, 24*, 1053–1064.

Sanna, L. J., & Schwarz, N. (in press). Debiasing hindsight: The role of accessibility experiences and attributions. *Journal of Experimental Social Psychology.*

Sanna, L. J., Schwarz, N., & Stocker, S. L. (2002). When debiasing backfires: Accessible content and accessibility experiences in debiasing hindsight. *Journal of Experimental Psychology: Learning, Memory, Cognition, 28*, 497–502.

Schwarz, N. (1994). Judgment in a social context: Biases, shortcomings, and the logic of conversation. In M. Zanna (Ed.), Advances in experimental social psychology (Vol. 26, pp. 123–162). San Diego, CA: Academic Press.

Schwarz, N. (1996). *Cognition and communication: Judgmental biases, research methods and the logic of conversation.* Mahwah, NJ: Lawrence Erlbaum Associates.

Schwarz, N. (1998). Accessible content and accessibility experiences: The interplay of declarative and experiential information in judgment. *Personality and Social Psychology Review, 2,* 87–99.

Schwarz, N. (2000). Attitudes and social judgment: Warmer, more social, and less conscious. *European Journal of Social Psychology, 30,* 149–176.

Schwarz, N., & Bless, H. (1992a). Constructing reality and its alternatives: Assimilation and contrast effects in social judgment. In L. L. Martin & A. Tesser (Eds.), *The construction of social judgment* (pp. 217–245). Hillsdale, NJ: Lawrence Erlbaum Associates.

Schwarz, N., & Bless, H. (1992b). Scandals and the public's trust in politicians: Assimilation and contrast effects. *Personality and Social Psychology Bulletin, 18,* 574–579.

Schwarz, N., Bless, H., Strack, F., Klumpp, G., Rittenauer-Schatka, H., & Simons, A. (1991). Ease of retrieval as information: Another look at the availability heuristic. *Journal of Personality and Social Psychology, 61,* 195–202.

Schwarz, N., & Clore, G. L. (1983). Mood, misattribution, and judgments of well-being: Informative and directive functions of affective states. *Journal of Personality and Social Psychology, 45,* 513–523.

Schwarz, N., & Clore, G. L. (1996). Feelings and phenomenal experiences. In E. T. Higgins, & A. W. Kruglanski (Eds.), *Social psychology: Handbook of basic principles.* New York: Guilford Press.

Schwarz, N., & Strack, F. (1981). Manipulating salience: Causal assessment in natural settings. *Personality and Social Psychology Bulletin, 6,* 554–558.

Schwarz, N., Strack, F., & Mai, H. P. (1991). Assimilation and contrast effects in part-whole question sequences: A conversational logic analysis. *Public Opinion Quarterly, 55,* 3–23.

Schwarz, N., & Vaughn, L. A. (2002). The availability heuristic revisited: Recalled content and ease of recall as information. In T. Gilovich, D. Griffin, & D. Kahneman (Eds.), *The psychology of intuitive judgment: Heuristics and biases.* pp. 103–119. Cambridge, UK: Cambridge University Press.

Shavitt, S., & Wänke, M. (2001). Consumer behavior. In A. Tesser & N. Schwarz (Eds.), *Blackwell handbook of social psychology: Intraindividual processes* (pp. 569–589). Oxford, UK: Blackwell.

Skurnik, I., Schwarz, N., & Winkielman, P. (2000). Drawing inferences from feelings: The role of naive beliefs. In H. Bless & J. Forgas (Eds.), *The message within: The role of subjective experience in social cognition and behavior* (pp. 162–175). Philadelphia: Psychology Press.

Srull, T. K., & Wyer, R. S. (1979). The role of category accessibility in the interpretation of information about persons. *Journal of Personality and Social Psychology, 38,* 841–856.

Stapel, D. A., & Schwarz, N. (1998). The Republican who did not want to become President: An inclusion/exclusion analysis of Colin Powell's impact on evaluations of the Republican Party and Bob Dole. *Personality and Social Psychology Bulletin, 24,* 690–698.

Stepper, S., & Strack, F. (1993). Proprioceptive determinants of emotional and nonemotional feelings. *Journal of Personality and Social Psychology, 64,* 211–220.

Strack, F., Martin, L. L., & Schwarz, N. (1988). Priming and communication: The social determinants of information use in judgments of life-satisfaction. *European Journal of Social Psychology, 18,* 429–442.

Strack, F., Schwarz, N., Bless, H., Kübler, A., & Wänke, M. (1993). Awareness of the influence as a determinant of assimilation versus contrast. *European Journal of Social Psychology, 23,* 53–62.

Sudman, S., Bradburn, N., & Schwarz, N. (1996). *Thinking about answers: The application of cognitive processes to survey methodology.* San Francisco, CA: Jossey-Bass.

Tourangeau, R., Rips, L. J., & Rasinski, K. (2000). *The psychology of survey response.* Cambridge, UK: Cambridge University Press.

Tversky, A., & Kahneman, D. (1973). Availability: A heuristic for judging frequency and probability. *Cognitive Psychology, 5,* 207–232.

Wänke, M., & Bless, H. (2000). The effects of subjective ease of retrieval on attitudinal judgments: The moderating role of processing motivation. In H. Bless, & J. P. Forgas (Eds.), *The message within: The role of subjective experience in social cognition and behavior* (pp. 143–161). Philadelphia: Psychology Press.

Wänke, M., Bless, H., & Biller, B. (1996). Subjective experience versus content of information in the construction of attitude judgments. *Personality and Social Psychology Bulletin, 22,* 1105–1113.

Wänke, M., Bless, H., & Igou, E. (2001). Next to a star: Paling, shining, or both? Turning inter-exemplar contrast into inter-exemplar assimilation. *Personality and Social Psychology, 27,* 14–29.

Wänke, M., Bless, H., & Schwarz, N. (1998). Context effects in product line extensions: Context is not destiny. *Journal of Consumer Psychology, 7,* 299–322.

Wänke, M., Bohner, G., & Jurkowitsch, A. (1997). There are many reasons to drive a BMW—Surely you know one: Ease of Argument Generation influences Brand Attitudes. *Journal of Consumer Research, 24,* 70–77

Wänke, M., Schwarz, N., & Bless, H. (1995). The availability heuristic revisited: Experienced ease of retrieval in mundane frequency estimates. *Acta Psychologica, 89,* 83–90.

Winkielman, P., & Cacioppo, J. T. (2001). Mind at ease puts a smile on the face: Psychophysiological evidence that processing facilitation increases positive affect. *Journal of Personality and Social Psychology. 81,* 989–1000.

Winkielman, P., & Fazendeiro, T. A. (2001). *The role of conceptual fluency in preference and memory.* Unpublished manuscript.

Winkielman, P., & Schwarz, N. (2001). How pleasant was your childhood? Beliefs about memory shape inferences from experienced difficulty of recall. *Psychological Science, 12,* 176–179.

Winkielman, P., Schwarz, N., & Belli, R. F. (1998). The role of ease of retrieval and attribution in memory judgments: Judging your memory as worse despite recalling more events. *Psychological Science, 9,* 124–126.

Winkielman, P., Schwarz, N., Fazendeiro, T. & Reber, R. (2003). The hedonic marking of processing fluency: Implications for evaluative judgment. In J. Musch &

K.C. Klauer (Eds.), *The psychology of evaluation: Affective processes in cognition and emotion.* (pp. 189–217). Mahwah, NJ: Lawrence Erlbaum Associates.

Winkielman, P., Schwarz, N., Reber, R., Fazendeiro, T., (in press). Cognitive and affective consequences of visual fluency: When seeing is easy on the mind. In L. Scott & R. Batra (Eds.), *Persuasive imagery: A consumer response perspective.* Mahwah, NJ: Lawrence Erlbaum Associates.

Wyer, R. S. (1974). *Cognitive organization and change: An information processing approach.* Hillsdale, NJ: Lawrence Erlbaum Associates.

Wyer, R. S., & Carlston, D. E. (1979). *Social cognition, inference, and attribution.* Hillsdale, NJ: Lawrence Erlbaum Associates.

Wyer, R. S., Clore, G. L., & Isbell, L. (1999). Affect and information processing. In M. P. Zanna (Eds.), *Advances in experimental social psychology* (Vol. 31, pp. 3–78). San Diego, CA: Academic Press.

Wyer, R. S., & Gruenfeld, D. H. (1995). Information processing in social contexts: Implications for social memory and judgment. In M. P. Zanna (Ed.), *Advances in experimental social psychology* (Vol. 27, pp. 49–89). San Diego, CA: Academic Press.

Wyer, R. S., & Srull, T. K. (1989). *Memory and cognition in its social context.* Hillsdale, NJ: Lawrence Erlbaum Associates.

Zajonc, R. B. (1968). Attitudinal effects of mere exposure. *Journal of Personality and Social Psychology: Monograph Supplement, 9,* 1–27.

5

Heuristic Strategies for Estimation Under Uncertainty: The Enigmatic Case of Anchoring

Fritz Strack
Thomas Mussweiler
University of Würzburg

When individuals are asked to judge themselves or another person, they are unlikely to perform an exhaustive search of memory [....] Rather, they are likely to base their judgment on some subset of these cognitions that is most readily accessible. (Srull & Wyer, 1979)

More than 20 years later, the insight that judgments are based on accessible information seems almost trivial. Of course, information only enters into a judgment if it can be accessed from memory. But at the time Bob Wyer and Tom Srull conducted the studies that supported their statement, social psychology was still far removed from asking how judgments were formed. Instead, it was the cognitive structure that was the focus of researchers' attention, not the process that led to the outcome. Cognitions were assumed to be "just there," and hardly anybody asked about the conditions under which they became an input to further processing. To be sure, the accessibility principle was implied in other programs of research (e.g., Bruner, 1957; Higgins, Rholes, & Jones, 1977; Taylor & Fiske, 1978; Tversky & Kahneman, 1973). However, it is Srull and Wyer's merit to recognize that the accessibility principle applies not only to selected tasks but is perhaps the most basic law in social cognition, and its apparent triviality speaks to its tremendous success (for a more elaborate account of social information processing, see also Wyer & Srull, 1986, 1989).

The power of this principle can be recognized by the vast number of research programs that are based on it (for a recent conceptualization and review of findings, see Higgins, 1996). Influences of accessible knowledge, it seems, become particularly apparent in situations of judgmental uncertainty. If the information we have available about a target object is ambiguous, if the time or the mental resources we have available are scarce, or if we are distracted while forming our judgment—in short, if we have to make judgments under suboptimal conditions, we are particularly likely to use what is at the top of our minds as a basis for our judgments. Accessible knowledge may thus be particularly influential under the same conditions that are typically seen as the hatchery of judgmental heuristics (Tversky & Kahneman, 1974). This similarity in the conditions that trigger and foster the effects of knowledge accessibility on the one hand and judgmental heuristics on the other hand suggests that there may also be a similarity in the underlying psychological processes. Can the core social cognition principle of knowledge accessibility also help us understand the mechanisms that underlie estimation under uncertainty? Are the effects of judgmental heuristics essentially knowledge accessibility effects? This chapter we examine these questions regarding one of the three classic heuristics, which for a long time has been the easiest to demonstrate and the hardest to explain: the enigmatic anchoring heuristic.

Described by Amos Tversky and Daniel Kahneman (1974) as a mechanism of "anchoring and adjustment," the anchoring phenomenon consists of an assimilation of a judgment toward the value that was first considered. In other words, the number that starts the generation of a judgment exerts a stronger impact than do subsequent pieces of numeric information. In one of the most dramatic demonstrations of this numeric assimilation, Tversky and Kahneman had participants estimate the proportion of African countries in the United Nations. But before this absolute estimate was generated, they had to generate a comparative judgment and to indicate whether the true percentage was higher or lower than a specific number. As a result, the absolute judgment was assimilated toward the standard of the comparison. For example, the estimates of the percentage of African states were 25 and 45 for participants who had received 10 and 65, respectively, as comparison values.

How can this striking assimilation effect be accounted for? Perhaps the most straightforward explanation is one that not only considers the value of the comparison standard but also the social implications of providing such information. Given that the contents of communications come with a guarantee of relevance (Sperber & Wilson, 1986; see also Bless, Strack, & Schwarz, 1993; Schwarz, 1996), the fact that one is provided with such information suggests that the true value is somewhere in the vicinity of the standard. While such a conversational influence is likely to operate under social conditions in which the standard for the comparison task is intentionally provided, this explanation does not apply to the described study by Tversky and Kahneman. In this experiment, the comparison value was *not* intentionally provided by the experimenter but was randomly generated by a spinning wheel of fortune in front of the participants' eyes. In this case, it is difficult to explain the absolute estimate as a conversational inference. Rather, a more basic cognitive mechanism must be invoked to explain the anchoring effect.

One such basic mechanism was suggested by Jacowitz and Kahneman (1995; see also Wilson, Houston, Etling, & Brekke, 1996; Wong & Kwong, 2000), who proposed that the comparative judgment will increase the likelihood that the standard will be a candidate for the absolute response. That is, the comparative judgment increases the accessibility of the numeric value in the absolute judgment. This mechanism of "numeric priming" operates without the assumption of an intention on the part of the experimenter. Rather, it is based exclusively on mechanisms of increased accessibility.

The assumption, however, that the accessibility of a numerical value causes judgments to be assimilated toward this number is difficult to reconcile with the fact that a mere number is void of any factual content. Unless it is associated with a semantic dimension, it is difficult to conceive how a numeric value can by itself become the basis of a judgment. At the same time, many findings demonstrate that the accessibility of a *semantic* content is a strong and systematic determinant of social and nonsocial judgments (for a recent review, see Higgins, 1996). The abundant research demonstrating such semantic influences suggests that a similar mechanism may also be responsible for assimilation effects in the anchoring paradigm.

Such a semantic-accessibility perspective on anchoring, however, begs the question of how the information that leads to an assimilation of the absolute judgment toward the standard of comparison is activated. Specifically, a process must be identified that selectively activates the assimilating information. Such a mechanism can be found by applying the procedures that are used for hypothesis testing to the anchoring paradigm. It has been demonstrated that judges who test the validity of a singular hypothesis adopt a "positive test strategy" (see Hawkins & Hastie, 1990; Klayman & Ha, 1987). That is, people seek information that is consistent with the focal hypothesis; they entertain the possibility that the hypothesis might be true. The actual decision, however, depends on the outcome of this search. If the result of the search does not meet the criterion, the hypothesis will be rejected.

This procedure is reasonable in situations where only one hypothesis has to be tested and where no alternative hypotheses are included in the decision (see Sanbonmatsu, Posavac, Kardes, & Mantel, 1998). One might argue that in the case of a single hypothesis, judges should actively generate alternative possibilities and seek confirmatory information for them as well. However, given that there is an infinite number of alternative hypotheses, the resulting lack of supporting evidence for the alternatives would greatly inflate the probability that the focal hypothesis will be confirmed.

While the positive test strategy does not necessarily bias the solution of the focal task, it produces cognitive consequences that may affect subsequent judgments. In particular, the search for "positive" evidence may selectively activate information that is consistent with the tested hypothesis. That is, even if it is rejected, the information that was found is still more likely to be in favor of the entertained possibility. For example, assume that you are asked to decide whether the extension of the Mississippi River is between 3000 and 3500 miles. You take this as a hypothesis and seek information that is consistent with this possibility. You may for instance, construct a mental map that depicts the river as it flows from the Canadian border to the Gulf of Mexico (2350 miles). But knowing that this distance is below 3000 miles, you reject the hypothesis. Assume, in contrast, that the hypothesis is between 1000 and 1500 miles. While you will also reject the hypothesis, you may not think about the river in its full extension. Thus both types of rejections have different cognitive consequences. In the first case, information is activated that implies a big extension of the target, while the information that is activated in the second case implies a small extension. A subsequent assessment of length will therefore be based on different "subsets of cognitions" and will result in judgments that are assimilated toward the values of the original hypothesis.

Applied to the case of anchoring, a comparative judgment can be understood as a qualified rejection of a hypothesis. This view implies that a person who is asked to generate a comparative judgment will solve this task by seeking information that is consistent with the possibility that the target possesses the value of the standard. The rejection of this hypothesis is followed by a directional judgment, indicating whether the target possesses more or less of the property in question. Thus before judges will decide whether the Mississippi River is longer or shorter than 3300 miles, they will entertain and reject the possibility that the actual extension lies around this value. However, the cognitive consequences remain the same. That is, even though the possibility that a target possesses the property implied by the standard is rejected and qualified, information that is consistent with this possibility will be activated and thereby be more accessible for subsequent use. As a consequence, the absolute judgment will be assimilated toward the standard of comparison.

In contrast to the proposed mechanism of numeric priming, the present model of selective accessibility (Mussweiler & Strack, 1999a, 1999b, 2000a; Strack & Mussweiler, 1997; see also Chapman & Johnson, 1999) suggests that the anchoring-assimilation effect is not brought about by an increased activation potential (Higgins, 1996) of a particular number, but by the increased accessibility of semantic information as a consequence of a presumed hypothesis test.

While the two processes may seem highly similar at first glance, they may be put to test under experimental conditions that allow for divergent predictions.

VARYING THE JUDGMENTAL DIMENSION

The first such test we would like to report rests on the assumption that in a strict sense, the effect of a primed number should be independent of its semantic association. That is, if a numeric value comes to mind, it should affect the judgment independent of the judgmental dimension. For example, if the number 500 is highly accessible, judgments of both 500 feet and 500 miles should become more likely, depending on the dimension that is being used. In contrast, the semantic accessibility model suggests that the response dimension matters because the activated information has different implications for the different dimensions.

This simple derivation was tested in a study in which we systematically varied the response dimension (Strack & Mussweiler, 1997, Study 1). For example, participants were given the assignment to indicate if Berlin's Brandenburg Gate was taller or shorter than 150 meters. In a typical anchoring task, the assessment of the monument's actual height would be assimilated toward the numeric value of the comparison standard. Because the response dimensions of both tasks are identical, it is not possible to tell if the impact of the comparative judgment is caused by the activated number or by the activation of consistent semantic information. However, if participants were asked to assess Brandenburg Gate's width instead of being asked to provide an absolute estimate for its height, the two mechanisms would be expected to produce different results. Thus varying judgmental dimensions should not matter if a numeric priming produces the effect. If, however, semantic priming is operating as an underlying mechanism, the assimilation effect should be reduced, because the information that is applicable (see Higgins et al., 1977) for one content domain is less applicable for another, even if the two are conceptually related.

This reasoning was clearly confirmed in the described study. For the two targets that were used (the Brandenburg Gate and Cologne Cathedral), the anchoring assimilation effects were replicated if the judgmental dimensions were identical for the comparative and the absolute judgments. That is, a high comparison standard ("anchor") led to higher estimates than did a low standard. However, if these dimensions changed from the comparative to the absolute judgment task (height/width or height/length), the assimilation effect was greatly reduced. Because these findings demonstrate that depending on the semantic context of the anchoring task, the same anchor value may have different judgmental consequences. This finding is difficult to account for by mechanisms of "numeric priming." At the same time, it is clearly consistent with mechanisms of semantic priming. The semantic accessibility perspective on the anchoring phenomenon is further supported by research examining the influences of implausible anchor values.

IMPLAUSIBLE ANCHORS

Assume you were asked to indicate whether the Mississippi River is longer or shorter than 20,000 miles. Of course, "shorter" is the correct answer. Because the answer to such a comparative question involving an implausible anchor is so obvious, you should be able to generate your answer faster than you would in a situation in which you consider a more plausible standard, such as 3300 miles. That is, the time needed to compare a target to an implausible anchor should be shorter. Indeed, this was the case in a study (Strack & Mussweiler, 1997, Study 3) in which response latencies were compared for plausible and implausible anchors. Guided by our selective accessibility model, we assume that this is the case because for implausible anchors, judges do not engage in a selective search for specific information about the target. Rather, they use the category to which the target belongs as a basis for their decision. In our example, judges would not apply what they know about the Mississippi River to decide if it is longer or shorter, but information about rivers in general. If the judge knows that no river approaches the length of 20,000 miles, the knowledge that the Mississippi belongs to this category suffices to decide that it is shorter.

Moreover, the selective-accessibility model of anchoring permits an additional prediction. Specifically, it implies that there is a trade-off between the facilitation of the comparative judgment and the speed with which the absolute judgment is generated. That is, if a judgment can be reached without accessing relevant individuating information, no advantage is gained when it comes to recalling such information for the absolute judgment. As a consequence, the generation of the absolute judgment will require more time if the target is compared to an implausible anchor than if it is compared to a plausible anchor. This prediction was also confirmed by the results of the described experiment. Thus the response latencies showed a cross-over interaction between the type of the judgment (comparative versus absolute) and the type of the anchor (plausible versus implausible), such that for comparative judgments, response latencies were slower for plausible than for implausible anchors. For the subsequent absolute judgments, this pattern of response latencies was reversed such that plausible anchors led to faster responses than did implausible ones. This pattern is consistent with predictions derived from the selective-accessibility model. Through the time-consuming search for individuating information during the target-standard comparison, this information will be rendered easily accessible for the subsequent assessment of the target's absolute value.

In this experiment (Strack & Mussweiler, 1997), plausibility was varied through the extremity of the anchors. This, however, is not the only way in which this construct can be manipulated. Because the plausibility of a characteristic depends on the category to which it belongs, a change of category should lead to the same results. For example, 3000 meters is a plausible height for a mountain but an implausible height for an African steppe animal. In contrast, two meters is a plausible height for African animals but not for mountains. This consideration was used in an experiment (Mussweiler & Strack, 2000b) in which participants assessed the height of a fictitious and ambiguous target named "Lowumbo." To disambiguate this concept, it was embedded in different questionnaire contexts (see Strack, Schwarz, & Wänke, 1991). In one condition, Lowumbo's height had to be compared to one of the two standards (2 meters and 3000 meters) after a series of questions about African steppe animals (e.g., gnu); in another condition, the critical item was preceded by context questions about mountains (e.g., Kilimanjaro). Subsequently, the absolute height had to be indicated.

As expected, the height estimates showed the typical anchoring-assimilation effect and proved the effectiveness of the context manipulation. That is, higher estimates were provided for the mountain context than for the animal context. More important, however, were the response latencies for the comparative and the absolute judgments. We found the same interaction between the plausibility of the anchor and the nature of the judgment as in the previous study. That is, if the category that was suggested by the context yielded a plausible characteristic, participants took more time comparing the target to the same standard than if the suggested category yielded an implausible characteristic. Again, the reverse was found for the absolute judgment. That is, a plausible anchor-category combination led to a faster absolute judgment, presumably because the activation of individuating target information for the comparative judgment increased its accessibility, thereby facilitating the subsequent judgment. This facilitation of the absolute judgment was not found when the implausible characteristic prevented participants from selectively activating such features for the comparative task.

Taken together, the two plausibility studies demonstrate that the participant's response latencies for the comparative and the absolute anchoring tasks are inversely related. The longer judges take to compare the target to the anchor, and the more target knowledge that can be used for the subsequent absolute estimate they generate, the faster they are in providing this absolute estimate. In this respect, the present findings provide converging support for the notion that the activation and the subsequent accessibility of anchor-consistent information serves as an underlying mechanism for the typical anchoring assimilation effect. Notably, these results are also difficult to explain by mechanisms of numeric priming. If it were indeed the numeric anchor value rather than the semantic knowledge that is activated during the comparison with this value that produces the effect, then response latencies for the absolute judgment should be independent of those for the comparison.

The presumed inverse relation between the amount of judgment-relevant knowledge that is activated during the comparative task and the amount of knowledge that still needs to be generated to provide an absolute estimate, however, can be tested in a more direct way. We assumed that an implausible standard prevents judges from considering individuating information about the target at the expense of category information. If this is indeed the case, then putting people under time pressure while doing the comparisons should be functionally equivalent. Under such conditions, relevant information should be activated to a lesser degree and, as a consequence, more time should be spent on generating the absolute judgment. Again, our results confirmed this prediction: absolute judgments took more time if the comparative judgment had to be generated under time pressure (Mussweiler & Strack, 1999b, Study 3). This result is also consistent with findings by Kruglanski and colleagues (e.g., Kruglanski & Webster, 1996), who found that time pressure increases a "need for closure" and leads to less elaborate processing (for related findings, see Strack, Erber, & Wicklund, 1982).

Together with our research on implausible anchors, this finding suggests that judges do indeed use the knowledge that was generated during the comparative anchoring task as a basis for their absolute estimates. The more time judges spend on the comparative task and the more judgment-relevant knowledge they activate, the less knowledge they need to generate while working on the absolute judgment. This facilitation of absolute estimates by an elaborate preceding comparison of the target and the anchor is apparent in shorter response latencies.

SELECTIVE ACCESSIBILITY

Although this research shows that mechanisms of knowledge accessibility play an important role in the genesis of anchoring, they are mute with respect to the core notion of our selective accessibility proposal. In particular, they do not speak to the nature of the knowledge that is generated during the comparative anchoring task. From the current perspective, absolute estimates are assimilated toward the anchor value because judges selectively activate anchor-consistent target knowledge during the comparison, and then use this knowledge as a basis for the absolute estimate. We examined this assumed selectivity in the implications of accessible knowledge with the help of a lexical decision paradigm (e.g., Neely, 1977).

This paradigm is based on the assumption that excitation activation is spread along semantic links in associative memory such that the accessibility of a concept is not only influenced by its prior use, but also by activation of semantically related concepts. This mechanism was typically tested using a task that required participants to indicate whether a letter string was a word. The described mechanism predicts that such lexical decisions will be faster if a semantically related word has been activated before.

If the anchoring-assimilation effect is in fact caused by the selective accessibility of semantic contents, then a comparative judgment should also accelerate a lexical decision. This was the prediction of a further study (Mussweiler & Strack, 2000a, Study 1) in which participants had to compare the average temperature in Germany with a given standard. In one condition, the standard of comparison was 20°C (68° Fahrenheit) or 5°C (41° Fahrenheit). As expected, most participants correctly believed that Germany's average temperature was lower than 20°C and higher than 5°C. However, instead of being asked to estimate the actual average temperature, participants were asked to solve a lexical decision task. Specifically, letter strings were presented on a computer screen that were readable nonwords, words related to wintertime (e.g., snow, cold, etc.), words related to summertime (e.g., beach, hot, etc.) or words that were unrelated to the two seasons (e.g., pencil, hair). The task was to decide for each letter string if it was a word or not.

On the basis of our selective-accessibility model, we assumed that when participants were given the high standard, they would consider the possibility that the average temperature was fairly high, and selectively activate information that is consistent with this hypothesis. As a consequence, semantic knowledge indicating high temperatures is more accessible; thus judges should be able to respond faster to words that are associated with high rather than low temperatures. For judges who had considered the low anchor values, however, the reverse should be the case. Consistent with these predictions, the results clearly indicated that people were faster at identifying words that were semantically related to the implications of the anchor value. That is, lexical decisions were accelerated for words related to summertime if the standard was 20°C, and for words related to wintertime if the standard was 5°C.

As with the previous results, this finding demonstrates which cognitive mechanisms are involved in a comparative judgment and what consequences they have for the solution of subsequent tasks. Specifically, in comparing the target to the anchor value, judges appear to test the possibility that the target extension is similar to the anchor. To do so, they selectively generate target knowledge that is consistent with this assumption so that the accessibility of anchor-consistent target knowledge is selectively increased. Because this knowledge is used as a basis for the absolute estimate, this estimate is assimilated towards the anchor value.

Notably, the operation of this basic mechanism is not limited to the anchoring situation. Rather, it applies to all circumstances in which entertaining and testing a possible characteristic of a target precedes a judgment of the same target (cf., Koehler, 1991). For example, explaining or imagining a hypothetical event may increase the subjective probability that this event will actually come about (Carroll, 1978; Ross, Lepper, Strack, & Steinmetz, 1977).

ANCHORING CONTRAST

On a more abstract level, the present findings demonstrate that to understand the mechanisms that underlie judgmental heuristics in general and the anchoring heuristic specifically, it may be useful to take a social cognition perspective on these phenomena. To the extent that the basic social cognition principle of knowledge accessibility underlies the anchoring phenomenon, those factors that moderate knowledge accessibility effects in general should also influence anchoring. One particularly interesting case in point relates to the direction of knowledge accessibility effects. Although judgments are often assimilated toward the implications of accessible knowledge, this is not necessarily the case. Rather, under specific conditions, accessible knowledge may also influence subsequent judgments in contrastive ways. For judgmental anchoring, this suggests that absolute estimates may not always be assimilated toward the anchor. Under specific conditions, contrast may also result.

To demonstrate the directional variability of the influence, experimental variations must be created that generate assimilation versus contrast. However, the creation of such conditions requires a conceptual basis to generate the divergent predictions.

Representativeness

While there exist various notions about the mediating conditions of assimilation versus contrast (e.g., Martin, 1986; Schwarz & Bless, 1992), the present predictions were derived from the idea of "representativeness" (Strack, 1992). It implies that to predict a judgmental influence, it is not sufficient to know the activation potential of a piece of information; one must also know how representative it is of a given judgment. For example, people who are asked to assess their general happiness with life will be more likely to base their judgment on information about events from the recent past than about events from the distant past, because for judgments about the present, information about the present is more representative than is information about the past (see, Strack, Schwarz, & Gschneidinger, 1985). Thus even if the less representative information about the past were highly accessible, it would not be used as a basis for the judgment. Instead, it would either be excluded from the judgment generation (cf., Schwarz & Bless, 1992) or used as a standard of comparison (Strack, 1992). In either case, the judgment would not be assimilated toward the activated information, but contrasted away from it. The same logic applies to subjective experiences as a basis for inferences. If a feeling is not representative because its source is unrelated to the judgment, the feeling will not be used as a judgmental basis (see, e.g., Schwarz & Clore, 1996). Finally, conversational determinants may render an activated information nonrepresentative. That is, if the use of an accessible information violates a conversational norm (Grice, 1975), it will not be included into the judgment (for evidence, see Strack, Martin, & Schwarz, 1988).

Activating concepts of varying representativeness has repeatedly been found to differentially affect judgments in the priming paradigm. Typically, priming representative concepts leads to assimilation, whereas priming nonrepresentative concepts leads to contrast. A set of studies by Herr, Sherman, and Fazio (1983; see also, Herr 1986) may serve as an example. In this research, participants had to judge the ferocity of animals (e.g., fox) after being exposed to animals that were similar (e.g., wolf) or dissimilar (e.g., tiger) to the target. Herr found that similar primes resulted in assimilation, whereas dissimilar primes led to contrast effects. Because similarity is a determinant of representativeness (cf. Kahneman & Tversky, 1972), these findings are consistent with the proposed notion. Moreover, they allow us to apply this reasoning to the anchoring paradigm. In particular, if the comparative judgment activates knowledge that is similar to the target, which is typically the case because the comparative and absolute judgments pertain to the same target, then assimilation should result. If, however, the comparison activates knowledge that is extremely dissimilar from the target, then the subsequent absolute judgment will be contrasted away from the comparison standard. In the latter case, instead of the typical anchoring-assimilation effect, a contrast effect may occur.

This prediction was tested in another study (Strack & Mussweiler, 1997, Study 2) in which the similarity between the knowledge that was activated during the comparison and the target of the absolute judgment was varied. In particular, the absolute judgment pertained either to the same target that had previously been compared to the anchor value, and for which anchor-consistent knowledge had thus been activated, or to a largely disparate target. In one condition, for example, judges were first asked to compare the annual mean temperature in the Antarctic to a low anchor value of –50°C (–58°F). They subsequently provided an absolute estimate for the mean temperature in either the Antarctic or on Hawaii. In the first case, the knowledge pertaining to the Antarctic that is activated during the comparison is highly representative of estimates of the temperature in the Antarctic, such that assimilation should result. In the second case, the knowledge about the Antarctic is not representative of estimates of temperatures on Hawaii; thus contrast should resume. This was, in fact, the result of our study (Strack & Mussweiler, 1997, Study 2). If the targets of both judgments were the same, the anchoring-assimilation effect was replicated. If the two targets were not identical however, contrast resulted.

These results demonstrate that a knowledge accessibility perspective on anchoring allows us to derive novel predictions about the direction of the effect. As is true for knowledge accessibility effects in general, the direction of anchoring effects depends on how representative the accessible knowledge is for the critical judgment.

Conversational Cue

Anchoring contrast, however, may be induced not only by manipulations of representativeness. Another example of how assimilation effects that result from a comparative judgment can be turned into contrast can be derived from another psychological mechanism that takes the social situation into account. Specifically, judgments are often generated and communicated in a social context, which has its own rules that need to be obeyed. For social communication, a set of rules or "maxims" has been identified by Paul Grice (1975). From his background as a linguist, Grice has stated that people who want to communicate smoothly need to cooperate by following a set of principles. One of them is the Maxim of Quantity that requires people to find the right level of specificity for their contributions to a communication. That is, they should not be more or less specific than is required. Very often, exact numeric judgments are more specific than is required in most situations. For example, the answer that the Mississippi River is 2353 miles long is probably more informative than is required in the situation. Thus we often resort to vague quantifiers, such as "around 2000 miles" or even "very long." While vague numeric quantifiers have a generic reference point that generalizes across different contents, vague verbal quantifiers (VVQs) need to be calibrated to be correctly understood. For example, the extension of a "very long" snake is shorter than that of a "very short" river.

The calibration of vague verbal quantifiers occurs implicitly in social interactions. Its exact processes have been identified by Ostrom, Upshaw, and Wyer (e.g., Ostrom & Upshaw, 1968; for a discussion, see Wyer & Srull, 1989) in a program of research that builds another foundation of social cognition. These researchers have argued and demonstrated that VVQs are calibrated by "anchoring" the reference system of a communicator and by establishing an ordinal structure of targets on a response scale. For example, if I know that the quantifier refers to a river, the range of exact quantifiers is categorically determined. Often, however, the relevant range of phenomena is determined by communicative cues. For example, if it is clear that a conversation is about a specific country, the reference to a "big river" means something else than if all the world's rivers are the topic. Typically, the intended range is not explicitly determined in a natural conversation. Rather, conversational cues are used to infer it. For example, if a participant refers to the Amazon River, one would assume that the conversation is not only about German rivers but about rivers in general. As a consequence, one would not refer to the Rhine as a "very long" river but perhaps only as a "long" or "rather long" river. Alternatively, if a conversant were to ask if a potential target has a certain characteristic, one would assume that this characteristic is part of the range of objects. For example, if the question is raised as to whether the Rhine is longer or shorter than 3000 miles, the respondent can assume that rivers of this length are being considered, even though the Rhine is much shorter.

This is, of course, the anchoring situation in which the consideration of a given value affects the subsequent quantitative judgments in an assimilative fashion. However, when it comes to vague verbal quantifiers, the effect goes in the opposite direction. That is, considering a high value will cause the target to be judged as less high, and vice versa. Because this contrast effect is conversationally determined, it should depend not only on the use of vague verbal quantifiers that need to be disambiguated, but also on the intentionality with which the numeric value is provided. That is, only if the recipient can assume that a standard of comparison is not selected randomly but reflects the user's intention will a contrast effect obtain. As the classic anchoring study by Tversky and Kahneman (1974) demonstrates, this is not true for the assimilation effect, which also occurs for anchors which are randomly determined by spinning a wheel of fortune, and are thus clearly not provided intentionally.

Results of a recent study on the consequences of anchoring for self-evaluative judgments are consistent with this reasoning (Mussweiler & Strack, 2000c, Study 5). Participants were given an attention-load test that consisted of a number of individual tasks, and received a numeric anchor against which they were to evaluate their prospective performance. Half of the participants ostensibly determined this anchor themselves by rolling dice. Thus for them, the anchor did not appear to be intentionally provided by the experimenter. The other half were given an anchor and told that this standard represented an average student's performance in the task. For this group, the anchor thus appeared to be intentional. We expected that, consistent with the above reasoning, exact numeric judgments would be assimilated to the random as well as to the intentional anchor. VVQs, however, should only be contrasted away from intentional anchors.

Participants received an attention-load test and were asked to estimate whether they would be able to solve more or fewer than either 562 or 365 of the individual tasks. They then estimated the number of tasks they would be able to solve, went on to solve as many tasks as they could within five minutes, and finally judged their ability to concentrate on a nine-point rating scale. Our results indicate that exact numeric judgments were assimilated to the standards and that this was true with random and intentional anchors alike. In contrast, VVQ judgments were contrasted away from the anchors. This was only the case, however, if the anchor was perceived as intentionally provided. If the standard was ostensibly determined at random, then this contrast effect vanished.

These findings indicate that conversational cues may also produce contrast effects in judgmental anchoring, at least for VVQ judgments. The fact that contrast occurred only for those anchors that could be seen as informative (because they were not selected at random) indicates that it is indeed conversational influences that underlie this contrastive effect on VVQs. Thus as we note the qualities of alternative judgment types, there appear to be different and even parallel routes to contrast as a result of judgmental anchoring. By the same token, the fact that the assimilative effect that was apparent on absolute judgments occurred for informative and random anchors alike further demonstrates that conversational influences do not contribute to the classic anchoring assimilation effect. In light of the accumulated evidence, anchoring assimilation effects appear to be produced by the described selective accessibility mechanism. The accessibility principle thus indeed appears to be at the heart of the anchoring heuristic—providing yet another demonstration of the power, breadth, and ubiquity of this core mechanism of social cognition.

CONCLUSION

The power of social psychology's most basic laws has often proven to be fruitful far beyond its original application. Like the mechanisms of cognitive dissonance (Festinger, 1957), the law of cognitive accessibility has been demonstrated to account for a multitude of phenomena other than the categorization of behavior—and anchoring is one of them. Starting out as a heuristic and originally described as an undue adherence to an initial value, principles of social cognition have now embedded the phenomenon of judgmental anchoring into a rich theoretical framework that allows us to gain a deeper understanding of the underlying processes, and to generate new predictions. As a result of this theoretical integration, however, the definition of anchoring as a judgmental assimilation after considering an initial value must be qualified. In fact, both assimilation and contrast may occur depending on theoretically meaningful conditions. In retrospect, anchoring has lost its status as a unique phenomenon with its own regularities. Instead, it has found its place as a special case of basic principles that served as the pillars of a psychological subdiscipline whose explanatory power has proven to be exceptionally strong. It has its place as a phenomenon whose underlying mechanisms speak to the "sovereignty of social cognition" (Ostrom, 1984).

REFERENCES

Bless, H., Strack, F., & Schwarz, N. (1993). The informative functions of research procedures: Bias and the logic of conversation. *European Journal of Social Psychology, 23*, 149–165.

Bruner, J. S. (1957). Going beyond the information given. In H. Gruber et al. (Ed.), *Contemporary approaches to cognition.*

Carroll, J. S. (1978). The effect of imagining an event on expectations for the event: An interpretation in terms of the availability heuristic. *Journal of Experimental Social Psychology, 14*, 88–96.

Chapman, G. B., & Johnson, E. J. (1999). Anchoring, activation, and the construction of values. *Organizational Behavior and Human Decision Processes, 79*, 1–39.

Festinger, L. (1957). *A theory of cognitive dissonance.* Stanford, CA: Stanford University Press.

Grice, H. P. (1975). Logic and conversation. In P. Cole & J. L. Morgan (Eds.), *Syntax and semantics 3: Speech acts* (pp. 41–58). New York: Academic Press.

Hawkins, S. A., & Hastie, R. (1990). Hindsight: Biased judgments of past events after the outcomes are known. *Psychological Bulletin, 107*, 311–327.

Herr, P. M. (1986). Consequences of priming: Judgment and behavior. *Journal of Personality and Social Psychology, 51*, 1106–1115.

Herr, P. M., Sherman, S. J., & Fazio, R. H. (1983). On the consequences of priming: Assimilation and contrast effects. *Journal of Experimental Social Psychology, 19*, 323–340.

Higgins, E. T. (1996). Knowledge activation: Accessibility, applicability, and salience. In E. T. Higgins & A. W. Kruglanski (Eds.), *Social psychology: Handbook of basic principles* (pp. 133–168). New York: Guilford.

Higgins, E. T., Rholes, W. S., & Jones, C. R. (1977). Category accessibility and impression formation. *Journal of Experimental Social Psychology, 13*, 141–154.

Jacowitz, K. E., & Kahneman, D. (1995). Measures of anchoring in estimation tasks. *Personality and Social Psychology Bulletin, 21*, 1161–1166.

Kahneman, D., & Tversky, A. (1972). Subjective probability: A judgment of representativeness. *Cognitive Psychology, 3*, 430–454.

Klayman, J., & Ha, Y. W. (1987). Confirmation, disconfirmation, and information in hypotheses testing. *Psychological Review, 94*, 211–228.

Koehler, D. J. (1991). Explanation, imagination, and confidence in judgment. *Psychological Bulletin, 110*, 499–519.

Kruglanski, A. W., & Webster, D. M. (1996). Motivated closing of the mind: "Seizing" and "Freezing." *Psychological Review, 103*, 263–283.

Martin, L. L. (1986). Set/reset: The use and disuse of concepts in impression formation. *Journal of Personality and Social Psychology, 51*, 493–504.

Mussweiler, T., & Strack, F. (1999a). Comparing is believing: A selective accessibility model of judgmental anchoring. In W. Stroebe & M. Hewstone (Eds.), *European review of social psychology*. (Vol. 10, pp. 135–167). Chichester, UK: Wiley.

Mussweiler, T., & Strack, F. (1999b). Hypothesis-consistent testing and semantic priming in the anchoring paradigm: A selective accessibility model. *Journal of Experimental Social Psychology, 35,* 136–164.

Mussweiler, T., & Strack, F. (2000a). The use of category and exemplar knowledge in the solution of anchoring tasks. *Journal of Personality and Social Psychology, 78,* 1038–1052.

Mussweiler, T., & Strack, F. (2000b). Numeric judgment under uncertainty: The role of knowledge in anchoring. *Journal of Experimental Social Psychology, 36,* 495–518.

Mussweiler, T., & Strack, F. (2000c). The "relative self": Informational and judgmental consequences of comparative self-evaluation. *Journal of Personality and Social Psychology, 79,* 23–38.

Neely, J. H. (1977). Semantic priming and retrieval from lexical memory: Roles of inhibitionless spreading activation and limited-capacity attention. *Journal of Experimental Psychology, 106,* 226–254.

Ostrom, T. M. (1984). The sovereignty of social cognition. In R. S. Wyer & T. K. Srull (Eds.), *Handbook of social cognition* (Vol. 1,(pp. 1–38). Hillsdale, NJ: Lawrence Erlbaum Associates.

Ostrom, T. M., & Upshaw, H. S. (1968). Psychological perspectives and attitude change. In A. G. Greenwald, T. C. Brock, & T. M. Ostrom (Eds.), *Psychological foundations of attitudes* (pp. 217–242). New York: Academic Press.

Ross, L., Lepper, M., Strack, F., & Steinmetz, J. L. (1977). Social explanation and social expectation: The effects of real and hypothetical explanations upon subjective likelihood. *Journal of Personality and Social Psychology, 35,* 817–829.

Sanbonmatsu, D. M., Posavac, S. S., Kardes, F. R., & Mantel, S. P. (1998). Selective hypothesis testing. *Psychonomic Bulletin & Review, 5,* 197–220.

Schwarz, N. (1996). *Cognition and communication: Judgmental biases, research methods, and the logic of conversation.* Mahwah, NJ: Lawrence Erlbaum Associates.

Schwarz, N., & Bless, H. (1992). Constructing reality and its alternatives: An inclusion/exclusion model of assimilation and contrast effects in social judgment. In L. L. Martin & A. Tesser (Eds.), *The construction of social judgments* (pp. 217–245). Hillsdale, NJ: Lawrence Erlbaum Associates.

Schwarz, N. & Clore, G. L. (1996). Feelings and phenomenal experiences. In E. T. Higgins & A. W. Kruglanski (Eds.), *Social psychology. Handbook of basic principles* (pp. 433–465). New York: Guilford.

Sperber, D., & Wilson, D. (1986). *Relevance. Communication and cognition.* Cambridge, MA: Cambridge University Press.

Srull, T. K., & Wyer, R. S. (1979). The role of category accessibility in the interpretation of information about persons: Some determinants and implications. *Journal of Personality and Social Psychology, 37,* 1660–1672.

Strack, F. (1992). The different routes to social judgments: Experiential vs. informational strategies. In L. L. Martin & A. Tesser (Eds.), *The construction of social judgment* (pp. 249–275). Hillsdale: Lawrence Erlbaum Associates.

Strack, F., Erber, R., & Wicklund, R. (1982). Effects of salience and time pressure on ratings of social causality. *Journal of Experimental Social Psychology, 18*, 581–594.

Strack, F., Martin, L. L., & Schwarz, N. (1988). Priming and communication: Social determinants of information use in judgments of life satisfaction. *European Journal of Social Psychology, 18*, 429–442.

Strack, F., & Mussweiler, T. (1997). Explaining the enigmatic anchoring effect: Mechanisms of selective accessibility. *Journal of Personality and Social Psychology, 73*, 437–446.

Strack, F., Schwarz, N., & Gschneidinger, E. (1985). Happiness and reminiscing: The role of time perspective, affect, and mode of thinking. *Journal of Personality and Social Psychology, 49*, 1460–1469.

Strack, F., Schwarz, N., & Wänke, M. (1991). Semantic and pragmatic aspects of context effects in social and psychological research. *Social Cognition, 9*, 111–125.

Taylor, S. E., & Fiske, S. T. (1978). Salience, attention, and attribution: Top-of-the-head phenomena. In L. Berkowitz (Ed.), *Advances in experimental social psychology* (Vol. 11, pp. 249–288). New York: Academic Press.

Tversky, A., & Kahneman, D. (1973). Availability: A heuristic for judging frequency and probability. *Cognitive Psychology, 4*, 207–232.

Tversky, A., & Kahneman, D. (1974). Judgment under uncertainty: Heuristics and biases. *Science, 185*, 1124–1131.

Wilson, T. D., Houston, C., Etling, K. M., & Brekke, N. (1996). A new look at anchoring effects: Basic anchoring and its antecedents. *Journal of Experimental Psychology: General, 4*, 387–402.

Wong, K. F. E., & Kwong, J. Y. Y. (2000). Is 7300 m equal to 7.3 km? Same semantics but different anchoring effects. *Organizational Behavior and Human Decision Processes, 82*, 314–333.

Wyer, R. S., & Srull, T. K. (1986). Human cognition in its social context. *Psychological Review, 93*, 322–359.

Wyer, R. S., & Srull, T. K. (1989). *Memory and cognition in its social context*. Hillsdale, NJ: Lawrence Erlbaum Associates.

6

The Accidental Tourist
Capturing Incidental (Versus
Intentional) Impressions

Donal E. Carlston
Purdue University

Lynda Mae
University of Southern Mississippi

Every venture into public is essentially a tour of the human race, as people encounter and observe numerous other individuals. Sometimes we are purposeful sight-seekers, seeking to meet others, to learn what they are like, to evaluate or appraise them. At other times we resemble Ann Taylor's main character in *The Accidental Tourist*, traveling though life without real engagement and learning about others as an incidental by-product of other pursuits. In this chapter, we argue that most impressions are formed "accidentally," making it surprising that research to date has focused almost exclusively on impressions formed purposefully.

Accidental tourism provides an appropriate metaphor for this chapter's excursion through the passive, incidental side of impression formation. Bob Wyer has been a leading researcher in the general area of impression formation area for at least 25 years, and as Bob's academic son and granddaughter, we have been privileged to benefit (both directly and indirectly) from his training. Thus a strong Wyeresque influence is evident in our approach to this area. We are pleased to write this chapter as a tribute to Bob, introducing our theory of the "accidental tourist" in person impression, identifying some over-looked issues that are highlighted by this approach, and describing the incidental impression paradigm we employ for studying this phenomenon.[1]

CHAPTER OBJECTIVES

Before getting to the heart of our argument, we wish to set a context for what follows. First, although this chapter reviews work on intentional and inciden-tal impression formation, it is intended as more of a thought piece than a comprehensive review of an area of social cognition. We acknowledge from the start that much of this chapter is speculative: It is intended to reflect our ideas about our research, and about incidental impression formation more generally, rather than to neatly detail what has already been learned.

Second, this chapter is largely forward-looking, rather than back-ward-looking: It suggests more of where our research is currently headed than where it has been. In a sense, it represents our plans for clarification and expansion of our work on incidental impression formation.

Third, this chapter focuses primarily on the promise of a research para-digm that we call the incidental impression paradigm. Of course, we recog-nize the desirability of employing a variety of paradigms to triangulate on social cognition processes. But examining incidental impressions requires a special form of undercover investigative work, and we think that our inci-dental impression paradigm has some unique features that make it particu-larly suitable for this endeavor.

Fourth, we are concerned with issues of external validity, and the extent to which "real" nonlaboratory impression processes are captured by con-trolled laboratory paradigms, such as our own. These concerns do not push us towards increased "mundane realism" (Berkowitz & Donnerstein, 1982), but rather toward specific steps designed to encourage more "natural" moti-vations and processing.

And finally, we confess that our ambitions in this piece may be somewhat grandiose. We believe the phenomena we emphasize are pervasive and cen-tral to social interactions, and that our approach therefore has the potential to illuminate a major part of the field. Moreover, we believe that our ap-proach raises a number of important issues about the nature of impressions, which we touch on throughout this chapter.

---

[1]We now recognize the procedures used in some of our earlier work on spontaneous trait inference (Carlston & Skowronski, 1994; Carlston, Skowronski, & Sparks, 1995) and spontaneous trait transfer-ence (Mae, Carlston, & Skowronski, 1999; Skowronski, Carlston, Mae, & Crawford, 1998) as specific implementations of a more general method for studying incidental impression formation. We wish to ac-knowledge our frequent collaborator, John Skowronski (another academic descendant of Bob Wyer), for his role in developing some of the procedures and logic that underlie the incidental impression paradigm.

INCIDENTAL VERSUS INTENTIONAL
IMPRESSION FORMATION

People clearly form impressions of others when they intend to do so. But do people also form impressions without intention, simply as a consequence of ordinary associative and cognitive processes? In other words, do people who are engaged in other kinds of activities (or perhaps, altogether unengaged) form impressions by accident?

In the field of social cognition, such issues have generally been framed in terms of the spontaneity of trait inference (e.g., Winter & Uleman, 1984): It has been argued that perceivers may "automatically" or "spontaneously" make trait inferences from observed behaviors even when they are not instructed to do so. There is now substantial empirical support for this possibility (Bassili, 1993; Carlston & Skowronski, 1994; Carlston, Skowronski, & Sparks, 1995; Uleman, Newman, & Moskowitz, 1996), suggesting that attributional processes can occur unintentionally as well as intentionally. However, this perspective oversimplifies by focusing primarily on trait representations and emphasizing the possible equivalence of spontaneous and intentional impression processes. Consequently, the perspective diverts attention from other interesting issues such as potential differences between such processes.

Intentional and incidental impression formation may differ in fundamental ways. For example, incidental impressions may derive from different cues, be less systematic or more vulnerable to irrational influences, differ in accessibility or endurability, and involve different forms of mental representation than intentional impressions. Admittedly, such possibilities are under-researched and consequently speculative. However, they serve to emphasize our central focus, which is not on whether people do incidentally what they also do intentionally, but rather whether this involves different processes, and results in notably different impressional content.

Formal Definitions

It may be helpful to provide more formal definitions of intentional and incidental impression formation before continuing further. We define "intentional impression formation" as the process of consciously and willfully making inferences, attributions, or appraisals of a target individual either during the processing of stimulus information or later, during its recall. In contrast, we define incidental impression formation as knowledge about an individual that is acquired inadvertently, during the course of activities that are not directed at forming an impression. We recognize that these processes may lie at opposite poles of a continuum, so that intermediate forms of "somewhat intentional" processing may be possible. However, like most dual-process theorists, we find it useful to discuss a dichotomy involving the two extreme cases (which we suspect are most frequent, in any case).

Although intentional impression formation is certainly common in contexts ranging from job interviews to romantic encounters, we suspect that incidental impression formation is even more so. This is difficult to prove, given the current state of research in this area. But it seems apparent that many social interactions are relatively casual and shallow, and that even deeper relationships often begin that way. For reasons to be described later, people often lack the motivation and/or the capacity to purposefully analyze the personalities of others. In fact, it seems likely that many (if not most) interactions are motivated by goals other than impression formation. People may be busy networking, obtaining or conveying information, maintaining their public image, buying groceries, or avoiding others along a sidewalk. True, in some instances, having impressions of others may facilitate such interactions. But often, it is sufficient for us to sense whether our own social maneuvers seem to be accomplishing our nonimpressional goals. Indeed, intentional impression formation may reflect relatively rare instances in which our interest is piqued to a level that makes us want to ensure that our social maneuvers are especially efficacious, or in which we have special reasons for wanting to get to know someone. In any case, one premise of our approach is that "real world" impression formation commonly involves incidental processes, even though impression research has largely focused on intentional ones.

Intentional and Incidental Memory

There is an obvious parallel between our reference to intentional versus incidental impression formation and the distinction in cognitive psychology between intentional and incidental learning. It was once thought that intentional learning was virtually always superior to incidental learning (Gleitman & Gillett, 1957), suggesting that motivation might play a key role in memory. However, it is now generally agreed that the critical factor in learning is not the underlying motivation, but the extent to which intentionality increases memory-enhancing processes such as rehearsal or organization. When experimental participants engage in the same processes to the same degree, even without any intention to learn the material, their memory for the material is equivalent to that of participants engaged in intentional learning. As Baddeley (1990) states, "the critical feature appears to be exactly how you process the material to be remembered, not why you process it" (p. 149).

By analogy, then, it would appear that intentionality per se might be similarly dismissed by impression formation researchers. Along these lines, one study (Carlston & Skowronski, 1994, Study 4) demonstrated that impressional associations were equally strong whether experimental participants were instructed to form impressions, to memorize the stimulus information, or simply to familiarize themselves with the stimuli. Moreover, even when stimuli were structured to preclude intentional impression processes, similar (though weaker) effects were obtained (Skowronski, Carlston, Mae, & Crawford, 1998, Study 3; see also Brown & Bassili, 2002), suggesting that the effects of intentionality might differ in degree, but not in direction. Why, then, should social psychologists care about the intentionality of impression information?

There are at least three reasons. First, there is too little evidence at this point to conclude that incidental and intentional impression formation differ only in the degree to which they implicate the same underlying processes. Incidental impression formation may depend more on simple associative processes, and intentional impression formation may depend more on complex attributional ones (e.g., Jones & Davis, 1965; Kelley, 1967). Intentional impression formation may also bring into play additional processes, such as situational correction (Gilbert, Pelham & Krull, 1988) or editing for social desirability (Devine, 1989); such processes seem less likely in incidental impression formation.

Second, even if incidental and intentional impression formation involve essentially the same processes, they may differ in the kinds of information processed. For example, incidental impression formation might be more influenced by a person's appearance (a "politically incorrect" source of information) or the weather (an illogical source of information), compared to intentional impression formation, which may be influenced more by his or her behavior (a logical and socially acceptable source of information). Or the processes might differ in their ultimate outputs. Incidental impression formation might result in affect or general evaluative impressions, and intentional impression formation in more specific, trait impressions (see Carlston, 1994). Third, even if incidental and intentional impression formation were ultimately shown to differ only in the degree to which certain processes are engaged, such differences in degree would be important. Differences in degree can have significant consequences in the real world; they may affect relative attention to, interpretation of, and memory for subsequent information, along with confidence, communication, and behavior. Thus if our assumption is correct that the incidental form is the most prevalent kind of impression formation, then the concentration of social psychological research on intentional impression formation may mislead about the nature of many social phenomena.

Relationship of Intentional/Incidental Impression Formation to Other Classic Distinctions

The distinction proposed here between intentional and incidental impression formation connects with, and serves to tie together, a number of other formulations in the psychological literature. Among these are theories of spontaneous versus intentional inference-making, automaticity versus control, on-line versus post-hoc impression formation, episodic versus semantic memory, explicit versus implicit memory, and systematic versus heuristic processing. Consideration of the connections between these approaches and ours helps to lay the theoretical groundwork for our ideas.

Spontaneous Trait Inference.   First, as briefly discussed earlier, there is considerable similarity between our distinction and Uleman's (1999) distinction between intentional and spontaneous trait inferences. Uleman now defines spontaneous trait inferences essentially as those that are not intentional, noting also that these tend to be "linked to actors by mere association," sometimes inappropriately, to be "promiscuous and unfocused" and to be "guided by chronically accessible constructs and procedures" (p. 147). In contrast, intentional trait inferences are guided more by goals and deliberative processes, are more coherent, and involve explicit links to actors.

We find Uleman's characterizations to be highly appropriate and useful, and the convergence with our ideas is more evident than are the divergences. However, we believe that the framing of "spontaneous trait inference" is unnecessarily limiting, primarily because it encompasses only one of many kinds of content (traits) that may comprise impressions. In fact, research suggests that other kinds of content may also be generated spontaneously; for example, evaluations (Bargh, Chaiken, Raymond, & Hymes, 1996; Fazio, Sanbonmatsu, Powell, & Kardes, 1986) and categorizations (Brewer, 1988; DeCoster & Smith, 2000; Fazio & Dunton, 1997). Our approach embraces the possibility that any form of impressional content may be generated incidentally. We also diverge from the spontaneous trait inference approach, in that it focuses on the spontaneity of impressions, whereas our approach focuses on the differences between incidental and intentional processing. As a consequence, our perspective evokes broader and different issues.

Automaticity.   Second, there are strong parallels between our distinction and conceptions of automaticity and control (e.g., Bargh, 1994, 1996; Bargh & Ferguson, 2000; Wegner & Bargh, 1998). As we have defined them, intentional impression processes are largely controlled, whereas incidental impression processes are largely automatic. In other words, incidental impressions may be formed involuntarily, without using limited cognitive resources, and perhaps without awareness or control. In addition to the spontaneous trait inference work discussed earlier, other research has confirmed that impression processes are sometimes automatic in one or more senses of that term (Bargh & Thein, 1985; Higgins & King, 1981; Smith & Lerner, 1986; Taylor & Fiske, 1978). However, the issues addressed here are somewhat more complex, focusing not just on whether people engage in incidental impression formation but also on how the processes and resultant impressions differ from those that are intentional.

On-line Versus Post-hoc Processing. Our distinction between intentional and incidental impressions overlaps partially with Hastie and Park's (1986) contrast between on-line versus post-hoc (or memory-based) impression processes. On-line impressions are formed as stimulus information is processed, and post-hoc impressions are formed later, based on memories of the stimulus information. The key finding in this area is that post hoc impressions tend to correlate with stimulus memory, whereas on-line impressions may or may not do so.

Intentional impressions can seemingly be made either on-line or post hoc, depending on when the perceiver has the motivation and capacity to do so. If motivation and capacity are sufficient when information is encountered, intentional impressions may be formed then; if not, they may be formed from memory later, when need and resources are greater. Alternately, incidental impressions require little motivation or capacity, and consequently seem likely to be formed whenever impression-relevant information is first encountered (i.e., on-line). Consequently, incidental impressions are likely to be formed even when intentional impressions are deferred.

Episodic Versus Semantic Memories. Tulving's (1972) distinction between episodic and semantic memories is also related to our formulation. In impression formation research, episodic memory generally involves memory for the stimulus events or behaviors that may underlie impressions of target individuals, and semantic (or impression) memory generally involves memory for abstracted knowledge, such as trait inferences or evaluations that derive from presented stimulus information.[2] Similar distinctions were common in early theories of person memory (Carlston, 1978, 1980; Lingle & Ostrom, 1979; Wyer & Carlston, 1979; Wyer & Srull, 1989). The present approach assumes that episodic/stimulus recall is a prerequisite for the formation of post hoc (memory-based) impressions, although not for on-line ones (Hastie & Park, 1986). Consequently, evidence for impressions in the absence of stimulus recall indicates that those impressions must have been formed on-line, rather than post-hoc. However, whether those on-line impressions were intentional or incidental can only be determined through additional analysis.

Implicit Versus Explicit Memory. Our conception of intentional versus incidental processing is loosely related to cognitive theories of explicit versus implicit memory (Roediger, 1990; Schachter, 1987). Just as the

---

[2]Carlston (1992, 1994) defined impressions as amalgamations of cognitive constructs that include episodic memory. However, it is more useful in the present context to reserve the term only for more abstract representations, such as trait inferences or associations.

distinction between explicit versus implicit memory hinges on whether people intentionally try to recall information or do so in the course of other activities, our distinction between intentional and incidental processing hinges on whether people intentionally try to form impressions or do so in the course of other activities. Moreover, recent research suggests that when attention is divided (a circumstance that we assume contributes to incidental impression formation), explicit memory tasks are disrupted more than are implicit ones (Mulligan, 1998). We also speculate that procedures or activities that provoke explicit memories about a stimulus person may be more likely to instigate intentional impression formation than those that require only the implicit use of memory. More generally, it would seem that intentional impression formation relates more closely to explicit memories, and incidental ones more closely to implicit memories.

Implicit and Explicit Processing.   The present distinction is somewhat similar to Skowronski, Carlston, & Isham's (1993) distinction between implicit and explicit processing. In the context of priming research, these authors characterized implicit processes as being instigated by covert primes, involving the activation of traits without effort or intention, and having some of the characteristics of automatic processes. In contrast, they defined explicit processes as being instigated by overt primes or expectancies, and engaging deliberate or controlled impressional processing. Although the context (and consequently the hypotheses) described in this work differ from our present concerns, the underlying mechanisms are obviously quite similar.

Greenwald and Banaji (1995) similarly distinguish between implicit and explicit social cognitions, based primarily on participants' awareness of the cognition and its impact. An implicit cognition is described as "the introspectively unidentified (or inaccurately defined) trace of past experience that mediates" responses (p. 5). Although this overlaps somewhat with our present distinction, it places considerably more emphasis on awareness and effects of the cognition, whereas our emphasis is more on the nature and awareness of the impression formation process.

Dual Process Models.   Finally, the present formulation relates to dual process models of attitudes, such as those described by Chaiken (1980) and Petty and Cacioppo (1984). We assume that intentional impression formation is often systematic (involving attributional analyses of central, diagnostic cues, for example), but that it may sometimes be heuristic, relying on stereotypes or other peripheral cues. In contrast, it is difficult to conceive of incidental impression processes as ever being systematic. In general, we feel that incidental processes might best be characterized as associative, perhaps focusing equally on central and peripheral cues, and involving rather simple mechanisms somewhat akin to the heuristic mechanisms suggested in dual process models.

It is important to recognize that just as both systematic and heuristic attitudinal processes can produce logical or illogical outcomes (Petty, 2001), so can both intentional and incidental impression processes. Both intentional and incidental processes may sometimes accurately reflect past experiences, and at other times reflect stereotypes, misperceptions and illusory correlations. However, incidental impressions may be especially vulnerable to bias by peripheral cues and simple heuristics. Additionally, because correcting for situational influences on behavior ordinarily requires awareness, capacity, and effort (Strack & Hannover, 1996; Trope & Gaunt, 1999; Wegener & Petty, 1995), such corrections may be less common in incidental than in intentional impression formation.

More generally, whenever people are associated with information that is not logically diagnostic about their personalities, that information may be more likely to affect incidental than intentional impression processes. A good example is provided by research on spontaneous trait transference (Skowronski et al., 1998), which demonstrated that people become associated with traits that they merely describe in others. Notably, the "real world" may provide many more illogical, peripheral, or random pairings between stimulus individuals and impression-implying information than does the typical laboratory experiment. For example, in the real world, people may become associated with background music, the weather, random objects in the environment, and so on. Notably, laboratory researchers generally think of such variables as extraneous contaminants and attempt to control them or exclude them from their experiments. But these sorts of illogical associates play an important role in real world contexts, where it seems likely that they would have more of an effect on incidental than intentional impressions.

IMPRESSION FORMATION IN THE REAL WORLD

Decades ago, Langer, Blank, and Chanowitz (1978) argued that people often approach everyday life mindlessly, going through the motions as though on cruise control. More recently, Gilbert et al. (1988) suggested that the demands of everyday life leave people "cognitively busy," with their limited mental resources focused on the most immediate demands of conversation and interaction. Although these characterizations differ, both imply a kind of passivity and distractedness that we believe characterizes many impression formation contexts. The cognitive resources that people bring to situations are often reserved for more pressing demands than generating elaborate impressions of others.

A number of features of the real world may promote this kind of mindless passivity; These include indifference, overload, time pressure, busyness, futility, forgetfulness, and satisficing. First, *indifference*: Many of the people we interact with are simply not relevant enough to merit extensive processing (see Brewer, 1988). Note that in contrast, a target individual in a typical laboratory setting is probably assumed by most participants to be relevant to the experiment. Consequently, many lab experiments may encourage more intentional impression processing than is normally elicited in the outside world. Second, *overload*: We encounter so many individuals during normal activities that we are probably overwhelmed and disinclined to focus too much attention on any one. Moreover, given multiple targets, we may tend to confuse who said or did what (Fiske, Haslam, & Fiske, 1991), and as a consequence we may tend to rely more on global reactions than on specific attributions or memories. Third, *time pressure*: In the outside world, events and other stimuli may occur without sufficient time for careful or extensive processing. In the lab, this is more often the exception than the rule. Fourth, *busyness*: We approach many nonexperimental tasks with motivations and objectives other than forming impressions. In fact, we suspect that self-presentation may be a more common, and often stronger, goal than that of forming impressions of others. In other words, people may be more concerned with the impressions they are "giving off" than with the impressions they are forming in social situations. Whether our goal is to present ourselves positively, to keep a conversation going, or to buy groceries, we may be preoccupied with any number of other activities that are more pressing and more intentional than making systematic judgments of others. Fifth, *futility*: In the "real world," a great many of the people we observe appear nondescript, the behaviors they engage in are non-diagnostic, and the things they are associated with appear noninformative. Consequently, the default mind set may be to process others superficially rather than to form impressions of them. Sixth, *forgetfulness*: Although in the lab, person perception and person judgment are usually compressed into one-hour experimental sessions, such activities may be far more extended outside of the laboratory. We often have time to forget the details of our interactions before our impressions of the interactants become relevant. And finally, *satisficing*: Despite the apparent assumption among social cognition theorists that people desire specific knowledge of the many traits and characteristics of others, vague and nonspecific impressions probably suffice much of the time. Certainly, there are times when it would pay to know whether someone is honest, adventurous, stubborn, or conceited, and times when we cannot help but notice such characteristics. But probably there are just as many times when it is sufficient to know simply that someone can be approached or should be avoided.

Our concern with features of the real world that may encourage passive processing derives directly from Bob Wyer's own lifelong interest in issues of "real world" processing. Wyer and Carlston (1979) wrote, "We feel additional emphasis needs to be placed on the cognitive representations of social information that people actually and spontaneously use" (p. 364). This concern with real world impression processes remains evident in Bob's subsequent work on the cognitive representation of mundane social events (Trafimow & Wyer, 1993; see also Wyer, 1997) and impression formation in informal conversations (e.g., Wyer, Budesheim, & Lambert, 1990; Wyer, Swan, & Gruenfeld, 1995; see also Wyer & Carlston, 1994).

One approach to dealing with such concerns is to increase the realism of laboratory experiments on impression formation. Thus for example, written descriptions of stimulus targets (presented either by computer or in booklets) might be replaced by videotapes (e.g., Carlston & Skowronski, 1986) or even by actual interactions with target individuals (e.g., Lewicki, 1985; Park, 1986). Such procedures clearly have utility in expanding the study of impressions beyond traditional impression paradigms. More generally, however, research needs to move beyond procedures that directly or indirectly encourage intentional impression formation, and to adopt those that promote and capture incidental impressions. We propose our incidental impression paradigm to do just that, not by mimicking reality, but by incorporating many of the features (e.g., preoccupation with alternative goals, exposure to multiple target individuals, time pressure, and delay) that probably account for the ubiquity of incidental impression formation in the real world.

THE INCIDENTAL IMPRESSION PARADIGM

It is easy to take pictures of a typical tourist, who willingly poses for photograph after photograph with the focus of his or her interest looming in the background. However, recording unposed images of the accidental tourist is more challenging. Essentially, this individual must be subtly maneuvered into position and impressions recorded with a kind of "candid camera," so that suspicion and self-consciousness are minimized. Should the accidental tourist become aware of being photographed, the opportunity to capture spontaneous impressions will be lost. Similarly, to assess incidental impressions, one must manipulate the situation and disguise one's objectives. The unique challenge is to structure the situation so that it allows incidental impressions to be formed and measured without prompting intentional ones.

Our intentional impression paradigm was designed for this purpose. In general terms, the features of this methodology are designed to expose participants to stimulus information about target individuals without promoting intentional impression formation on-line, and then to assess impressions after the specific details of the stimulus information are no longer accessible, so that intentional impressions cannot be formed post hoc. These objectives are accomplished in the incidental impression paradigm through the following specific procedures.

Specific Procedures

First, some participants are exposed to stimulus individuals (usually through photos or videos) in combination with paired information. Such paired information can include anything from logical influences, such as spoken utterances or observed acts, to illogical influences such as weather conditions or environmental odors. Second, comparison or control participants are exposed to these same people in combination with paired information having neutral or differing implications, eventually allowing the impact of the paired information to be assessed while controlling for other characteristics of the people.[3] Third, the stimulus situation is structured to minimize participants' motivation to form intentional impressions of the stimulus individuals. This involves the provision of a suitably passive or diversionary instructional set and the deferment of all impression-related questions until later in the procedure. Fourth, as often occurs in the real world, participants are exposed to multiple target individuals over a relatively short period of time. This serves to de-emphasize the importance of each individual, further discouraging intentional impression formation. It also creates realistic overload and confusion, diminishing recall for the specific information that was originally paired with each stimulus individual, and leaving only traces of any impressions that might already have been formed. Fifth, additional steps are often included to reduce memory for specific information about stimulus targets. Such steps include filler tasks, interference tasks, and time delays ranging from minutes to weeks. Sixth, after specific details of the paired information have been forgotten, participants' incidental impressions are finally, and unexpectedly, assessed. Because multiple stimulus targets are involved, this assessment is accomplished by providing participants with cues (usually photos) of each stimulus person. To avoid demand effects, we take steps to mask our interest in the implications of the original paired material. For example, if trait rating scales are used, they might be provided for a number of different traits, only one of which was implied by the original paired information.

Finally, it is desirable to add a recall or recognition task to demonstrate that participants' memory for the paired information is poor. If participants demonstrate poor recall for this information, they presumably cannot use it to form intentional, post-hoc impressions. Instead, any impact of the originally paired information must be due to incidental impressions formed during the original exposure to the target person.

These steps work together in a way that substantially reduces the likelihood of intentional impression formation and permits incidental impressions to be captured. An application of the complete paradigm is illustrated in the following section.

---

[3]Experimental and control trials can be varied within subjects as well as between subjects. In other words, sometimes individual participants receive impression-relevant stimuli on some trials and control stimuli on other trials, though of course they never view the same target individual more than once.

An Illustration of the Method

Suppose that the incidental impression paradigm was to be used to examine the possibility that our impressions of people can be incidentally influenced by the weather at the time we initially meet them. First, participants would be "introduced" to a number of different people, perhaps through videos. In the background of some videos, a specific kind of weather (e.g., rain) would be superimposed, whereas in the control versions of these, a different kind of weather (e.g., sunshine) would be evident. Participants would receive instructions designed to divert them from intentional impression formation (perhaps by suggesting that their task is to judge the quality of the filming in each video), and would be exposed to multiple individuals (perhaps 30), during a short period of time (perhaps eight seconds each). These procedures should make it difficult for participants to recall the type of weather present when they "encountered" each specific individual.

Next, participants might engage in a short, unrelated filler task (perhaps searching for words in a letter matrix puzzle for four minutes), further clearing their short-term memory for the presented videos. Then participants would be shown stills of the stimulus individuals with all background weather information deleted, and would be unexpectedly asked to report their impressions of each individual (e.g., by rating this individual on personality scales theorized to be weather-affected). Finally, participants would be shown the stills yet again, but this time with instructions to guess the background weather depicted in each original stimulus video.

If participants who viewed targets in the context of weather information rate their personalities differently from those who watched the control video of the same people, this would confirm the impact of weather on incidental impressions. And if participants in the experimental condition reveal poor memory for the originally depicted weather, this would further indicate that these weather effects reflect incidental impressions rather than intentional inferences made at the time impressions were reported.

NUANCES OF THE METHOD

The preceding discussion covers some of the considerations underlying our basic method. Other aspects of our rationale require more elaborate discussion. In this section, we discuss our procedures in more detail, attempting to clarify both variations and theoretical underpinnings of our method. The key difference between intentional and incidental impression formation, as we have defined them, is whether the perceivers are purposefully engaged in trying to form person impressions. Consequently, it is essential to consider the kinds of perceptions and motivations aroused by the situations in which impression formation might take place. Do the explicit or implicit demands of the situation encourage perceivers to form impressions of others?

Instructional Manipulations

The instructions used in past impression formation research fall into four basic categories: explicit, implicit, passive, and diversionary. Most commonly,
participants are simply given explicit impression formation instructions. Virtually all research on classic phenomena in impression formation fall into this
category including, for example, the literatures on halo effects (e.g., Asch,
1946; Dion, Berscheid, & Walster, 1972), trait attribution (e.g., Jones, Davis,
& Gergen, 1961), environmental effects (e.g., Griffitt, 1970), diagnosticity
effects (e.g., Reeder & Coovert, 1986; Skowronski & Carlston, 1987), transference (e.g., Andersen & Cole, 1990; Andersen, Reznik, & Manzella, 1996;
Chen, Andersen, & Hinkley, 1999), companion effects (e.g., Kernis &
Wheeler, 1981; Meiners & Sheposh, 1977; Sigall & Landy, 1973), role confu-
sion (e.g., Fiske et al., 1991), kill-the-messenger effects (Manis, Cornell, &
Moore, 1974), and priming effects (e.g., Higgins, Bargh, & Lombardi, 1985;
Srull & Wyer, 1979; but see Higgins, Rholes, & Jones, 1977).

Explicit impression formation instructions may seem straightforward
enough on the surface; however, little is known about how participants actually
interpret instructions to "form an impression." Some participants may see this
as calling for some kind of mental image, some as mandating highly systematic
trait attribution processes, some as permitting more heuristic processes such as
stereotyping, and still others as encouraging reliance on intuition or gut feelings.
The interpretation adopted may depend on individual differences, examples
provided by the experimenter or cues provided in the stimuli. Regardless of
which of these processes are elicited however, the resultant processes would be
clearly characterized as intentional impression formation.

Implicit instructions lead participants to engage in impression formation
without explicitly telling them to do so. Examples would include instructing
participants to expect future interaction (Conway, Carroll, Pushkar,
Arbuckle, & Foisy, 1997; Devine, Sedikides, & Fuhrman, 1989), to compare
others to oneself (Devine et al., 1989; Symons & Johnson, 1997), or to prepare to describe, or answer questions about,[4] an individual (Cohen, 1961;
Harkins, Harvey, Keithly, & Rich, 1977; Higgins, Rholes, & Jones, 1977).
The effects of such tasks may be even more variable than explicit instructions to form impressions, because participants are largely free to determine
for themselves what kinds of processing to engage in. However, it seems
likely that, as with explicit instructions, implicit ones usually encourage intentional impression formation.

Passive instructions imply that the stimuli should be observed without
goal-related processing. For example, we have sometimes led participants to

---

[4]When instructions prepare participants to later answer questions about stimulus material, it is not
evident whether this prompts impression formation or memory goals. We assume that when participants
anticipate questions about *people,* this encourages impression formation.

believe that the stimuli were simply examples of materials to be used later in the experiment. Such instructions plausibly lead to passive observation, provided that other cues in the experiment (e.g., the stimuli) do not prompt intentional impression formation. Consequently, if such passivity is adopted, then any effects of associated stimuli on impressions of the target individual should reflect incidental impression formation processes.

Finally, diversionary instructions direct participants to engage in processing activities other than impression formation. For example, participants might be asked to memorize stimulus materials (Whitney, Waring, & Zingmark, 1992; Winter & Uleman, 1984), to comprehend them (Richter & Kruglanski,1998), or to evaluate their authenticity (Skowronski et al., 1998, Study 4), or they might be told that the stimulus materials are distractors for the actual, focal task (Lupfer, Clark, & Hutcherson, 1990). By providing a reasonable alternative goal to participants, such instructions may divert them from intentionally pursuing impression formation goals. However, care must be taken to ensure that the diversionary task does not implicitly encourage impression formation on the one hand (as it probably did in some of the earlier-mentioned cases) or interfere with it on the other. Then any effects of the associated stimuli should again reflect incidental impression processes.

In general, then, explicit and implicit impression formation instructions can be assumed to prompt intentional impression formation, whereas passive and diversionary instructions do not, allowing only incidental impression formation. However, to work effectively, passive and diversionary instructions must be supported by other features of the experiment that encourage incidental impression formation. Such features are described in the following section.

Experimental Demands

The potential for experimental situations to create "demands" that can prompt particular kinds of responding is well documented by social psychologists (Carlston & Cohen, 1980; Orne, 1962; Weber & Cook, 1972). Strangely, despite their apparent relevance, such possibilities have not been systematically considered in the impression formation realm. Participants presented with stimulus information in the laboratory almost certainly assume that this information is given to them for a reason (Wyer, Budesheim, Lambert, & Swan, 1994). Moreover, this is probably particularly true when the stimulus information has no apparent or logical source, so that it appears to have been fabricated for research purposes. In our research, we generally provide a plausible explanation for such information to avoid any implication that it was created or selected for its impressional relevance. For example, when studying the effects of behavioral descriptions, we led participants to believe that these were comments drawn from longer interviews with the targets; when studying the effects of vehicles on impressions, we gave participants a diversionary cover story that we were interested in studying people in an impatience-inducing situation (i.e., in line at a car wash); and when studying the effects of pets on owners' impressions, we initially engaged participants in an entirely different, diversionary task (judging how much owners and their pets look alike) to account for the presence of the pet photos. However, most person perception research provides no explanations regarding the origins of stimuli, implicitly encouraging the (correct) assumption that this information was created or selected because participants are expected to find it informative and useful.

In the absence of special precautions, we suspect that participants tend to assume, by default, that their goal is to learn the information presented, sometimes in anticipation of a memory test, but often in anticipation of impression questions. Our intuition is that many features of the experimental situation can serve to push participants toward one or the other of these expectations. For example, we suspect that many experiment titles in ads or "sign-up" sheets may imply one objective or the other, although the extent to which participants attend to or remember these is virtually unknown. Any references to facts, memory, learning, or tests may incline participants towards memorization processes; in contrast, references to meeting or getting to know people may incline them towards impression formation.

Other features of experiments can also create demands for intentional impression processes. For example, when only a single stimulus target is presented, this likely suggests that the individual is important, and that it may be valuable to form an impression of what this individual is like. Alternatively, when trait or evaluation ratings are made after each trial of a multiple trial study, this certainly creates a demand for impression formation, whether or not such goals are ever mentioned in instructions. If the researcher's objective is to examine incidental impressions, procedures that might make impression formation intentional must be avoided. However, the challenge here is dual-faceted. Although it is important not to prompt intentional impressions, it is nonetheless essential that the experimental situation be conducive to incidental impression formation, or no impressions will be formed at all. The next section focuses on the second facet; specifically, the role that experimental stimulus materials play in creating situations that are conducive to incidental impression formation.

Stimulus Characteristics

Target Photographs. The importance of facial appearance in impression formation has been documented in a great deal of research (Dion et al., 1972; Zebrowitz, 1997; see also Rhodes & Zebrowitz, 2002). Seeing a person's facial appearance may contribute to impressional processes in several different ways. Knowledge of a person's appearance probably makes him or her appear more "real," relevant, and worthy of attention. Seeing a face may cue cognitive processes (e.g., those underlying impression formation) that ordinarily occur in the presence of faces. More specifically, appearance cues may automatically bring to mind specific characteristics with which similar-looking people are associated (Zebrowitz, 1997). And finally, appearance provides a strong mnemonic cue that may serve to embody and to prime previously formed impressions. In real life, people's faces are usually evident, providing a natural cue for impression formation. Because of their richness and ubiquity, we have generally used facial photographs to represent our stimulus individuals, although intentional impression studies could be constructed to identify target individuals in other ways (e.g., through proper names).

Paired Information. The information that accompanies target individuals is also likely to play an important role in the instigation of impression processes. As with facial cues, those stimuli that are frequently present during impression formation processes may serve to cue such processes. Behavioral observations or information probably fall into this category, as demonstrated by research suggesting that such stimuli tend to lead to spontaneous trait inferences (Uleman, 1999). Some other forms of information (speech, companions, pets, clothing, etc.) may also indirectly provide information about individuals, and thus may cue such processes when presented with a target individual. Finally, myriad other forms of information (e.g., background weather, music, smells, noise, etc.) do not logically tell us anything about others but often still bias impressions. Thus there is no limit to the type of paired information that can be used in our incidental impression paradigm. However, to produce reliable effects, paired information must have reasonably clear and unambiguous implications for traits, evaluations, or other impressional judgments. Thus for example, a target's alleged behavior is likely to elicit trait impressions only if it has strong implications for one or more traits. A problem is created, however, when such implications are so obvious and regular across a set of experimental stimuli that they stimulate purposeful efforts to identify those implications. For example, if each behavior in a set obviously implies some personality trait, participants are likely to note this pattern and to play a game of "guess the intended trait" as they process each new item. Consequently, it is generally important to include numerous fillers that lack clear implications (or use other diversionary methods) to break set and inhibit intentional impression formation processes.

Post-Observational Activities

In most impression formation studies, relatively little occurs between exposure to stimulus information and assessment of impressions. Consequently, the likelihood of interference or forgetting is fairly small. As a result, the stimulus information is likely to remain memorable and salient, permitting intentional memory-based impression formation even if impression measures are completely unexpected.

On the other hand, in non-experimental situations, a great deal may occur between observation of an individual and thoughtful consideration of that person's characteristics. For example, interactions with a new acquaintance at a cocktail party may take place over a period of hours, and may be interspersed with numerous other conversations and activities. One effect of such post-observational activities may be to reduce access to the grist from which impressions are ordinarily milled: episodic memories. As a consequence, people may become more dependent on their vague intuitions about others.

Surprisingly, there is little direct evidence about the effects of delay on impressional representations. The few exceptions indicate that event memories do tend to have diminishing effects, and initial inferences tend to have increasing effects, over time (Carlston, 1980; Higgins et al., 1977). However, other research (e.g., Carlston & Skowronski, 1994) suggests that initial impressions also tend to weaken with time, though perhaps not as quickly as episodic memories. The critical consideration, in terms of the incidental impression paradigm, is that the delay be long enough to preclude using recalled paired information as a basis for forming post-hoc impressions. Although we have used delays as long as two weeks, we have generally found that delays of even a few minutes are sufficient, given the other procedures that we have adopted in our incidental impression studies.

In general, then, time delays can be used in the incidental impression paradigm to diminish intentional, memory-based impression formation, but such procedures may not be necessary when other design features already attain the same objective. Whatever procedures are used, it can be useful to use pre- or post-experimental memory measures to confirm that the specific paired information could not be reliably and explicitly recalled, ensuring that impressions were not intentionally formed post hoc.[5]

Dependent Measures

The assessment of impressions through trait scales obviously cues participants to focus on impressions of previously observed target individuals. In general, however, such cuing cannot prompt intentional impression formation processes if the specific stimulus material necessary for intentional processes is no longer accessible. Incidental impression procedures are designed to ensure that this is true. Nonetheless, participants may bias their

---

[5]Pre- and post-experimental memory tests have different pros and cons. The pretest, conducted with different participants, allows for the opportunity to test participants' memory at the *exact time* that impressions will be collected from experimental participants. However, the post-test, conducted with the same participants, allows one to compare the effects for participants who show varying degrees of memory.

trait ratings of target individuals if they perceive that the provided trait scales indicate dimensions about which inferences were supposed to have been made. To diminish such perceptions, we generally bury trait scales for which results are expected among others for which no results are expected. This reduces the cue value of the rating scales themselves.

Another technique for reducing the cue value of trait scales is to eschew them altogether in favor of more implicit measures of impressions. One example is the savings-in-relearning measure developed by Carlston and Skowronski (1994). This measure involves presenting participants with photograph-trait pairs, some of which correspond to inferences they presumably made incidentally during prior exposure. Participants are asked to memorize these pairs for a later recall test, and it is assumed that they will be more successful doing so when the stimulus pairings represent associations that participants have previously formed on their own. Evidence for "savings effects" indicates that incidental impressions have been formed previously. Burying the traits of interest and using implicit measures are thus two examples of dependent measures that avoid cuing intentional impressions.

Research on Incidental Impressions

A search of the early impression formation literature turns up only a few isolated studies that have some, but not all, of the characteristics composing incidental impression procedures. Thus for example, some naturalistic studies carefully avoided creating impression formation goals (e.g., Stephan & Tully, 1977; Walster, Aronson, Abrahams, & Rottmann, 1966), but their reliance on a single, important target in a judgmental context probably provoked intentional processes nonetheless. Other studies have used grouped presentations of person stimuli followed by deferred impression ratings (e.g., Moreland & Zajonc, 1982), although the goal was to examine the effects of familiarity rather than incidental learning of impression information. Only recently have some concerted efforts been made to adopt the whole range of procedures necessary to allow incidental processes to be examined.

As previously noted, the most systematic past attempts to explore incidental impressions of persons focused on the issue of whether people spontaneously infer traits from actors' behaviors (Bassili, 1993; Lupfer et al., 1990; Winter & Uleman, 1984). Winter and Uleman first addressed the challenge of capturing spontaneous (or incidental) impressions, using an adaptation of the encoding specificity principle (Tulving & Thomson, 1973). After participants read multiple actors' trait-related behaviors under memory instructions, the existence of incidental impressions was suggested by the relative superiority of trait terms as retrieval cues. However, critics (e.g. Bassili & Smith, 1986) suggested that this result simply indicates that traits were activated during stimulus interpretation, and not that traits were in any way associated with actors, let alone attributed to them. Thus it is not clear that impressions were even formed.

This controversy was largely settled by the first studies using what we now view as a variation of the incidental impression paradigm (Carlston & Skowronski, 1994; Carlston et al., 1995). In these studies, participants were given familiarization instructions, exposed to 30 photo-behavior stimulus pairs (fewer than half of which had clear trait implications), put through delays and interference tasks, and then tested for savings in "relearning" photo-trait pairs that matched the original stimulus implications. Even when participants could not explicitly recall the original pairings, they showed superior learning for these photo-trait pairs compared to control pairs, indicating that the traits were already associated with the individuals in the photos. Furthermore, other work (Skowronski et al., 1998) has shown that spontaneous trait inferences are actually attributed to the targets.

Our subsequent work on spontaneous trait transference investigated the formation of incidental impressions under circumstances in which the stimulus information should not logically have had an influence (Skowronski et al., 1998). In these studies, we paired targets with descriptions they allegedly provided of other people. A series of studies using a variation of the incidental impression paradigm showed that the targets became associated with the traits they described in other people, and also that the targets were ultimately viewed as actually possessing these traits. Furthermore, the evidence suggested that these results reflected simple associative processes rather than higher level attributional processes, such as believing that people choose to talk about others who are similar to themselves (see also Brown & Bassili, 2002). A subsequent series of studies (Mae, Carlston, & Skowronski, 1999) demonstrated that trait transference occurred even when the perceivers possessed prior knowledge of the targets.

Recently we have used the incidental impression paradigm to study impressions of those who engage in bigoted speech. The method is ideal for studying socially sensitive issues such as bigotry, because participants are not aware that their impressions will be assessed until they have formed incidental impressions and forgotten the underlying stimuli. At this point, unaware of the basis for their impressions, they are less able to recognize or correct for any socially unacceptable influences that may have affected them. In a number of studies, we found that those who engage in bigoted speech were liked less by audiences, surprisingly even by audience members who agreed with the prejudiced remarks. We are currently exploring some of the underlying mechanisms that may be responsible for this counterintuitive effect.

We have two studies in progress that constitute our first attempts to compare and contrast logical versus illogical effects on incidental impressions. In one study, we pair trait-laden symbols (e.g., guns, peace symbols, swastikas) with target individuals under conditions in which those symbols either do or do not provide a logical basis for impressions. Some participants are told that the symbols were chosen by targets' friends as somehow indicative of these individuals' personalities (a logical influence), whereas other participants are told that the symbols were randomly paired with the targets (an illogical influence). Similarly, in a second study, we have "introduced" participants to targets photographed in vehicles. Some participants are told that the vehicles are owned by the target, whereas others are informed that the individuals were randomly assigned vehicles to sit in. Our preliminary analyses suggest that incidental impressions are affected by both illogical and logical associates, though the effects of the latter appear significantly stronger.

Finally, we are also using the incidental impression paradigm to explore whether impressions of owners are affected by the personalities of their pets. For example, a person who owns a collie might be seen as more heroic, one who owns a Doberman as more aggressive, and one who owns a bulldog as lazier. This study employs some novel variations on the incidental impression method. First, participants engage in an unusual diversionary task during stimulus exposure: specifically, they are asked to judge how much the owners and pets look alike. Additionally, we are incorporating the separate study paradigm: When participants finish the exposure and filler task, they are told that, for another study, we are interested in determining how much we can tell about people from their appearances alone. To this end, participants are asked to flip back through the photos of the pet owners and to report their impressions; this time, however, the owners' pets are covered up.

Researchers have only begun to capture incidental impressions in laboratory work on impression formation. This work illustrates the broad range of phenomena that may be discovered as laboratory work shifts from the intentional impression domain to the kinds of incidental impressions that we feel predominate in the real world. But research has not yet addressed some of the more systematic questions that arise about differences between incidental and intentional impressions. Those questions are outlined in the following section.

FUTURE RESEARCH

Virtually nothing concrete is known about the differences between intentional and incidental impressions, though educated guesses can be made from prior work in related literatures. Obviously, to quote an oft-stated conclusion, "more research is needed." To provide some structure to the following discussion of such research possibilities, we advance a number of hypotheses about ways in which incidental impression formation differs from intentional impression formation. These hypotheses, which are grouped into general themes, provide the outline of a comprehensive theory of incidental impressions. For the sake of simplicity, the comparative "intentional impressions" is not explicitly stated, but is implicit in each hypothesis.

Contributing Cues

1. *Incidental impressions may be more vulnerable to socially sensitive cues.* Just as Robert Zajonc (1980) suggested that different cues form the basis for identification and for preferences, we propose that different cues are likely to form the basis for intentional and incidental impressions. Specifically, compared to intentional impression formation, incidental impression formation may be more strongly affected by information that is socially sensitive. As a consequence, the incidental impression paradigm is particularly suitable for capturing uncensored impressions in contexts in which people might otherwise bias their responses. Thus for example, incidental impressions may be more affected by a target person's race, gender, or sexual orientation than those formed intentionally.

Testing such possibilities would be relatively simple. For example, participants could be given diversionary or explicit impression instructions, and then presented with a half-dozen person photos, depicting varying races, each paired with a race-neutral first name. Next, all participants would be put through a series of practice and memory tests to ensure that they learned the face-name pairs. Finally, they would be cued only by the first names and asked to report their impressions of each individual. We predict that race will affect incidental impressions more than intentional ones, because of participants' inability to censure such information in the incidental impression paradigm.

2. *Incidental impressions may be more vulnerable to peripheral cues.* In the attitudes literature, it is not always evident which cues are peripheral, and which are more central (Petty & Wegener, 1999). We would argue that the most central cues for impression formation are those that are most diagnostic (see Skowronski & Carlston, 1987), such as actors' trait-relevant behaviors. Peripheral cues would involve information that only indirectly implies the trait of interest, including, for example, the setting in which a person is observed.

Imagine an experiment involving numerous videotaped clips of skilled or unskilled dancers performing either on stage (a professional setting) or in residential rooms (a nonprofessional setting). Intentional impression participants receive impression instructions and judge the dancers' skills after viewing each videotaped clip; incidental impression participants are preoccupied by instructions to count the number of pirouettes each dancer makes, and then are asked to make skill judgments only after viewing all the tapes. Presumably, intentional impressions would primarily reflect the central cue; namely, the dancers' gracefulness and performance, with the setting having a lesser influence. Incidental impressions would undoubtedly also reflect the central cue, but the peripheral cue (the setting) should affect them more than it does intentional impressions. Consequently, the dancers performing of stage should be viewed as more skilled than those performing in residential rooms.

3.   *Incidental impressions may be more vulnerable to illogical cues.* Just as people should be less able to censor incidental impressions to avoid socially sensitive influences, they should also be less able to counter-argue irrational ones. For example, consider a study we are currently running to examine this possibility. We have collected videotaped segments of television newscasters reporting positive and negative news stories. To promote intentional impressions, some participants will be asked to report their impressions of each newscaster immediately following their stories. To promote incidental impressions, others will be focused on the content of the news stories and will be asked to report their impressions only after they have been exposed to all of the newscasters. Clearly, the stories assigned to newscasters are not rational reflections of their personalities. However, past research (Manis et al., 1974; Veitch & Griffitt, 1976) has shown that impressions of messengers are influenced by the valence of their messages. We predict that impressions of the newscasters formed incidentally will be more likely to reflect the valence of the news stories than those formed intentionally.

Implicated Processes

4.   *Incidental impressions may be more likely to involve associative processes.* We propose that incidental impressions may involve associative processes, whereas intentional ones are more likely to involve inferential processes. Demonstrating that a process involves associations rather than inferences may not be as simple as it first seems. Trait-rating dependent measures may prompt participants to access their associations and intentionally translate them into explicit inferences. And implicit measures, such as word completion tasks, may be affected by inferences as well as by associations. One strategy for disentangling the two is to create situations in which it is highly unlikely that people would make inferences (Skowronski et al., 1998, Study 3; see also Brown & Bassili, 2002). Any impressions formed under these circumstances presumably implicate lower level associations. However, in research where intentional impressions are more likely, additional assumptions must be made about the precise nature of associative versus inferential impression processes in order to distinguish the two.

One plausible assumption is that associations may be less sensitive than inferences to situational indicators that specify the exact nature of the link between a target person and associated information. Suppose, for example, that target persons are paired with affect-laden symbols (e.g., flags, swastikas, guns, etc.) that they are sometimes said to love and sometimes said to hate. Inferential processes seem likely to take such contingencies into account, leading the target individual who loves the American flag to be judged as more patriotic than the individual who hates it. Irrespective of the love/hate linkage, however, associations may be formed between the target person and the American flag. Should that association persist after the linkage fades from memory, then both the flag hater and the flag lover may be viewed as patriotic. (We predict that incidental processes result in associations that fail to take the nature of the link into account.) Similar processes have been demonstrated in relation to the sleeper effect (Cook, Gruder, Hennigan, & Flay, 1979; Kelman & Hovland, 1953), source monitoring (Johnson, Hastroudi, & Lindsay, 1993), and instructions to disregard information (Isbell, Smith, & Wyer, 1998; Wyer & Budesheim, 1987).

    5.   *Incidental impressions may be less likely to involve correction processes.* Research indicates that people generally do not engage in correction processes unless they possess awareness, capacity, and motivation to do so (Strack & Hannover, 1996; Trope & Gaunt, 1999; Wegener & Petty, 1995). Thus, for example, when these criteria are not met, people fail to correct for situational influences on behavior (Gilbert et al., 1988). Logically, then, they should also be less likely to engage in such correction processes when they are forming impressions incidentally rather than intentionally. More generally, people should engage in less sophisticated and comprehensive attributional processes when processing incidentally. Uleman (1999) makes an essentially identical prediction in discussing spontaneous versus intentional trait inference.

    Numerous means exist for examining such possibilities. Consider the following "hybrid" experiment based on point-of-view work by Taylor and Fiske (1975) and situational-discounting work by Gilbert et al. (1988). Participants would observe one of two different interactions between two individuals, each of whom would evidence a different trait. In one version, each would also reveal the existence of a situational cause or constraint that logically discounts the trait, whereas in the other version, no such discounting cue would be presented. Participants would be instructed in advance to form an impression of one or the other individual. After a sufficient delay, trait ratings would be elicited for both the focal and the non-focal individual.

    It would be predicted that intentional processing of the focal individual would lead to more trait attribution in the absence of a discounting cue, and more discounting (reflected in less trait attribution) in the presence of the cue. Incidental processing of the non-focal individual, however, should be less affected by the discounting cue, leading to modest levels of attribution in all conditions. Moreover, the incidental (non-focal) targets might also be viewed as having some of the traits actually characteristic of the intentional (focal) targets (see Skowronski et al., 1998), whereas the reverse would be less likely to occur.

6.   *Incidental impressions are less likely to involve reconciliation processes.* Researchers have also shown that capacity and motivation are required for the reconciliation processes assumed to underlie incongruity effects (Srull, 1981). Consequently, such reconciliation processes should also be more characteristic of intentional than incidental impression processes.

Imagine an experiment where ten different stimulus targets are each seen performing six behaviors: four implying one trait, and two implying an incongruent trait. Intentional impression participants are given impression formation instructions and make trait judgments after viewing each target individual. Incidental impression participants are given diversionary instructions and make their trait judgments later, following procedures of the incidental impression paradigm. Later, both groups might also be given a memory task, cued with photos of the target individuals. Superior memory for incongruent information is generally presumed to be an indication that reconciliation processes have occurred (Srull, 1981).

We would predict that intentional impression participants will make more of an effort to reconcile and integrate incongruent information, and consequently will report more moderate impressions, than incidental impression participants. Additionally, on the memory task, intentional impression participants should show better recall for incongruent than congruent behaviors, whereas incidental impression participants (whose memory for the behaviors is likely to be abysmal, in any case) should not.

Resultant Impressions

7.   *Incidental impressions may reflect less extremity and/or confidence.* In general, it seems that incidental impressions should be less extreme, and held with less confidence, than those that are intentional. To examine this possibility, one might present participants with photos of artists standing beside their beautiful or grotesque works of art. Intentional impression participants would be instructed to form impressions of the artists trial by trial, as the photos are presented. Incidental impression participants would be diverted from forming impressions by being focused on judging the quality of the artwork, using post-stimulus interference, and other components of the incidental impression method. Then, after a brief delay, all participants would be shown photos of the artists and asked to rate them on personality

---

[6]It is necessary to control for delay across intentional and incidental conditions, because delay alone is likely to affect both extremity and confidence. Delays are usually a feature of the incidental impressions paradigm, though they do not by themselves promote incidental processing. Thus intentional impressions would still be relatively more intentional than incidental ones.

traits, and to report their confidence in these impressions.[6] We predict that the resultant incidental impressions would be less extreme and confidently held than those formed under intentional instructions.

A possible exception to this predicted pattern may occur for impressions formed from contextual information that logically has no implications for targets' traits. As discussed earlier, such information seems more likely to affect incidental impressions than intentional ones. Suppose, for example, that participants were told that the depicted works of art were found by the targets in their attics. Under this circumstance, we might expect a reversal of the usual pattern, with incidental impressions evidencing more extremity and confidence than intentional ones.

8. *Incidental impressions may be less accessible and less enduring.* Because intentional impressions are formed consciously, sometimes through extensive cognitive work, one might expect these to be more accessible, more readily and often retrieved, and ultimately more enduring. A simple experiment comparing the accessibility of intentional and incidental impressions over time could demonstrate such differences. For example, participants induced to make intentional or incidental impressions could have their response times to trait measures assessed after varying delays. We predict that incidental impressions will be less accessible than intentional ones initially, and possibly even decay faster than those that are intentional.

In follow-up work, one might equate the initial strength of the intentional and incidental impressions, perhaps by repeating trials for specific target individuals in the incidental impression procedure until initial effects are comparable to those obtained through intentional processes. With initial strength equated, would incidental impressions still be less enduring? Perhaps they would, because intentional inferential processes may create more linkages with other knowledge, increasing routes of access.

9. *Incidental impressions may involve different forms of mental representation.* There has been a widespread tendency for social psychologists to equate impressions with traits (Wyer & Lambert, 1994). However, as several theorists (e.g., Carlston, 1994; Carlston & Smith, 1996; Wyer & Srull, 1986) have noted, traits are only one of many possible forms of person representation. Consequently, it is plausible that intentional and incidental impression processes may tend to produce different forms of mental representation. One method for detecting such differences involves soliciting free descriptions that are later coded for descriptors likely to reflect different underlying representations. Thus for example, participants might be given either explicit impression instructions or diversionary instructions and then exposed to videos of a series of actors performing different behaviors. Then, after a delay, they would be shown photos of the actors and asked to describe their impressions of each.

We hypothesize that traits would predominate in the descriptions reported by intentional impression participants, but that evaluative feelings might be more common in those reported by incidental impression participants. This speculation is simply based on the guess that participants tend to interpret impression formation instructions as demanding specific, trait/personality descriptions, whereas incidental associations may be likely to involve more general evaluations.

CONCLUSIONS

We have described the typical individual forming a person impression as a kind of accidental tourist, passively meandering through life in a somewhat detached manner, forming impressions as an incidental by-product of other goals and pursuits. Moreover, we have suggested that capturing these incidental impressions requires more stealth and finesse than measuring the intentional impressions so readily elicited in the laboratory. To continue with the tourist metaphor, we have proposed that researchers employ a kind of "candid camera," surreptitiously recording incidental impressions without the heavy-handed encouragement typifying much impression research. For just as an unposed snapshot of an individual may carry little resemblance to his or her posed portrait, we believe that the examination of incidental impressions, through methods such as the incidental impression paradigm, will develop a different picture of the social perceiver.

Past conceptions, largely based on intentional impression formation, characterized the social perceiver as a naive scientist (desiring to learn about others and going about this by testing hypotheses), a cognitive miser (doing so by exerting as little effort as possible), and a motivated tactician (driven by multiple needs and desires; Fiske & Taylor, 1991). We believe our "accidental tourist" metaphor better captures the social perceiver under typical real-world conditions, in which impression formation is not a primary or intended motivation, and in which knowledge of others is acquired incidentally. We believe this metaphor encourages examination of many interesting issues regarding the causation, processing, and nature of incidental impressions, and we invite others to join us in stalking the accidental tourist.

So What About Bob?

Bob has toured a great deal of the world and of the realm of person perception. Does our approach follow in Bob Wyer's footsteps? Well, Bob is a hard act to follow.

We've certainly wandered off the track from time to time. But there is little question that he has inspired and provoked us with his creativity and speculations in numerous thought pieces of the sort to which this one aspires. Like Bob, we are preoccupied with the nature of impression formation out in the real world, where life's priorities place numerous activities above forming impressions and life's little instruction booklet doesn't include an impression formation chapter. And like Bob, we are convinced that impressions are complex entities, composed of myriad inferences and concepts that change shape and influence depending on how the information is processed. Of course, there are many differences between our perspective and Bob's, including the fact that (as clearly reflected in this chapter) we adopt an unabashedly associationistic approach, which he does not. But then, aren't children notorious for being rebellious?

REFERENCES

Andersen, S. M., & Cole, S. W. (1990). "Do I know you?": The role of significant others in general social perception. *Journal of Personality and Social Psychology, 59*, 384–399.

Andersen, S. M., Reznik, I., & Manzella, L. M. (1996). Eliciting facial affect, motivation, and expectancies in transference: Significant-other representations in social relations. *Journal of Personality and Social Psychology, 71*, 1108–1129.

Asch, S. E. (1946). Forming impressions of personality. *Journal of Abnormal and Social Psychology, 41*, 258–290.

Baddeley, A. (1990). *Human Memory*. Boston: Allyn & Bacon.

Bargh, J. A. (1994). The four horsemen of automaticity: Awareness, intention, efficiency, and control in social cognition. In R. S. Wyer, Jr. & Srull, T. K. (Eds.), *Handbook of social cognition: Vol. 1. Basic processes* (2nd ed., pp. 1–40). Hillsdale, NJ: Lawrence Erlbaum Associates.

Bargh, J. A. (1996). Automaticity in social psychology. In E. T. Higgins & A. W. Kruglanski (Eds.), *Social psychology: Handbook of basic principles* (pp. 169–183). New York: The Guilford Press.

Bargh, J. A, Chaiken, S., Raymond, P., & Hymes, C. (1996). The automatic evaluation effect: Unconditional automatic attitude activation with a pronunciation task. *Journal of Experimental Social Psychology, 32*, 104–128.

Bargh, J. A., & Ferguson, M. J. (2000). Beyond behaviorism: On the automaticity of higher mental processes. *Psychological Bulletin, 126*, 925–945.

Bargh, J. A., & Thein, R. D. (1985). Individual construct accessibility, person memory, and the recall-judgment link: The case of information overload. *Journal of Personality and Social Psychology, 49*, 1129–1146.

Bassili, J. N. (1993). Procedural efficiency and the spontaneity of trait inference. *Personality & Social Psychology Bulletin, 19*, 200–205.

Bassili, J. N., & Smith, M. C. (1986). On the spontaneity of trait attribution: Converging evidence for the role of cognitive strategy. *Journal of Personality & Social Psychology, 50*, 239–245.

Berkowitz, L., & Donnerstein, E. (1982). External validity is more than skin deep: Some answers to criticisms of laboratory experiments. *American Psychologist, 37,* 245–257.

Brewer, M. (1988). A dual process model of impression formation. In. T. K. Srull & R. S. Wyer, Jr. (Eds.), *Advances in social cognition* (Vol. 1, pp. 1–36). Hillsdale, NJ: Lawrence Erlbaum Associates.

Brown, R. D., & Bassili, J. N. (2002). Spontaneous trait associations and the case of the superstitious banana. *Journal of Experimental Social Psychology, 38,* 87–92.

Carlston, D. E. (1978). The recall and use of observed behaviors and inferred traits in social inference processes (Doctoral Dissertation, Purdue University, 1978). *Dissertation Abstracts International, 38,* 5088.

Carlston, D. E. (1980). The recall and use of traits and events in social inference processes. *Journal of Experimental Social Psychology, 16,* 303–328.

Carlston, D. E. (1992). Impression formation and the modular mind: The associated systems theory. In L. L. Martin, & A. Tesser (Eds.), *The construction of social judgments* (pp. 301–341). Hillsdale, NJ: Lawrence Erlbaum Associates.

Carlston, D. E. (1994). Associated Systems Theory: A systematic approach to cognitive representations of persons. In R. S. Wyer, Jr. (Ed), *Advances in social cognition,* (Vol. 7, pp. 1–78). Hillsdale, NJ: Lawrence Erlbaum Associates.

Carlston, D. E., & Cohen, J. L. (1980). A closer examination of subject roles. *Journal of Personality and Social Psychology, 38,* 857–870.

Carlston, D. E., & Skowronski, J. J. (1986). Trait memory and behavior memory: The effects of alternative pathways on impression judgment response times. *Journal of Personality and Social Psychology, 50,* 5–13.

Carlston, D. E., & Skowronski, J. J. (1994). Savings in the relearning of trait information as evidence for spontaneous inference generation. *Journal of Personality and Social Psychology, 66,* 840–856.

Carlston, D. E., Skowronski, J. J., & Sparks, C. (1995). Savings in relearning: II. On the formation of behavior-based trait associations and inferences. *Journal of Personality and Social Psychology, 69,* 429–436.

Carlston, D. E., & Smith, E. R. (1996). Principles of mental representation. In T. E. Higgins & A. W. Kruglanski (Eds.), *Social psychology: Handbook of basic principles* (pp. 184–210). New York: Guilford Press.

Chaiken, S. (1980). Heuristic versus systematic information processing and the use of source versus message cues in persuasion. *Journal of Personality and Social Psychology, 39,* 752–766.

Chen, S., Andersen, S. M., & Hinkley, K. (1999). Triggering transference: Examining the role of applicability in the activation and use of significant-other representations in social perception. *Social Cognition, 17,* 332–365.

Cohen, A. R. (1961). Cognitive tuning as a factor affecting impression formation. *Journal of Personality, 29,* 235–245.

Conway, M., Carroll, J. M., Pusukar, D., Arbuckle, T., & Foisy, P. (1996). Anticipated interaction, individual differences in attentional resources, and elaboration of behavior. *Social Cognition, 14,* 338–366.

Cook, T. D., Gruder, C. L., Hennigan, K. M., & Flay, B. R. (1979). History of the sleeper effect: Some logical pitfalls in accepting the null hypothesis. *Psychological Bulletin, 86,* 662–679.

DeCoster, J., & Smith, E. R. (2000). Savings in relearning through exposure to same-group exemplars. *Current Research in Social Psychology, 5,* 17–32.

Devine, P. G. (1989). Stereotypes and prejudice: Their automatic and controlled components. *Journal of Personality and Social Psychology, 56,* 5–18.

Devine, P. G., Sedikides, C., & Fuhrman, R. W. (1989). Goals in social information processing: The case of anticipated interaction. *Journal of Personality & Social Psychology, 56,* 680–690.

Dion, K., Berscheid, E., & Walster, E. (1972). What is beautiful is good. *Journal of Personality and Social Psychology, 24,* 285–290.

Fazio, R. H., & Dunton, B. C. (1997). Categorization by race: The impact of automatic and controlled components of racial prejudice. *Journal of Experimental Social Psychology, 33,* 451–470.

Fazio, R. H., Sanbonmatsu, D. M., Powell, M. C., & Kardes, F. R. (1986). On the automatic activation of attitudes. *Journal of Personality and Social Psychology, 50,* 229–238.

Fiske, A. P., Haslam, N., & Fiske, S. T. (1991). Confusing one person with another: What errors reveal about the elementary forms of social relations. *Journal of Personality and Social Psychology, 60,* 656–674.

Fiske, S. T., & Taylor, S. E. (1991). *Social Cognition* (2nd ed.). New York: McGraw-Hill.

Gleitman, H., & Gillett, E. (1957). The effect of intention upon learning. *Journal of General Psychology, 57,* 137–149.

Gilbert, D. T., Pelham, B. W., & Krull, D. S. (1988). On cognitive busyness: When person perceivers meet persons perceived. *Journal of Personality and Social Psychology, 54,* 733–740.

Greenwald, A. G., & Banaji, M. R. (1995). Implicit social cognition: Attitudes, self-esteem, and stereotypes. *Psychological Review, 102,* 4–27.

Griffitt, W. (1970). Environmental effects on interpersonal affective behavior: Ambient effective temperature and attraction. *Journal of Personality & Social Psychology, 15,* 240–244.

Harkins, S. G., Harvey, J. H., Keithly, L., & Rich, M. (1977). Cognitive tuning, encoding, and the attribution of causality. *Memory & Cognition, 5,* 561–565.

Hastie, R., & Park, B. (1986). The relationship between memory and judgment depends on whether the judgment task is memory-based or on-line. *Psychological Review, 93,* 258–268.

Higgins, E. T., Bargh, J. A., & Lombardi, W. (1985). Nature of priming effects on categorization. *Journal of Experimental Social Psychology, 11,* 59–69.

Higgins, E. T., & King, G. (1981). Accessibility of social constructs: Information-processing consequences of individual and contextual variability. In N. Cantor & J. F. Kihlstrom (Eds.), *Personality, cognition, and social interaction* (pp. 69–122). Hillsdale, NJ: Lawrence Erlbaum Associates.

Higgins, E. T., Rholes, W. S., & Jones, C. R. (1977). Category accessibility and impression formation. *Journal of Experimental Social Psychology, 13,* 141–154.

Isbell, L. M., Smith, H. L., & Wyer, R. S., Jr. (1998). Consequences of attempts to disregard social information. In J. M. Golding & C. M. MacLeod (Eds.), *Inten-*

tional forgetting: Interdisciplinary approaches (pp. 289–320). Mahwah, NJ: Lawrence Erlbaum Associates.

Johnson, M. K., Hashtroudi, S., & Lindsay, D. S. (1993). Source monitoring. *Psychological Bulletin, 114*, 3–28.

Jones, E. E., & Davis, K. E. (1965). From acts to dispositions: The attribution process in person perception. In L. Berkowitz (Ed.), *Advances in experimental social psychology* (Vol. 2, pp. 220–266). New York: Academic Press.

Jones, E. E., Davis, K. E., & Gergen, K. J. (1961). Role playing variations and their informational value for person perception. *Journal of Abnormal and Social Psychology, 63*, 302–310.

Kelman, H. C., & Hovland, C. I. (1953). "Reinstatement" of the communicator in delayed measurement of opinion change. *Journal of Abnormal and Social Psychology, 48*, 327–335.

Kelley, H. H. (1967). Attribution theory in social psychology. *Nebraska Symposium on Motivation, 15*, 192–238.

Kernis, M. H., & Wheeler, L. (1981). Beautiful friends and ugly strangers: Radiation and contrast effects in perception of same-sex pairs. *Personality and Social Psychology Bulletin, 7*, 617–620.

Langer, E. J., Blank, A., & Chanowitz, B. (1978). The mindlessness of ostensibly thoughtful action: The role of "placebic" information in interpersonal interaction. *Journal of Personality and Social Psychology, 36*, 635–642.

Lewicki, P. (1985). Nonconscious biasing effects of single instances on subsequent judgments. *Journal of Personality and Social Psychology, 48*, 563–574.

Lingle, J. H., & Ostrom, T. M. (1979). Retrieval selectivity in memory-based impression judgments. *Journal of Personality and Social Psychology, 37*, 180–194.

Lupfer, M. B., Clark, L. F., & Hutcherson, H. W. (1990). Impact of context on spontaneous trait and situational attributions. *Journal of Personality and Social Psychology, 58*, 239–249.

Mae, L., Carlston, D. E., & Skowronski, J. J. (1999). Spontaneous trait transference to familiar communications: Is a little knowledge a dangerous thing? *Journal of Personality and Social Psychology, 77*, 233–246.

Manis, M., Cornell, S. D., & Moore, J. C. (1974). Transmission of attitude-relevant information through a communication chain. *Journal of Personality and Social Psychology, 30*, 81–94.

Meiners, M. L., & Sheposh, J. P. (1977). Beauty or brains: Which image for your mate? *Personality and Social Psychology Bulletin, 3*, 262–265.

Moreland, R. L., & Zajonc, R. B. (1982). Exposure effects in person perception: Familiarity, similarity, and attraction. *Journal of Experimental Social Psychology, 18*, 395–415.

Mulligan, N. W. (1998). The role of attention during encoding in implicit and explicit memory. *Journal of Experimental Psychology: Learning, Memory, & Cognition, 24*, 27–47.

Orne, M. T. (1962) On the social psychology of the psychological experiment: With particular reference to demand characteristics and their implications. *American Psychologist, 17*, 776–783.

Park, B. (1986). A method for studying the development of impressions of real people. *Journal of Personality and Social Psychology, 51*, 907–917.

Petty, R. E. (2001). Subtle influences on judgment and behavior: Who is most susceptible? In J. P. Forgas & K. D. Williams (Eds.), *Social influence: Direct and indirect processes. The Sydney symposium of social psychology* (pp. 129–146). Philadelphia: Psychology Press.

Petty, R. E., & Cacioppo, J. T. (1984). The effects of involvement on responses to argument quantity and quality: Central and peripheral routes to persuasion. *Journal of Personality and Social Psychology, 46*, 69–81.

Petty, R. E., & Wegener, D. T. (1999). The elaboration likelihood model: Current status and controversies. In S. Chaiken & Y. Trope (Eds.), *Dual-process theories in social psychology* (pp. 37–72). New York: Guilford Press.

Reeder, G. D., & Coovert, M. D. (1986). Revising an impression of morality. *Social Cognition, 4*, 1–17.

Rhodes, G., & Zebrowitz, L. A. (Eds.). (2002). *Facial attractiveness: Evolutionary, cognitive and social perspectives* [Advances in Visual Cognition (Vol. 1)]. Westport, CT: Ablex.

Richter, L., & Kruglanski, A. W. (1998). Seizing on the latest: Motivationally driven recency effects in impression formation. *Journal of Experimental Social Psychology, 34*, 313–329.

Roediger, H. L., III. (1990). Implicit memory: Retention without remembering. *American Psychologist, 45*, 1043–1056.

Schachter, D. L. (1987). Implicit memory: History and current status. *Journal of Experimental Psychology: Learning, Memory & Cognition, 13*, 501–518.

Sigall, H., & Landy, D. (1973). Radiating beauty: Effects of having a physically attractive partner in person perception. *Journal of Personality and Social Psychology, 28*, 218–224.

Skowronski, J. J., & Carlston, D. E. (1987). Social judgment and social memory: The role of cue diagnosticity in negativity, positivity, and extremity biases. *Journal of Personality and Social Psychology, 52*, 689–699.

Skowronski, J. J., Carlston, D. E., Mae, L., & Crawford, M. T. (1998). Spontaneous trait transference: Communicators take on the qualities they describe in others. *Journal of Personality and Social Psychology, 74*, 837–848.

Skowronski, J. J., Carlston, D. E., & Isham, J. T. (1993). Implicit versus explicit impression formation: The differing effects of overt labeling and covert priming on memory and impressions. *Journal of Experimental Social Psychology, 29*, 17–41.

Smith, E. R., & Lerner, M. (1986). Development of automatism of social judgments. *Journal of Personality and Social Psychology, 50*, 246–259.

Srull, T. K. (1981). Person memory: Some tests of associative storage and retrieval models. *Journal of Experimental Psychology: Human Learning & Memory, 7*, 440–463.

Srull, T. K., & Wyer, T. S. (1979). The role of category accessibility in the interpretation of information about persons: Some determinants and implications. *Journal of Personality and Social Psychology, 37*, 1660–1672.

Stephan, C., & Tully, J. C. (1977). The influence of physical attractiveness of a plaintiff on the decisions of simulated jurors. *Journal of Social Psychology, 101*, 149–150.

Strack, F., & Hannover, B. (1996). Awareness of influence as a precondition for implementing correctional goals. In P. M. Gollwitzer & J. A. Bargh (Eds.), *The psy-*

chology of action: Linking cognition and motivation to behavior (pp. 579–596). New York: Guilford Press.

Symons, C. S., & Johnson, B. T. (1997). The self-reference effect in memory: A meta-analysis. *Psychological Bulletin, 121,* 371–394.

Taylor, S. E., & Fiske, S. T. (1975). Point of view and perceptions of causality. *Journal of Personality and Social Psychology, 32,* 439–445.

Taylor, S. E., & Fiske, S. T. (1978). Salience, attention, and attribution: The top of the head phenomena. In L. Berkowitz (Ed.), *Advances in experimental social psychology* (Vol. 11, pp. 249–288). New York: Academic Press.

Trafimow, D., & Wyer, R. S., Jr. (1993). Cognitive representation of mundane social events. *Journal of Personality & Social Psychology, 64,* 365–376.

Trope, Y., & Gaunt, R. (1999). A dual-process model of overconfident attributional inferences. In S. Chaiken & Y. Trope (Eds.) *Dual-process theories in social psychology.* New York: Guilford Press.

Tulving, E. (1972). Episodic and semantic memory. In E. Tulving & W. Donaldson (Eds.), *Organization of memory.* New York: Academic Press.

Tulving, E., & Donaldson, W. (1972). *Organization of memory.* New York: Academic Press.

Tulving, E., & Thomson, D. M. (1973). Encoding specificity and retrieval processes in episodic memory. *Psychological Bulletin, 30,* 352–373.

Uleman, J. S., (1999). Spontaneous versus intentional inferences in impression formation. In S. Chaiken (Ed.), *Dual-process theories in social psychology* (pp. 141–160). New York: Guilford Press.

Uleman, J. S. & Bargh, J. A. (Eds.). (1989). *Unintended thought.* New York: The Guilford Press.

Uleman, J. S., Newman, L. S., & Moskowitz, G. B. (1996). People as flexible interpreters: Evidence and issues from spontaneous trait inference. In M. P. Zanna (Ed.), *Advances in experimental social psychology* (Vol. 28, pp. 211–279). San Diego: Academic Press.

Veitch, R., & Griffitt, W. (1976). Good news-bad news: Affective and interpersonal effects. *Journal of Applied Social Psychology, 6,* 69–75.

Walster, E., Aronson, V., Abrahams, D., & Rottmann, L. (1966). Importance of physical attractiveness in dating behavior. *Journal of Personality and Social Psychology, 4,* 508–516.

Weber, S. J., & Cook, T. D. (1972). Subject effects in laboratory research: An examination of subject roles, demand characteristics, and valid inference. *Psychological Bulletin, 77,* 273–295.

Wegener, D. T., & Petty, R. E. (1995). Flexible correction processes in social judgment: The role of naive theories in corrections for perceived bias. *Journal of Personality & Social Psychology, 68,* 36–51.

Wegner, D. M., & Bargh, J. A. (1998). Control and automaticity in social life. In D. T. Gilbert & S. T. Fiske (Eds.), *The handbook of social psychology* (4th ed., Vol. 1, pp. 446–496). New York: McGraw-Hill.

Whitney, P., Waring, D. A., & Zingmark, B. (1992). Task effects on the spontaneous activation of trait concepts. *Social Cognition, 10,* 377–396.

Winter, L., & Uleman, J. S. (1984). When are social judgments made? Evidence for the spontaneousness of trait inferences. *Journal of Personality and Social Psychology, 47*, 237–252.

Wyer, R. S., Jr. (Ed.). (1997). The automaticity of everyday life: Advances in social cognition. *Advances in social cognition* (Vol. 10). Mahwah, NJ: Lawrence Erlbaum Associates.

Wyer, R. S., Jr., & Budesheim, T. L. (1987). Person memory and judgments: The impact of information that one is told to disregard. *Journal of Personality & Social Psychology, 53*, 14–29.

Wyer, R. S., Jr., Budesheim, T. L., & Lambert, A. J. (1990). Cognitive representation of conversations about persons. *Journal of Personality & Social Psychology, 58*, 218–238.

Wyer, R. S., Jr., Budesheim, T. L., Lambert, A. J., & Swan, S. (1994). Person memory and judgment: Pragmatic influences on impressions formed in a social context. *Journal of Personality & Social Psychology, 66*, 254–267.

Wyer, R. S., Jr., & Carlston, D. E. (1979). *Social cognition, inference, and attribution.* Hillsdale, NJ: Lawrence Erlbaum Associates.

Wyer R. S., Jr., & Carlston, D. E. (1994). The cognitive representation of persons and events. In R. S. Wyer, Jr., & T. K. Srull (Eds.), *Handbook of social cognition: Vol. 1. Basic Processes* (2nd ed., pp. 41–98). Hillsdale, NJ: Lawrence Erlbaum Associates.

Wyer, R. S., Jr., & Gruenfeld, D. H. (1995). Information processing in interpersonal communication. In D. Hewes (Ed.), *The cognitive bases of interpersonal communication* (pp. 7–47). Hillsdale, NJ: Lawrence Erlbaum Associates.

Wyer, R. S., Jr., & Lambert, A. J. (1994). The role of trait constructs in person perception: An historical perspective. In P. G. Devine & D. L. Hamilton (Eds.), *Social cognition: Impact on social psychology* (pp. 109–142). San Diego, CA: Academic Press.

Wyer, R. S., Jr., & Srull, T. K. (1986). Human cognition in its social context. *Psychological Review, 93*, 322–359.

Wyer, R. S., Jr., & Srull, T. K. (1989). *Memory and cognition in its social context.* Hillsdale, NJ: Lawrence Erlbaum Associates.

Wyer, R. S., Jr., Swan, S., & Gruenfeld, D. H. (1995). Impression formation in informal conversations. *Social Cognition, 13*, 243–272.

Zajonc, R. B. (1980). Feeling and thinking: Preferences need no inferences. *American Psychologist, 35*, 151–175.

Zebrowitz, L. A. (1997). *Reading faces: Window to the soul?* Boulder, CO: Westview Press.

7

Activating and Inhibiting Social Identities: Implications for Perceiving the Self and Others

Galen V. Bodenhausen
Northwestern University

C. Neil Macrae
Dartmouth College

Kurt Hugenberg
Northwestern University

The phenomena that interest social psychologists show considerable variability across situations. Stereotyping, aggression, conformity, and most other entries in the lexicon of social psychology are fundamentally dynamic in their manifestations. A central goal of social psychological theory, then, is the specification of the key variables that regulate social behavior, allowing us to select from the vast repertoire of possible responses the ones that ultimately emerge. We take it as an uncontestable assumption that this channeling of behavior, from innumerable possibilities to specific actuali-

131

ties, is accomplished by the information-processing capacities of the central nervous system. Although the specific neural mediation of human social behavior is only beginning to be explored (Klein & Kihlstrom, 1998; Ochsner & Lieberman, 2001), much has been learned in recent decades about the properties of the social information-processing system. As developed by pioneering scholars like Bob Wyer, social cognition research has begun to shed light on the general cognitive factors that orient, bias, and otherwise constrain social conduct.

Consider the famous case of Kitty Genovese, a young woman living in New York who was pursued and eventually brutally murdered in the presence of several witnesses watching from their windows. The witnesses might have responded in any number of ways to this horrifying event. They might have attempted to subdue the attacker, or phone the police, or rush to Ms. Genovese's aid once the attacker left the scene. They did none of these things, however. They watched the events unfold, but did not take action. Many psychological factors undoubtedly contributed to this behavior (Latané & Darley, 1970), but one of the most critically important involves the subjective interpretation of the event sequence that was constructed by the witnesses. Some witnesses mistakenly interpreted the situation as involving harmless teenage horseplay, or as a lover's quarrel. Because the events transpired at night and the bystanders were observing from a distance, there was undeniably a degree of ambiguity in the situation. Given that multiple interpretations of the situation were possible, why might the "lover's quarrel" interpretation have arisen in the minds of some bystanders? In all likelihood, the most frequently experienced episodes of adult male-female conflict do involve disagreements between romantic partners. As such, this interpretation may spring to mind quite readily, unless there are clear cues suggesting its poor fit to the current situation (for empirical confirmation of this intuition, see Shotland & Straw, 1976).

It is this "springing to mind" of certain interpretations of the social environment that is of great interest to the social cognition researcher. In attempting to understand how certain ideas come to dominate our construals of ambiguous social stimuli, early research emphasized the concepts of *activation* and *accessibility* (Higgins, Rholes, & Jones, 1977; Srull & Wyer, 1979). This research demonstrated that social impressions tend to be biased in the direction of whatever concepts happen to be most readily accessible in the perceiver's mind. Using a priming methodology, the researchers surreptitiously activated specific concepts (e.g., "hostile"), and they discovered that the impressions that participants ultimately formed were indeed assimilated to the activated concepts. This pattern held even though the relevant concepts were activated surreptitiously, and in a context that was apparently unrelated to the impression formation task. Indeed, similar results emerged even when the target concept was activated subliminally (Bargh &

Pietromonaco, 1982). Citing findings such as these, social cognition researchers began to give a central role to knowledge activation in models of social perception, cognition, and behavior (e.g., Higgins, 1996; Wyer & Srull, 1989; for a state-of-the-art overview, see Schwarz, Bless, Wänke, & Winkielman, this volume). In this view, once an idea becomes cognitively accessible, it enters working memory and can be applied to the task of disambiguating incoming information. The problem of response selection, from this perspective, is most fruitfully addressed by understanding the factors that lead particular concepts and response options to become activated, thus gaining the accessibility necessary to influence subsequent information processing. Thus, returning to the example of Kitty Genovese, to understand the responses of the inactive bystanders, we must understand what caused those bystanders to construe the situation as, for example, a lover's spat, rather than a brutal murder.

As fruitful as this approach to the dynamics of social cognition has been, it runs into a fundamental conceptual difficulty. Specifically, in a system in which multiple potentially relevant ideas can be simultaneously activated, when both time and cognitive resources are limited to the point that a minimal number of possible interpretations can be entertained, there needs to be some way to constrain which of the activated concepts will prevail. If concept A gains more activation than concept B, but B nevertheless gains a substantial degree of activation, what will happen? The question is especially acute when A and B imply very different views of the target stimulus. It is also possible that concepts that are initially activated ultimately prove to be irrelevant to the target. In practice, a plethora of concepts can potentially be activated in any given context, yet only a small subset is actually relevant and useful in parsing the situation. The complexity of this situation is further compounded when one considers that interpretations must be made in real time in a potentially distracting environment. With distracting and competing concepts in an increasingly burdened working memory, how can a coherent interpretation of impinging social stimuli be constructed? The necessity of selecting from among multiple competing representations has been dubbed the MAC/FAC problem ("Many Are Called, but Few Are Chosen"; see Forbus, Gentner, & Law, 1995). It arises because of the ready capability of our mental systems to sustain multiple, simultaneous (or parallel) activations of memory, while conscious reflection and action are subject to much more limited (and largely serial) patterns of activation (e.g., Simon, 1994).

To deal with this challenge, it makes sense that our cognitive architecture would have evolved in such a way that it not only permits some concepts to gain greater activation than others, but it also permits the *active inhibition* of other concepts that, although initially activated to some degree, prove to be irrelevant to, or in conflict with, a dominant interpretation of incoming stimuli. From this perspective, the construction of a particular construal of the immediate social situation (and the behavioral response it implies) would arise from the dynamic interplay of both excitatory forces that make certain interpretations more accessible, and inhibitory forces that make alternative interpretations less accessible. Although relatively new to social psychologists, this way of thinking actually has a rich history in psychology (e.g., Herbart, 1891; Wundt, 1904) and has informed research in a wide variety of content domains (see Bodenhausen & Macrae, 1998, for a survey). Moreover, this approach fits with our emerging understanding of the neural dynamics of the cerebral cortex (e.g., Houghton & Tipper, 1996), which clearly involve both excitatory and inhibitory mechanisms.

An example from psycholinguistics research may be useful in conveying the fundamental importance of inhibitory mechanisms in creating coherent mental representations. Consider the sentence, "Bob Wyer ate a steak." Upon hearing this sentence, the listener might be tempted to activate some semantic representations that are associated with homophones of the sentence elements (e.g., "wire," "eight," and "stake"), but the complete context of the sentence makes it obvious that these alternative meanings are inappropriate. Psychologists have shown that in such situations, the contextually inappropriate meanings are not merely ignored, they are actively inhibited (e.g., Gernsbacher & Faust, 1991); that is, they are rendered even less cognitively accessible than they would be in the absence of any related linguistic stimuli. Similar issues arise with respect to polysemous words encountered in reading. Skilled readers show evidence of actively inhibiting contextually inappropriate interpretations of words such as "lead" when used in a phrase like "lead poisoning" versus "she will lead." Analogously, the social perceiver must find a contextually appropriate interpretation of social stimuli that are, at least potentially, open to alternative interpretations. Once such an interpretation is selected, competing alternatives must be dampened if coherence is to emerge. Whereas earlier approaches to understanding the contingencies of social cognition emphasized the role of activation in "tuning in" a particular meaning, the present approach additionally stipulates a key role for inhibition in "tuning out" the potentially distracting alternatives. In the rest of this chapter, we explore some of the implications of this view of the dynamics of social cognition. We first discuss one of the most fundamental sources of variability in the perception of others (and of the self), namely, the multiplicity of social identity. The fact that people can be categorized in numerous alternative ways creates functional flexibility, but it also complicates the process of social perception. We consider how category selection unfolds, with a focus on the factors that influence category activation, and we then examine the role that inhibition may play in dealing with alternative, unselected bases for categorization. We next explore the implications of such a view of categorization processes for fundamental aspects of person perception and self-regulation. We conclude by reflecting upon the many intellectual debts of our approach to the seminal insights of Bob Wyer and by considering some of the unresolved issues that will confront social cognition researchers of the future.

THE MULTIPLICITY OF SOCIAL IDENTITY

It is seemingly trite to observe that every person can be categorized in many different ways, such as by sex, ethnicity, age, nationality, religion, occupation, handedness, body size, hair color, or countless other human groupings. Yet most social psychological research on stereotyping has largely bypassed this inherent complexity by reducing the stimulus presented to research participants to one or, at most, a few possible categories. For example, by presenting just a name, the target's sex and ethnicity may be conveyed, but little else can be discerned. Although useful for certain research purposes, this practice of simplifying the stimulus person has led researchers to overlook some fairly basic questions about social perception. In particular, how does the perceiver select relevant categories when the set of contenders is large? Do we routinely categorize people simultaneously along multiple dimensions, or does a single category tend to dominate our perceptions in many everyday circumstances? If one category does gain dominance, what happens to the alternative identities of the target that are not the focus of impression formation? Are they merely ignored, or are they actively inhibited? Might these same issues arise in situations in which it is the self that is being categorized?

We developed an example of a fat Irish priest who might be stereotyped in terms of his sex, his body type, his nationality, his religion, or his vocation (Bodenhausen & Macrae, 1998). To form an impression of this person, the perceiver might activate general stereotypes about men, about fat people, about the Irish, and so on, and the resulting amalgamation of associations might then be used to construct a sense of what the person is like. However, the task of discerning how all of these pieces fit together might be a daunting one, especially given that there are inherent contradictions among the various elements (e.g., the alleged violent tendencies of the Irish may not jibe with the alleged non-violence of priests; "pugilistic pacifist" is not an especially coherent notion!). Although perceivers may sometimes be motivated enough by a desire to know the individual that they will work to integrate a diverse set of facts and suppositions about him or her, we assume that the perceiver routinely seeks a more streamlined and efficient basis for impression formation (e.g., Allport, 1954; Fiske & Taylor, 1991; for a detailed review, see Sherman, Macrae, & Bodenhausen, 2000). Whether because of limited motivation for engaging in the cognitive work of individuation, or because of limited attentional capacity for such work, the perceiver may often choose to construct social impressions upon the scaffolding provided by a single relevant category. Such a representation is more likely to be internally consistent, and can be efficiently derived from generic knowledge about the group in question. Thus simply stereotyping our hypothetical target as a "typical priest" may be sufficient for the perceiver's purposes. We refer to this assumption that perceivers routinely prefer simpler, well-structured, unidimensional bases for social impressions as the *category dominance hypothesis*.

While admittedly involving some degree of information loss, such category inhibition can frequently provide a basis for impressions that are of *sufficient* accuracy to navigate the social environment successfully, and to do so with a minimum of cognitive effort. Indeed, category dominance is a means of satisficing (Simon & Kadane, 1975), providing a less than perfect answer to the problem of forming impressions, but doing so with very low cognitive costs. Most of the situations that we encounter in our daily lives do not require anything but an approximate answer. This is not to say, however, that category dominance is a necessary outcome of categorization. In line with Fiske and Taylor's (1991) motivated tactician model of information processing, we assume that when motivation and sufficient cognitive capacity are available, perceivers can use both combinations of categories (Bodenhausen, Macrae, & Sherman, 1999; Kunda, Miller, & Claire, 1990) or individuating, non-category information (e.g., Neuberg & Fiske, 1987) to make impressions of and draw inferences about others in the social environment. For example, Neuberg and Fiske (1987) found that outcome-dependency and accuracy-motivation lead to individuating processes in person perception. Thus when the costs of inferential imprecision are salient and substantial, the drive toward category dominance can be overcome, leading to the simultaneous use of multiple categories as well as individuating information.

Given these benefits of category dominance, the immediate question raised by the category dominance hypothesis is this: Which category will come to dominate social impressions in any given situation? Here, the classic research on social perception is illuminating. Bob Wyer's research has, in particular, examined many relevant factors. His priming research (e.g., Srull & Wyer, 1979; Wyer & Srull, 1989) confirmed that recent activation (even in a seemingly unrelated context) of a particular concept can increase the probability that the concept will be used, if it is applicable, in a subsequent context. Thus for example, if one has been recently thinking about the topic of sex differences, then when later encountering a target person, that individual's sex may dominate the impression that is formed, rather than age, occupation, and so on. Similarly, those categories that have been used frequently in the past will also tend to be relatively more accessible, hence more likely to dominate social impressions. An extremely religious person, for example, who routinely relates to life in terms of religious concepts, may be especially likely to categorize others principally in terms of their religious affiliations, rather than their occupation, nationality, and so on. Alternatively, an extremely racist person may tend to categorize people largely on the basis of ethnicity rather than sex or age (see Stangor, Lynch, Duan, & Glass, 1992). In demonstrating that recency and frequency of activation influence the probability of a concept's future use, research by Wyer and colleagues has helped to identify one important answer to the question of which category will dominate social impressions.

The goals of social perceivers also direct their attention toward goal-relevant categorizations of social stimuli (Bruner, 1957; Jones & Thibaut, 1958; for a comprehensive review, see Srull & Wyer, 1986). For example, when pursuing professional objectives, we may categorize our coworkers in terms of their organizational roles instead of their ages, religions, or sexual orientations. These other factors are not merely irrelevant; they may be downright distracting, and thus may deflect attention from focal considerations that are important for goal attainment.

Category dominance also emerges from the background context in which a person is encountered. For example, McGuire, McGuire, Child, and Fujioka (1978) showed that categories that stand out from the background will naturally draw attention. Thus, being the only woman at a convention of middle-aged tax attorneys will likely result in categorizations of the target focusing on her sex, rather than her age or occupation, because it is on the former dimension that the person stands out from the social background (see also Biernat & Vescio, 1993; Taylor, Fiske, Etcoff, & Ruderman, 1978). Related evidence for category dominance is provided by Nelson and Miller (1995), who found that people tend not to use all available social categories at once when making social inferences. Instead, certain social categories gain ascendancy over others. In this case, participants had two alternate bases on which to categorize a social target. One category was statistically distinctive and the other was non-distinctive (e.g., skydiver and tennis player). Nelson and Miller found that the category that offers the most distinctiveness in the situation wins out against the other available social categories, achieving a "master status," which Hughes (1945) defined as "a category membership that tends to overpower … any other characteristics that might run counter to it" (p. 357).

Self-categorization theory (e.g., Turner, Oakes, Haslam, & McGarty, 1994) similarly assumes that context drives categorization processes. For example, the concept of "normative fit" implies that categories will be selected when stereotypic expectancies derived from the category provide a sensible fit to observed features of the stimulus person. Imagine observing a group of friends discussing whether to spend a Saturday afternoon at a baseball game. If the men are enthusiastic about this proposal and the women resist it, then gender stereotypes "fit" the situation well, and the individuals may be categorized and evaluated by reference to their sex, rather than their other social identities (see also van Knippenberg & Dijksterhuis, 2000). In short, some categories achieve a high level of contextual salience, either because of their situational distinctiveness or their stereotypic affinity with the salient features of the immediate situation.

In past research investigating these various determinants of category selection, the (often implicit) assumption has been that once a given category becomes salient, the alternative bases for categorization are simply passively ignored. If an alternative categorical identity were initially activated to some degree, this activation would, it is assumed, gradually decay as a function of its subsequent neglect. An arguably more plausible model derives from the "MAC/FAC" perspective described above. In this view, initial encounters with a social target are likely to result in the parallel activation of multiple categories, at least initially.

In essence, the various salient categories enter into a race for dominance. As we have noted, a given category gains an advantage in this race to the extent that it has been recently or frequently used, is relevant to the perceiver's goals and current concerns, or is contextually salient or distinctive. A certain threshold of activation must be surpassed in order for the category to win the race and become the dominant framework for organizing the impression formation process. Once this ascendancy has occurred, the rivals are assumed to be actively inhibited. Rather than simply being ignored or left to slowly decay, this inhibition process results in immediate, marked reductions in the level of activation given to the alternative categories. That is, the losing categories are "tuned out" in a manner that often results in below-baseline levels of activation. In this way, the potential distractions and contradictions inherent in these alternative ways of thinking about the target are rapidly eliminated.

One empirical implication of the theoretical perspective we are proposing is that whereas stereotypes associated with a dominant category will tend to be more accessible after exposure to the category memory, stereotypes associated with non-dominant, but otherwise salient, categories will be even less accessible than they would have been in the absence of exposure to any category member(s). In the next section, we examine the evidence for this way of thinking about the process of social perception, and consider some of the implications it may have for social judgment and social behavior.

CATEGORY ACTIVATION AND INHIBITION IN SOCIAL PERCEPTION

Because of the apparent ubiquity of inhibitory processes in human cognition (Clark, 1996; Kimble, 1994), it is plausible that social perception will also be shaped, at least to some extent, by inhibition. Category inhibition is, however, more than merely plausible. There is increasing evidence from a number of sources that category inhibition not only occurs, but it also has a powerful effect on the way in which we see others in our social milieu.

Macrae, Bodenhausen, and Milne (1995) provided some of the first empirical evidence suggesting that active inhibition, as opposed to simple decay, is the mechanism by which we deal with social categories that compete for, yet lose, the mental race for dominance. Macrae et al. found that, when presented with a person who could fit into more than one social category, stereotypes associated with the most contextually meaningful social identity were activated. Further, in support of the inhibition hypothesis, they also found that stereotypes associated with the non-activated category were actively inhibited. In one study, Macrae et al. (1995) presented participants with a Chinese woman (a multiply categorizable target, as either "Chinese" or "female") and primed participants with either the category "Chinese" or the category "woman." As would be expected, participants then showed facilitation in a lexical decision task that involved recognizing words that are stereotypical of the primed category; importantly, they simultaneously showed inhibition in the same task when recognizing words that are stereotypical of the non-primed category. That is, they were slower to recognize these words than were subjects who were not presented with an Asian woman target at all. The activation level of these associates of the non-primed category was thus below baseline levels. These results are consistent with the claim that social perception tends to focus on a single, dominant category at a given time and that competing, but non-activated, categories are actively inhibited, thus providing a mechanism by which category dominance occurs.

In a related vein, Sinclair and Kunda (1999) showed that category-based stereotype inhibition can vary as a function of the perceiver's goals and motivations. Their findings provide further support of both category dominance and inhibition of social categories that lose the race to activation. In their study, white participants were given either affirming or threatening feedback from a black or white confederate. Sinclair and Kunda (1999) found that, when motivated to esteem a black confederate after receiving positive feedback from him, participants showed inhibited access to the black stereotype (as evidenced by their performance on a word-fragment completion task), as compared to when the feedback was given by a white confederate. Similarly, after receiving negative feedback from the black confederate, participants showed greater activation of the black stereotype as compared to when they received the same feedback from a white confederate. Similar results were found with a black doctor confederate in that positive feedback led to activation of the category "doctor" and inhibition of the category "Black" using a lexical decision task. Conversely, negative feedback led to activation of the categorical associates of "Black" and inhibition of the associates of "doctor." While somewhat confounding the valence of the categories in question with the valence of the affect induced by the positive and negative feedback, it does provide at least initial evidence that motivation can lead to both activation and inhibition of social categories.

There is also preliminary evidence from a number of other sources that category inhibition can affect relatively early, perceptual processing of social stimuli. Specifically, we have found promising preliminary evidence for inhibitory processes regarding attention to human faces. In an attempt to conceptually replicate and extend the results of Macrae et al. (1995) in a markedly different processing domain, we (Hugenberg & Bodenhausen, 2001a) adapted recent change-blindness techniques pioneered by Simons, Levin (e.g., Simons & Levin, 1998), and others (e.g., Henderson & Hollingworth, 1999). In our experimental paradigm, after exposure to a subliminal prime of either the category "Race," the category "Gender," or a neutral prime, participants were briefly exposed to a picture of a naturalistic scene in which an assortment of people are facing the camera and smiling. All scenes involved numerous people of both sexes and various ethnicities, and many different objects. Participants were instructed to pay close attention to each scene and were told that they would be asked to describe in specific detail one person or object in the scene. Each scene was presented for three seconds, after which the entire scene was briefly occluded and then restored, but with one person or object in the scene masked with a solid black box. Participants were then asked to recall as much information about the target covered with the box as possible, including (in the case of persons) ethnicity and gender. Using this visual detection paradigm, we found preliminary evidence that participants tend to show enhanced recall of ethnicity information about an individual when ethnicity is contextually salient (i.e., it has been primed), compared to the control condition. However, their recall of target ethnicity decreases below baseline when a rival category (i.e., gender) has been primed. Interestingly, a converse pattern did not hold true for gender; instead, regardless of context, gender appears to be universally visually salient. However, the results with respect to ethnicity salience are consistent with the category inhibition hypothesis, as they indicate that visual detection of social identities can also be actively inhibited. Interestingly, though, these results also provide preliminary evidence that some categories, especially very basic and important social categories such as gender, may be relatively immune to inhibition in this low-level, perceptual sense.

While using different experimental paradigms, Macrae et al. (1995), Sinclair and Kunda (1999), and Hugenberg and Bodenhausen (2001a) share the same focus on categorization processes that occur relatively quickly after a multiply categorizable target is encountered. Categorization, however, does not happen for its own sake. Instead, categorization serves a number of important roles in cognition, not the least of which is to facilitate clear predictions and inferences about others in our social world (Smith & Medin, 1981). Malt, Ross, and Murphy (1995) examined whether multiple categories are used simultaneously in making inductive predictions. Participants were asked to make predictions about both social and non-social targets (e.g., doctors, burglars, and dogs) presented in short vignettes. Although the targets were always multiply categorizable (e.g., a target could be either a burglar or an insurance adjustor), participants consistently showed a pattern of using only one of the two possible social categories when generating inductive inferences, indicating that one of the social categories became dominant. Later research by Ross and Murphy (1996; see also Murphy & Ross, 1994) similarly found that, when making predictions, people tend to use a single category as opposed to multiple relevant categories, even when multiple categories are available and potentially applicable.

Again using multiply categorizable social targets, Ross and Murphy (1996) replicated and extended Malt et al.'s (1995) findings, showing that alternative categories are used only when they are specifically evoked by the inference to be made (i.e., when the alternative category becomes situationally important). Specifically, Ross and Murphy (1996) presented participants with multiply categorizable targets and then asked a number of questions about the target, designed to indicate whether participants categorized using only one of the categories or an admixture of both when making inferences about the target. When questioned in a manner that made a particular categorization salient, participants strongly tended to use only that category in generating predictions. Interestingly, once participants had answered this "leading" question, the alternative category went unused for the subsequent non-leading questions. Indeed, unless a dual-categorization was specifically elicited by the question, using only one of the available categories seemed to be the default in categorization.

Using a paradigm similar to Ross, Murphy, and colleagues, Hugenberg and Bodenhausen (2001b) sought to extend the potential impact of inhibitory processes to predictions and inferences about social targets. While technically multiply categorizable, many of Ross and Murphy's (1996) targets belonged to categories that were likely to be mutually exclusive for the task at hand. For example, while the man inspecting the window locks on a house could be either an insurance adjustor or a burglar, it is likely that he is either one or the other. Many social categories, however, are not mutually exclusive. Indeed, many of the important social categories to which we belong, such as ethnicity, gender, occupation, and sexual orientation, are (relatively) orthogonal to one another. As such, we are currently constructing targets embedded in short vignettes that have two salient social identities, such as age and occupation. Similar to Ross and Murphy (1996), once participants had read the vignette about the target, they were asked questions relevant to the salient categories. For example, when age and occupation are the salient categories, a question regarding how the target would perform on a speeded memory task is posed. The target's age (young adult vs. senior citizen) and occupation (lawyer vs. janitor) were both stereotypically associated with memory performance, so both aspects of his or her identity could be useful in inductive inferences about the target's memory performance. The target vignettes were preceded by a vignette designed to make one of the social categories salient. For example, occupation was primed by a prior vignette about an individual experiencing work-related stress. By manipulating the category memberships and the primed category between subjects, we were able to examine whether the heightened incidental activation of one possible basis for categorizing a target would lead to the neglect of alternative bases that may be just as relevant in making predictions about the target. For example, in the age/occupation scenario previously described, inductive inferences were influenced only by the target's standing on the primed category dimension, and not by his standing on the alternative one. This result is consistent with the possibility that the non-primed category became inductively impotent because of its relative inaccessibility, due to inhibition. While these studies are still preliminary, when considered in light of increasing evidence in favor of the category inhibition hypothesis, it becomes increasingly clear that category inhibition can and does play a powerful role in our perceptions of others.

ACTIVATING AND INHIBITING THE SELF: IMPLICATIONS FOR SELF-PERCEPTION AND SELF-REGULATION

Inhibitory processes, however, may play out in domains a bit more personal than those concerning the perceptions of others. Indeed, there is good reason to entertain the hypothesis that inhibitory processes may also occur in the perception of the self. For instance, self-relevant goals and motives seem to be subject to the same excitatory and inhibitory forces as other mental representations. Shah, Friedman, and Kruglanski (2002) recently showed over the course of several studies that activating one goal can inhibit the accessibility of other goals. As per the usual inhibition pattern, Shah et al. showed that inhibition of personal goals tends to be greater when the inhibited goals serve the same purpose as the dominant goal. Thus goals that are relevant to the situation all race to activation, but goals that do not become the focal or situationally dominant goal become actively inhibited in order to shield the activated goal from potential distraction. There are, however, reasons to believe that this same process of inhibition of self-relevant mental representations may not be limited to goals, but instead may apply to entire social identities.

According to Turner, Hogg, Oakes, Reicher, and Wetherell's (1987) self-categorization theory, we categorize ourselves into social categories in a manner similar to how we categorize others; if so, perhaps the same cognitive processes of category dominance and category inhibition may occur in self-categorization. Self-categorization theory claims that the self can be dissected into a large number of self-concepts or self-categorizations. These self-categories can range from an individual level, which is defined by attributes that serve to differentiate the self from other individuals, to a social level, in which we categorize ourselves in terms of an ingroup membership that serves to differentiate us from relevant outgroup(s). Further, self-categorizations can be at different levels of inclusion, ranging from quite superordinate ("humanity") to the very subordinate ("the 'real' me").

The self-category that is salient at any given time is determined by both *comparative fit* and *normative fit* (e.g., see Oakes, 1987; van Knippenberg & Dijksterhuis, 2000). Comparative fit refers to the extent to which a particular categorization tends to minimize within-group differences while maximizing intergroup differences. For example, if one found oneself at a professional conference associating with one group of colleagues (e.g., social psychologists), while not interacting with another group (e.g., clinical psychologists), then the identity associated with one's "professional specialty area" would be salient because it would provide a categorization scheme in which the members of the ingroup are all similar to one another, while being quite different from outgroup members. Other aspects of one's identity (e.g., sex, age, ethnicity) may provide relatively poor comparative fit, as both groups may show considerable heterogeneity (while not differing much, on average, from one another) in terms of these characteristics. In this situation, the professional specialty identity is said to provide a strong meta-contrast between the groups (i.e., an augmenting of the degree of inter category differentiation relative to the degree of intra category homogeneity), whereas the other potential identity dimensions do not. In general, a particular categorization scheme is expected to be salient to the degree that it maximizes this meta-contrast. As previously mentioned, category salience is also enhanced by normative fit, which is defined by the congruence between stereotypic expectations and observable data. It is high when our stereotypes are fulfilled by what is occurring in the social situation. To return to our example, if one stereotypically expects clinical psychologists to spend their time exploring and sharing their feelings, while expecting social psychologists to drink margaritas and dance enthusiastically (but poorly), then normative fit would be enhanced to the extent that the groups one observed at a professional conference were actually engaging in these expected behaviors.

Self-categorization is also determined by the current accessibility of any one self-category relative to other self-categories (which can be modified by recent or frequent activation of this self-category, as can social categories of others). Moreover, as is the case in the categorization of others, self-categorization can also be affected by our current goals and motives. For example, Mussweiler, Gabriel, and Bodenhausen (2000) showed that self-enhancement goals can determine which of two competing group-level self-categorizations become activated. Female European-American participants were presented with bogus, threatening, or non-threatening feedback, indicating that another participant (an Asian woman) happened to score better or worse than they did on an experimental task. The threatening feedback led high-self-esteem participants to shift the importance of their social identities, in order to protect themselves from the threat of being outperformed, by favoring an identity that was not shared with their comparison standard. Specifically, if they had been outperformed by an Asian woman, they emphasized their ethnic identity more strongly, but if they had done better than the Asian woman, then they emphasized their gender identity more strongly. Because comparisons with similar targets are considered to be a more diagnostic source for self-evaluation, focusing on an unshared identity renders the superior standard less relevant for purposes of social comparison. Conversely, focusing on a shared identity makes the inferior target more relevant for such comparisons. These findings indicate that current goal states may also play an important role in self-categorization, just as it does in the perception of others. Self-categorization theory further hypothesizes that people can and do move fluidly among these multiple social identities. Thus from moment to moment, depending on the conjunction of situational and chronic factors, we see ourselves as belonging to different groups, or perhaps as an individual, rather than as a group member (Turner, 1991; Turner et al., 1994). Indeed, the findings of Mussweiler et al. (2000) only strengthen this claim, as their participants were able to shift the importance of their identities in response to situational contingencies.

According to self-categorization theorists, this process of self-categorization has a number of important consequences, the first of which is that an individual comes to see the self as more similar to the group (Hogg & Turner, 1987). Turner hypothesizes that activating a social identity will cause people to *depersonalize*, or to tend to "perceive themselves more in terms of the shared stereotypes that define their social category membership (the attributes that define their common social identity) and less in terms of their personal differences and individuality" (p. 157; see also Haslam, Oakes, Turner, & McGarty, 1996; Hogg & Turner, 1987). According to Turner (1987), this emphasis on the shared stereotypes of the activated social identity is a very basic cognitive process, which he claims happens even at the "perceptual" level. Indeed, Hogg and Turner (1987) conducted two studies that sought to illustrate the phenomenon of depersonalization (also known as self-stereotyping). They showed that making a particular self-categorization did indeed lead participants to self-stereotype, which was manifested as participants thinking of themselves as possessing characteristics that were considered typical of that group.

Categorizing the self in terms of a social identity has repercussions not only for perceptions of similarity to the group standard, but also for the norms to which one adheres (Hogg & Turner, 1987). Different groups have different social norms, values, and beliefs that group members consensually validate. Such norms can be especially powerful in guiding behavior (for a review, see Cialdini & Trost, 1998). Indeed, even groups that are defined primarily by physical characteristics (such as male and female) also frequently have attendant normative or ideological characteristics (such as masculine or feminine attitudes, traits, and behaviors) that guide behavior (Marques & Paez, 1994; Marques, Abrams, Paez, & Martinez-Taboada, 1998). Thus when a group membership is made salient and is used to categorize the self, certain norms, beliefs, and attitudes that are held by that group become activated as well. As one "shifts" from one identity to another, self-categorization theory hypothesizes that group norms become activated, and behavior then tends to reflect the emergent social norms of the activated identity (Hogg & Turner, 1987; Turner et al., 1994). However, while there is ample data suggesting that the process of self-stereotyping occurs and leads to stereotypic self perceptions (e.g., Biernat, Vescio, & Green, 1996; Hardie & McMurray, 1992; Simon, Glaessner-Bayerl, & Stratenwerth, 1991; Simon & Hamilton, 1994), there is relatively little evidence that self-categorization leads to a shift in the norms and attitudes to which people adhere behaviorally.

In one of the few examples of this effect, Verkuyten and Hagendoorn (1998), in two studies, manipulated the level of self-categorization of Dutch participants. Of interest was how the differing self-categorizations of the participants affected the importance of factors that cause prejudice. Verkuyten and Hagendoorn (1998) showed that, when operating at an individual level of self-categorization, the individual difference of authoritarianism affected prejudice. But when the national (i.e., Dutch) identity was activated, consensual stereotypes held by the ingroup (Dutch) about an outgroup (Turks & Germans) affected prejudice and the individual difference of authoritarianism had no effect on it.

Another example of norm activation concomitant with self-categorization is recent work by Shih, Pittinsky, and Ambady (1999), who showed that the salience of an identity influenced intellectual performance. Using a stereotype threat paradigm, Shih et al. subtly primed Asian-American women with their gender identity, their ethnic identity, or a neutral prime. Participants primed to think of themselves in terms of their gender identity (i.e. woman) performed more poorly on the mathematics test as compared to participants primed to think of themselves in terms of their ethnic identity (i.e. Asian); the baseline condition fell in between these two prime conditions. While Shih et al. (1999) do not provide clear mediational evidence, self-categorization theory might provide one potential mediator. By activating participants' Asian identity, the norms, beliefs, and expectations attendant to that identity are also activated, thus providing Asian-primed participants with positive expectations of success.

Cheryan and Bodenhausen (2000), in an extension of Shih et al. (1999), also showed that identity salience could affect performance; however, this study provides mediational evidence indicating that the group norm was likely to have contributed to observed changes in performance. Specifically, Cheryan and Bodenhausen (2000) primed either the Asian or the gender identity of female Asian-American participants in a way that made explicit reference to how others viewed the group, after which participants performed a mathematical reasoning test. Contrary to Shih et al. (1999), Cheryan and Bodenhausen (2000) found that Asian-primed participants actually performed worse than baseline. Further, they provided evidence that the deleterious impact of ethnicity focus on mathematical performance was mediated through impaired concentration. Because of the high expectations for mathematical prowess that go with the Asian identity, it appears that concerns about living up to the group standards produced a tendency to choke under the pressure of high expectations (Baumeister, Hamilton, & Tice, 1985). Indeed, it seems that activating the group norms for high performance can lead to rumination, just as can activating the norms for low group performance. Most important for our concerns, however, is that both Shih et al.'s (1999) and Cheryan and Bodenhausen's (2000) results indicate that the performance increases and decreases are likely due to activation of the group norms that occurs due to self-categorization.

Interpreting self-categorization theory, especially the evidence that group norms are activated concomitantly with self-categories (e.g. Verkuyten & Hagendoorn, 1998) and in light of Macrae et al.'s (1995) findings, may offer new insight as to the specific cognitive functioning of our multifaceted social identities. Macrae et al. (1995) found evidence of identity inhibition when perceiving others. Just as when we perceive others, we actively inhibit the facets of their social identities that do not have the best fit with the situation, so too may we be inhibiting contextually inappropriate aspects of our *own* social identities. Thus when the social situation activates one of our own social identities, we may actively inhibit the other competing social identities.

Inhibiting our own social identities may serve a number of beneficial functions, the most important of which would arguably be the maintenance of a subjectively stable self-concept. Indeed, maintaining a consistent self-concept has been shown to be a strong motive, and cognitive inconsistency can lead to a host of strategies to regain a consistent self-concept (Higgins, 1989; Higgins, Bond, Klein, & Strauman, 1986; Swann, 1990, 1996; Swann & Schroeder, 1995). If, as self-categorization theory posits, identity-congruent norms, beliefs, and attitudes are activated when a social identity is activated, we may, depending on the social identities to which we belong, frequently have some conflicting or incompatible attitudes activated. Thus as we shift from one social identity to another, we are constantly activating different, and possibly conflicting, sets of norms and values.

Consider the example of a career-oriented mother. There are certainly powerful norms driving mothers to spend as much time as possible with their children. In addition, however, the workplace puts rather demanding norms on career-oriented persons by requiring a great investment of time and energy. It would certainly be anxiety-producing to be confronted with the fact that our norms, attitudes, and even behaviors were inconsistent across different situations. If we were to inhibit competing but inactive social identities, we would also inhibit the norms, beliefs, and attitudes that are part of that social identity, thus making it more difficult to notice or be bothered by these inconsistencies.

Apart from providing a basis for maintaining a stable sense of identity, inhibition of alternative aspects of the self could prove to be enormously valuable in managing the tasks of self-regulation. If each social identity carries its own associated norms and behavioral tendencies, then the simultaneous activation of multiple identities could pose serious self-regulatory problems, particularly if the relevant norms are in conflict with one another. For example, the norms of relative formality and decorum that operate when one self-categorizes on the basis of a workplace identity would certainly clash with norms of boozing and carousing that may be activated when one self-categorizes on the basis of alternative identities (such as "conventioneer"). It would certainly seem to be self-defeating if both self-aspects were simultaneously activated—thus perhaps when one identity achieves dominance and directs self-regulatory efforts, the alternative aspects may be actively inhibited. In this way, the goals of self-regulation are clarified and well-structured, just as our social impressions of others can be clarified and structured by the inhibition of alternative bases for categorizing them.

We recently attempted to test the hypothesis that our own social identities can be activated and inhibited in the same way that we activate and inhibit social categories when categorizing others (Hugenberg & Bodenhausen, 2001c). This study was similar to Macrae et al. (1995) in that it used lexical decision procedures to attempt to show category-based stereotype inhibition. We selected as participants for this study individuals who were both undergraduate students at Northwestern University and members of a fraternity or sorority (i.e., "Greeks"). Pretesting confirmed that the norms for NU students and Greeks were conflicting: The student identity was associated with norms of achievement and hard work, but the Greek identity was associated with socializing and partying. Participants were primed with either their student identity or their Greek identity (through the administration of a collective self-esteem scale), or they were given a control prime (specifically, a personal self-esteem scale). Participants then completed a lexical decision task designed to test activation and inhibition of the norms associated with the participants' own social identities. Specifically, it was anticipated that participants primed with their Greek identity would self-categorize as Greeks, and would inhibit their (conflicting) student identity. Conversely, participants primed with "student" were expected to self-categorize as students, and inhibit their (conflicting) Greek identity. As predicted, participants who had their student identity primed showed faster performance for student-related words (e.g., *study, reading*) than did those who had an activated Greek identity, with the neutral, baseline condition falling squarely in between. Similarly, participants with an activated Greek identity responded faster to Greek-related words (e.g., *party, hazing*) than did those primed with their student identity, again with the baseline condition falling between the two.

These findings imply that processes of activation and inhibition can occur in the domain of *self*-categorization. That activation and inhibition of social categories in self-categorization does occur has important implications for self-categorization theory. While tentative, these findings are a first step in more clearly specifying potential mechanisms by which social categories come to impact behavior and the self, in addition to providing a clearer understanding of important self-related processes.

One potential problem with the current research is that the findings could be interpreted as occurring merely as a result of category activation, without implicating the self. Indeed, perhaps the requirement to complete a collective self-esteem scale led participants to activate the concept suggested by the prime (either Greek or student), without actually perceiving the self as part of that group. The norms, or stereotypes, associated with the groups might thus be activated without any direct ties to processes of self-perception or self-regulation. We regard this alternate explanation as unlikely, considering the attendant inhibition effects. As they are currently understood, in order for inhibition effects of this nature to occur, there must be competing alternatives that lost a race to activation. Along these lines, Macrae et al. (1995, Study 2) showed that activating, for example, the "Asian" category produced inhibition only of the "female" category when participants had actually considered an Asian woman; in the absence of such a target, activating one category produced enhanced accessibility of that category's associates, but it had absolutely no effect on accessibility of the other category. Analogously, if our identity prime led to activation of the relevant concept, but not to a self-categorization, then there would be no "competing" category requiring inhibition. Only in the context of self-regulatory concerns does the category "student" come into conflict with the category "Greek." Thus an explanation based solely on classical notions of category activation seems insufficient to account for these findings.

Interestingly, self-categorization theory already proposes a functional antagonism between identities, or more specifically, between levels of identity. While our own findings tentatively suggest a trade-off between different social identities, Turner (1987) proposes that there is a "mutual antagonism" between different *levels* of self-categorization, meaning it is difficult, if not impossible, to have both an individual level and a social level of identity simultaneously active. While the evidence is inconclusive (see Spears, 2001 for a review), there does appear to be a good case for assuming that a functional antagonism exists between the individual and social levels of identity. For example, Jetten, Branscombe, and Spears (2002) showed a trade-off between personal and collective self-esteem. By informing participants who were marginal group members that they would become either more marginalized or more prototypical of the group, Jetten et al. showed that differences in collective and personal self-esteem occurred. For those who became more prototypical, collective self-esteem was boosted (relative to personal self-esteem), whereas for those who became more marginalized, personal self-esteem rose relative to collective self-esteem. Thus it appears that people can and do strategically manage their personal and collective levels of self-esteem in order to buffer against the threat of being a marginal group member. Perhaps more important to the concept of functional antagonism, this research also provides evidence that personal and collective self-esteem are dissociated and can function in a hydraulic manner. Gaertner, Sedikides, and Graetz (1999) similarly showed that shifting to a collective level of identification can be a means of buffering against threats to the individual self. These and other similar findings (e.g., Barnes et al., 1988) indicate that inhibition can occur both between conflicting social identities and between levels of identity that vary in their breadth or inclusiveness.

CONCLUSIONS

We have reviewed much evidence supporting the general notion of category dominance in the domains of both social perception and self-perception. Research has begun to document the role of inhibitory mechanisms in making category dominance feasible within a cognitive system in which multiple, parallel activations are not only possible but commonplace. Inhibition, moreover, appears to operate at several levels of information processing, including low-level perceptual parsing of visual social stimuli, stereotype activation evaluation, inference, and even behavioral intention. Given the array of initial evidence, it appears that the phenomenon of cognitive inhibition is a fruitful avenue for future social-cognitive explorations.

Our intellectual debts to Bob Wyer will be obvious to anyone familiar with the field of social cognition. His prolific contributions to the field are legendary (and have been empirically well-documented; see Gordon & Vicari, 1992, who showed Wyer to be the single most prolific contributor to the *Journal of Personality and Social Psychology*, the *Journal of Experimental Social Psychology*, and *Personality and Social Psychology Bulletin* between the years of 1980 and 1989). More than anyone else, he has advocated and popularized the rigorous, information-processing analysis of social perception and action. Somewhat ironically, his enormous contributions to the field may stem in large part from his relative lack of inhibitory mechanisms. From his remarkable ability to see alternative interpretations, to his complete inability to say "no" to a request for feedback or discussion, Wyer has been an enthusiastic facilitator of social psychological scholarship, perhaps in large part because he simply refuses to foreclose viable possibilities. His personal generosity is just as limitless as his scholarly output. Like the other contributors to this volume, we owe Bob much more than we can ever repay.

REFERENCES

Allport, G. W. (1954). The nature of prejudice. Reading, MA: Addison-Wesley.

Bargh, J. A., & Pietromonaco, P. (1982). Automatic information processing and social perception: The influence of trait information presented outside of conscious awareness on impression formation. Journal of Personality and Social Psychology, 43, 437–449.

Barnes, B. D., Mason, E., Leary, M. R., Laurent, J., Griebel, C., & Bergman, A. (1988). Reactions to social vs. self-evaluation: Moderating effects of personal and social identity. Journal of Research in Personality, 22, 513–524.

Baumeister, R. F., Hamilton, J. C., & Tice, D. M. (1985). Public versus private expectancy of success: Confidence booster or performance pressure? Journal of Personality and Social Psychology, 48, 1447–1457.

Biernat, M., & Vescio, T. K. (1993). Categorization and stereotyping: Effects of group context on memory and social judgment. Journal of Experimental Social Psychology, 29, 166–202.

Biernat, M., Vescio, T. K., & Green, M. L. (1996). Selective self-stereotyping. Journal of Personality and Social Psychology, 71, 1194–1209.

Bodenhausen, G. V., & Macrae, C. N. (1998). Stereotype activation and inhibition. In R. S. Wyer, Jr. (Ed.), Stereotype activation and inhibition: Advances in social cognition (Vol. 11, pp. 1–52). Mahwah, NJ: Lawrence Erlbaum Associates.

Bodenhausen, G. V., Macrae, C. N., & Sherman, J. S. (1999). On the dialectics of discrimination: Dual processes in social stereotyping. In S. Chaiken & Y. Trope (Eds.), Dual-process theories in social psychology (pp. 271–290). New York: Guilford Press.

Bruner, J. S. (1957). On perceptual readiness. Psychological Review, 64, 123–152.

Cheryan, S., & Bodenhausen, G. V. (2000). When positive stereotypes threaten intellectual performance: The psychological hazards of "model minority" status. Psychological Science, 11, 399–402.

Cialdini, R. B., & Trost, M. R. (1998). Social influence: Social norms, conformity, and compliance. In D. T. Gilbert, S. T. Fiske, & F. Lindzey (Eds.), The handbook of social psychology (4th ed., Vol. 2, pp. 151–192). Boston: McGraw-Hill.

Clark, J. M. (1996). Contributions of inhibitory mechanisms to unified theory in neuroscience and psychology. Brain and Cognition, 30, 127–152.

Fiske, S. T., & Taylor, S. E. (1991). Social cognition, (2nd ed.). New York: McGraw-Hill.

Forbus, K. D., Gentner, D., & Law, K. (1995). MAC/FAC: A model of similarity-based retrieval. *Cognitive Science, 19*, 141–205.

Gaertner, L., Sedikides, C., & Graetz, K. (1999). In search of self-definition: Motivational primacy of the individual self, motivational primacy of the collective self, or contextual primacy? *Journal of Personality and Social Psychology, 76*, 5–18.

Gernsbacher, M. A., & Faust, M. E. (1991). The mechanism of suppression: A component of general comprehension skill. *Journal of Experimental Psychology: Learning, Memory, and Cognition, 17*, 245–262.

Gordon, R. A., & Vicari, P. J. (1992). Eminence in social psychology: A comparison of textbook citation, *Social Sciences Citation Index*, and research productivity rankings. *Personality and Social Psychology Bulletin, 18*, 26–38.

Hardie, E. A., & McMurray, N. E. (1992). Self stereotyping, sex role ideology, and menstrual attitudes: A social identity approach. *Sex Roles, 27*, 17–37.

Haslam, S. A., Oakes, P. J., Turner, J. C., & McGarty, C. (1996). Social categorization and group homogeneity: Changes in the perceived applicability of stereotype content as a function of comparative context and trait favourableness. *British Journal of Social Psychology, 34*, 139–160.

Henderson, J. M., & Hollingworth, A. (1999). High-level scene perception. *Annual Review of Psychology, 50*, 243–271.

Herbart, J. F. (1891). *A textbook in psychology* (2nd ed.). New York: Appleton.

Higgins, E. T. (1989). Continuities and discontinuities in self-regulatory and self-evaluative processes: A developmental theory relating self and affect. *Journal of Personality, 57*, 407–444.

Higgins, E. T. (1996). Knowledge activation: Accessibility, applicability, and salience. In E. T. Higgins & A. W. Kruglanski (Eds.), *Social psychology: Handbook of basic principles* (pp. 133–168). New York: Guilford Press.

Higgins, E. T., Bond, R. N., Klein, R., & Strauman, T. (1986). Self-discrepancies and emotional vulnerability: How magnitude, accessibility, and type of discrepancy influence affect. *Journal of Personality and Social Psychology, 51*, 5–15.

Higgins, E. T., Rholes, W. S., & Jones, C. R. (1977). Category accessibility and impression formation. *Journal of Experimental Social Psychology, 13*, 141–154.

Hogg, M. A., & Turner, J. C. (1987). Intergroup behaviour, self-stereotyping and the salience of social categories. *British Journal of Social Psychology, 26*, 325–340.

Houghton, G., & Tipper, S. P. (1996). Inhibitory mechanisms of neural and cognitive control: Applications to selective attention and sequential action. *Brain and Cognition, 30*, 20–43.

Hugenberg, K., & Bodenhausen, G. V. (2001a). *Visual category identification of multiply categorizable persons*. Manuscript in preparation, Northwestern University.

Hugenberg, K., & Bodenhausen, G. V. (2001b). *Category dominance effects in inductive inferences about multiply categorizable targets*. Manuscript in preparation, Northwestern University.

Hugenberg, K., & Bodenhausen, G. V. (2001c). *Inhibitory processes in self-categorization*. Paper presented at the annual convention of the Society for Personality and Social Psychology, San Antonio, TX.

Hughes, E. C. (1945). Dilemmas and contradictions of status. *American Journal of Sociology, 50*, 353–359.

Jetten, J., Branscombe, N. R., & Spears, R. (2002). On being peripheral: Effects of identity insecurity on personal and collective self-esteem. *European Journal of Social Psychology, 32,* 105–123.

Jones, E. E., & Thibaut, J. W. (1958). Interaction goals as bases of inference in interpersonal perception. In R. Taguiri & L. Petrullo (Eds.), *Person perception and interpersonal behavior* (pp. 151–178). Stanford, CA: Stanford University Press.

Kimble, G. A. (1994). A frame of reference for psychology. *American Psychologist, 49,* 510–519.

Klein, S. B., & Kihlstrom, J. F. (1998). On bridging the gap between social-personality psychology and neuropsychology. *Personality and Social Psychology Review, 2,* 228–242.

Kunda, Z., Miller, D. T., & Claire, T. (1990). Combining social concepts: The role of causal reasoning. *Cognitive Science, 14,* 551–577.

Latané, B., & Darley, J. M. (1970). *The unresponsive bystander: Why doesn't he help?* Englewood Cliffs, NJ: Prentice-Hall.

Macrae, C. N., Bodenhausen, G. V., & Milne, A. B. (1995). The dissection of selection in person perception: Inhibitory processes in social stereotyping. *Journal of Personality and Social Psychology, 69,* 397–407.

Malt, B. C., Ross, B. H., & Murphy, G. L. (1995). Predicting features for members of natural categories when categorization is uncertain. *Journal of Experimental Psychology: Learning, Memory, and Cognition, 21,* 646–661.

Marques, J. M., Abrams, D., Paez, D., & Martinez-Taboada, C. (1998). The role of categorization and in-group norms in judgments of groups and their members. *Journal of Personality and Social Psychology, 75,* 976–988.

Marques, J. M., & Paez, D. (1994). The "black sheep effect": Social categorization, rejection of ingroup deviates, and perception of group variability. *European Review of Social Psychology, 5,* 37–68.

McGuire, W. J., McGuire, C. V., Child, P., & Fujioka, T. (1978). Salience of ethnicity in the spontaneous self-concept as a function of one's ethnic distinctiveness in the social environment. *Journal of Personality and Social Psychology, 36,* 511–520.

Murphy, G. L., & Ross, B. H. (1994). Predictions from uncertain categorizations. *Cognitive Psychology, 27,* 148–193.

Mussweiler, T., Gabriel, S., & Bodenhausen, G. V. (2000). Shifting social identities as a strategy for deflecting threatening social comparisons. *Journal of Personality and Social Psychology, 79,* 398–409.

Nelson L. J., & Miller, D. T. (1995). The distinctiveness effect in social categorization: You are what makes you unusual. *Psychological Science, 6,* 246–249.

Neuberg, S. L., & Fiske, S. T. (1987). Motivational influences on impression formation: Outcome dependency, accuracy-driven attention, and individuating processes. *Journal of Personality and Social Psychology, 53,* 431–444.

Oakes, P. J. (1987). The salience of social categories. In J. Turner, M. A. Hogg, P. J. Oakes, S. D. Reicher, & M. Wetherell (Eds.), *Rediscovering the social group: A self-categorization theory* (pp. 117–141). Oxford: Basil Blackwell.

Ochsner, K. N., & Lieberman, M. D. (2001). The emergence of social cognitive neuroscience. *American Psychologist, 56,* 717–734.

Ross, B. H., & Murphy, G. L. (1996). Category-based predictions: Influence of uncertainty and feature associations. *Journal of Experimental Psychology: Learning, Memory and Cognition, 22*, 736–753.

Shah, J. Y., Friedman, R., & Kruglanski, A. W. (2002). Forgetting all else: On the antecedents and consequences of goal shielding. *Journal of Personality and Social Psychology, 83*, 1261–1280.

Sherman, J. W., Macrae, C. N., & Bodenhausen, G. V. (2000). Attention and stereotyping: Cognitive constraints on the construction of meaningful social impressions. *European Journal of Social Psychology, 11*, 145–175.

Shih, M., Pittinsky, T. L., & Ambady, N. (1999). Stereotype susceptibility: Identity salience and shifts in quantitative performance. *Psychological Science, 10*, 80–83.

Shotland, R. L., & Straw, M. K. (1976). Bystander response to an assault: When a man attacks a woman. *Journal of Personality and Social Psychology, 34*, 990–999.

Simon, B., Glaessner-Bayerl, B., & Stratenwerth, I. (1991). Stereotyping and self-stereotyping in a natural intergroup context: The case of heterosexual and homosexual men. *Social Psychology Quarterly, 54*, 252–266.

Simon, B., & Hamilton, D. L. (1994). Self-stereotyping and social context: The effects of relative in-group size and in-group status. *Journal of Personality and Social Psychology, 66*, 699–711.

Simon, H. A. (1994). The bottleneck of attention: Connecting thought with motivation. In W. D. Spaulding (Ed.), *Integrative views of cognition, emotion, and action: Nebraska symposium on motivation* (Vol. 41, pp. 1–21). Lincoln, NE: University of Nebraska Press.

Simon, H. A., & Kadane, J. B. (1975). Optimal problem-solving search: All-or-none solutions. *Artificial Intelligence, 6*, 235–247.

Simons, D. J., & Levin, D. T. (1998). Failure to detect changes to people during a real-world interaction. *Psychonomic Bulletin and Review, 5*, 644–649.

Sinclair, L., & Kunda, Z. (1999). Reactions to a black professional: Motivated inhibition and activation of conflicting stereotypes. *Journal of Personality and Social Psychology, 77*, 885–904.

Smith, E. E., & Medin, D. L. (1981). *Categories and concepts.* Cambridge, MA: Harvard University Press.

Spears, R. (2001). The interaction between the individual and the collective self: Self-categorization in context. In C. Sedikides & M. B. Brewer (Eds.), *Individual self, relational self, collective self* (pp. 171–198). Philadelphia: Psychology Press.

Srull, T. K., & Wyer, R. S., Jr. (1979). The role of category accessibility in the interpretation of information about persons: Some determinants and implications. *Journal of Personality and Social Psychology, 37*, 1660–1672.

Srull, T. K., & Wyer, R. S., Jr. (1986). The role of chronic and temporary goals in social information processing. In R. M. Sorrentino & E. T. Higgins (Eds.), *Handbook of motivation and cognition: Foundations of social behavior* (Vol. 1, pp. 503–549). New York: Guilford Press.

Stangor, C., Lynch, L., Duan, C., & Glass, B. (1992). Categorization of individuals on the basis of multiple social features. *Journal of Personality and Social Psychology, 62*, 207–218.

Swann, W. B., Jr. (1996). *Self-traps: The elusive quest for higher self-esteem.* New York: W. H. Freeman & Co.

Swann, W. B., Jr. (1990). To be adored or to be known? The interplay of self-enhancement and self-verification. In R. M. Sorrentino & E. T. Higgins (Eds.), *Handbook of motivation and cognition* (Vol. 2, pp. 404–448). New York: Guilford Press.

Swann, W. B., Jr., & Schroeder, D. B. (1995). The search for beauty and truth: A framework for understanding reactions to evaluations. *Personality and Social Psychology Bulletin, 21,* 1307–1318.

Taylor, S. E., Fiske, S. T., Etcoff, N.L., & Ruderman, A. J. (1978). Categorical and contextual bases of person memory and stereotyping. *Journal of Personality and Social Psychology, 36,* 778–793.

Turner, J. C. (1991). *Social influence.* Pacific Grove, CA: Brooks/Cole.

Turner, J. C., Hogg, M. A., Oakes, P. J., Reicher, S. D., & Wetherell, M. S. (1987). *Rediscovering the social group: A self-categorization theory.* New York: Basil Blackwell.

Turner, J. C., Oakes, P. J., Haslam, S. A., & McGarty, C. (1994). Self and collective: Cognition and social context. *Personality and Social Psychology Bulletin, 20,* 454–463.

van Knippenberg, A., & Dijksterhuis, A. (2000). Social categorization and stereotyping: A functional perspective. In W. Stroebe & M. Hewstone (Eds.), *European review of social psychology* (Vol. 11, pp. 105–144). Chichester, England: Wiley.

Verkuyten, M., & Hagendoorn, L. (1998). Prejudice and self-categorization: The variable role of authoritarianism and in-group stereotypes. *Personality and Social Psychology Bulletin, 24,* 99–110.

Wundt, W. (1904). *Principles of physiological psychology* (5th ed.). New York: Macmillan.

Wyer, R. S., Jr., & Srull, T. K. (1989). *Memory and cognition in its social context.* Hillsdale, NJ: Lawrence Erlbaum Associates.

8

Perceiving Groups:
How, What, and Why?

Steven J. Sherman
Amy L. Johnson
Indiana University

Perhaps it seems strange to write a chapter that focuses on groups for a book that is dedicated to Bob Wyer and his work. After all, Bob was surely firmly entrenched in the Attitudes and Social Cognition section of the *Journal of Personality and Social Psychology*, rather than in the Interpersonal Relations and Group Processes section. Bob's research focused heavily on the perception of individuals by individuals. Yet there are clearly three ways in which this chapter is very much tied to Bob's work and relies heavily on that work.

First, our interest in groups is not primarily about intergroup relations, interpersonal relations of group members, or the group dynamics principles that help to explain how groups function, how they make decisions, or how they set group goals. Rather, our interest is in the perception of groups by individuals. We focus on how information about groups, as social targets, is attended to, processed, encoded, represented, and remembered. This focus on the encoding, storage, and retrieval of social information has been, of course, the focus of Bob's work over many years. No one has taught us more about the representations and retrieval of social information than Bob.

Second, although it is true that Bob's primary interest has been in the perception of individual social targets, he and his colleagues have at times been concerned with the perception of group social targets. One of the major

155

themes of our work has been the identification and explanation of similarities and differences between the processing of information about individual versus group social targets. Our key assumption about these similarities and differences concerns the degree of unity, cohesiveness, or entitativity that social perceivers attribute to individual or group targets. This assumption and where it has led us owes much to some earlier work by Bob and his colleagues. Srull (1981) considered impressions of groups based on information about the members of these groups. He concluded that, when a group was highly cohesive, representation of and memory for information about group members were similar to representation of and memory for information about individual social targets. However, when a group was a loosely knit aggregate, different processes and outcomes emerged. This idea was expanded upon by Wyer, Bodenhausen, and Srull (1984), who developed a comprehensive conceptualization of how trait and behavioral information is organized in memory for individuals and groups, and how this stored information is subsequently recalled and recognized. Their conceptualization served as an important part of our initial thinking about similarities and differences in the perceptions of individuals and groups (Hamilton & Sherman, 1996).

Third, in addition to his important theoretical, conceptual, and empirical contributions, Bob developed and pushed all of us to develop and use methods that were designed to reveal the cognitive representation of social information, and to clarify the social cognitive processes that were employed in the encoding, storing, and retrieval of this information. Many of the methods that we have used in the research presented in this chapter were employed to achieve exactly these goals. The specific methods were not necessarily developed by Bob, but they are clearly methods that were developed because of Bob's early leadership and vision in the general area of social cognition.

INDIVIDUAL AND GROUP PERCEPTION

The topics of individual and group perception have been historically segregated in social psychology (Hamilton & Sherman, 1996). The person perception and person memory literature has reported extensively on specific mechanisms underlying impression formation of individual targets, emphasizing the ways in which information is encoded, integrated, and represented in memory. It has generally been concluded that people, often spontaneously, integrate trait or behavioral knowledge about an individual into a strong dispositional impression (Anderson, 1966, 1981; Asch, 1946; Burnstein & Schul, 1982; Hastie & Park, 1986). Research focused on memory for evaluative and descriptive traits and behaviors of individual targets, especially memory for impression-congruent versus impression-incongruent traits, has shown that impression-incongruent traits and behaviors are preferentially recalled (Hamilton, Katz, & Leirer, 1980; Hastie & Kumar, 1979; Srull, 1981;

Srull & Wyer, 1989; Wyer et al., 1984). The structure and function of mental representations of person information have also been examined, primarily by Bob and his colleagues (Wyer & Carlston, 1979; Wyer & Srull, 1989).

Processes governing group perceptions and stereotyping have been studied rather independently from the work on person perception. Group perception and stereotype researchers have focused on processes of categorization (Allport, 1954; Bruner, 1957; Tajfel, 1969), perceptions of variability in groups (Linville, Fischer, & Salovey, 1989; Park & Hastie, 1987), mental representations of group-level information (Klein & Loftus, 1990; Posner & Keele, 1968; Smith & Zarate, 1990), and the information processing and social judgment consequences of stereotypes (e.g., Bodenhausen & Wyer, 1985). Until recently, few researchers have attempted to assemble person impression formation and group perception into a single, more parsimonious framework (Hamilton & Sherman, 1996; Wyer et al., 1984).

Compatible with the separate treatment of person and group perception, research on the processes guiding individual impression formation and group impression formation has suggested that the two processes are often distinct. Person perception involves an on-line, integrative impression formation process, with incoming information organized into a coherent, dispositional inference about a target person as the information is received (Hastie & Park, 1986). As incoming information is assimilated to fit earlier information, a summary evaluation and trait-behavior clusters are formed and consulted in making judgments (Srull & Wyer, 1989; Wyer & Srull, 1989). Alternatively, in forming impressions of groups, processing is generally less integrative. Judgments about group targets tend to be based on memory for specific behavioral exemplars, due to the absence of a strong, coherent impression upon which to rely (Hastie & Park, 1986). This less integrative processing involves storing information as it is received, with less assimilation of new information into previously encountered group-level knowledge, at least initially, before a stereotype of the group is formed. Thus as new information is received, it is not shaped to form a coherent impression of a group to the same degree as it is for an individual.

Because individual impression formation processes are typically more integrative than are group impression processes, traits and dispositions are quickly extracted from early information, and in turn serve as a basis for integrating subsequent knowledge. Thus primacy effects in recall are characteristic of individual impressions; and because global impressions become independent from the information upon which they are based, correlations between memory for impression-based information and judgments of the target are typically low. As a result of the memory-based judgments in group impressions, recency effects in recall are characteristic, and memory-judgment correlations are typically quite high. Overall recall of the trait or behavioral information upon which impressions are based is better for individuals than for groups (Hamilton et al., 1980), and person memory research has consistently found that, due to the integrative nature of the impression formation process, memory is better for impression-inconsistent, rather than impression-consistent, information (Garcia-Marques & Hamilton, 1996; Gordon & Wyer, 1987; Hastie, 1984; Hastie & Kumar, 1979; Srull, 1981; Wyer & Gordon, 1982). Conversely, impression-consistent information is typically better recalled than impression-inconsistent information in the formation of group impressions (Stangor & McMillan, 1992; Wyer & Gordon, 1982).

Perceivers also tend to make more extreme trait inferences about individuals, and they draw these conclusions more quickly and on the basis of less information than for group inferences (Susskind, Maurer, Thakkar, Hamilton, & J. Sherman, 1999). Also, distinctiveness-based illusory correlations are often observed with group information. Illusory correlation occurs when people overestimate the frequency with which distinctive traits or behaviors are associated with distinctive groups. Because of their distinctiveness, these trait/group pairings necessitate additional encoding and are, consequently, strongly associated in memory. Thus illusory correlations are the result of a reliance on individual exemplars in memory-based judgments (Hamilton & Gifford, 1976). Illusory correlations are absent when the social targets are individuals (Sanbonmatsu, Sherman, & Hamilton, 1987).

PERCEIVED ENTITATIVITY

At first glance, it appears as if the processing systems that govern impressions of individuals and groups are quite distinct. However, Hamilton and Sherman (1996) maintain that the same underlying processing system is actually at work in perceiving both individual and group targets. This system is mediated by assumptions of the perceived level of unity and consistency, or the perceived degree of entitativity of the impression target. Perceived entitativity is the degree to which a social aggregate is perceived as a meaningful entity (Campbell, 1958). Individuals are the quintessence of high perceived entitativity, as we tend to assume a great deal of consistency in their behaviors and traits across time and situations. Groups, in general, are perceived as less consistent and less entitative than a single individual. There is logically much more variability within the members of a group than within an individual; thus the same degree of consistency and unity is not expected in a group, resulting in less of a tendency for group impressions to be unified. Hence a target's level of perceived entitativity appears to be responsible for guiding impression formation toward more or less integrative processes (Hamilton & Sherman, 1996).

Several studies have tested the notion that the degree of perceived entitativity accounts for the apparent differences between processes of person and group perceptions, typically by manipulating the information processing goals given to participants, or by manipulating the perceived entitativity of a target. In one study (McConnell, Sherman, & Hamilton, 1994), on-line or memory-based processes were invoked using instructions to form an impression of the target or to simply memorize the presented information for a later recall test (e.g., Hamilton et al., 1980; Wyer & Gordon, 1982). The same behavior-descriptive sentences were attributed to either a single individual or to several individual members of a group. Under impression formation instructions, information was actively integrated into a coherent impression, yielding no illusory correlation effects. This occurred whether the behaviors were attributed to an individual or to members of a group. Under memory instructions, judgments were subsequently memory-based, and illusory correlations were formed between low-frequency targets and low-frequency traits. Again, this occurred regardless of whether the target was an individual or a group. These results showed that the way in which information is processed underlies the apparent differences between individual and group impression formation.

A similar study (McConnell, Sherman, & Hamilton, 1997) manipulated target entitativity, and again used the presence or absence of illusory correlation as a dependent variable. Descriptions of high or low target entitativity were applied to individual or to group targets. The results showed that information about targets described as high in entitativity was processed on-line, regardless of whether the description was applied to an individual or to a group. Similarly, when low entitativity descriptions were applied to individual or to group targets, the accompanying information processing was less integrative, yielding illusory correlation effects. Thus assumptions about target entitativity seem to spontaneously invoke more or less integrative information processing strategies. When these assumptions are given to participants through entitativity manipulations, the individual or group status of the target is inconsequential. It is the expected consistency, or perceived entitativity of a target, that leads to differential impression formation mechanisms.

More recent studies have also manipulated the perceived entitativity of a target and examined indicators of integrative processing. Yzerbyt, Rogier, and Fiske (1998) have shown that the fundamental attribution error is far more prevalent toward targets with high levels of perceived entitativity. Also, Welbourne (1999) demonstrated greater effort exerted toward inconsistency resolution in the impressions of targets described as high, relative to low, in entitativity.

TYPES OF GROUPS AND THEIR MENTAL REPRESENTATION

Individuals and general groups are two extreme ends of the entitativity continuum. The concept of entitativity, as originally proposed by Campbell (1958), referred to the perceived "groupness" of various aggregates, and the properties that might lead us to expect more or less unity in those groups. A family, social psychologists, and people who drive red cars are all social entities, but they obviously vary in the extent to which they are seen as meaningful groups. The family members are likely perceived as quite similar and as more important to each other than are social psychologists or people who drive red cars. Whereas social psychologists constitute a fairly meaningful entity, their union is based more on interaction and common goals than on similarity or importance. Owners of red cars are a much less meaningful group than either a family or social psychologists, for their membership is based solely on a low-level surface cue, the color of their car. Thus distinct patterns of features exist for different groups, and determine the extent to which the group is perceived as a meaningful and cohesive entity.

Lickel et al. (2000) examined the levels of perceived entitativity assigned to various social entities through a series of rating and sorting tasks. Participants in the United States and Poland were asked to rate 40 groups on several properties, including the extent to which they were each perceived as a meaningful group (entitativity), before sorting those same 40 groups into categories. Sorting tasks in both samples resulted in four distinct clusters. The first cluster consisted of small groups with high levels of interaction, similarity, importance to their members, and entitativity. Membership in these groups is typically of long duration, and the groups are characterized as impermeable and as having goals and outcomes that members share. Lickel et al. (2000) called this cluster *intimacy groups*. Examples of intimacy groups are members of a family, groups of close friends, street gangs, and fraternities and sororities. A second cluster included groups such as labor unions, juries, co-workers, and students studying for an exam together, and were referred to as *task-oriented groups*. Task-oriented groups are typically fairly small and are together for modest duration. Like intimacy groups, members of task groups share common goals and outcomes and are seen as rather high in interaction, importance, and similarity. These groups are rated as moderate in entitativity. The third cluster of groups consists of social categories such as Women, Blacks, and Jews. *Social category groups* are large, long-lasting, and impermeable. Unlike intimacy and task-oriented groups, social categories are rated as being low in interaction, importance to members, and common goals and outcomes. Social categories are also rated as relatively low in perceived entitativity, and low in perceived similarity between members. Given the outgroup homogeneity effect, the low perceived similarity between members of social categories might seem paradoxical, and is discussed later in the chapter. A fourth, semi-meaningful cluster is made up of groups termed *loose associations*, barely considered a real group. Some examples of loose associations are people in the same neighborhood, people who like classical music, or those who drive red cars. Loose associations are typically of short or moderate duration, and membership is highly permeable. They are rated as lower than intimacy, task-oriented, and social category groups on interaction, importance, common goals and outcomes, similarity, and entitativity.

Thus the 40 groups rated by participants appear to fall into four types: intimacy groups, task-oriented groups, social categories, and loose associations, with the first three perceived as possessing some real unity, or entitativity. Like person typologies (Anderson & Sedikides, 1991; Sedikides & Anderson, 1994), this research uncovered clear group typologies, each with a unique pattern of associated features. The Lickel et al. (2000) data, replicated in two countries as well as with respect to both outgroups (Studies 1 and 2) and ingroups (Study 3), strongly suggest that this categorization into these group types is quite reliable. That is, we know that participants consistently sort lists of various groups into the four specific clusters outlined above, and dependably associate the same patterns of properties and levels of perceived entitativity with each group type.

To provide further evidence that the group typologies are meaningful for perceiving groups in less contrived settings, Sherman, Castelli, and Hamilton (2002) considered the spontaneous organization and representation of groups in memory by examining errors in recognition when groups of various types were presented (Taylor, Fiske, Etcoff, & Ruderman, 1978). In a first phase of their initial experiments, participants were shown a series of 60 faces or 60 behaviors in random order, and each face or behavior was paired with one of six possible group labels. Two of the six labels were intimacy groups (family member and friend), two were of task groups (jury and co-worker), and two signified social categories (French and Presbyterian). Thus the labels indicated the group membership of the presented face or of the person who performed the presented behavior. In the following phase, only the faces or behaviors from the first phase were presented, and participants were asked to recall and supply the correct group label. If members of various groups are spontaneously classified according to their superordinate group typology, errors in recognition should reveal this. Specifically, members of groups of the same type should be more easily confused than members of groups of different types. Indeed, this was the case. Results showed that participants made significantly more within-group-type errors than between-group-types errors. That is, confusions of members of different groups within the same type (a face labeled as French in the first phase mislabeled as Presbyterian in the second phase) were more common than confusions of members of groups of different types (a face labeled French in the first phase mislabeled as co-worker, jury member, family member, or friend in the second phase).

Response latencies and order effects in a free recall task were also analyzed. Across four studies, response latency data typically revealed the shortest latencies for correct responses, followed by slightly longer latencies for incorrect within-group-type errors, and the longest latencies for between-group-types errors. Response latencies were taken as additional evidence of higher degrees of confusability between groups of the same type relative to groups of different types. In another study, participants were presented with behaviors and group labels, and were subsequently given a surprise free recall task. Participants were asked to recall as many of the previously presented behaviors as possible so that the organization of recalled behaviors, with regard to within-group-type versus between-group-types transitions in recall, could be examined. If behaviors are clustered in memory by group type, there should be more within-group-type transitions (i.e., recalling behaviors performed by groups of a single type sequentially) than between-group-types transitions (i.e., transitioning from a behavior performed by a group of one type to a behavior performed by a group of a different type). As expected, within-group-type transitions occurred significantly more than between-group-types transitions.

Finally, Sherman et al. (2002) varied their description of a group, a softball team, to participants. In one case, the softball team was described in terms usually associated with task-oriented groups. That is, the focus was on the achievement goals of the team, the division of labor, and the importance of success and competition. In the other case, the team was described in terms that are usually associated with intimacy groups. The interpersonal relations and affiliative goals of playing on a team were emphasized in the description. The framing of the team as a task-oriented or intimacy group very much affected the false inclusions of members of other groups as softball team members. With a task-oriented description, errors of inclusion were far greater for members of other task-oriented groups (e.g., labor unions). With an intimacy group description, there was a relatively greater number of false inclusions into the softball team from members of other intimacy groups (e.g., social clubs). Thus the way in which a group is framed determines how it is categorized, and determines the other groups with which it is closely represented in memory.

Taken together, the results of the Sherman et al. (2002) studies provide compelling evidence that the mental representation of groups is organized by group type. Further, these findings indicate that this organization is seen not only in intentional sorting tasks, but also in timed tasks of a less intentional nature, providing evidence that this organization by group type occurs spontaneously. These data speak to the meaningfulness of the typological view of groups, based on perceived attributes and entitativity, as identified by Lickel et al. (2000).

It should be noted that our identification of a lay conception of group types corresponds with other data-based group typologies. Deaux, Reid, Mizrahi, and Ethier (1995), using a methodology similar to that used in the Lickel et al. (2000) work, found distinct traits associated with five major group types: relationships, vocation, political affiliation, stigmatized groups, and ethnicity and religion groups. Their first type, relationships, consists of groups such as mother, friend, and roommate. The groups in this type closely mirror Lickel et al.'s (2000) intimacy groups. Vocation groups were groups such as student, supervisor, or teacher, similar to our task-oriented groups. Political affiliation (e.g., feminist, conservative) and ethnicity and religion (e.g., Mormon, Hispanic) yielded two separate factors in the Deaux et al. (1995) work, but were combined into one type, social categories, in the Lickel et al. research. The Deaux et al. (1995) and Lickel et al. (2000) data emphasize the significance of distinguishing among types of groups, and highlight the discrete properties of groups within various types.

In addition to these data-based group typologies, McGrath (1984) has proposed a theory-based typology of groups that emphasizes some practical and methodological strengths and limitations of studying groups of various types. Included in his typology are natural groups, concocted groups, and quasi-groups. Natural groups are those that naturally exist in the world, such as friendship groups, work crews, and families; concocted groups are those created for the purpose of research, such as mock juries or work groups performing practice drills; and quasi-groups are those formed for extensive study, in which the behaviors of group members are highly restricted for the sake of research. McGrath's (1984) typology makes clear the distinction between groups in his three types, especially in terms of issues for the group researcher.

FUNCTIONS SERVED BY DIFFERENT GROUP TYPES

Given the emergence of meaningful group types (Lickel et al., 2000), and evidence that group-level information is spontaneously organized in terms of these types (Sherman et al., 2002), a logical next question concerns the way in which this group typology is functional for the perceiver. How does our attentiveness to and use of these group types benefit us, both as perceivers in everyday life and as members of those groups ourselves? An answer may be found by investigating the psychological needs fulfilled by membership in the types of groups. We believe that the functions served by intimacy, task-oriented, and social category groups, in particular the specific psychological needs fulfilled by membership in each type of group, can help us to understand why groups are spontaneously categorized into these group types.

Intimacy groups are small, close groups of people such as friends and family, with high perceived levels of interaction, similarity, importance, and entitativity. We hypothesize that membership in intimacy groups primarily satisfies affiliation needs such as emotional attachment and belongingness. Intimacy groups promote attachments and feelings of closeness among members (Karasawa, 1991), and they allow members to learn much about each other and influence each other (Prentice, Miller, & Lightdale, 1994). Research on attachment needs supports our hypothesis. Bowlby (1958) has written much on attachment as an innate, fundamental human motive, stating that the need is primarily satisfied through relationships with caregivers. In addition, Baumeister and Leary (1995) have discussed the need to belong as a fundamental human motive, also claiming that membership in intimacy groups such as friends, family, and romantic relationships allow this need to be realized. Further, Maslow (1962) discusses love and belongingness needs as fulfilled through intimacy groups, as do Rushton (1989) and Stevens and Fiske (1995), in terms of an evolutionary perspective.

It seems quite logical that membership in task-oriented groups—groups that have a specific purpose and that are characterized by high interaction, importance, shared common goals and outcomes, and moderate entitativity—help to fulfill achievement-type needs. In line with this contention, White (1959) has discussed the need for competence, and explores how this need might be most likely fulfilled through membership in therapy and work groups. Similarly, McClelland and his colleagues (McClelland, 1951; McClelland, Atkinson, Clark, & Lowell, 1953) have theorized that achievement needs, such as mastery are fundamental human motives often satisfied in groups that fit the task-oriented nature of our typology.

Finally, social categories, perceived as large, impermeable groups with relatively low levels of similarity, interaction, importance, and entitativity, are expected to fulfill identity-type needs. Most notably, social identity theory (Tajfel & Turner, 1979) supports this proposition. Social identity theory has shown that even minimal groups—groups constructed in the laboratory on the basis of seemingly insignificant group differences (e.g., dot over- and under-estimators)—can serve to provide social identity value to their members. If these apparently meaningless and unimportant categorizations can satisfy identity needs, so should more meaningful social categories. These groups are typically low in interaction, importance, and similarity among members, but are much more meaningful in terms of low-level surface cues.

Indeed, membership in broad social categories is often found to fulfill social identity needs (Blascovich, N. Wyer, Swart, & Kibler, 1997; Gaskell & Smith, 1986). Hogg and Hardie (1991) maintain that social categories provide members with a connection to the group that provides a sense of social and personal identity to them. Related to this, social categorization theory (Turner, Hogg, Oakes, Reicher, & Wetherell, 1987) holds that self-categorization, particularly into social category groups, helps to fulfill salient identity needs. Also, optimal distinctiveness theory (Brewer, 1991) stresses that optimal levels of both assimilation and differentiation with regard to social category membership are required to attain the most functional sense of identity.

Recent research in our laboratory has begun to test the functions of intimacy, task-oriented, and social category groups in terms of the respective attachment, achievement, and identity needs that they are predicted to fulfill. In a questionnaire study, participants were presented with a list of 28 needs (e.g., emotional attachment, mastery, uniqueness) chosen a priori as likely to fall into each of the three need-type categories. Participants were given examples of intimacy, task-oriented, and social category groups, were asked to consider their own memberships in groups of each type, and then were asked to rate the extent to which each of the 28 needs was fulfilled by those memberships. Factor analyses confirmed that the needs initially considered attachment-, achievement-, and identity-type needs comprised three factors accordingly. From the factor analyses, several needs of each type (those best fitting each factor) were used as indices for each function. The attachment needs were comfort, emotional attachment, belongingness, support, connectedness, and acceptance; achievement needs were achievement, mastery, success, accomplishment of goals, and competence; and identity needs were identity, distinctiveness, uniqueness, and individuality. Means were compared to test the types of needs that were most fulfilled by each type of group. Results revealed an overall main effect of group type, in that intimacy groups fulfilled needs in general more than did task-oriented groups and social categories. There was also a main effect of need type in that attachment-type needs were fulfilled by all group memberships to a greater extent than were achievement or identity needs. Most important, and as predicted, intimacy groups primarily fulfilled attachment needs, and task-oriented groups primarily fulfilled achievement needs. Largely because of the main effect of attachment needs being fulfilled overall, and the small proportion of distinct needs being fulfilled by social categories, social categories were found to primarily fulfill attachment needs, followed closely by identity needs.

A second study presented participants with the 15 needs derived from the factor analyses of the previous study, and asked them to list up to three groups to which they turned for fulfillment of each specific need. Consistent with the above research, the same main effects of group and need type emerged. More importantly, intimacy groups were listed in response to attachment needs more than were the other group types; task-oriented groups were reported as more likely to fulfill achievement needs than were groups of the other types; and social categories were listed as helping to fulfill identity needs more often than were intimacy or task groups.

Finally, a third study required that participants consider the specific group of each type that was most important to them, and to rate the three groups on the extent to which each of the 15 needs was fulfilled by membership. Results revealed the same pattern as the previous studies. Thus asking participants to generate specific groups themselves in response to attachment, achievement, and identity needs and to rate self-generated groups on their capacity for fulfilling the needs provided further support for our hypotheses.

In the future, it will be important to examine the extent to which these needs are satisfied by specific groups within each of the three group types, allowing us to take other factors, such as the perceived entitativity of the group and the importance of the group to the member, into account as possible mediators of need fulfillment. Studies of a more experimental nature might manipulate particular needs and allow us to examine the types of real groups that are relied upon to fulfill those needs. For example, a need for achievement might be induced through negative feedback on an achievement test. Participants would subsequently be asked to simply list several groups to which they belong. With a need for achievement made salient, it would be expected that groups that satisfy this need (i.e., task-oriented groups) would be listed before, and more often than, other types of groups. Such findings would provide support for the idea that groups are organized into the three major types so that people will know where to go when important social motives are aroused. These contextually aroused social needs would have much in common with the goal-driven categories studied by Barsalou (1983). Just as people have a category of "things to save from a burning house," they have categories of "groups to which to go when needs for affiliation, achievement, or identity are aroused."

GROUP TYPES, INTERPERSONAL RELATIONS, AND SOCIAL INFLUENCE

Because the different group types serve different functions and have different properties, it is likely that certain aspects of interpersonal relations for group members will differ in the different types of groups. For example, different qualities or styles of interaction have been shown to be reflected in the principles by which people regulate their interactions (Fiske, 1991). These relational styles should differ according to the different group types and their properties and functions.

Fiske (1991, 1992) has identified four types of relational styles:

1. Communal sharing is a relational style marked by fusion of the individual to the group. Individuality is minimized, and exchange is regulated simply through group membership. Members can use the resources of the group without the expectation of paying back. The principle of unity underlies decisions.
2. Equality matching as a relational style is marked by principles of neighborly balancing. The goal is to balance exchanges between individuals in the long run without immediate payment or formal bookkeeping. However, unlike communal sharing, where the needs of each individual predominate, equality matching assumes that there will be turn-taking in contributions, and that all members will contribute equally in the long run.
3. Market pricing, the third relational style, is geared toward maximizing the value of exchange, work, and other interactions. The key

motivations are efficiency and maximization. Individuals attempt to maximize their own outcomes from the interaction.

4. Authority ranking is a relational style where status differences between individuals are the basis for regulating social interaction. Higher-status individuals can take what they want from lower-ranking individuals, but they must also care for and protect the low-status individuals. Decision-making is achieved by a chain of command.

Interestingly, research has shown that the four relational styles are used to cognitively organize information about social relationships. Fiske, Haslam, and Fiske (1991) examined the natural errors that people make when they do things such as call a person by an incorrect name, or misremember who in a group may have engaged in a certain behavior. Errors of confusing one person with another are typically made between people who share the same type of relationship (e.g., communal) with the perceiver or with each other. This is reminiscent of the findings of Sherman et al. (2002), who reported confusions between groups of the same type. Both sets of findings observed the spontaneous nature of confusions, and both sets of findings were indicative of the spontaneous organization of social information. Perceivers appear to spontaneously encode groups (and their members) in terms of group type, and to spontaneously encode group members by the relational styles that govern their interaction.

These findings suggest that there may be a relation between the different group types that we have identified and the different relational styles. Because intimacy groups are long-lasting and the members are highly interdependent, communal sharing should be a likely relational style, and market pricing should be an unlikely style. Task groups are generally hierarchically organized, and they should involve authority ranking and market pricing as relational styles. Social categories should show greater authority ranking than other types of relational styles, because leaders of social categories are often elected or ordained.

In order to explore these possibilities, Lickel, Rutchick, Hamilton, and Sherman (2001) presented descriptions of groups in terms of four of the properties that were typical of the different group types (size, permeability, duration, and amount of interaction). For example, one of the groups was described as being small, impermeable, long in duration, and marked by high levels of interaction among members. This is the pattern of factors associated with intimacy groups. After reading each group description, participants evaluated how they thought people in the group would relate to one another by completing a rating scale that was developed by Haslam (1994). Items were indexed to refer to the four relational styles. The group property information (signifying the type of group) did affect inferences of how the people within each of the groups would relate to one another. As expected, groups with the properties of intimacy groups (i.e., small, impermeable, long duration, and high interaction) were seen as very high in communal sharing, but low in authority ranking. Groups described with the properties of task-oriented groups (i.e., small, permeable, short duration, and high interaction) were seen as having relations among members regulated by authority ranking.

In another study, we presented participants with relational styles used by members of a group, and asked them to make inferences about other properties of the group. Again there was a relation between relational style and group type. The manipulation of relational style information greatly affected perceivers' inferences about other group properties. The group described in terms of communal sharing was rated as likely to have higher levels of interaction than groups described in terms of other relational styles, and was also perceived as small and impermeable. These are the factors associated with intimacy groups. The group described in terms of market pricing was perceived as large and permeable, qualities of task-oriented groups. In terms of perceived entitativity, describing the group in communal sharing terms led to the perception of the highest level of entitativity, whereas a market pricing description led to the lowest level of perceived entitativity.

Thus people clearly see relations between the properties that define the different types of groups and the way in which the group members relate to each other. These inferences were made in both directions—from group type properties to relational styles, and from relational styles to properties indicative of the different group types.

In addition to relational styles, the differences among the different group types may be related to other aspects of the interactions between group members. For example, the different group types may foster different types of attitudes in the members, and involve different styles of interpersonal influence. Attitudes have been portrayed as serving three major functions: value-expressive, instrumental, and social adjustment (Katz, 1960; Shavitt, 1990; Smith, Bruner, & White, 1956). These three functions of attitudes would appear to map nicely onto the three major group types. Intimacy groups, with their focus on interaction and attachment, would likely foster the development of value-expressive attitudes. Task-oriented groups, with their focus on goals and achievement, should be related to instrumental attitudes. Because social categories are involved in the social identity function, social adjustment attitudes would be likely to develop in conjunction with social category membership.

In addition, Kelman (1961) has identified three types of social influence, based on the motivational significance of an individual's relationship to the agent of influence. This typology of interpersonal social influence might well be related to the group typology identified in our work. Kelman's typology of social influence includes internalization, compliance, and identification. In the internalization process, individuals adopt a particular attitude position because it is congruent with their overall values. The ideas and actions associated with the attitude are intrinsically rewarding. The position comes to be both publicly and privately accepted, and it is assumed to be the credibility of the influence agent that precipitates the attitude change. The internalization of attitudes seems most likely in tight-knit intimacy groups comprised of significant others, such as friends and family, in which perceived credibility is often high and the overall values of members are typically congruent.

Compliance is marked by public agreement but private disagreement, when the agent eliciting compliance possesses means control, or the ability to give and withhold the means an individual needs to achieve particular goals. Attitudes and associated behaviors are adopted not because a group member believes in the content of the attitude, but because adopting the attitude has social effects in the attaining of rewards and the avoidance of punishment. Compliance behavior (i.e., public acceptance) occurs only in the presence of the influencing agent. This type of social influence appears especially likely in task-oriented groups, in which group membership primarily serves an achievement function and membership revolves around accomplishing particular goals. Rewards and punishment are key aspects of task-oriented groups.

In identification processes, the yielding to social influence helps to establish or maintain an individual's positive, self-defining relationship with the influence agent. The agent, in this case, is said to possess attractiveness. The group is important to the member's self-identity. Influence through identification is accepted publicly and privately, but only insofar as the group remains attractive as a source of association or self-definition for the individual. Emphasizing a need for positive identity, social influence processes based on identification appear especially likely in social categories, which are primarily important for establishing social identity. Future empirical work will help to determine whether the internalization of attitudes is most likely in intimacy groups, whether compliance with group pressures for external reward is most prevalent in task-oriented groups, and whether influence attempts in the form of identification occur most often in social category groups. If so, type of influence and social control, in addition to motivational function and relationship style, would bear a strong relation to group type.

THE REPRESENTATION OF MEMBERS OF A GROUP

We have focused so far on the perception of groups as a whole. We have identified the different types of groups and the properties perceived as descriptive of the different group types. In addition, we have demonstrated that groups of the same type are confusable and thus must be represented together in memory. Moreover, we have presented evidence that groups of each of the different major types are associated with unique functions and unique relational styles, and we have speculated that the different group types are associated with different types of member attitudes and different modes of social influence. Now we shall focus on how members of the same group are represented in memory and on the factors that determine the closeness with which different members of the same group are represented.

As indicated earlier, groups differ in the degree to which they are perceived as a unified entity. To the extent that a group is perceived as highly entitative, several important consequences follow. We have already discussed how high perceived entitativity of a group leads to the processing of information about the group and its members in an on-line, integrative manner, and we have identified the effects of such on-line processing: High levels of recall, primacy effects in recall, a lack of the traditional illusory correlation effect, and low recall–judgment correlations (McConnell et al., 1994, 1997). In addition, groups with high perceived entitativity are viewed as more threatening (Abelson, Dasgupta, Park, & Banaji, 1998; Dasgupta, Banaji, & Abelson, 1999) and as more extreme (Thakkar, 2000). High perceived entitativity also leads to stronger dispositional inferences (Yzerbyt, Rogier, & Fiske, 1998) and greater correspondence bias (Rogier & Yzerbyt, 1999). Thus perceived entitativity affects both the processes and the content of group impressions.

Recent work in our laboratory (Crawford, Sherman, & Hamilton, 2002) has focused on another consequence of perceived group entitativity: Its relation to the degree to which information about individual group members is integrated to form an impression of the group as a whole, and, once formed, the degree to which this group impression is applied to other group members. The main operating assumption of this work is that the members of highly entitative groups are treated as collections of interchangeable parts, and information about any member is easily transferred to other members. On the other hand, information about members of low entitativity groups or aggregates of individuals must be processed and learned only in conjunction with the individual to whom the information directly applies. This information is not transferred to other members easily.

Thus we have proposed that, when processing behaviors performed by members of a highly entitative group, not only are direct behavior-trait associations made to the specific individuals who engaged in the behaviors, but two other types of associations are made as well. First, the traits become associated with the group to which the individual members belong through the process of stereotyping. Second, the traits become associated with all other members of the group. These greater perceived associations among members of high entitative groups provide greater inductive potential within the group, allowing perceivers to go beyond the characteristics of individual members. However, this gain in inductive potential comes with a loss. The extent of associations to other group members causes individuals to lose their unique identities, and weakens the associations between individual members and specific information about them.

In order to explore these ideas, Crawford et al. (2002) employed a modified "Savings-in-Relearning" inference paradigm (Carlston & Skowronski, 1994). This savings paradigm has been shown to be a powerful implicit memory measure of spontaneous social inference (Carlston & Skowronski, 1994) and associations (Skowronski, Carlston, Mae, & Crawford, 1998). The main assumption of this approach is that, if a trait inference is made during the first phase of the experiment (exposure to a person engaging in a behavior), then the learning of that person being associated with the implied trait should be facilitated.

In our experiments, participants first viewed photographs and read behaviors performed by members of two different groups. Each group contained sixteen members. For each group, eight of the sixteen members were paired with behaviors that implied one trait (e.g., aggressive), and the other eight members engaged in behaviors that implied a different trait (e.g., intelligent). Thus each group could be characterized by two traits. The two groups were both described as high in entitativity, low in entitativity, or as unrelated individuals. In the next phase, each photograph was paired with a trait term that either matched the behavior that was originally paired with that particular photograph (trait inference), or with a trait that matched the behaviors of other members of the same group, but not the behavior originally paired with that specific photograph (trait transference). Our goal was to examine the relative ease of trait inference and trait transference for social targets that were either high or low in entitativity.

As predicted, trait inference was significantly easier for low entitativity groups and for unrelated individuals. On the other hand, trait transference was significantly easier for high entitative groups. These results confirm that, for highly entitative groups, the trait implications of behaviors of each member of the group are abstracted, and generalized across all other members of the group. All members of a highly entitative group are seen as alike and as interchangeable. This renders trait transference from one member to another quite easy. On the other hand, the interchangeability of members of a high entitative group means that each individual loses his or her unique identity, and the degree of association between any individual and his or her own behavior is weak. It is because of this loss of individuality that trait inference trials (where perceivers must learn to associate a trait with an individual when that individual has already engaged in a behavior that implies that trait) are more difficult for highly entitative groups.

These results are consistent with the findings of other recent work. Pickett (2001) showed that the presentation of a set of faces produced a greater Ebbinghaus illusion (an indicator of greater implicit comparisons among the faces) when the faces were described as members of a highly entitative group (fraternity members) than as members of a low entitative group (people with birthdays in May). Brewer, Weber, and Carini (1995) explored the effects of perceived entitativity on the extent to which information about the group is organized at the level of the individual or at the social category level. Participants viewed a videotaped discussion among six people who were identifiable as two separate groups of three members each. The groups were both described as either high or low in entitativity. After viewing the videotape, participants had to identify which person had made which comments. Errors were coded as within-group or between-groups errors. The relative number of within-group to between-groups errors was significantly greater for high entitative groups, indicating that high perceived entitativity leads to the representation of individual members as category-based.

In another line of work, Lickel (2000) investigated the extent to which individual group members might be held responsible for the negative acts of other group members, even when they were not directly involved in these acts. The blaming of members other than the directly responsible member is referred to as collective responsibility. Lickel's major prediction was that collective responsibility would be based on the perception that the members of a group are interpersonally interdependent with the person who committed the wrongdoing. The factors that determine perceived interdependence are entitativity, amount of interaction, affective bonds, and the sharing of common goals and norms. Lickel conducted several studies in order to test this hypothesis.

First, a simple correlational study revealed a strong association between perceived interdependence and collective responsibility. In groups where there was high interpersonal interdependence, members not directly responsible for an act of wrongdoing were nonetheless seen as collectively responsible. In a second study, perceptions of group interdependence were manipulated. In addition, the wrongdoing was described as either relevant to the group's sphere of activity or as irrelevant. The combination of high member interdependence and event relevance led to the greatest degree of perceived collective responsibility for members not directly involved in the act of wrongdoing.

Finally, Lickel studied collective responsibility for a real world event, the shootings at Columbine High School in Littleton, Colorado, where two students killed thirteen other students and then killed themselves. Lickel studied the degree of perceived collective responsibility for the killings. Participants judged the amount of collective responsibility for the Trenchcoat Mafia (a friendship group or gang to which the boys belonged) and by the boys' parents. Measures of perceived interdependence of these groups as well as perceived collective responsibility were taken. In addition, Lickel distinguished between responsibility due to acts of commission (other members of a group may have encouraged or tacitly facilitated the murders) and acts of omission (a failure by members of the group to prevent a fellow member from engaging in a wrongdoing). Results indicated that perceived interdependence in the groups predicted collective responsibility. In addition, inferences of commission and omission were distinct in their effects. Inferences of commission strongly predicted the collective responsibility of the Trenchcoat Mafia, whereas inferences of omission predicted the collective responsibility of the families. The results of these studies indicate that the responsibility that group members share for the acts of other group members depends on the degree to which the group is perceived as entitative.

CONCLUDING REMARKS

In this chapter, we have explored many aspects of the perception of groups. We have been especially concerned with perceptions of the entitativity of groups and the variety of effects that follow from perceiving a group as a cohesive and entitative unit. In addition, we have been concerned with the processes involved in group perception and the representation of groups and group members in memory. We have seen how important group type is for both the processes involved in group perception and the representation of groups and their members. The empirical work that has been done to address these issues has employed a variety of methods in order to clarify the questions of process and representation. Response latency, recognition and recall data, clustering in memory, sorting tasks, and savings-in-relearning, as well as paper and pencil measures, have all played a role in this work.

Although we believe that a lot of progress has been made in the understanding of the perception of groups and in the clarification of the similarities and differences between impression formation of individuals versus groups, there is much more to be done. Two areas that should prove to be important in the future in our laboratory involve a clarification of the relationships among the related but independent concepts of entitativity, homogeneity, essentiality, and stereotyping (see Hamilton, Sherman, & Rodgers, in press, for a more complete discussion of this topic), and longitudinal work that can demonstrate, in a direct way, the development of and changes in perceptions of groups and their members over time.

With regard to the relationship among the concepts of entitativity, homogeneity, essentiality, and stereotyping, some progress has already been made. Entitativity and homogeneity are clearly related to each other. In fact, homogeneity is one of the important bases of entitativity (Lickel et al., 2000). However, there are also many other antecedents of perceptions of entitativity. Thus entitativity and homogeneity are far from synonymous (Hamilton, Sherman, & Lickel, 1998; Sherman, Hamilton, & Lewis, 1999). Whereas similarity, proximity, and boundedness best express the concept of homogeneity, the factors of common fate, structure, and organization better express the concept of entitativity. To make matters more complex, research on the per-

ceived essentiality of groups (Haslam, Rothschild, & Ernst, 2000) has identified two factors of group characteristics. The first factor includes the
attributes of natural kinds (Rothbart & Taylor, 1992), such as discreteness,
stability, and naturalness. The second factor involves the perception of coherence, and it contains attributes relevant to both entitativity and homogeneity.

The relation between entitativity and stereotyping is also a very important, but complex, issue. On one hand, the work that we discussed earlier by
Crawford et al. (2002) demonstrated that perceptions of entitativity lead to
the abstraction of group characteristics from the behaviors of individual
members, and to the transfer of attributes from one group member to all
other members of the group. This suggests that perceived entitativity and
stereotyping are positively related. On the other hand, research on the
Outgroup Homogeneity Effect (Linville & Fischer, 1993; Park & Hastie,
1987) has shown that outgroups are generally perceived as having greater
similarity among members than ingroups. This finding implies greater stereotyping of outgroups. Because it is likely that ingroups are perceived as
higher in entitativity than outgroups, there is an inverse relation between
entitativity and stereotyping. In addition, the work of Rothbart and Taylor
(1992) suggests that certain social categories, especially those with a clear
biological differentiation, such as race or gender, are the kind of group most
likely to be perceived as natural kinds, with a perceived essence and a good
deal of inductive potential. The perception of essentialism and inductive
potential of a group should be related to the extent to which the group is stereotyped. Yet social categories (including gender and race) are generally
perceived as quite low in entitativity (Lickel et al., 2000). On the other
hand, families (an example of intimacy groups) are very high in perceived
entitativity, and clearly have an essentialistic basis (the sharing of genes).
Yet our intuition tells us that sweeping stereotypic generalizations about
families and their members seem less likely than broad generalizations about
social categories. People seem more comfortable making generalizations
about "what Asians are like" than they are about "what members of the
Jones family are like." Thus groups that are high in entitativity and
essentialism may not be the best candidates for stereotyping. It is also possible that perceptions of social categories as high or low in similarity might depend on the attribute dimension on which they are focused. Social
categories may be perceived as homogeneous with respect to function-rele-
vant (i.e., identity) dimensions, but heterogeneous with respect to func-
tion-irrelevant dimensions. In any case, it will require careful research to
effectively understand the similarities and differences among the concepts
of entitativity, homogeneity, essentialism, and stereotyping.

Another avenue of future research concerns changes in the perceptions
of in- and outgroup entitativity over time, as new members become social-
ized into a pre-existing group. New members of seven sororities at Indiana

University are currently participating in a two-year longitudinal study. Once per month for their first year of membership and twice per semester for their second year of membership, new members will complete a questionnaire assessing perceptions of their own sorority and other sororities on campus. Specifically, the questionnaire measures the perceived entitativity, perceived homogeneity, favorability, and stereotyping of their in- and outgroups. Earlier work by Ryan and Bogart (1997) demonstrated that new group members perceived their ingroup as more homogeneous than their outgroups initially, but as they transition from new to full-fledged members of their group, outgroup homogeneity increased to levels greater than that seen in the ingroup. At all waves in their research, members rated outgroups more stereotypically than ingroups, and their own ingroup more positively than outgroups. Our work will examine similar variables, with a greater number of groups and over a longer period of time. More important, we will be able to examine the role of perceived entitativity in these other impressions at various points during group socialization and membership.

We expect that, as members undergo the socialization process and become full members of their group, perceptions of ingroup entitativity will increase. Indeed, Ryan and Bogart's finding that ingroup homogeneity increased as membership length increased may have been due, at least in part, to increasing perceptions of ingroup entitativity over time. It is conceivable, however, that perceptions of ingroup entitativity could be quite high at the outset, even before members have had much experience with their group. New members might be particularly motivated to believe that their group is quite entitative in order to justify the effort exerted toward becoming a member, and to view their new group in positive terms (Moreland & Levine, 1982). Overall, perceived outgroup entitativity is predicted to be lower than ingroup entitativity. However, perceptions of outgroups might be related to perceptions of ingroup entitativity, especially if members use their own group as a standard of comparison against which to judge outgroups. Thus if perceived ingroup entitativity increases over time, perceptions of outgroup entitativity may decrease. In addition to examining perceived entitativity across time and at various points in group membership, this work will allow comparisons of in- and outgroup entitativity, as well as the relationships among stereotyping, self-stereotyping, and perceived entitativity.

One thing should be very clear from our consideration of how groups are perceived—namely, that our work in this area, as well as the work of many others, owes a great deal to earlier theorizing and research by Bob Wyer. At the broad level, Bob has allowed us to understand that social cognition is not a narrow content area of social psychology, but is an approach that can be used to understand social behavior and social relations in a wide variety of areas as diverse as individual impression formation, attitude change, self theory, close relationships, cross-cultural work, and group perception. At the more specific level, Bob has developed methods and has pushed others to develop and adopt methods that can help us to understand how social information of all kinds is processed and represented in memory. The study of group perception is far better off today because of Bob's vision.

REFERENCES

Abelson, R. P., Dasgupta, N., Park, J., & Banaji, M. R. (1998). Perception of the collective other. *Personality and Social Psychological Review, 2,* 243–250.

Allport, G. W. (1954). *The nature of prejudice.* Reading, MA: Addison-Wesley.

Anderson, N. H. (1966). Component ratings in impression formation. *Psychonomic Science, 6,* 179–180.

Anderson, N. H. (1981). *Foundations of information integration theory.* New York: Academic Press.

Anderson, C. A., & Sedikides, C. (1991). Thinking about people: Contributions of a typological alternative to associationistic and dimensional models of person perception. *Journal of Personality and Social Psychology, 60,* 203–217.

Asch, S. E. (1946). Forming impressions of personality. *Journal of Abnormal and Social Psychology, 41,* 1230–1240.

Barsalou, L. W. (1983). Ad hoc categories. *Memory and Cognition, 11,* 211–227.

Baumeister, R. F., & Leary, M. R. (1995). The need to belong: Desire for interpersonal attachments as a fundamental human motivation. *Psychological Bulletin, 117,* 497–529.

Blascovich, J., Wyer, N. A., Swart, L. A., & Kibler, J. L. (1997). Racism and racial categorization. *Journal of Personality and Social Psychology, 72,* 1364–1372.

Bodenhausen, G. V., & Wyer, R. S. (1985). Effects of stereotypes on decision making and information processing strategies. *Journal of Personality and Social Psychology, 48,* 267–282.

Bowlby, J. (1958). The nature of the child's tie to his mother. *International Journal of Psychoanalysis, 39,* 350–373.

Brewer, M. B. (1991). The social self: On being the same and different at the same time. *Personality and Social Psychology Bulletin, 17,* 475–482.

Brewer, M. B., Weber, J. G., & Carini, B. (1995). Person memory in intergroup contexts: Categorization versus individuation. *Journal of Personality and Social Psychology, 69,* 29–40.

Bruner, J. S. (1957). On perceptual readiness. *Psychological Review, 64,* 123–152.

Burnstein, E., & Schul, Y. (1982). The informational basis of social judgments: Operations in forming an impression of another person. *Journal of Experimental Social Psychology, 18,* 217–234.

Campbell, D. T. (1958). Common fate, similarity, and other indices of the status of aggregates as social entities. *Behavioral Science, 3,* 14–25.

Carlston, D. E., & Skowronski, J. J. (1994). Savings in the relearning of trait information as evidence for spontaneous inference generation. *Journal of Personality and Social Psychology, 66,* 840–856.

Crawford, M. T., Sherman, S. J., & Hamilton, D. L. (2002). Perceiving entitativity stereotype formation and the interchangeability of group members. *Journal of Personality and Social Psychology, 83, 1076–1094.*

Dasgupta, N., Banaji, M. R., & Abelson, R. P. (1999). Group entitativity and group perception: Associations between physical featuares and psychological judgment. *Journal of Personality and Social Psychology, 77, 991–1003.*

Deaux, K., Reid, A., Mizrahi, K., & Ethier, K. A. (1995). Parameters of social identity. *Journal of Personality and Social Psychology, 68, 280–291.*

Fiske, A. P. (1991). *Structures of social life: The four elementary forms of human relations: Communal sharing, authority ranking, equality matching, market pricing.* New York: Free Press.

Fiske, A. P. (1992). The four elementary forms of sociality: Framework for a unified theory of social relations. *Psychological Review, 99, 689–723.*

Garcia-Marques, L., & Hamilton, D. L. (1996). Resolving the apparent discrepancy between the incongruency effect and the expectancy-based illusory correlation effect: The TRAP model. *Journal of Personality and Social Psychology, 71, 845–860.*

Gaskell, G., & Smith, P. (1986). Group membership and social attitudes of youth: An investigation of some implications of social identity theory. *Social Behaviour, 1, 67–77.*

Gordon, S. E., & Wyer, R. S. (1987). Person memory: Category-set-size effects on the recall of a person's behaviors. *Journal of Personality and Social Psychology, 53, 648–662.*

Hamilton, D. L., & Gifford, R. K. (1976). Illusory correlation in interpersonal perception: A cognitive basis of stereotypic judgments. *Journal of Experimental Social Psychology, 12, 392–407.*

Hamilton, D. L., Katz, L. B., & Leirer, V. O. (1980). Cognitive representation of personality impressions: Organizational processes in first impression formation. *Journal of Personality and Social Psychology, 39, 1050–1063.*

Hamilton, D. L., & Sherman S. J. (1996). Perceiving persons and groups. *Psychological Review, 103, 336–355.*

Hamilton, D. L., Sherman, S. J., & Lickel, B. (1998). Perceptions of groups: The importance of the entitativity continuum. In C. Sedikides, J. Schopler, & C. A. Insko (Eds.), *Intergroup cognition and intergroup behavior* (pp. 47–74). Mahwah, NJ: Lawrence Erlbaum Associates.

Hamilton, D. L., Sherman, S. J., & Rodgers, J. S. (in press). Perceiving the groupness of groups: Entitativity, homogeneity, essentialism, and stereotypes. In V. Yzerbyt, C. M. Judd, & O. Corneille (Eds.), *The psychology of group perception: Contributions to the study of homogeneity, entitativity, and essentialism.* Philadelphia: Psychology Press.

Haslam, N. (1994). Categories of social relationship. *Cognition, 53, 59–90.*

Haslam, N., Rothschild, L., & Ernst, D. (2000). Essentialist beliefs about social categories. *British Journal of Social Psychology, 39, 113–127.*

Hastie, R. (1984). Causes and effects of causal attribution. *Journal of Personality and Social Psychology, 46, 44–56.*

Hastie, R., & Kumar, P. (1979). Person memory: Personality traits as organizing principles in memory for behavior. *Journal of Personality and Social Psychology, 37, 25–38.*

Hastie, R., & Park, B. (1986). The relationship between memory and judgment depends on whether the judgment task is memory-based or on-line. *Psychological Review, 93*, 258–268.

Hogg, M. A., & Hardie, E. A. (1991). Social attraction, personal attraction, and self-categorization: A field study. *Personality and Social Psychology Bulletin, 17*, 175–180.

Karasawa, M. (1991). Toward an assessment of social identity: The structure of group identification and its effects on in-group evaluations. *British Journal of Social Psychology, 30*, 293–307.

Katz, D. (1960). The functions approach to the study of attitudes. *Public Opinion Quarterly, 24*, 163–204.

Kelman, H. C. (1961). Processes of opinion change. *Public Opinion Quarterly, 25*, 57–78.

Klein, S. B., & Loftus, J. (1990). Rethinking the role of organization in person memory: An independent trace storage model. *Journal of Personality and Social Psychology, 59*, 400–410.

Lickel, B. (2000). *Perceptions of interdependence and judgments of collective responsibility.* Unpublished doctoral dissertation, University of California, Santa Barbara.

Lickel, B., Hamilton, D. L., Wieczorkowska, G., Lewis, A., Sherman, S. J., & Uhles, A. N. (2000). Varieties of groups and the perception of group entitativity. *Journal of Personality and Social Psychology, 78*, 223–246.

Lickel, B., Rutchick, A., Hamilton, D. L., & Sherman, S. J. (2001). *The association of structural and relational elements within lay people's intuitive theory of social groups.* Unpublished manuscript.

Linville, P. W., & Fischer, G. W. (1993). Exemplar and abstraction models of perceived group variability and stereotypicality. *Social Cognition, 11*, 92–125.

Linville, P. W., Fischer, G. W., & Salovey, P. (1989). Perceived distributions of the characteristics of in-group and out-group members: Empirical evidence and a computer simulation. *Journal of Personality and Social Psychology, 57*, 165–188.

Maslow, A. H. (1962). Some basic propositions of a growth and self-actualization psychology. In A. W. Combs (Ed.), *Perceiving, behaving, becoming: A new focus for education* (pp. 34–49). Washington, DC: Yearbook of the Association for Supervision and Curriculum Development.

McClelland, D. C. (1951). *Personality.* New York: William Sloane.

McClelland, D. C., Atkinson, J. W., Clark, R. A., & Lowell, E. L. (1953). *The achievement motive.* East Norwalk, CT: Appleton Century Crofts.

McConnell, A. R., Sherman, S. J., & Hamilton, D. L. (1994). On-line and memory-based aspects of individual and group target judgments. *Journal of Personality and Social Psychology, 67*, 173–185.

McConnell, A. R., Sherman, S. J., & Hamilton, D. L. (1997). Target entitativity: implications for information processing about individual and group targets. *Journal of Personality and Social Psychology, 72*, 750–762.

McGrath, J. E. (1984). *Groups: Interaction and performance.* Englewood Cliffs, NJ: Prentice-Hall.

Moreland, R. L., & Levine, J. M. (1982). Socialization in small groups: Temporal changes in individual-group relations. In L. Berkowitz (Ed.), *Advances in experimental social psychology* (Vol. 15, pp. 137–192). New York: Academic Press.

Park, B., & Hastie, R. (1987). Perception of variability in category development: Instance- versus abstraction-based stereotypes. *Journal of Personality and Social Psychology, 53,* 621–635.

Pickett, C. L. (2001). The effects of entitativity beliefs on implicit comparisons between group members. *Personality and Social Psychology Bulletin, 27,* 515–525.

Posner, M. I., & Keele, S. W. (1968). On the genesis of abstract ideas. *Journal of Experimental Psychology, 77,* 353–363.

Prentice, D. A., Miller, D. T., & Lightdale, J. R. (1994). Asymmetries in attachments to groups and to their members: Distinguishing between common-identity and common-bond groups. *Personality and Social Psychology Bulletin, 20,* 484–493.

Rogier, A., & Yzerbyt, V. (1999). Social attribution, correspondence bias, and the emergence of stereotypes. *Swiss Journal of Psychology, 58,* 233–240.

Rothbart, M., & Taylor, M. (1992). Social categories and social reality: Do we view social categories as natural kinds? In G. R. Semin & K. Fiedler (Eds.), *Language, interaction, and social cognition* (pp. 11–36). Newbury Park, CA: Sage.

Rushton, J. P. (1989). Genetic similarity, human altruism, and group selection. *Behavioral and Brain Sciences, 12,* 503–559.

Ryan, C. S., & Bogart, L. M. (1997). Development of new group members' in-group and out-group stereotypes: Changes in perceived group variability and ethnocentrism. *Journal of Personality and Social Psychology, 73,* 719–732.

Sanbonmatsu, D. M., Sherman, S. J., & Hamilton, D. L. (1987). Illusory correlation in the perception of individuals and groups. *Social Cognition, 5,* 1–25.

Sedikides, C., & Anderson, C. A. (1994). Causal perceptions of intertrait relations: The glue that holds person types together. *Personality and Social Psychology Bulletin, 20,* 294–302.

Shavitt, S. (1990). The role of attitude objects in attitude functions. *Journal of Experimental Social Psychology, 26,* 124–148.

Sherman, S. J., Castelli, L., & Hamilton, D. L. (2002). The spontaneous use of a group typology as an organizing principle in memory. *Journal of Personality and Social Psychology. 82,* 328–342.

Sherman, S. J., Hamilton, D. L., & Lewis, A. C. (1999). Perceived entitativity and the social identity value of group memberships. In D. Abrams & M. Hogg (Eds.), *Social identity and social cognition* (pp. 80–110). Oxford, UK: Blackwell.

Skowronski, J. J., Carlston, D. E., Mae, L., & Crawford, M. T. (1998). Spontaneous trait transference: Communicators take on the qualities they describe in others. *Journal of Personality and Social Psychology, 74,* 837–848.

Smith, E. R., & Zarate, M. A. (1990). Exemplar and prototype use in social categorization. *Social Cognition, 8,* 243–262.

Smith, M. B., Bruner, J. S., & White, R. W. (1956). *Opinions and personality.* New York: Wiley.

Srull, T. K. (1981). Person memory: Some tests of associative storage and retrieval models. *Journal of Experimental Psychology: Human Learning and Memory, 7,* 440–462.

Srull, T. K., & Wyer, R. S. (1989). Person memory and judgment. *Psychological Review, 96,* 58–83.

Stangor, C., & McMillan, D. (1992). Memory for expectancy-congruent and expectancy-incongruent social information: A meta-analytic review of the social psychological and social developmental literature. *Psychological Bulletin, 111,* 42–61.

Stevens, L. E., & Fiske, S. T. (1995). Motivation and cognition in social life: A social survival perspective. *Social Cognition, 13*, 189–214.

Susskind, J., Maurer, K., Thakkar, V., Hamilton, D. L., & Sherman, J. W. (1999). Perceiving individuals and groups: Expectancies, dispositional inferences, and causal attributions. *Journal of Personality and Social Psychology, 76*, 181–191.

Tajfel, H. (1969). Cognitive aspects of prejudice. *Journal of Social Issues, 25*, 79–97.

Tajfel, H., & Turner, J. (1979). An integrative theory of intergroup conflict. In W. Austin & S. Worchel (Eds.), *The social psychology of intergroup relations* (pp. 33–47). Monterey, CA: Brooks/Cole.

Taylor, S. E., Fiske, S. T., Etcoff, N. L., & Ruderman, A. J. (1978). Categorical and contextual bases of person memory and stereotyping. *Journal of Personality and Social Psychology, 36*, 778–793.

Thakkar, V. (2000). *The role of entitativity in judgments about groups.* Unpublished doctoral dissertation, University of California, Santa Barbara.

Turner, J. C., Hogg, M. A., Oakes, P. J., Reicher, S. D., & Wetherell, M. S. (1987). *Rediscovering the social group: A social-categorization theory.* Oxford, UK: Basil Blackwell.

Welbourne, J. L. (1999). The impact of perceived entitativity on inconsistency resolution for groups and individuals. *Journal of Experimental Social Psychology, 35*, 481–508.

White, R. (1959). Motivation reconsidered: The concept of competence. *Psychological Review, 66*, 297–333.

Wyer, R. S., & Carlston, D. W. (1979). *Social cognition, inference, and attribution.* Hillsdale, NJ: Lawrence Erlbaum Associates.

Wyer, R. S., & Gordon, S. E. (1982). The recall of information about persons and groups. *Journal of Experimental Social Psychology, 18*, 128–164.

Wyer, R. S., Bodenhausen, G. V., & Srull, T. K. (1984). The cognitive representation of persons and groups and its effects on recall and recognition memory. *Journal of Experimental Social Psychology, 20*, 445–469.

Wyer, R. S., & Srull, T. K. (1989). *Memory and cognition in its social context.* Hillsdale, NJ: Lawrence Erlbaum Associates.

Yzerbyt, V. Y., Rogier, A., & Fiske, S. T. (1998). Group entitativity and social attribution: On translating situational constraints into stereotypes. *Personality and Social Psychology Bulletin, 24*, 1089–1103.

AUTHORS' NOTE

Preparation of this chapter was facilitated by National Institute of Mental Health Grant MH-40058 and National Institute on Drug Abuse Grant K05 DA00492 to the first author. Address correspondence to Steven J. Sherman, Department of Psychology, Indiana University, 1101 E. 10th St., Bloomington, IN 47405-7007. Electronic mail may be sent via Internet to sherman@indiana.edu

9

Finding Prejudice in all the Wrong Places: On the "Social Facilitation" of Stereotypes in Anticipated Public Settings

Alan J. Lambert
Washington University

Alison Chasteen
University of Toronto

B. Keith Payne
Ohio State University

As readers of this volume can see, Bob Wyer's far-reaching influence on the field of social psychology spans many theoretical and substantive terrains. One of his better-known contributions concerns insights into the way that expectancies are represented in long-term memory, and how expectancy-consistent vs. -inconsistent information evoke different cognitive processing. This work produced precise models articulating, for example, when and why people might recall information better if it violates expectancies than if it does not (Wyer, Bodenhausen, & Srull, 1984; Wyer & Srull, 1989).

As we have learned from Bob's work, one reason why we remember such inconsistencies is that the incongruent event stimulates efforts to understand why it might have occurred in the first place. For example, a person holding expectancies about professors being boring and sedentary might be surprised to learn that Bob Wyer enjoyed climbing up the side of volcanoes during his summer treks to Asia. As with other violations of our expectancies, acquiring this information is likely to stimulate efforts to understand the incongruency. (Of course, for the people who really know him, an image of Bob trudging up active volcanoes is not surprising at all, but we digress.) These and other considerations lead not only to predictions for superior recall of expectancy-inconsistent information, but a host of fine-grained propositions addressing such factors as conditional recall probabilities and the contingency of retrieval processes on evaluative versus descriptive consistency (Wyer & Srull, 1989; Srull, 1981).

In one sense, this chapter is also about expectancy violations. Like anyone else, psychologists have expectations that guide how they make sense of their world. These expectations are often reflected in the predictions that we generate for our own experiments. Naturally, these expectations might derive from a variety of sources, ranging from the most intuitive "gut" feelings to formal theoretical models. Regardless of where these expectancies come from, data that violate them certainly grab one's attention. Depending on the circumstance, these inconsistencies might often engender frustration (back to the drawing board on our favorite theory), puzzlement (we were so sure that 3-way interaction would replicate!), or increased resolve (maybe next time …). Like anyone else, psychologists are somewhat uneasy with having their expectations violated, and are often driven to try to understand why, exactly, this might have occurred.

ON FINDING PREJUDICE
IN ALL THE WRONG PLACES

Recent work in our laboratory has been concerned with one notion about stereotypes that falls squarely into what some authors have referred to as "bubba psychology": propositions that are so obviously true that our grandmothers could (perhaps with a little background in Psychology 101) have reached the same conclusion. It certainly seems trivially obvious to suggest that people are less likely to act in prejudicial ways in public, compared to private, contexts. Everything we have learned in social psychology, beginning with the classic studies on conformity by Asch (1955), suggests that prejudicial behavior, like other unpopular acts, should be less likely to emerge when others are privy to our behaviors than if they are not. As we describe in more detail below, this expectation was strongly violated by some initial studies. Specifically, we discovered consistent tendencies for our participants to display greater levels of stereotypic judgment in public, compared to private contexts.

Our response to these expectancy violations could not have made Bob Wyer happier, for two reasons. First, we did what his model would have predicted: the inconsistency certainly grabbed our attention and stimulated us to figure out why it might have occurred. Second—and less flattering to us—our initial efforts to resolve the inconsistency met a series of dead-ends, with several of our hunches receiving absolutely no support from the data. We eventually reached greater theoretical understanding of these matters, but only through much trial and error. Although we didn't realize it at the time, our strategy was heavily influenced by one of Bob's favorite maxims (Wyerism #1), that unexpected outcomes in the data can sometimes be quite useful and perhaps even more interesting than the results one expected all along. (Actually, Bob seems to have a warm spot in his heart for counterintuitive findings, perhaps reflecting a more general dispositional delight at upsetting the status quo, in psychology as well as in politics). As Bob often emphasized, counterintuitive findings can be quite useful, especially if researchers stay the course and continue to work in the same research paradigm, rather than abandon ship in search of more promising areas of research (see Wyer, Lambert, Budesheim, & Gruenfeld, 1992, p. 33, for a relevant discussion). In retrospect, we are glad that we followed the former rather than the latter strategy. Thus although much of the research to be discussed below has little direct connection with Bob's own work, our intellectual debt to him is far greater than it might appear.

MCGUIRE'S LAMENT: ON THE "STRANGE NEGLECT" OF INTERPERSONAL PROCESSES IN SOCIAL PSYCHOLOGY

Because this chapter is largely about surprise and expectancy violation, it seems fitting to begin with a more general point made by Bill McGuire (see chapter 2 of this volume), regarding the "strange neglect" (p. 7) of interpersonal processes by social psychologists since the 1960s, including social cognition researchers. As McGuire notes, certain periods in our field (e.g., in the 1940s through the mid-1950s) reflected a strong and active interest in interpersonal social psychology. We use *interpersonal* in a deliberately broad sense here (as does McGuire), embracing a large class of paradigms generally oriented toward understanding the cognitive, behavioral, and affective responses elicited by or associated with actual or anticipated interactions with one or more other individuals. Since the late 1950s, however, the general trend has been toward the study of intrapersonal mechanisms, that is, those not directly involving interactions with others (Neisser, 1980). This is especially surprising, given that at least one famous definition of our field framed social psychology as the study of how the actual or imagined presence of others affects thoughts, feelings, and behaviors (Allport, 1985).

It is interesting to speculate why this trend might have developed, and McGuire has his own thoughts on this matter. Although we have little to add to his insightful commentary, we might add that many social cognition theorists (including Bob Wyer) have been particularly impressed by the power and precision offered by measures traditionally used by cognitive psychologists (e.g., reaction time, free recall) to study a range of important social phenomena, such as impression formation (Srull, 1984). To be sure, the whole purpose in using these measures was to gain a better understanding of the underlying processes guiding manifestly interpersonal phenomena. (What is more "social" than impression formation?)

Nevertheless, McGuire's "strange neglect" comment certainly rings true, in the sense that the typical social cognition experiment has been aimed at understanding "in the head" phenomena (e.g., cognitive representation of persons and groups) that can be studied without having to include interpersonal contact as a literal component of the experimental design. This trend can be seen as an outgrowth of a number of intrinsic values held by many social cognition researchers, including high premium on precision of measurement and experimental control and reliance on methods (e.g., RTs) of measuring internal processes (e.g., cognitive accessibility, representation of knowledge in long-term memory) that are best used when the participants are isolated from others. In combination, these factors all point to the fact that social cognition has, admittedly, strayed somewhat from Allport's view of the field insofar as there has been a less explicit focus on how the actual and imagined presence of others might affect how we think about and respond to our social world.

HISTORICAL TRENDS IN THE STUDY OF PRIVATE VS. PUBLIC CONTEXTS IN EXPERIMENTAL SOCIAL PSYCHOLOGY

It is useful at this point to take a few steps backward and consider how previous generations of social psychologists might have studied interpersonal processes (defined broadly) in experimental contexts. One key aspect of "interpersonal settings" is that other people are privy to our behavior. For purposes of this chapter, we broadly characterize such settings as "public contexts." Social psychologists have known for quite some time that people act in predictably different ways in public, compared to how they act in more private settings, and indeed this assumption lies at the heart of at least four major subdisciplines in our field: Conformity (Asch, 1955), impression management (Schlenker, Britt, & Pennington, 1996), accountability (Tetlock, 1992), and the social facilitation literature (Baron, 1986; Zajonc, 1965).

There are many ways to manipulate the private versus public contexts in the laboratory. One obvious solution is to have all participants perform the same task, but have them do so either alone or in the physical presence of others. In fact, this simple manipulation was used in what is regarded as one of the first experiments in social psychology (Triplett, 1898). This famous study found that children performed a well-learned task (reeling in a fishing line) faster if they performed the task in public, compared to a private context, and eventually sparked widespread interest in the effect of audiences on task performance (Geen & Gange, 1977).

Although operationalizations of private settings are straightforward, public contexts pose somewhat greater methodological challenges. This is because researchers have many choices as to what the "other people" might be doing (from the perspective of the participant, that is). For example, these others might observe the participant, creating a context of one "actor" and multiple members of an "audience." (In most cases, the audiences play a relatively passive role and are often hired by the experimenter as confederates.) Alternatively, one might employ a "co-actor" paradigm in which all of the "real" participants are physically present in the same room, performing the same task.

Of the two methodologies noted above, co-actor methodologies arguably introduce more experimental noise, because there is no control over how the "co-actors" might perform from session to session. (Participants in one session might, on average, perform the task significantly better than participants in another session, making it difficult to compare the two experimental sessions directly.) In contrast, one has more control over the behavior of the audiences, in that one can instruct them to respond to the single actor-participant in the same manner (e.g., "Please strike an air of mild interest but please do not smile at the participant or say anything during the task."). However, this latter approach still creates some worries because it is impossible to fully eliminate differences from session to session in terms of how these live audiences might be responding to the real participant.

There is a third, classic approach to instantiating public settings that represents something of a compromise of the previous two: anticipated public contexts (Zajonc, 1960; Tetlock, 1992). In such settings, participants expect to share and discuss their responses with other participants who had engaged in the same task. This task represents a blending of the two approaches above, in that participants believe that other participants (technically co-actors) will have the opportunity to appraise and evaluate their own work. However, it has more experimental control, in that all participants actually perform the same task under the same physical conditions: it is the mental expectation of the impending discussion that is different across conditions, even though all participants actually perform the task in isolation from others.

SOCIAL VS. "NON-SOCIAL" SOCIAL PSYCHOLOGY

Anticipated public settings are not the same thing as actual public settings. But the two settings are not as different as one might think, at least in terms of the behavioral consequences of placing people in them. Indeed, there is ample evidence that several classic findings generalize across anticipated and actual public settings. For example, although though most classic demonstrations of social facilitation effects have been conducted in actual public settings, such effects also occur when participants expect that other people will be evaluating their performance in the future (Baron, 1986). This convergence is easily explained: Compared to private settings, anticipated as well as actual public settings trigger significantly greater levels of attentional conflict, evaluation apprehension, and social anxiety (Baron, 1986), all of which are thought to drive social facilitation effects to varying degrees. (We discuss the competing explanations for social facilitation effects later in this chapter.)

In our view, therefore, one might argue that the question of whether the public setting is actual or anticipated is not the key issue. Rather, the question is whether the experimental manipulation is able to successfully instantiate the processes presumed to mediate the effect of interest. In the case of social facilitation, for example, it appears (ironically enough) that the underlying mechanism is not so "social" after all. Indeed, one striking conclusion reached in this area is that classic social facilitation effects can be produced by simply introducing a distracting inanimate stimulus, such as a flashing light (Baron, 1986). Does this mean that social facilitation effects have nothing to do with audiences or co-actor settings? Obviously not. Rather, the point is that psychologists can gain greater understanding of a manifestly "social" and interpersonal phenomenon through methodologies that seem rather "non-social" at first blush.

STRANGE NEGLECT, REDUX: THE CURIOUS ABSENCE OF EXPERIMENTAL RESEARCH ON PRIVATE VS. PUBLIC EXPRESSIONS OF PREJUDICE

Setting aside these methodological issues, it is certainly clear that many important branches of social psychology (e.g., conformity, accountability, and impression management) have long relied on manipulations of private versus public contexts, broadly defined. One might imagine that stereotyping researchers would have been especially likely to use this methodology. Contemporary and classic models of stereotyping (Allport, 1954; Bodenhausen & Macrae, 1998; Brewer, 1988; Dovidio & Gaertner, 1986; Fiske & Neuberg, 1990) assume that people are often motivated to avoid open expression of their prejudicial views about others. This is especially true with respect to racial prejudice in the post-civil rights era in American society, in which "it is no longer merely immoral to discriminate against Blacks, it is also illegal" (Gaertner & Dovidio, 1986; p. 66). It seems reasonable to assume, therefore, that the private versus public nature of the judgmental setting might powerfully moderate how people express versus suppress (conceal) their prejudicial views. Given the theoretical and practical importance of this idea, one might imagine there to be a plethora of studies to investigate this idea empirically.

Surprisingly, this is not the case. Although situational context is often discussed as a likely moderator of stereotyping effects, there is only a small handful of studies to actually investigate the moderating effects of private versus public contexts empirically (Blanchard, Lilly, & Vaughn, 1991; Dutton & Yee, 1974; Plant & Devine, 1998; Monteith, Deneen, & Tooman, 1996). Thus there is actually only a small amount of data that speak directly to this issue. Moreover, among these few studies, there is a surprisingly mixed pattern of data. Of the studies noted above, for example, two (Dutton & Yee, 1974; Plant & Devine, 1998) yielded a fairly intuitive pattern (greater evidence of concealment in public), but the other two studies (Blanchard et al., 1991; Monteith et al., 1996) found no effect of situational context at all.

Curiouser and Curiouser

Nevertheless, given what we know about normative pressures to conform (Asch, 1955) one might imagine that people should be more motivated to hide their prejudicial views in public compared to private contexts. Indeed, our first effort in this area (Lambert, Cronen, Chasteen, & Lickel, 1996) was based on this very assumption. Our original objective was to investigate whether stereotype inhibition (suppression) might be mediated by conscious, or unconscious, processes. As a first step in this research, we sought initially to simply find evidence for public inhibition. To this end, we initially measured participants' racial attitudes and, in an ostensibly unrelated study two months later, they were asked to form an impression of a single Black individual in one of two settings. Half of the participants were told that their responses would be confidential, but the other participants were told that they would be asked to share and discuss their impressions with the other participants in the testing session. Following this, all participants were asked to form an impression of a single Black individual whose race was subtly cued in the context of an evaluatively ambiguous passage about this individual similar to that used by Srull and Wyer (1979).

The only problem with our plan to understand public inhibition is that participants did not inhibit. In fact, participants were even more likely to use their own stereotypic attitudes as a basis for responding to the target in the anticipated public context. This was revealed by the stronger pattern of correlations between group attitudes and judgments of the target (so-called "attitude-behavior relations") in the public, compared to the private, condition. It is important to note that the greater role of stereotypic attitudes was symmetric, and did not depend on whether participants actually held pro- or anti-Black views. In other words, we found that among the pro-Black participants, they used their "pro" attitudes more if they were assigned to the anticipated public rather than to the private context. But the same was true of the anti-Black participants: their negative views played a larger role in reactions to the target if these judgments were rendered in the public context. In other words, the public context polarized differences between how the "pros" and the "antis" reacted to the target, moving the former group in a more favorable direction, and the latter group in a more unfavorable direction relative to the private context. Evidence for this effect was obtained across two studies.

What's Not Going On

Another of Bob's favorite maxims (Wyerism #2) was to insist on addressing the processes underlying an intriguing pattern of data (rather than simply describing it), expressing this vocally (in his trademark booming/raspy voice) with the question, "What's really going on here?" Nevertheless, it may be useful in this context to put somewhat of a Popperian spin on the question, in the sense of ruling out potential explanations. A series of studies in our lab ruled out two of these. First, given the tendency for people to assume that their views are widely shared by others (Ross, Greene, & House, 1977), such "false consensus" effects might conceivably have encouraged participants in the anticipated public condition to express their own underlying views through a kind of "consensual validation." We were able to rule this explanation out in different ways. In one study, we found that participants still expressed their racial attitudes in anticipated public settings, even when they expected to disclose their judgments to a single individual whose explicitly pro- or anti-Black racial views were known in advance (Lambert, Cronen, Chasteen, & Manier, 1997). For example, contrary to what a false consensus-based explanation might predict, anti-Black participants still judged the Black target in a relatively negative manner, regardless of whether their "discussion partner" was known to hold strongly positive or negative racial attitudes.

Another explanation for our findings derives from previous work in the accountability area (Tetlock, 1992), which suggests that when people anticipate a public discussion of their views, they sometimes engage in a "bolstering" process, in which they actively generate reasons why they think their views are correct. To the extent that such bolstering mechanisms are less likely to occur in a private context (in which there is little need to justify one's responses), this could explain why public contexts might tend to polarize responses by the pro- and anti-Black participants. Although we offered some speculative discussion of the viability of this explanation (Lambert, Chasteen, Khan, & Manier, 1998) we subsequently were unable to generate any definitive evidence in support of it.

Thus we had on our hands a highly counterintuitive but replicable effect with little clue as to exactly why it might be occurring. As it turned out, we have only recently discovered what is really going on, and it is much different from what we thought at first.

A BRIEF REVIEW OF THE SOCIAL FACILITATION LITERATURE

Habit represents one of the oldest constructs in psychology (Hull, 1943; James, 1980), but it gained renewed prominence in the mid-1960s with the publication of Robert Zajonc's (1965) landmark paper. Earlier we had noted the classic finding by Triplett (1898), who found that performance was enhanced in a public setting. However, psychologists discovered that public settings could also impair performance relative to private contexts (Allport, 1924). Drawing from drive theory (Hull, 1943), Zajonc argued that people are more likely to rely on habitual behavior (or "dominant responses," as they are referred to in this area) if they perform these tasks along with, or are being observed by, other people than if they are not. If so, one should expect public audiences to facilitate task performance only to the extent that the dominant response would yield the correct answer. Although there is lively debate as to the exact mechanisms underlying social facilitation, research over the last 30 years has generated impressive support for Zajonc's formulation with both human and non-human species (Zajonc, Heingartner, & Herman, 1969; for reviews, see Geen & Gange, 1977; Sanders, 1981).

For human studies, at least, there is some disagreement as to whether experimental manipulation of private versus public contexts is sufficient to produce social facilitation in its own right, independent of individual differences in social anxiety. Anxiety is relevant to drive-based accounts, insofar as this represents a specific type of arousal that is theorized to energize well-learned, dominant responses. Some studies show strong moderation effects, such that reliable social facilitation effects arise only among high anxious participants (for whom the "drive" state is presumably greater). When one collapses over, or ignores, individual differences in anxiety, social facilitation emerges only in relatively weak form. Other studies have shown "weak moderation," in the sense that social facilitation effects are reliably obtained collapsing over social anxiety (although such effects may well be stronger among high anxious participants). This point is relevant for present concerns because in our research, the strength of anxiety in moderating our observed social facilitation effects appears to vary across different studies.

STEREOTYPES AS DOMINANT RESPONSES

Perhaps because of its historical ties to neo-behaviorism, the social facilitation literature has focused almost exclusively on the facilitating effects of audiences on behavioral performance (Geen & Gange, 1977). There is no reason, however that one could not broaden conceptualization of well-learned procedures to the cognitive domain, as in the formation of social stereotypes or strong attitudes. In other words, attitudes (strong ones, at least) are dominant responses, in the sense that they represent well-learned associations between a particular attitude object (e.g.; Blacks, grandmothers, Bob Wyer), and one's cognitive or affective appraisal of it.

Taken on its own, conceptualizing stereotypes as well-learned mental associations is not an especially novel idea (Devine, 1989). Nevertheless, we are not aware of any theorist who explicitly conceptualizes stereotypes (or strong attitudes) as a dominant response with specific reference to a social facilitation framework. Indeed, we were unable to find even one passing mention of the social facilitation area in two edited volumes on stereotyping (Dovidio & Gaertner, 1986; Wyer, 1998), two advanced texts in attitudes and information processing (Ajzen, 1988; Petty & Krosnick, 1995), two comprehensive overviews of the social cognition area (Fiske & Taylor, 1991; Wyer & Srull, 1994), or a dozen or so current social psychology texts. Similarly, decades of research in the social facilitation literature contains only a few scattered papers (e.g. Baron, 1986) that have empirically extended the dominant response framework to mental habits, such as stereotypes or attitudes.

We believe that conceptualizing stereotypes as dominant responses has value insofar as it fosters yet-unrealized connections between the attitude and social facilitation literatures. Moreover, when applied to the specific case of stereotypes, this framework leads to an extremely counterintuitive prediction. Most contemporary stereotyping models stipulate that people should be less likely to express their stereotypic views in public compared to private settings, but our model makes the exact opposite prediction. Note that this provides an (admittedly post-hoc) explanation of the results obtained by Lambert et al. (1996) who, it will be recalled, found greater impact of racial attitudes in an anticipated public context. However, our earlier work was not designed to provide a definitive test of this framework. A series of studies, to be described, were designed to do just that. We first describe a recent study patterned after the general methodology of our earlier work.

AN IMPRESSION FORMATION STUDY

There is ample empirical evidence showing that White Americans differ in terms of whether they associate positive or negative sentiments with Blacks. When such data are viewed through the lens of social facilitation, therefore, it is apparent that the "dominant response" towards Blacks might vary from individual to individual. There is strong debate as to the best way to capture this variance across individuals, and at the present time there is no single "best" measure of racial sentiment. In our recent work we sidestep this conundrum by using several different well-validated measures, all of which have been shown to reliably capture meaningful variation (albeit in different ways) in the extent to which people personally view Blacks in a positive or negative fashion. These included the modern racism (McConahay, 1986), social dominance orientation (Sidanius, Pratto, & Bobo, 1996), and humanism egalitarianism scales (Katz & Hass, 1988). This multi-method approach stands in contrast to our earlier work, which measured racial attitudes using only the modern racism scale. Obviously, a rigorous test of our "dominant response" model requires that we show evidence for it, generalizing about the specific way that stereotypic beliefs are operationalized.

As in our earlier studies, we first had our participants ($N = 48$) complete the battery of individual difference measures (as mentioned previously). Two months later, they were brought back into the laboratory and were randomly assigned to judge a Black target in either a private or anticipated public setting. As before, our main interest was in the pattern of correlations between individual differences in racial sentiment and participants' overall reactions to the target. After rendering their impressions of the target person, participants completed a measure of social (trait) anxiety on the basis of their reactions to a six-item anxiety subscale of an instrument developed by Fenigstein, Scheier, and Buss (1975). Items on the survey referred to general anxiety about public settings and evaluation apprehension (e.g., I have trouble working when someone is watching me; large groups make me nervous.) Scores on the composite trait-anxiety measure did not vary as a function of the context (private vs. anticipated public) to which participants had been assigned, and did not correlate with any of the measures of racial sentiment noted above.

Results

We expected to generally replicate previous findings by Lambert et al. (1996) insofar as we expected stronger correlations in the anticipated public compared to the private setting. However, we had some reason to suppose that the "public expression effect" would be especially pronounced among the high anxiety participants. In contrast, low anxiety participants should show little variation in their responses across the two types of contexts. Another way of stating this prediction is that high and low anxiety participants should differ in the use of their stereotypic attitudes only in the anticipated public condition, since this is the context that primarily "draws out" the relevance of their different levels of social anxiety. This is precisely what we found. Moreover, as it turned out, our results generalized across the different measures of racial attitudes. For ease of exposition, therefore, we formed a general index of stereotypic attitudes averaging across the modern racism, social dominance, and egalitarianism scales (after standardization and reverse scoring, where appropriate); higher numbers on this index correspond to more favorable views toward Blacks.

As seen in Fig. 9.1, a pattern of modest positive correlations emerged among participants assigned to the private condition, regardless of whether participants were high ($r = .22$) or low (.13) in social anxiety, both correlations ns. When participants were assigned to anticipated public settings, the attitude-behavior relation was, as predicted, greatly strengthened in the case of the high anxiety participants ($r = .70, p < .01$), but not the low anxiety participants ($r = -.17$, ns.). Another way of looking at these data is that the difference between high versus low anxiety participants was evident only in the anticipated public, but not the private, condition. This conclusion is reflected by the fact that the Racial Attitude X Anxiety interaction was highly significant in the public setting, but not the private setting. Closer inspection of Fig. 9.1 shows that, as in Lambert et al. (1996), the findings were symmetrical in that the effect of the anticipated public set was similar, regardless of whether participants held relatively pro or anti-Black participants. In other words, the public setting seemed to accentuate the extent to which participants used their racial attitudes as a basis for responding to the target, and this was true regardless of whether participants held favorable, or unfavorable, views toward the group to which he or she belonged.

But What's Really Going On?

If stereotypic attitudes can be thought of as dominant responses, why, exactly, might people be more likely to express them in public? Given that our framework is rooted in the social facilitation literature, one might expect us to draw from this literature in seeking answers to this question. Unfortunately, the social facilitation literature has never resolved why dominant responses might be more likely to occur in public compared to private settings. Although several specific models have been proposed (Baron, 1986), our reading of this literature reveals two general classes of explanations, as described below.

Drive-Based (Habit-Strengthening) Models

One class of explanations is rooted in Hullian views of drive, primarily emphasizing the energizing role of arousal on dominant responses.

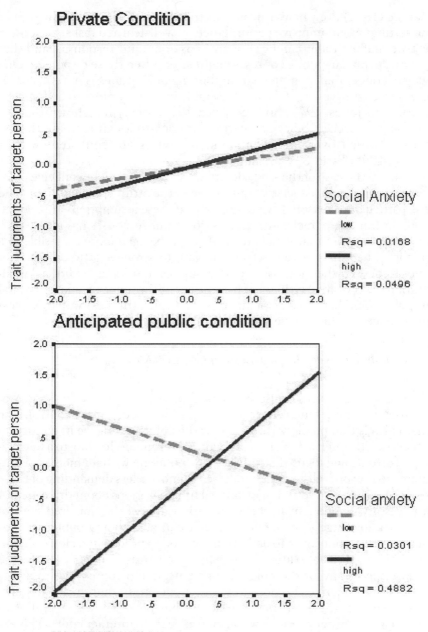

FIG. 9.1   Best-fitting regression lines corresponding to the regression of target judge-ments on racial attitudes for private and anticipated public condition as a function of trait anxiety level. Experiment 1. Values respresent standardized scores.

Zajonc (1965) drew heavily from this framework in explaining why public settings might improve performance on well-learned tasks. Suppose it is true that attitudes can be conceived as dominant responses, and that placing people in public contexts might strengthen these responses. One way of conceptualizing such strengthening of attitudes is in terms of increased cognitive accessibility. Research in the priming area (Higgins, Rholes, & Jones, 1977; Srull & Wyer, 1979, 1980) has shown that increasing the accessibility of a particular construct can increase the extent to which overt judgments and behaviors are consistent with it (Fazio, 1995; Fazio & Williams, 1986).

Thus in the case of the study described above, one might conceive of racial attitudes as an associative link between the attitude object Blacks and the participants' personal evaluation of it. If these assumptions are correct, and our framing of racial attitudes as dominant responses has merit, then one could predict that racial attitudes might become more accessible in a public rather than private setting, leading to stronger attitude-behavior consistency. Furthermore, one could easily account for an additional moderating effect of anxiety, inasmuch as the energizing force of anxiety/arousal in public (and hence, accessibility of stereotypic attitudes) would be most pronounced for high anxiety participants.

Cognitive-Based (Impairment-of-Control) Models

A second hypothesis also predicts greater reliance on dominant responses, but frames such effects in terms of a loss of cognitive control. The main idea is that public settings impair the ability to engage in controlled processing through a depletion of cognitive resources, leading to a narrowing of attentional focus (Easterbrook, 1959) along with an increased tendency to rely on well-learned processes which are less demanding of these resources (Baron, 1986). Importantly, Hullian notions about drive are not a necessary component in this view. Advocates of the impaired-control view acknowledge that the arousal that can accompany public settings may, in itself, contribute to deficits in controlled processing. However, impaired control can also arise through more "cognitive" factors, such as the distracting nature of the public context itself and ruminative thoughts about the evaluative reactions from other persons in that setting (regardless of whether these others are co-actors, passive observers, or part of an unseen group of persons with whom one expects to interact later). This explanation could also account for our findings, insofar as the depletion of cognitive resources through any or all of the factors noted above presumably would lead to greater reliance on stereotypic attitudes as a heuristic basis for responding to the target person.

On the "Plusses" and "Minuses" of Social Facilitation

A heuristically useful contrast between the two views concerns their emphasis on whether key processes are being augmented (added) or impaired (taken away). The habit-strengthening view stresses that something is being added, the strength of the dominant response, fueled by the dynamic, motivating force of arousal. On the other hand, the impaired-control view stresses that something is being taken away, the ability to effectively engage in controlled processes. As social facilitation theorists have long acknowledged, drive-based and control-based models often lead, despite their theoretical differences, to very similar predictions. Indeed, as we have seen, both can account for the findings presented thus far.

We appreciate the fact that to some readers, the "strengthened stereotype" and "weakened control" explanations may sound like different ways of saying the same thing. A football metaphor is useful in terms of illustrating this distinction. Consider two fans who are watching the same football game and who both are trying to explain why, in the second half of play, team X suddenly starts scoring touchdowns against team Y after a miserable first half of play. One fan could plausibly argue that these touchdowns reflect the augmented power of X's offense. However, the other fan could just as easily account for the sudden surge in terms of an impaired defense of team Y. (Of course, it could reflect both effects in combination.) As football fans know, however, a sudden surge in touchdowns leaves it unclear as to whether the offense is getting stronger, or the defense is getting weaker.

Most studies in the social facilitation literature predated the recent surge of interest in the social cognition literature in separating automatic from controlled processes (e.g., Bargh, 1994; Chaiken & Trope, 1999; Fazio, Jackson, Dunton, & Williams, 1995). Even so, the social facilitation literature may be viewed as grappling with many of the same issues, even though details of the theoretical models and some crucial terminology may be different. In other words, the inherent difficulty of cleanly separating automatic from controlled processes lies at the heart of the long-running debate regarding the viability of "pure" drive accounts as articulated by a Hull/Zajonc perspective (which embrace the idea of strengthened activation) from the kind of deficits-in-control account advanced by Baron (1986). Thus we turn to a new paradigm that holds some promise as a way of gaining greater clarity on these matters.

STEREOTYPIC ERRORS
IN PERCEPTUAL IDENTIFICATION

In a recent experimental paradigm developed by Payne and colleagues (Payne, 2001; Payne et al., 2002; in press), participants are presented with pictures of handguns and hand tools on a computer monitor. Their assignment was to correctly identify each item by pressing either a key labeled "gun" or "tool" on the keyboard. Immediately before each target item, faces of Black and White persons are flashed briefly (but visibly) for a duration of 200 ms. Participants are told that they should be as accurate as they can, but that they were allowed only a very brief "response window" of 550 ms to make their responses. Failure to respond within this interval results in the display of a large red exclamation point, indicating to participants that they had not responded fast enough. After a series of practice trials, most participants typically become fairly adept at the task, at least in terms of responding within the response window. However, participants often make errors, and the types of errors they make are disproportionally stereotypic in nature. For example, when participants are actually presented with a tool, they are more likely to mistakenly respond "gun" if they were primed with a Black rather than a White face (Payne, 2001).

This paradigm is obviously different from the impression-formation task presented earlier. In the first study, our major focus was on individual differences in racial attitudes. In that study, all participants were presented with the same Black target, and the impact of stereotypic processing was assessed by measuring the relation between participants' own evaluations of Blacks and their evaluation of a single group member. In contrast, this perceptual identification task focuses on widely shared stereotypes. In this case, we measure the impact of stereotypes as the average difference between behavior in the presence of a Black prime compared to a White prime. Thus whereas the first study held constant the target stimuli and measured individual variability in responses, the second study averages across individuals and compares across experimental conditions. Central to both, however, is the effect of race on participants' judgments.

Our theoretical model suggests that people should be more likely to make stereotypic errors when they complete this task in an anticipated public, compared to a private, setting. We recently conducted a study ($N = 127$) to test this prediction. All participants completed the "guns and tools task" under either a private or anticipated public context. Operationalization of the private/public context was very similar to the first study reported earlier. Other things being equal, we expected that stereotypic errors would be more likely under anticipated public compared to private settings.

This was in fact the case, as shown in Fig. 9.2. This figure shows the pattern of errors as function of prime type (Black vs. White face) and the actual identity of the object. As seen here, the tendency to make stereotypic errors (e.g., mistakenly identifying a tool as a gun when primed with a Black face) was exacerbated in the anticipated public condition, which was reflected in a significant three-way Prime X Object X Context interaction. (Note also that the overall proportion of errors was greater in the public set, suggesting

Private Condition

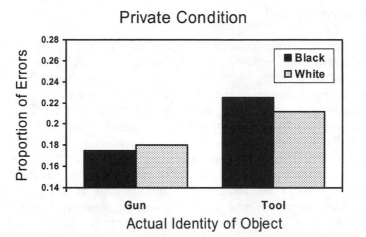

Anticipated Public Condition

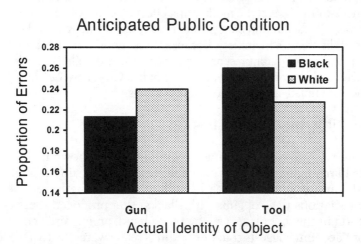

FIG. 9.2   Proportion of erros as a function of situational context (private vs. antici-pated public), actual idenity of object (gun vs. tool), and prime race (Black vs. White). Experiment 2.

that participants were less able to concentrate on the task in this condition; this point becomes important. Thus once again we found that participants responded in a more stereotypical way if they expected to share their re-sponses with others than if they did not.

Anxiety Analyses

Although the first study operationalized anxiety as a trait variable, our main focus in this study was on so-called "state" anxiety (i.e., with regard to participants' worries or concerns about the specific situational context). State anxiety arguably represents the more critical variable, because our framework suggests that the context-specific, "local" anxiety about the specifics of the task might provide the most proximal determinant of whether the anticipated public context actually elicits stereotypic responding. Two findings of interest emerged from these data. First, state anxiety was significantly higher in the anticipated public setting. This confirms our assumptions about the potential for the public setting to increase greater arousal and/or potentially distracting worries relative to the private context. Further analyses revealed a somewhat complex mediated-moderator effect, such that the greater surge in stereotypic errors in the public condition was somewhat more pronounced among participants experiencing greater-than-average amounts of anxiety in that condition. However, as one can see from Fig. 9.2, the moderating effect of anxiety was relatively weak, insofar as social facilitation effects were readily apparent, even collapsing over individual differences in anxiety. Because these modest moderator effects are not of critical concern for present purposes, we defer detailed consideration of them here. (See Lambert, Payne, Jacoby, Shaffer, Chasteen, & Khan, in press, for a more complete discussion of these findings.)

Addressing the Process Issue

There are two ways of explaining the kind of effects shown in Fig. 9.2. On the one hand, a drive-based account suggests that our findings reflected a strengthening of habit, insofar as the public setting strengthened the stereotypic associations (e.g., of guns with Blacks) that produced these errors of perception in the first place. On the other hand, an impaired control (distraction) account suggests that our findings really were due to a loss of participants' ability to expend the cognitive effort in tracking and responding correctly to the veridical properties of the target stimuli. This is where Jacoby's (1991) process dissociation procedure comes into play.

Both Payne (2001) and Payne, Lambert, and Jacoby (in press) have used this perceptual identification task in conjunction with the process dissociation procedure (Jacoby, 1991; Jacoby, Begg, & Toth, 1997; Jacoby, Kelley, & McElree, 1999). Importantly, this procedure permits decomposition of participants' responses to the same task into estimates of automatic and controlled processing. This approach differs from that of most current work in the social cognition area, which uses different tasks and measures to tease apart the influences of automatic and controlled mechanisms (e.g., Fazio et al., 1995; Wittenbrink et al. 1997).

As in other applications of process dissociation, this task has both congruent and incongruent trials. Congruent conditions are the White-tool pairs and the Black-gun pairs. In these cases, responding either on the basis of the racial category or on the basis of the actual target will lead to the correct answer. For example, when a Black face is followed by a gun, responding either in a controlled way using the objectively correct information or responding based on the stereotype in the absence of control would lead to the "gun" response. The incongruent conditions include the White-gun and Black-tool pairs. In these conditions, the racial stereotypes and controlled processing of the target object lead to contradictory responses. For example, when a Black face is followed by a tool, race stereotypes would lead to an erroneous "gun" response, while the objective information would lead to the "tool" response. A stereotypic response in this condition is clearly unintentional, as it leads to a "gun" response even as a tool sits before the participant's eyes.

The process dissociation approach entails systematically analyzing the pattern of "hits" and "false alarms" to congruent and incongruent trials by decomposing performance on a single task into two estimates: cognitive control and accessibility bias. As the terms imply, cognitive control represents an estimate of intentionally controlled processing, whereas accessibility bias provides an estimate of automatic processing. In this paradigm, control refers to the ability of participants to respond based on the objective features of the target stimulus. That is, it reflects the ability to respond "gun" when guns are actually presented, and to respond "tool" when tools are presented. Perfect control means that there would be no errors, regardless of the nature of the primes. On any given trial, however, control may fail, raising the question of how the presence of the Black versus White prime might influence responses. This is where accessibility bias comes into play. In this study, accessibility bias estimates were constructed so that higher values reflect a greater bias toward responding "gun." Therefore a stereotypical bias is shown if bias estimates are higher (i.e., reflecting greater tendencies to respond "gun") when primed with Black rather than White faces. Space does not permit extensive discussion of the computation of control and accessibility bias, but essentially it involves solving algebraically, for the two parameters given, the pattern of hits and false alarms on congruent versus incongruent trials. (For details and illustrative examples pertaining to the computation of accessibility bias and control estimates, see Payne, 2001; Payne et al., 2002, in press).

These matters are important for present concerns because deriving estimates of cognitive control and accessibility bias provides leverage in teasing apart why anticipated public settings might have increased the tendency to respond in a stereotypic manner, as shown in Fig. 9.2. Was it due to a strengthening of stereotypic bias, as a drive-based account might suggest? If so, this should show up in the accessibility parameter, conceptually reflecting a strengthening of the stereotypic association between, for example, Blacks and guns. On the other hand, our findings could also reflect impairment of cognitive control. In this latter case, the tendency to find more stereotypic responding in the public context would not entail strengthening of the stereotype per se. Rather, this account suggests that public settings impair control, leading to more responses based on the most accessible piece of information at the time, ultimately producing greater reliance on the stereotype, and less on the veridical features of the target.

Estimates of Control and Bias

Table 9.1 shows the estimates of control (top row) and bias (second row) as a function of race of the prime and situational context. Estimates of control range from theoretical minimum of 0 (chance responding) to a theoretical maximum of 1 (perfect accuracy, with no errors). Bias estimates also range from a hypothetical minimum and maximum of 0 and 1, respectively, with higher numbers indicating a greater probability of responding "gun" when control fails.

These estimates were analyzed as a function of situational context and race of the prime. These analyses yielded three primary findings, the first two of which replicated earlier results by Payne (2001). First, race of the prime did not affect estimates of control, meaning that the ability to correctly attend to the features of the target (tool or gun) was not contingent on the race of the prime per se. Second, race of the prime significantly affected accessibility bias. In other words, when participants did make an error on any given trial, they were much more likely to respond "gun" when primed with the Black rather than the White prime, and more likely to respond "tool" when primed with the White compared to the Black prime.

TABLE 9.1
Estimates of Control and Accessibility Bias

	Context			
	Private		Anticipated Public	
	Prime Race		Prime Race	
	Black	White	Black	White
Cognitive control	.60	.61	.53	.53
Accessibility bias	.56	.53	.56	.49

Third, and most important for present concerns, control was significantly lower in the anticipated public compared to the private condition (.53 vs. .60), but accessibility bias was completely unaffected by context. These findings are critical for our purposes, because they speak to the viability of the two competing explanations for social facilitation. On the one hand, these findings do not support a drive-based account. This explanation suggests that stereotypic bias should have been strengthened in the public context, but it was not. Stereotypic bias was only affected by the race of the prime. In contrast, cognitive control was lower in the public setting, thus supporting the impaired control account.

If we had not used process dissociation in this study, the fact that stereotypic errors reliably increased in the anticipated public condition (see Fig. 9.2) might be interpreted to suggest that race information was being processed to a greater extent when time was limited, possibly as an effort-saving strategy (e.g., Bodenhausen & Lichtenstein, 1987). Or, more colloquially, that the public setting had increased the strength of heuristic processing. This is not what our data show. Instead, race information was processed to the same extent, regardless of situational context. Thus the observed increase in stereotype-congruent errors in the anticipated public condition was wholly due to the fact that cognitive control failed and, when this happened, participants' responses were determined by accessibility bias.

GENERAL DISCUSSION

Several lines of work in social psychology suggest that people should "be on their best behavior" when they are in public compared to private contexts. This idea is certainly prevalent in the impression management literature, which assumes that people are generally motivated to act in socially desirable ways when others are privy to our actions (Schlenker et al., 1996), and a similar implication can be drawn from work on conformity and normative influence (Asch, 1955). Finally, several stereotyping models implicitly or explicitly assume that public settings should lead people to act in less prejudicial ways. This is especially true of the aversive racism framework, which explicitly assumes that people are motivated to "avoid acting in recognizably unfavorably or normatively inappropriate ways" (Gaertner & Dovidio, 1986, p. 66). For all of these reasons, it seems odd to suggest that stereotypes and prejudice might actually be more pronounced in public compared to private settings. Yet this is exactly what our findings show.

Relation of our Findings to the "Cognitive Load" Literature

Although current stereotyping models do not explicitly predict that prejudice can be exacerbated by public settings, one might argue that our findings are not completely incompatible with the stereotyping literature, either. The process dissociation analyses reported earlier suggested that there was a greater impairment of control in the anticipated public compared to the private setting, thus leading to greater reliance on stereotypes in the former compared to the latter condition. This explanation appears to overlap with the implications of the "cognitive load" literature (e.g., Bodenhausen & Wyer, 1985; Rothbart et al., 1978; Gilbert & Hixon, 1991; Macrae, Milne, & Bodenhausen, 1994). In other words, the notion that people rely on dominant responses in response to the attentional demands of public settings certainly seems compatible with the notion that people rely on stereotypes as labor-saving devices to save cognitive effort (Allport, 1954). To the extent that anticipated public settings deplete cognitive resources, one might explain greater impact of stereotypic attitudes in this condition as an important and yet unexplored consequence of the well-known cognitive efficiency principle.

On one hand, we readily agree that there is likely to be important overlap between the mechanisms underlying our findings with those obtained in the cognitive load literature. On the other hand, this does not diminish the importance of our findings, because they suggest (at the very least) that current models of stereotyping, as well as impression management, may need to be revised in at least one important way. In particular, these models will need to take into account what we believe to be a heretofore unknown and ironic consequence of anticipated public contexts: Warning people that others are (or might be) privy to their behavior might actually increase the likelihood of people openly displaying their bad habits, including prejudice. Moreover, to the extent that such effects may be more pronounced for socially anxious people, this might be especially true among the very people who are most worried about saying or doing the wrong thing in public.

Furthermore, even granting the similarity of our findings to previous work on the cognitive efficiency principle, our research provides an interpretation of this literature that is different from that typically offered. A common assumption in this area is that heuristic-based processing becomes stronger under conditions of diminished cognitive capacity. This assumption may not be correct. Returning to our football metaphor, concluding that stereotypes must be getting stronger under conditions of diminished cognitive capacity is akin to concluding that the offense of a football team must be getting stronger if they start scoring more touchdowns against the opposing team. Greater evidence of stereotypic processing may not have anything to do with greater stereotyping strength. Rather, it may be due to diminished cognitive control. Together with recent work by Payne (2001; see also Payne et al., 2002, in press) our work represents the first formal effort to make this distinction in the stereotyping literature.

Finally, it is worth noting that, despite some theoretical and methodological similarities cutting across the social facilitation and cognitive load literatures in stereotyping, there have been few, if any, connections made between these two literatures. This is especially surprising since, at least for the distraction-conflict version of social facilitation, these two literatures make essentially the same predictions (greater reliance on heuristic processing) through exactly the same mechanism (dwindling cognitive resources). Nevertheless, we are not aware of even one study in the stereotyping literature that cites or even mentions any aspect of social facilitation in any manner whatsoever. This strikes us as quite fertile ground for theoretical integration of these two areas.

Unresolved Issues

Although we are (for obvious reasons) interested in the counterintuitive findings reported here, it would be foolish to argue that public settings always lead to greater prejudice. Obviously, the key is to discover the boundary conditions that determine whether public settings stimulate higher versus lower amounts of prejudice compared to private contexts. One of the ideas we are currently exploring is that "public correction" is most likely when (1) the normatively correct answer is obvious, (2) participants can easily adjust their response to match normative standards, and (3) participants have ample ability and resources to make the needed correction. It should be noted that all three of these conditions are typically met in the classic studies on conformity (Asch, 1955). In contrast, our own studies tend not to meet all of these criteria. In the case of the second study, for example, the extremely short response window (550) makes it difficult for participants to initiate any correction to their initial impulse to respond in a stereotypic way, and the anticipated public setting apparently makes this even more difficult, as seen by the lower control estimates. As for the first study, participants do have more opportunity and resources to make any adjustments to their impressions, but the normatively correct answer in this paradigm is not obvious (i.e., what constitutes a truly "unbiased" response to the Black target?). We are currently exploring the viability of this line of reasoning by varying the extent to which participants in public contexts are, or are not, given easily-used cues as to how they might want to respond if they were interested in responding in a normatively acceptable (i.e., "safe") manner. Our model leads to the prediction of a two-way interaction: In the absence of such cues, public settings might produce greater prejudice compared to private settings (as in our studies to date), but this pattern might be reversed when readily-available normative guidelines are available.

Extensions of the Dominant Response Framework Into Other Research Domains

In our view, extending the boundaries of dominant responses from behavioral to mental habits is exciting insofar as it provides an alternative account of at least two now-classic findings in social psychology. The first is the group polarization effect (Stoner, 1961), which occurs "when an initial tendency of individual group members toward a given direction is enhanced following group discussion" (Isenberg, 1986, p. 1141) and would predict, for example, that people moderately in favor of capital punishment would be even more so following group discussion. There are three major explanations of this effect: persuasive arguments, normative influence, and self-categorization. However, our framework provides a fourth and yet unidentified explanation: To the extent that the initial tendency of individual group members represents a kind of dominant response, attitude polarization following exposure to a public forum is exactly the kind of effect predicted by social facilitation theorists.

The dominant response framework also provides an alternative and heretofore unexamined account of the well-known mirror manipulations, which show that people act more in accordance with their own attitudes if they are in the presence of a mirror than if they are not (e.g., Pryor et al., 1977). The currently accepted explanation is that enhanced attitude-behavior consistency is due to heightened self-awareness. However, to the extent that mirrors produce effects analogous to those of audiences (i.e., they are both arousing and/or distracting), a social facilitation framework makes the same prediction as self-awareness accounts.

CONCLUSION

We began this chapter talking about Bob Wyer and expectancy violations. As is evident by now, we encountered many surprises in this program of research. When we first started this program of research, we anticipated that many stereotyping studies had already investigated the moderating effects of private versus public contexts, but this turned out not to be the case. We also anticipated that strong connections had already been made between the stereotyping and social facilitation literature, but we were wrong about that, too. Finally, and most important, we found that people responded in a more prejudicial and stereotypic manner when they were placed in public rather than private contexts. Such findings clash with both intuition and several lines of work in social psychology.

As with all surprises, however, what is considered to be surprising (or not) depends entirely on one's expectations. Framed in the context of the prototypical college professor (reserved, staid, and, it must be admitted, a little boring), one could hardly imagine a more incongruous exemplar than Bob Wyer (not reserved, not staid, and definitely not boring). But for those lucky enough to know him, Bob is, well, typically Bob: a category unto himself and consistent only to his own true self.

In an analogous fashion, our own findings appear far less surprising when framed in terms of social facilitation. To be sure, a social facilitation framework is unlikely to explain everything about the impact of private versus public settings on stereotypes and prejudice. Indeed, there may well be consequences of private and public contexts on stereotyping that cannot be explained in terms of social facilitation models at all. Nevertheless, the social facilitation literature provides a firm base from which we can begin to make sense of some data that would otherwise seem far more puzzling.

A Final Word

It seems only fitting that we close by recognizing some remarkable "dominant responses" in Bob Wyer's repertoire of behavior that seem so easy for him, and so difficult for the rest of us: his astonishing devotion to his students, his intellectual passion, and his ability to recognize the distinct joys of interpreting a five-way interaction as much as appreciating the intricacies of the closing movement of a Mozart symphony, to name just a few. These skills are out of reach for most of us, but for those who have been lucky enough to meet Bob Wyer, at least we have had the pleasure in knowing that it can be done. It is preposterous to expect that any single human being could have so many atypically wonderful qualities, but this represents one expectancy violation that will surely be memorable for quite some time to come.

REFERENCES

Ajzen, I. (1988). *Attitudes, personality, and behavior.* Chicago: Dorsey Press.

Allport, F. H. (1924). *Social psychology.* Boston: Houghton Mifflin.

Allport, G. W. (1954). *The nature of prejudice.* Reading, MA: Addison-Wesley.

Allport, G. W. (1985). The historical background of social psychology. In G. Lindzey & E. Aronson (Eds.), *The handbook of social psychology* (Vol. 1, pp. 1–46). Reading, MA: Addison-Wesley.

Asch, S. E. (1955). Opinions and social pressure. *Scientific American, 193,* 31–25.

Bargh, J. A. (1994). The four horsemen of automaticity: Awareness, intention, efficiency, and control in social cognition. In R. S. Wyer & T. K. Srull (Eds.), *Handbook of Social Cognition,* Vol. 1, pp. 1–40. Hillsdale, NJ: Lawrence Erlbaum Associates.

Baron, R. S. (1986). Distraction-conflict theory: Progress and problems. In L. Berkowitz (Ed.), *Advances in experimental social psychology, 19,* pp. 1–40.

Blanchard, F. A., Lilly, T., & Vaughn, L. A. (1991). Reducing the expression of racial prejudice. *Psychological Science, 2,* 101–105.

Bodenhausen, G. V., & Lichtenstein, M. (1987). Social stereotypes and information-processing strategies: The impact of task complexity. *Journal of Personality and Social Psychology, 52,* 871–880.

Bodenhausen, G. V., & Macrae, C. N. (1998). Stereotype activation and inhibition. In R. S. Wyer, Jr. (Ed.), *Stereotype activation and inhibition.* Mahwah, NJ: Lawrence Erlbaum Associates.

Bodenhausen, G. V., & Wyer, R. S. (1985). Effects of stereotypes in decision making and information-processing strategies. *Journal of Personality and Social Psychology, 48,* 267–282.

Brewer, M. B. (1988). A dual process model of impression formation. In T. K. Srull & R. S. Wyer, Jr. (Eds.), *Advances in social cognition* (Vol. 1, pp. 1–36). Hillsdale, NJ: Lawrence Erlbaum Associates.

Chaiken, S., & Trope, Y. (1999). *Dual Process Theories in Social Psychology.* New York: Guilford Press.

Devine, P. G. (1989). Stereotypes and prejudice: Their automatic and controlled components. *Journal of Personality and Social Psychology, 56,* 5–18.

Dovidio, J. F., & Gaertner, S. L. (1986). *Prejudice, discrimination, and racism.* Orlando, FL: Academic Press.

Dutton, D. G., & Yee, P. (1974). The effects of subject liberalism, anonymity, and race of experimenter on subjects' rating of oriental and white photos. *Canadian Journal of Behavioral Science, 6,* 332–341.

Easterbrook, J. A. (1959). The effect of emotion on cue utilization and the organization of behavior. *Psychological Review, 66,* 183–201.

Fazio, R. H. (1995). Attitudes as object-evaluation associations: Determinants, consequences, and correlates of attitude accessibility. In R. E. Petty & J. A. Krosnik (Eds.), *Attitude strength: Antecedents and consequences* (pp. 247–282). Hillsdale, NJ: Lawrence Erlbaum Associates.

Fazio, R. H., Jackson, J. R., Dunton, B. C., & Williams, C. J. (1995). Variability in automatic activation as an unobtrusive measure of racial attitudes: A bona fide pipeline? *Journal of Personality and Social Psychology, 69,* 1013–1027.

Fazio, R. H., & Williams, C. J. (1986). Attitude accessibility as a moderator of the attitude-perception and the attitude-behavior relations: An examination of the 1984 presidential election. *Journal of Personality & Social Psychology, 51,* 505–514.

Fenigstein, A., Scheier, M. F., & Buss, A. H. (1975). Public and private self-consciousness: Assessment and theory. *Journal of Consulting & Clinical Psychology, 43,* 522–527.

Fiske, S. T., & Neuberg, S. L. (1990). A continuum of impression formation from category-based to individuating processes: Influences of information and motivation on attention and interpretation. In M. P. Zanna (Ed.), *Advances in experimental social psychology* (Vol. 23, pp. 1–74). New York: Academic Press.

Fiske, S. T., & Taylor, S. E. (1991). *Social cognition.* (2nd Ed.). New York: McGraw-Hill.

Gaertner, S. L., & Dovidio, J. F. (1986). The aversive form of racism. In J. F. Dovidio & S. L. Gaertner (Eds.), *Prejudice, discrimination, and racism* (pp. 61–89). Orlando, FL: Academic Press.

Geen, R. G., & Gange, J. J. (1977). Drive theory of social facilitation: Twelve years of theory and research. *Psychological Bulletin, 84,* 1267–1288.

Gilbert, D. T., & Hixon, J. G. (1991). The trouble of thinking: Activation and application of stereotypic beliefs. *Journal of Personality and Social Psychology, 60,* 509–517.

Higgins, E. T., Rholes, W. S., & Jones, C. R. (1977). Category accessibility and impression formation. *Journal of Experimental Social Psychology, 13,* 141–154.

Hull, C. L. (1943). *Principles of behavior: An introduction to behavior theory.* New York: Appleton-Century.

Isenberg, D. J. (1986). Group polarization: A critical review and meta-analysis. *Journal of Personality & Social Psychology, 50,* 1141–115.

Jacoby, L. L. (1991). A process dissociation framework: Separating automatic from intentional uses of memory. *Journal of Memory & Language, 30,* 513–541.

Jacoby, L. L., Begg, I. M., & Toth, J. P. (1997). In defense of functional independence: Violations of assumptions underlying the process-dissociation procedure? *Journal of Experimental Psychology: Learning, Memory, and Cognition, 23,* 484–495.

Jacoby, L. L., Kelley, C. M., & McElree, B. D. (1999). The role of cognitive control: Early selection vs. late correction. In S. Chaiken & Y. Trope (Eds.), *Dual-process theories in social psychology* (pp. 383–400). New York: Guilford Press.

James, W. (1980/1983). *The principles of psychology.* Cambridge, MA: Harvard University Press.

Katz, I., & Hass, R. G. (1988). Racial ambivalence and American value conflict: Correlational and priming studies of dual cognitive structures. *Journal of Personality and Social Psychology, 55,* 893–905.

Lambert, A. J., Chasteen, A. L., & Khan, S., & Manier, J. (1998). Rethinking assumptions about stereotype inhibition: Do we need to correct our theories about correction? In R. S. Wyer (Ed.), *Advances in social cognition* (Vol. 11). Mahwah, NJ: Lawrence Erlbaum Associates.

Lambert, A. J., Cronen, S., Chasteen, A., & Lickel, B. (1996). Private vs. public expressions of prejudice. *Journal of Experimental Social Psychology. 32,* 437–459.

Lambert, A. J., Cronen, S., Chasteen, A. L., & Manier, J. (1997). Responses to single Black targets as a function of pro-Black vs. anti-Black partners. Unpublished raw data.

Lambert, A. J., Payne, B. K., Jacoby, L. L. Shaffer, L. M., Chasteen, A. L., & Khan, S. K. (in press). Stereotypes as dominant responses: On the "social facilitation" of prejudice in anticipated public contexts. *Journal of Personality and Social Psychology.*

Macrae, C. N., Milne, A. B., & Bodenhausen, G. V. (1994). Stereotypes as energy-saving devices: A peek inside the cognitive toolbox. *Journal of Personality and Social Psychology, 66,* 37–47.

McConahay, J. B. (1986). Modern racism, ambivalence, and the modern racism scale. In J. Dovidio & S. L. Gaertner (Eds.), *Prejudice, discrimination, and racism: Theory and research.* New York: Academic Press.

Monteith, M. J., Deneen, N. E., & Tooman, G. D. (1996). The effect of social norm activation on the expression of opinions concerning gay men and Blacks. *Basic and Applied Social Psychology, 18,* 267–288.

Neisser, U. (1980). On "social knowing." *Personality and Social Psychology Bulletin, 64,* 601–605.

Payne, B. K. (2001). Prejudice and perception: The role of automatic and controlled processes in misperceiving a weapon. *Journal of Personality and Social Psychology, 81,* 181–192.

Payne B. K., Jacoby, L. L., & Lambert, A. J. (in press). Attitudes as accessibility bias: Dissociating automatic and controlled processes. In R. Hassan, J. A. Bargh, & J. Uleman (Eds.), *The New Unconscious.* New York: Oxford University Press.

Payne, B. K., Lambert, A. J., & Jacoby, L. L. (2002). Best laid plans: Effects of goals on accessibility bias and cognitive control in race-based perceptions of weapons. *Journal of Experimental Social Psychology, 38,* 384–396.

Petty, R. E., & Krosnick, J. A. (1995). *Attitude strength: Antecedents and consequences.* Hillsdale, NJ: Lawrence Erlbaum Associates.

Plant, E. A., & Devine, P. G. (1998). Internal and external motivation to respond without prejudice. *Journal of Personality and Social Psychology, 75,* 811–832.

Pryor, J. B., Gibbons, F. X., Wicklund, R. A., Fazio, R. H., & Hood, R. (1977). Self-focused attention and self-report validity. *Journal of Personality, 45,* 514–517.

Ross, L., Greene, D., & House, P. (1977). The false consensus effect: An egocentric bias in social perception and attribution processes. *Journal of Experimental Social Psychology, 13,* 279–301.

Rothbart, M., Fulero, S., Jensen, C., Howard, J., & Birrell, B. (1978). From individual to group impressions: Availability heuristics in stereotype formation. *Journal of Experimental Social Psychology, 14,* 237–255.

Sanders, G. S. (1981). Driven by distraction: An integrative review of social facilitation theory and research. *Journal of Experimental Social Psychology, 17,* 227–251.

Schlenker, B. R., Britt, T. W., & Pennington, J. (1996). Impression regulation and management: Highlights of a theory of self-identification. In R. M. Sorrentino & E. T. Higgins (Eds.), *Handbook of motivation and cognition: The interpersonal context* (Vol. 3). New York: Guilford Press.

Sidanius, J., Pratto, F., & Bobo, L. (1996). Racism, conservatism, affirmative action, and intellectual sophistication: A matter of principled conservatism or group dominance? *Journal of Personality and Social Psychology, 70,* 476–490.

Srull, T. K. (1981). Person memory: Some tests of associative storage and retrieval models. *Journal of Experimental Psychology, Human Learning and Memory, 7,* 440–463.

Srull, T. K., & Wyer, R. S. (1979). The role of category accessibility in the interpretation of information about persons: Some determinants and implications. *Journal of Personality and Social Psychology, 37,* 1660–1672.

Srull, T. K., & Wyer, R. S. (1980). Category accessibility and social perception: Some implications for the study of person memory and interpersonal judgments. *Journal of Personality and Social Psychology, 38,* 841–856.

Srull, T. K. (1984). Methodological techniques for the study of person memory and social cognition. In R. S. Wyer & T. K. Srull (Eds.), *Handbook of Social Cognition*, (Vol. 2, pp. 1–72). Hillsdale, NJ: Lawrence Erlbaum Associates.

Stoner, J. A. F. (1961). *A comparison of individual and group decisions involving risk.* Unpublished master's thesis, Massachusetts Institute of Technology, Cambridge, MA.

Tetlock, P. E. (1992). The impact of accountability on judgment and choice: Toward a social contingency model. In L. Berkowitz (Ed.), *Advances in experimental social psychology* (Vol. 25, pp. 331–376). Orlando, FL: Academic Press.

Triplett, N. (1898). The dynamogenic factors in pacemaking and competition. *American Journal of Psychology, 9*, 507–533.

Wittenbrink, B., Judd, C., & Park, B. (1997). Evidence for racial prejudice at the implicit level and its relationship with questionnaire measures. *Journal of Personality and Social Psychology, 72*, 262–274.

Wyer, R. S., (1998). *Stereotype activation and inhibition.* Mahwah, NJ: Lawrence Erlbaum Associates.

Wyer, R. S., & Srull, T. K. (1994). *Handbook of social cognition*, (Vol. 1). Hillsdale, NJ: Lawrence Erlbaum Associates.

Wyer, R. S., Jr., Bodenhausen, G. V., & Srull, T. K. (1984). The cognitive representation of persons and groups and its effects on recall and recognition memory. *Journal of Experimental Social Psychology, 20*, 445–469.

Wyer, R. S. & Srull, T. K. (1989). *Memory and cognition in social context.* Hillsdale, NJ: Lawrence Erlbaum Associates.

Wyer, R. S., Lambert, A. J., Budesheim, T. L., & Gruenfeld, D. H. (1992). Theory and research on person impression formation: A look to the future. In L. Martin & A. Tesser (Eds.), *The construction of social judgment* (pp. 3–36). Hillsdale, NJ: Lawrence Erlbaum Associates.

Zajonc, R. B. (1965). Social facilitation. *Science, 149*, 269–274.

Zajonc, R. B. (1960). The process of cognitive tuning in communications. *Journal of Abnormal and Social Psychology, 61*, 159–167.

Zajonc, R. B., Heingartner, A., & Herman, E. M. (1969). Social enhancement and impairment of performance in the cockroach. *Journal of Personality and Social Psychology, 13*, 83–92.

AUTHOR'S NOTE

This research was supported by grant # SBR 9817554 from the National Science Foundation to Alan J. Lambert.

10

How Strategies For Making Judgments and Decisions Affect Cognition: Motivated Cognition Revisited

E. Tory Higgins
Daniel C. Molden
Columbia University

Once seen as a dubious endeavor, the study of motivated reasoning has recently achieved new life and begun to reappear in many different areas of social psychology. One reason for this new life is that instead of revisiting old debates about whether people's judgments stem from their motivations or from cognitive processes, researchers have started to examine the complex interplay that occurs between these two systems as judgments are formed. As a result, a growing number of studies are examining the interface of motivation and cognition—especially how people's needs and desires to reach certain conclusions influence the cognitive processes that are involved in forming their judgments.

Our objective in this chapter is to present a complementary perspective on the *motivation-cognition interface*. We propose that, in addition to being motivated to reach certain conclusions, people are also motivated to adopt certain strategies as a means for arriving at these conclusions. That is, people care not only about the outcomes of their judgments, but also about the manner in which their judgments are made. Furthermore, we propose that, independent of the outcomes they are seeking, people's motivations for using specific means to make their judgments, or their *strategic preferences*, also influence their cognitive processing. We begin by briefly reviewing the outcome-based perspective on the motivation-cognition interface and, in so doing, noting Bob Wyer's important role in the development of this perspective. We then describe our recent research that takes a strategy-based perspective.

PREFERRED OUTCOMES
IN THE MOTIVATION-COGNITION INTERFACE

Not long ago, theories of motivated reasoning in social psychology were criticized by several prominent members of the field. Their collective position was that because people's judgments could be explained parsimoniously by purely cognitive mechanisms, the basic principles of which had long been studied, any additional speculation concerning poorly understood motivational mechanisms was unwise and unnecessary (e.g., Bem, 1967; Miller & M. Ross, 1975; Nisbett & L. Ross, 1980; Tetlock & Levi, 1982). At the time, these criticisms of motivational accounts of judgment were quite reasonable, given that there was little unambiguous evidence for motivated reasoning. In subsequent years, however, research on topics such as arousal during attitude change (Cooper & Fazio, 1984), self-affirmation (Steele, 1988), goal effects on information processing (Srull & Wyer, 1986), and the subjective costs and benefits that this information processing may involve (Cacioppo, Petty, Feinstein, & Jarvis, 1996; Kruglanski & Webster, 1996) has gone a long way toward constructing a set of basic principles for the influence of motivation on judgment. By so doing, this research has effectively rendered untenable arguments for the superiority of purely cognitive accounts of reasoning (see Kunda, 1990, 1999). Most objections have now faded, and the study of motivated reasoning has returned to the forefront of social psychology (see Dunning, 1999; Higgins & Sorrentino, 1990; Kruglanski, 1996; Kunda, 1990, 1999; Sorrentino & Higgins, 1986a, 1996).

This "second generation" of study has not merely revisited the original conceptions of motivated reasoning, however. No longer preoccupied with defining the boundaries between the operation of motivational and cognitive systems, as was once considered necessary, researchers have instead shifted their focus to the mutual interaction of these systems. Thus it is the interface that exists between motivation and cognition that has emerged as the central topic for investigation (see Kruglanski, 1996; Kunda 1990, 1999; Sorrentino & Higgins, 1986b).

How has the motivation-cognition interface been conceptualized by researchers? Although a number of different approaches have been used, there has been one dominant perspective in the area of judgment and decision making. This perspective views motivation in terms of people's needs and desires for *preferred outcomes* during judgment, such as drawing positive conclusions about oneself. These preferred outcomes are thought to influence people's cognitions by directing their information processing (including the encoding and retrieval of information in memory, the generation of alternatives, the testing of hypotheses, etc.) so as to facilitate the gathering of evidence that supports the desired conclusions.

Evidence for the preferred-outcome perspective on the motivation-cognition interface can be found in the effects of a wide variety of specific preferred conclusions. For example, (1) people's needs to believe positive things about themselves lead them to retrieve instances from memory and construct self-serving theories that support positive self beliefs (e.g., Dunning, Leuenberger, & D. Sherman, 1995; Santioso, Kunda, & Fong, 1990); (2) people's desires to view their own in-group as superior to other groups lead them to selectively apply inferential rules that support this viewpoint (e.g., Doosje, Spears, & Koomen, 1995; Schaller, 1992); and (3) people's goals to maintain a particular belief or opinion (e.g., support of, or feelings against, the death penalty) inspire them to invest extra effort in searching for evidence that undermines and refutes a threat to their belief or opinion (Edwards & Smith, 1996).

Evidence for the role of preferred outcomes in the motivation-cognition interface can also be found in the effects of preferred conclusions that are more general and abstract. For example, (1) people's needs to find a decisive answer (any answer) lead them to rely more heavily on simple heuristic rules in obtaining this answer (Dijksterhuis, van Knippenberg, Kruglanski, & Schaper, 1996; Webster, 1993); (2) people's desires to justify to others whatever conclusions they reach lead them to preferentially encode information that is less ambiguous and more easily articulated when forming their conclusions (Lerner, & Tetlock, 1999; Wilson & Schooler, 1991); and (3) people's goals to achieve the most accurate outcome in their judgments (whatever it may be) lead them to overcome biases that can be created by highly accessible knowledge structures (Ford & Kruglanski, 1995; Thompson, Roman, Moskowitz, Chaiken, & Bargh, 1994).

It is through his classic work on these more general types of motivation that Bob Wyer made historical contributions to current conceptions of the motivation-cognition interface. Wyer and his colleagues demonstrated that people's general processing goals or objectives, such as to remember a person's behaviors, to form an overall impression of this person, or to make a particular judgment about this person, can significantly influence how they encode and retrieve information in memory (e.g., Wyer, Bodenhausen, & Srull, 1984; Wyer & Gordon, 1982; Wyer, Srull, & Gordon, 1984; Wyer, Srull, Gordon, & Hartwick, 1982; for a review see Srull, & Wyer, 1986). In so doing, they were among the first to examine how people's general task goals can induce different mind-sets that determine how stimulus information is processed, and to extend the study of motivated cognition beyond people's specific beliefs and opinions.

PREFERRED STRATEGIES
IN THE MOTIVATION-COGNITION INTERFACE

Our brief review illustrates the value of studying the motivation-cognition interface (for more thorough treatments, see Kruglanski, 1996; Kunda, 1990, 1999). In addition, it provides strong evidence for the perspective that people's motivation to reach certain outcomes in their judgments (whether specific or general) can significantly alter their cognitive processing while forming these judgments. But are people's desires to reach preferred outcomes the only type of motivation involved in motivated cognition? We suggest that people are motivated not only with respect to the outcomes of their judgments, but also with respect to the manner in which they make their judgments. That is, not only do people have preferred conclusions, but they also have preferred strategies for reaching their conclusions. Therefore, beyond favoring particular conclusions, people may be independently motivated to reach these conclusions using strategies that "feel right" given their current motivational orientation, such as eagerly gathering positive evidence in support of a desired conclusion, or vigilantly suppressing negative evidence that could undermine a desired conclusion. We propose, then, that motivated cognition can also be examined in terms of such strategic preferences.

How might this be done? One possibility would be to examine the cognitive consequences of people's motivation to pursue preferred strategies in essentially the same way as their motivation to reach preferred conclusions. In this paradigm, the effects of individuals' strategic preferences on their information processing would be tested by measuring or manipulating these preferences, and examining their judgmental processes. Another possibility, which has not been used in outcome-based research, would be to examine the cognitive consequences of using strategies that either do or do not match one's current preferences. In this paradigm, the effects of the fit between individuals' motivational orientations and the strategies they use during judgment would be tested by measuring or manipulating this fit, and examining their judgmental processes. Our research on the cognitive consequences of preferred strategies has used both of these paradigms, and we describe examples of each in turn. Because people's strategic preferences vary as a function of their regulatory focus in all of the research we describe, we begin by discussing regulatory focus theory and the different types of strategic preferences it postulates.

Regulatory Focus Theory

Regulatory focus theory assumes that people have two distinct self-regulatory systems which serve fundamentally different survival needs—

nurturance (e.g., nourishment) and security (e.g., protection). Earlier papers on self-discrepancy theory (e.g., Higgins, 1987, 1989) have discussed how people represent nurturance and security needs in the course of self-regulation. Nurturance needs are expressed in individuals' hopes, wishes, and aspirations for themselves (i.e., their ideals). Meeting one's ideals is represented as the presence of positive outcomes, whereas failing to meet one's ideals is represented as the absence of positive outcomes. Ideal self-regulation is conceptualized as involving *promotion focus* concerns with advancements and accomplishments (see Higgins, 1997, 1998).

In contrast, security needs are expressed in individuals' beliefs about their duties, obligations, and responsibilities (i.e., their oughts). Meeting one's oughts is represented as the absence of negative outcomes, whereas failing to meet one's oughts is represented as the presence of negative outcomes (see Gould, 1939). Ought self-regulation is conceptualized as involving *prevention focus* concerns with protection and safety (see Higgins, 1997, 1998).

Because individuals' social upbringing can emphasize ideals (e.g., accomplishments are rewarded and failures to meet hopes are met with love withdrawal) or oughts (e.g., duties that are fulfilled remove threats, and failures to meet obligations are punished), a promotion focus or a prevention focus can become a chronic orientation, depending on one's socialization history (see Higgins & Silberman, 1998). However, momentary experiences of similar contingencies can also temporarily induce a promotion or prevention focus. For example, feedback or task instructions that create concerns with gain/non-gain outcomes versus non-loss/loss outcomes, or priming manipulations that activate people's ideals versus oughts, can place people in a promotion focus or a prevention focus, respectively. Thus the distinction between promotion focus concerns and prevention focus concerns applies both to individual differences that are chronic, and to those that are momentarily induced by situations and tasks.[1]

In addition to differentiating between concerns over the presence and absence of positive versus negative outcomes, regulatory focus theory also distinguishes between different strategies of goal attainment—*eager strategies* versus *vigilant strategies* (see Crowe & Higgins, 1997; Higgins, 1997, 1998). In signal detection terms (e.g., Tanner & Swets, 1954; see also Trope & Liberman, 1996), eager strategies involve ensuring *hits* and ensuring against *errors of omission* or *misses* (i.e., a *risky bias*), and vigilant strategies involve ensuring *correct rejections* and ensuring against *errors of commission* or

---

[1] At this point, it is worth noting that regulatory focus is not only conceptually but also empirically distinct from other motivational constructs that are commonly used to investigate the motivation-cognition interface, such as the need for cognition (Cacioppo et al., 1996) and the need for closure (Kruglanski & Webster, 1996). Our studies have found, for example, that the effects of the strategic differences between promotion and prevention on cognition are obtained, even when need for cognition and need for closure are statistically controlled (see Liberman, Molden, Idson, & Higgins, 2001; Molden & Higgins, 2001).

false alarms (i.e., a *conservative bias*). Regulatory focus theory (Higgins, 1997, 1998) proposes that there is a fit between promotion focus concerns and the use of eager strategies (i.e., that these strategies feel right), because eager strategies also emphasize the presence of positive outcomes (i.e., seeking advancement and ensuring against omitting possible hits; see Crowe & Higgins, 1997). Therefore individuals who are in a promotion focus should prefer eager means of goal pursuit. Regulatory focus theory also proposes that there is a fit between prevention focus concerns and the use of vigilant strategies, because vigilant strategies also emphasize the absence of negative outcomes (i.e., being careful and guarding against mistakes; see Crowe & Higgins, 1997). Therefore, individuals who are in a prevention focus should prefer vigilant means of goal pursuit.

Given these differences in their strategic preferences, people in a promotion focus or a prevention focus would be expected to differ in the biases they display during judgment. From a signal detection perspective, promotion-focused individuals favoring eager strategies over vigilant strategies should display a risky bias, whereas prevention-focused individuals favoring vigilant strategies over eager strategies should display a conservative bias. These hypotheses were tested in a recognition memory study by Crowe and Higgins (1997; see also Friedman & Förster, 2001). Participants were first shown a list of target items and, following a delay, were then given test items that included both old target items from the original list and new distracter items not from the original list. They were asked to respond "Yes" if they believed the test item was an old target item, and to respond "No" if they believed the test item was a new distracter item. In this task, favoring "Yes" responses reflects a risky bias of ensuring hits and ensuring against errors of omission (indicating a preference for strategic eagerness); and favoring "No" responses reflects a conservative bias of ensuring correct rejections and ensuring against errors of commission (indicating a preference for strategic vigilance).

Before performing the recognition memory task, participants were told that they would also be assigned a second, final task. A liked and a disliked activity had been selected earlier for each participant to serve as the final task. Everyone was informed that the activity he or she would work on at the end of the session depended on his or her performance on the recognition memory task. Although a contingency was thus created for all participants, the framing of this contingency varied as a function of both regulatory focus (i.e., promotion versus prevention) and outcome valence (i.e., success versus failure). The promotion framing of the contingency stated that by doing well on the memory task, the participant would get to do the liked task (or by not doing well, they would not get to do the liked task). The prevention framing of the contingency stated that by not doing poorly on the memory task, the participant would not have to do the disliked task (or by doing poorly, they would have to do the disliked task). The study found that, independent of success versus failure framing (which itself had no effect), participants framed to be in a promotion focus gave more "Yes" responses and showed a risky bias in the recognition memory task, whereas participants framed to be in a prevention focus gave more "No" responses and showed a conservative bias. These results support the hypothesized associations between a promotion focus and eagerness, and between a prevention focus and vigilance.

This and other evidence (see Higgins, 1997, 1998) of a relation between people's regulatory focus and their strategic preferences for eagerness or vigilance have inspired our new preferred-strategy perspective on motivated cognition that complements the preferred-outcome perspective. The first set of studies we review concerns how strategic preferences, analogous to outcome preferences, can influence people's cognitive systems by directing their information processing in a manner that reflects these preferences. These effects on information processing involve fundamental aspects of judgment and decision making. The second set of studies we review concerns the separate question of how strategic preferences can influence people's cognitive systems by affecting whether the strategies they use feel right, or *fit*, given their current motivational orientation. This fit also has important consequences during judgment and decision making.

Preferred Strategies and Judgmental Processes

There are a number of cognitive consequences of people's preferred strategies for making judgments and decisions that have been studied. Here we consider four: expectancy-value integration, generation of alternatives, counterfactual thinking, and the speed/accuracy trade-off.

Expectancy X Value Effects in Goal Commitment. Expectancy-value (or subjective utility) models have been, historically, the most influential models regarding the evaluative processes underlying decision making. They are also one of the oldest and most extensively studied examples of the motivation-cognition interface. A basic assumption shared by these models is that, beyond the additive effects of people's high or low expectancies of successful goal attainment and the high or low value of successful goal attainment, their commitment to goal pursuit will also be determined by a multiplicative combination of these two factors (i.e., an expectancy x value effect; for a review, see Feather, 1982). According to these models, as either people's expectancy or value for goal attainment increases, the impact of the other variable on their commitment also increases. For example, people should care more about high (versus low) expectancies of success when success has high value than when it has low value. This reflects a motivation to maximize the product of expectancy and value.

Expectancy-value models have received some experimental support, yet not all studies have found the positive interactive effect of people's expectancies and value as predicted by these models (e.g., Lynch & Cohen, 1978). Shah and Higgins (1997) proposed that one possible explanation for these inconsistent findings is variability across individuals or across situations (or both) in strategic preferences during decision making. How might a promotion focus preference for eager strategies and a prevention focus preference for vigilant strategies affect people's processing of expectancy and value information? As previously described, goal pursuit with eager strategies involves ensuring hits and advancement. This should lead people to attempt to maximize outcomes and to be especially motivated by high expectancies for success when this success is highly valued. People in a promotion focus would then be expected to show the classic expectancy x value effect, and be the most committed to goals that maximize this product. Thus for goal pursuit with a promotion focus, the difference between a high versus a low likelihood of success should have more impact on commitment as the value of goal attainment increases.

In the prevention system, however, goal attainment is seen as a necessity when the value of success becomes high. It becomes something one must try to do, regardless of difficulty or likelihood of success. That is, when a valued goal becomes a necessity, such as ensuring the safety of one's child, goal commitment is high, whether the likelihood of the outcome is high or low. For goal pursuit with a prevention focus, then, as value increases, goal attainment becomes a necessity and, once it is a necessity, the difference between a high versus a low likelihood of success is less important. Thus in the presence of strong prevention concerns, the difference between a high versus a low likelihood should have less impact on commitment as the value of goal attainment increases (see Shah & Higgins, 1997).

These predictions were tested in a set of studies in which participants were asked to make decisions about taking a class in their major. One study obtained measures of participants' subjective estimates of the value of, and their expectancies for success in, this class. The other two studies experimentally manipulated both of these factors. With respect to regulatory focus, two studies experimentally manipulated participants' focus using framing procedures similar to those described earlier, and the other study assessed participants' focus by measuring their chronic orientation toward a promotion focus or a prevention focus. Like previous work on attitude accessibility (see Bassili, 1995; Fazio, 1995), a promotion focus orientation was operationalized in terms of the chronic accessibility of people's hopes and aspirations (ideal strength), and a prevention focus orientation was operationalized in terms of the chronic accessibility of people's beliefs about their responsibilities and obligations (ought strength). Because knowledge structures with higher accessibility should produce faster responses to relevant inputs (see Higgins, 1996), a strong promotion focus or a strong prevention focus was defined by shorter response latencies when describing one's ideals or oughts, respectively (for more information on chronic measures of regulatory focus, see Higgins, et al., 2001; Higgins, Shah, & Friedman, 1997).

Participants in these studies were asked to evaluate the likelihood that they would take a course in their major. The value of doing well and the expectancy of doing well in the course varied. In the two studies that manipulated people's expectancies and values, high value was established by telling participants that 95% of previous majors were accepted into their honor society when they received a grade of "B" or higher, whereas low value was established by telling participants that 51% of previous majors were accepted into their honor society when they received a grade of "B" or higher. High expectancy was established by telling participants that 75% of previous majors received a grade of "B" or higher, whereas low expectancy was established by telling participants that 25% of previous majors received a grade of "B" or higher. All three studies found that for participants with a stronger promotion focus, high (versus low) expectancies for success had a greater influence on choosing to enroll in the course when this course was highly valued than when it was not highly valued (i.e., the classic positive expectancy x value interaction). However, for participants with a stronger prevention focus, high (versus low) expectancies for success had less influence on choosing to enroll in the course when the course was highly valued than when it was not highly valued (i.e., a negative expectancy x value interaction). These results demonstrate that even when people desire the same outcome (e.g., membership in an honor society), differences in their strategic preferences can affect how expectancy and value information is integrated in pursuit of this outcome.

Generation of Alternatives During Judgment.   Another fundamental component of judgment and decision making is the generation of alternatives. Because most basic forms of judgment, such as hypothesis generation, causal attribution, and categorization, require people to produce and evaluate a number of possible options, this process is an especially important aspect of the motivation-cognition interface. How might people's strategic preferences influence the way in which they generate alternatives?

This question was initially examined in a second study by Crowe and Higgins (1997). The study investigated how promotion and prevention orientations influence decisions to classify and characterize objects in the world. One task involved sorting a set of fruits and a set of vegetables. For this task, everyone was allowed to choose his or her own criteria for the groups created, and the only requirement was that, within each category, the sorting criterion had to be consistent across all members of that category (see Mikulincer, Kedem, & Paz, 1990). Another task involved listing characteristics of different pieces of furniture. For this task, everyone was presented with the names of furniture objects, such as "desk," "couch," or "bed," and was asked to write down all of the characteristics they could think of for each object (see Mikulincer, Kedem, & Paz, 1990). Prior to both of these tasks, participants were placed in a promotion or a prevention focus using an experimental framing technique such as those previously described.

For both of these tasks, the instructions allowed participants to complete them successfully in different ways. One possible approach was to generate many different alternatives across each task, i.e., use different criteria for sorting the fruits and vegetables (e.g., color for the fruits and shape for the vegetables), and use distinct dimensions for listing the characteristics of each piece of furniture (e.g., shape and size for the bed, function for the chair, etc.). Another possible approach was to generate only a few alternatives across each task, i.e., repeat the same criteria for sorting the fruits and vegetables (e.g., color), and use the same dimension for listing the characteristics of each piece of furniture (e.g., function).

Because the instructions did not say which answers were "correct," generating many different alternatives across each task increases one's chances of attaining a hit from using the right criteria (whatever they may be) and guards against a miss from omitting the right criteria. Therefore this represents an eager strategy and should have been preferred by participants in a promotion focus. In contrast, generating few alternatives across each task increases one's chances of attaining a correct rejection by not using the wrong criteria (again, whatever they may be) and guards against a false alarm from using the wrong criteria. Therefore this represents a vigilant strategy and should have been preferred by participants in a prevention focus.

Results confirmed these predictions and showed that promotion-focused participants generated a greater number of alternatives, using more criteria on the sorting task, and using a greater number of unique dimensions for the characteristic-listing task. In contrast, prevention-focused participants generated a smaller number of alternatives, using fewer criteria on the sorting task, and using a smaller number of unique dimensions for the characteristic-listing task. This indicates that even on a task where participants are not motivated to achieve any particular outcome (and where a successful outcome is not very well specified), their strategic preferences from a promotion or a prevention focus can affect their generation of alternatives. It should also be noted that recent research has shown that the greater generation of alternatives when individuals have a promotion focus (versus a prevention focus) is also reflected in their being more creative (see Friedman & Förster, 2001; Wing-hong Lam & Chiu, 2002).

The sorting and characteristic-listing tasks used by Crowe and Higgins (1997) are special cases of people generating alternatives. As Bruner, Goodnow, and Austin (1956) pointed out years ago, a more general form of generating alternatives occurs when people form hypotheses about what it is they are perceiving. Do differences in people's strategic preferences affect their generation of alternatives in this situation as well?

This question was addressed in several studies by Liberman, Molden, Idson, and Higgins (2001). In the first two studies, participants' strategic preferences were assessed either by measuring their chronic promotion and prevention orientations, or by framing success on the experimental task in terms of adding points and gaining a dollar (i.e., a promotion focus), or not subtracting points and not losing a dollar (i.e., a prevention focus). Participants performed an object-naming task in which they received a booklet with four pictures, each on a separate page. Each picture was of a familiar object taken from an unusual angle, making it difficult to recognize (see Mayseless & Kruglanski, 1987). The task was to guess what the object was in each picture, and participants were told that they could list as many or as few answers as they wanted.

Similar to the sorting and characteristic-listing tasks described above, it was not clear to participants viewing the pictures what the right hypotheses were. Generating more alternatives would again increase the likelihood of finding a correct hypothesis (i.e., attaining a hit), and decrease the likelihood of leaving out a correct hypothesis (i.e., suffering a miss). Alternatively, generating more alternatives would again increase the likelihood of including a wrong hypothesis (i.e., committing a false alarm), and decrease the likelihood of rejecting a wrong hypothesis (i.e., attaining a correct rejection). Because decision makers in a promotion focus prefer to use eager strategies and are more concerned with increasing hits and decreasing misses, they should be inclined to generate relatively more hypotheses for the identity of the pictures. In contrast, because decision makers in a prevention focus prefer to use vigilant strategies and are more concerned with decreasing false alarms and increasing correct rejections, they should be inclined to generate relatively fewer hypotheses for the identity of the pictures. The results of both studies confirmed these predictions. Similar to the results of the Crowe and Higgins (1997) study, participants with a stronger promotion focus generated more hypotheses about what the object was in each picture, whereas participants with a stronger prevention focus generated fewer hypotheses.

In addition to examining the effects of people's strategic preferences on generating alternative hypotheses for object perception, Liberman et al. (2001) investigated whether similar effects could also be found for social perception. Participants were placed in a promotion focus or a prevention focus by priming their ideals or oughts, respectively, and asked to read about the helpful behavior of a target person. They were then asked to select the possible causes of this behavior from among a number of alternatives they were given. The results were similar to those found for object perception—participants in a promotion focus selected more hypotheses about the causes of the target's behavior, whereas participants in a prevention focus selected fewer hypotheses about the causes of the target's behavior.

Beyond extending the study of strategic preferences to social perception, another goal of this third study was to investigate the consequences of such motivation for people's judgments of others. The generation of hypotheses is a fundamental component of causal attribution, including people's use of the *discounting principle*. Standard attribution models predict that, when perceiving others' behaviors, the more possible causes that people acknowledge for these behaviors, the more reluctant they will be to generalize to future situations (Kelley, 1973; Morris & Larrick, 1995). Therefore people in a promotion focus, who select more hypotheses for a target's behavior, should generalize less to future situations than people in a prevention focus who select fewer hypotheses (see Liberman et al., 2001).

To test this prediction, participants in the third study were also asked how helpful the target would be in future situations. As predicted, participants in a promotion focus were less likely than those in a prevention focus to make generalizations. This finding demonstrates that preferences for strategic eagerness versus vigilance not only affects the process of forming initial judgments (i.e., generating possible causes for a behavior), but it also affects the use of these judgments in subsequent inferences (i.e., generalizing current behavior to future situations).

The results of the Liberman et al. (2001) studies raised the possibility that strategic preferences might even affect people's basic categorization processes. Recent research by Molden and Higgins (2001) investigated this possibility. In one condition, participants were given a *vague* behavioral description of a target person and were asked to categorize the behavior. When an entity to be categorized is vague, the correct category is uncertain, and a number of possibilities could all be right (see Higgins, 1996). Like the stimuli used in the studies just described, in this vague condition it was uncertain what the right hypotheses were. Therefore participants in a promotion focus would be expected to generate multiple alternatives for categorization, which would maintain the vagueness of the behavior. In contrast, participants in a prevention focus would be expected to generate few alternatives for categorization, which would result in a clearer impression. The results supported these predictions.

In a second condition, participants were instead given an *ambiguous* behavioral description of the same target person, and again asked to categorize the behavior. When a behavior to be categorized is ambiguous, the correct category is also uncertain, but in a different way from when a behavior is vague. Ambiguity arises in situations in which there are a number of conflicting, and mutually exclusive, possibilities that all seem to be correct (see Higgins, 1996). Thus unlike the stimuli used in our previous studies, in this ambiguous condition the right hypotheses seem to be sufficiently clear, but they cannot all be endorsed simultaneously.

How might the strategic eagerness preferred by people in a promotion focus and the strategic vigilance preferred by people in a prevention focus affect their generation of alternatives under such ambiguous circumstances? Because a variety of alternatives appear to be right, but not all can be, an eager strategy consists of selecting a single alternative and eliminating the others. Although this strategy risks the error of choosing the wrong category, it also ensures against omitting an opportunity to select the right category, which would occur if a selection is not made. Therefore when categorizing ambiguous targets, people in a promotion focus should actually generate fewer alternatives, thereby forming a clearer impression of the behavior. In contrast, a vigilant strategy consists of selecting all of the possible categories and not choosing between them. Although this strategy forfeits any chance of selecting the right category, it also ensures against committing to an alternative that is wrong. Therefore when categorizing ambiguous targets, people in a prevention focus should actually generate more alternatives, thereby maintaining the ambiguity of the behavior. These predictions were also supported. Together, the findings of Molden and Higgins (2001) indicate that people's strategic preferences can influence even their basic categorization processes, and affect how and whether they resolve uncertainty in stimulus information.

In sum, people's strategic preferences play a significant role in their generation of alternatives during judgment and in their resolution of different kinds of uncertainty (e.g., vague versus ambiguous input). In turn, these differences in the number of alternatives considered by people in a promotion focus versus a prevention focus also affect the final conclusions they reach, such as their inferences about future behaviors.

Counterfactual Thinking.   During decision making, people sometimes imagine or simulate what would happen under different conditions (e.g., Kahneman & Tversky, 1982). For example, individuals may consider the possible outcomes if they were to perform or not perform particular behaviors, or, retrospectively, they might consider what might have happened "if only" they had taken certain actions or "if only" they had decided not to take certain actions (see Kahneman & Miller, 1986). These thoughts about alternatives to imagined, or previously experienced, outcomes have been termed *counterfactuals*, and have been shown to be an important judgmental process which aids people in understanding and learning from the events they experience (see Roese, 1997).

Recent studies by Roese, Hur, and Pennington (1999) have investigated whether people's promotion or prevention strategic preferences alter their use of counterfactuals. First, they proposed that promotion preferences for eager strategies are related to the formation of *additive* counterfactuals that concern the reversal of a previous inaction (e.g., if only I had acted, I wouldn't have missed that opportunity for advancement). Second, they proposed that prevention preferences for vigilance are related to the formation of *subtractive* counterfactuals that concern the reversal of a previous action (e.g., if I hadn't acted, I would have avoided that mistake). These relations were derived from the notion that simulating the correction of a past error of omission, which occurs with additive counterfactuals, would be more consistent with eager strategies than with vigilant strategies, and that simulating the correction of a past error of commission, which occurs with subtractive counterfactuals, would be more consistent with vigilant strategies than with eager strategies.

In one of the experiments testing these proposed interrelations, Roese et al. (1999) had participants read scenarios involving failure situations, with half of the scenarios involving promotion failure (e.g., failure to attain an accomplishment goal) and the other half involving prevention failure (e.g., failure to attain a safety goal). Each of these scenarios was constructed to be equally negative, so that the outcome of failing would be equivalent across both groups.

Immediately after each scenario, there was a measure of counterfactual thinking, adapted from Kahneman and Tversky (1982), in which participants completed sentences that began with the counterfactual stem, "If only ..." As predicted, participants were more likely to complete the sentence with additive counterfactuals when the scenario invoked promotion eagerness rather than prevention vigilance, and were more likely to complete the sentence with subtractive counterfactuals when the scenario invoked prevention vigilance rather than promotion eagerness.

Another study by Roese et al. (1999) manipulated participants' strategic preferences by inducing either a promotion focus or a prevention focus, and asked them to think of a negative event that they had experienced sometime during the past year. Like the other study, the participants were then asked to give "if only" thoughts about their negative experience. As before, participants were more likely to complete the sentence with additive counterfactuals when in a promotion rather than a prevention focus, and to complete it with subtractive counterfactuals when in a prevention rather than a promotion focus.

In the literature that exists on counterfactual thinking, it has been traditionally assumed that subtractive counterfactuals are more common than additive counterfactuals, and that failures associated with action inspire more regret than failures associated with inaction (Kahneman & Miller, 1986; see Gilovich & Medvec, 1995). However, the results of these two studies demonstrate that in some cases, people's strategic preferences can result in additive counterfactuals being more common, and perhaps being associated with greater regret (see also Seta, McElroy, & Seta, 2001). Another common finding in counterfactual research is that counterfactuals are generated more often in response to narrowly missing a success (i.e., "I would have succeeded if only ...") than in response to narrowly avoiding a failure (i.e., "I would have failed if only ...", see Roese, 1997). However, given the differences in the way that people with a promotion or a prevention focus represent success and failure (i.e., as gains versus non-gains or non-losses versus losses, respectively), it seems possible that individuals in a promotion focus would spend a greater amount of time ruminating about the lost gains of a near success, whereas individuals in a prevention focus would spend a greater amount of time ruminating about the successfully avoided losses of a near failure. This could be another topic for future studies in counterfactual thinking. What current research relating regulatory focus and counterfactual thinking demonstrates is that strategic preferences have important processing effects on people's evaluation and understanding of what happens to them.

Fast Versus Accurate Processing of Information.   One of the fundamental questions since the beginning of experimental psychology has been when and why people are fast or accurate (Woodworth, 1899). Across all areas of psychology, the so-called speed/accuracy trade-off, or quantity/quality conflict, has been of major concern. Given the extensive interest in people's decisions to favor either speed or accuracy when processing information, it is surprising that still so little is known about the basic principles underlying these decisions. How might a consideration of people's strategic preferences increase our understanding of why, at times, individuals are more concerned with speed and why, at other times, they are more concerned with accuracy?

Förster, Higgins, and Taylor (in press) recently proposed that promotion preferences for strategic eagerness would result in faster information processing and a higher quantity of output in a search for possible hits, whereas prevention preferences for strategic vigilance would result in more accurate information processing and a higher quality of output in an effort to avoid mistakes. In addition, Förster et al. further proposed that each of these tendencies would increase in intensity as people moved closer to goal completion, resulting in stronger effects of strategic preferences toward the end of a task than toward the beginning of a task. This second prediction was based on earlier research relating regulatory focus to the *goal looms larger* effect. The "goal looms larger" effect refers to the fact that motivation increases as one's distance to the completion of a goal decreases (see e.g., Lewin, 1935). Studies by Förster, Higgins, and Idson (1998) found that as the participants in their studies moved closer to completing a task, both the eagerness of people in a promotion focus and the vigilance of people in a prevention focus increased. Therefore, Förster et al. expected that the effects of strategic preferences on fast versus accurate processing would follow the same "goal looms larger" principle. If so, then the speed of people in a promotion focus (but not those in a prevention focus) should increase as they move toward the end of the task, whereas the accuracy of people in a prevention focus (but not those in a promotion focus) should increase as they move toward the end of the task.

In order to test these hypotheses, studies were conducted in which participants were given a task involving four pictures taken from a children's connect-the-dots drawing-book. For each picture, the objective was to connect sequentially numbered dots within a given time period in order to complete the outline of an image (which, if done correctly, depicted a cartoon animal). Participants' speed on each picture was assessed by the highest number dot they reached by the end of the time period for that picture, and their accuracy on each picture was assessed by the number of dots they missed (i.e., that were not connected) up to the highest number they reached at the end of the time period. Participants' tendency to increase in speed or accuracy closer to the completion of the task was examined by sequentially comparing their scores on these respective measures as they moved from the first picture to the fourth picture. In one study, people's strategic preferences were assessed by measuring their chronic promotion and prevention orientations, and in a second study, people's strategic preferences were manipulated by using gain/non-gain and non-loss/loss contingencies to induce promotion and prevention orientations, respectively.

Across both studies, as predicted, there were significant effects of people's strategic preferences on both the speed and accuracy of their information processing. Over the entire task, promotion-focused individuals were faster and produced a higher quantity of responses, whereas prevention-focused individuals were more accurate and produced a higher quality of responses. In addition, results showed that, again as predicted, as people with promotion preferences for eagerness moved closer to task completion (i.e., moved through each successive picture), their speed increased, whereas there was no increase in speed for people with prevention preferences for vigilance. In contrast, as people with prevention preferences for vigilance moved closer to task completion, their accuracy increased (i.e., they made fewer mistakes), whereas accuracy actually decreased for people with promotion preferences for eagerness. The results of these studies indicate that people's strategic preferences can alter their concerns with different aspects of information processing during goal pursuit (e.g., speed versus accuracy), especially as they get closer to goal completion.

Overall, the studies reviewed in this section demonstrate that people's preferred strategies can significantly influence their information processing during judgment and decision making. The processes in which these influences have been found thus far, including the integration of expectancy and value information when evaluating choices in decision making, the generation of alternatives in causal attribution and categorization, the use of counterfactual reasoning when reacting to life events, and the choice of fast versus accurate appraisals of information, are broad and fundamental. It is clear from this research, then, that preferred strategies are an important part of motivated cognition. Next, we consider another way in which preferred strategies can affect cognition. These studies use a different research paradigm that examines the cognitive consequences of the fit between the strategies used by individuals and their current motivational orientation.

Regulatory Fit and Judgmental Processes

What are the effects on judgmental processes of people pursuing strategies that do or do not feel right in terms of their current motivational orientation? To answer this question, we begin by discussing what it means to "feel right," according to the theory of regulatory fit (see Higgins, 2000).

Regulatory Fit. As we have seen thus far, individuals can pursue the same goal with different motivational orientations and with different strategies. To review, consider students in the same course who are working to attain an "A." Some students in this class may be oriented toward an "A" as an accomplishment (i.e., possess a promotion orientation), whereas others may be oriented toward an "A" as a responsibility (i.e., possess a prevention orientation). Moreover, one strategy to attain an "A" that might occur to these students would be to read material beyond the assigned readings (representing an eager strategy), whereas another strategy that might occur to them would be to make sure they fulfill all course requirements (representing a vigilant strategy).

From our previous discussion, most students who see an "A" as an accomplishment would be expected to adopt the eager strategy of reading extra, non-assigned material, whereas most students who see an "A" as a responsibility would be expected to adopt the vigilant strategy of paying careful attention to course requirements. These students, who are using the strategy that feels right and fits their current motivational orientation, would experience a regulatory fit in their pursuit of an "A" (Higgins, 2000). However, for whatever reasons, some people may pursue a strategy that does not feel right, and does not fit their current orientation (e.g., accomplishment-oriented students adopting vigilant strategies and responsibility-oriented students adopting eager strategies). These students would not experience a regulatory fit.

What might be the effects of such experiences of fit or non-fit? Higgins (2000) has proposed that one of the primary consequences of regulatory fit is to increase the experienced value of the goal one is pursuing. That is, if people feel right during goal pursuit, then they should experience the outcome of this pursuit as good, above and beyond whatever value the outcome may have on its own. Consider again our example of the students who are trying to attain an "A" in a course. Assuming that eager and vigilant strategies are, in general, equally effective routes toward this goal (i.e., equally instrumental), those students who use strategies (in their pursuit of an "A") that produce regulatory fit would be expected to place greater value on this "A" than those students who use strategies that do not produce regulatory fit (see Higgins, 2000).

Two separate studies by Higgins, Idson, Freitas, Spiegel, and Molden (in press) have tested this hypothesized *value transfer*. Both studies measured participants' chronic promotion and prevention orientations. In the experimental session, the participants chose between owning either a coffee mug or a pen. (The coffee mug was more valuable than the pen, and pre-testing had shown that it was clearly preferred.) The participants were asked to make their choice using one of two strategies. Half of them received an eager strategy—"Think about what you would gain by choosing the mug, and think about what you would gain by choosing the pen." The other half received a vigilant strategy—"Think about what you would lose by not choosing the mug, and think about what you would lose by not choosing the pen." The order in which the mug and pen were presented as choices was counterbalanced across all participants.

As expected, all of the participants chose the coffee mug. In one study, they were then asked to assess the price of the mug they had chosen, whereas in a second study, they were given the opportunity to buy the mug with the money they had received for participating in the study. If goal pursuits with regulatory fit have greater value than those without (i.e., if there is value transfer), then the participants in these studies should assign a greater monetary value to the same coffee mug when it was chosen with, as opposed to without, regulatory fit. The results of both studies supported this prediction. Promotion-oriented individuals assigned the mug a higher price and offered more money to buy it when they had chosen it using an eager strategy than a vigilant strategy, and prevention-oriented individuals assigned the mug a higher price and offered more money to buy it when they had chosen it using a vigilant strategy than an eager strategy. Across the two studies, the monetary value of the coffee mug was judged to be about 50% higher when there was regulatory fit than when there was non-fit. In addition, participants' chronic regulatory focus and their assigned choice strategy had no main effects, per se, on their perceptions of the monetary price of the mug.

Beyond altering how people value the outcomes of their decisions, are there other ways in which regulatory fit influences judgment? This question has been addressed in several recent programs of research. In one series of studies, Freitas and Higgins (2002) hypothesized that because people with regulatory fit feel right about the goals they are pursuing, they might also feel good while engaged in this pursuit. In a series of studies, participants' regulatory orientations were either assessed by measuring their chronic promotion and prevention orientation, or were primed experimentally. Participants were then given a perceptual task in which they had to circle all of the four-sided figures within a larger matrix of shapes using either an eager strategy (e.g., "find the helpful elements"), or a vigilant strategy (e.g., "eliminate the harmful elements"). Afterwards, everyone was asked how much he or she had enjoyed the activity as a whole. As predicted, participants with a promotion orientation enjoyed the task more when using an eager strategy (which created regulatory fit) than a vigilant strategy (which did not create regulatory fit), whereas participants with a prevention orientation enjoyed the task more when using a vigilant strategy (which created regulatory fit) than an eager strategy (which did not create regulatory fit). Similar to the Idson (in press) studies described above, there was no effect on enjoyment of either regulatory focus alone or the type of strategy used alone.

In another research program, Camacho, Higgins, and Lugar (in press) hypothesized that people with regulatory fit who feel right about their goal pursuit might also feel that what they are doing is right (i.e., that what feels right is right). Similarly, if people without regulatory fit do not feel right about their goal pursuit, then they could feel that what they are doing is not right (i.e., what feels wrong is wrong). As discussed earlier, when people are in a promotion focus, ensuring against errors of omission feels right and failing to do so feels wrong. However, when people are in a prevention focus, ensuring against errors of commission feels right and failing to do so feels wrong. Thus people in a promotion focus should feel greater guilt from their errors of omission than from their errors of commission, whereas the opposite should be true for people in a prevention focus.

To test this, several studies were performed where people's regulatory focus was either assessed by measuring their chronic orientation or primed experimentally, and they were then asked to recount an experience in which some harm had arisen because of their action (i.e., an error of commission), or where some harm had arisen because of their inaction (i.e., an error of omission). The primary dependent measure was how guilty they felt about what had happened. Results showed that, as predicted, participants with a promotion orientation felt more guilty about harm that had resulted from their inaction rather than from their action, whereas participants with a prevention orientation felt more guilty about harm that had resulted from their action rather than from their inaction (see also Seta, et al., 2001). As in earlier studies, this interaction was the only significant effect.

To further examine the question of whether people's strategic preferences influence what they consider to be inherently right, Camacho et. al., (in press) performed an additional study where participants, who varied in their chronic promotion and prevention orientations, were asked to read an essay about an educational program that was being designed for underprivileged youth. For half of the participants, the overall goals of this program were described as representing eager strategies (e.g., "to promote higher achievement and ensure that everyone moves ahead"), and for the other half, pursuit of these same goals were described as representing vigilant strategies (e.g., "to prevent students from failing and ensure that no one falls behind"). Afterwards, participants judged the morality of the school program. Consistent with the results of their earlier studies, Camacho et. al, (in press) found that participants with a promotion orientation felt that the program was more morally right when its goals were described in terms of eager rather than vigilant strategies, whereas the reverse was true for participants with a prevention orientation. Once again, this interaction was the only significant effect.

Overall, these studies demonstrate that, in addition to influencing information processing during judgment, people's strategic preferences can influence evaluative judgments through regulatory fit. Because regulatory fit leads people to feel right about their goal pursuit, this can lead them to (1) feel good while pursuing these goals (i.e., what feels right feels good); (2) experience the outcomes they are striving for as having more value or worth (i.e., what feels right is good); and (3) believe that the strategies they are using are right (i.e., what feels right is right). Additional research that measures the combined effects of each of these mechanisms on people's judgments and decisions could lead to a more thorough understanding of the role of regulatory fit in judgment and decision making.

Concluding Remarks

The interaction between the motivational and cognitive systems during judgment has gained increasing prominence in the social psychological literature, and is currently spawning a growing body of important research. For his seminal contributions in the 1980s to this new perspective on motivated cognition, we are all grateful to Bob Wyer. In this chapter, we have outlined an additional perspective on motivated cognition in an attempt to broaden the field's general approach to the motivation-cognition interface. Along with studying the cognitive consequences of people's motivations to achieve preferred outcomes during judgment, we propose that researchers also examine the cognitive consequences of people's motivations to use preferred strategies in the pursuit of such outcomes.

We believe that perspectives involving preferred outcomes and preferred strategies are complementary, and together can shed more light on motivated cognition than either could alone. Indeed, it is even possible to combine these perspectives in the same study. For example, an experiment was performed by Förster, Higgins, and Strack (2000) which examined the effects on memory of both people's motivation to achieve a preferred outcome (in the form of maintaining a prejudiced viewpoint of an out-group) and their preferred strategy for processing information (in the form of promotion eagerness and prevention vigilance). In this experiment, there was an interaction between the different types of motivation. The standard finding that people have better memory for stereotype-inconsistent behaviors (for a review, see Srull & Wyer, 1986; Stangor & McMillan, 1992) was greatly enhanced when high prejudiced individuals used vigilant prevention strategies to process information. This demonstrates how additional insight can be gained when both outcome-based and strategy-based approaches to motivated reasoning are employed simultaneously.

In conclusion, the studies reviewed here are a testament to the advantages of considering people's strategic preferences when attempting to explain and predict their judgments. These studies demonstrate the influence of such preferences on fundamental components of cognition, including causal attribution, categorization, and counterfactual thinking, as well as their effects through regulatory fit on people's evaluative judgments. Although all of the studies we reviewed used promotion and prevention strategies to examine the effects of strategic preferences, the perspective we have outlined is not limited to the principle of regulatory focus. Other self-regulatory principles could, and should, be examined. Hopefully, future research of this type will deepen our understanding of strategic preferences and their critical role in motivated cognition.

REFERENCES

Bassili, J. N. (1995). Response latency and the accessibility of voting intentions: What contributes to accessibility and how it affects vote choice. *Personality and Social Psychology Bulletin, 21,* 686–695.

Bem, D. J. (1967). Self-perception: An alternative interpretation of cognitive dissonance phenomena. *Psychological Review, 74,* 183–200.

Bruner, J. S., Goodnow, J. J., & Austin, G. A. (1956). *A study of thinking.* New York: Wiley.

Cacioppo, J. T., Petty, R. E., Feinstein, J. A., Jarvis, W. B. G. (1996). Dispositional differences in cognitive motivation: The life and times of individuals varying in need for cognition. *Psychological Bulletin, 119,* 197–253.

Camacho, C. J., Higgins, E. T., & Lugar, L. (in press). Moral value transfer from regulatory fit: "What feels right *is* right" and "what feels wrong *is* wrong," *Journal of Personality and Social Psychology.*

Cooper, J., & Fazio, R. H. (1984). A new look at dissonance theory. In L. Berkowitz (Ed.), *Advances in experimental social psychology* (Vol. 17, pp. 229–266). San Diego, CA: Academic Press.

Crowe, E., & Higgins, E. T. (1997). Regulatory focus and strategic inclinations: Promotion and prevention in decision-making. *Organizational Behavior and Human Decision Processes, 69,* 117–132.

Dijksterhuis, A., van Knippenberg, A., Kruglanski, A. W., & Schaper, C. (1996). Motivated social cognition: Need for closure effects on memory and judgment. *Journal of Experimental Social Psychology, 32,* 254–270.

Doosje, B., Spears, R., & Koomen, W. (1995). When bad isn't all bad: Strategic use of sample information in generalization and stereotyping. *Journal of Personality and Social Psychology, 69,* 642–655.

Dunning, D. (1999). A newer look: Motivated social cognition and the schematic representation of social concepts. *Psychological Inquiry, 10,* 1–11.

Dunning, D., Leuenberger, A., & Sherman, D. A. (1995). A new look at motivated inference: Are self serving theories of success a product of motivational forces? *Journal of Personality and Social Psychology, 69,* 58–68.

Edwards, K., & Smith, E. E. (1996). A disconfirmation bias in the evaluation of arguments. *Journal of Personality and Social Psychology, 71,* 5–24.

Fazio, R. H. (1995). Attitudes as object-evaluation associations: Determinants, consequences, and correlates of attitude accessibility. In R. E. Petty & J. A. Krosnick (Eds.), *Attitude strength: Antecedents and consequences* (pp. 247–282). Hillsdale, NJ: Lawrence Erlbaum Associates.

Feather, N. T. (Ed.). (1982). *Expectations and actions: Expectancy-value models in psychology.* Hillsdale, NJ: Lawrence Erlbaum Associates.

Ford, T. E., & Kruglanski, A. W. (1995) Effects of epistemic motivations on the use of accessible constructs in social judgment. *Personality & Social Psychology Bulletin, 21,* 950–962.

Förster, J., Higgins, E. T., & Idson, L. C. (1998). Approach and avoidance strength during goal attainment: Regulatory focus and the "goal loom larger" effect. *Journal of Personality and Social Psychology, 75,* 1115–1131.

Förster, J., Higgins, E. T., & Strack, F. (2000). When stereotype disconfirmation is a personal threat: How prejudice and prevention focus moderate incongruency effects. *Social Cognition, 18,* 178–197.

Förster, J., Higgins, E. T., & Taylor, A. (in press). Speed/accuracy decisions in task performance: Built-in trade-off or separate strategic concerns? *Organizational Behavior and Human Decision Processes.*

Freitas, A. L., & Higgins, E. T. (2002). Enjoying goal-directed action: The role of regulatory fit. *Psychological Science, 13,* 1–6.

Friedman, R. S., & Förster, J. (2001). The effects of promotion and prevention cues on creativity. *Journal of Personality and Social Psychology, 81,* 1001–1013.

Gilovich, T., & Medvec, V. H. (1995) The experience of regret: What, when, and why. *Psychological Review, 102,* 379–395.

Gould, R. (1939). An experimental analysis of "level of aspiration." *Genetic Psychology Monographs, 21,* 3–115.

Higgins, E. T. (1987). Self-discrepancy: A theory relating self and affect. *Psychological Review, 94,* 319–340.

Higgins, E. T. (1989). Self-discrepancy theory: What patterns of self-beliefs cause people to suffer? In L. Berkowitz (Ed.), *Advances in experimental social psychology* (Vol. 22, pp. 93–136). New York: Academic Press.

Higgins, E. T. (1996). Knowledge activation: Accessibility, applicability, and salience. In E. T. Higgins & A. W. Kruglanski (Eds.), *Social psychology: Handbook of basic principles* (pp. 133–168). New York: Guilford Press.

Higgins, E. T. (1997). Beyond pleasure and pain. *American Psychologist, 52,* 1280–1300.

Higgins, E. T. (1998). Promotion and prevention: Regulatory focus as a motivational principle. In M. P. Zanna (Ed.), *Advances in experimental social psychology* (Vol. 30, pp. 1–46). New York: Academic Press.

Higgins, E. T. (2000). Making a good decision: Value from "fit." *American Psychologist, 55*, 1217–1230.

Higgins, E. T., Friedman, R. S., Harlow, R. E., Idson, L. C., Ayduk, O. N., & Taylor, A. (2001). Achievement orientations from subjective histories of success: Promotion pride versus prevention pride. *European Journal of Social Psychology, 31*, 3–23.

Higgins, E. T., Idson, L. C., Freitas, A. L., Spiegel, S., & Molden, D. C. (in press). Transfer of value from fit. *Journal of Personality and Social Psychology.*

Higgins, E. T., Shah, J., & Friedman, R. (1997). Emotional responses to goal attainment: Strength of regulatory focus as moderator. *Journal of Personality and Social Psychology, 72*, 515–525.

Higgins, E. T., & Silberman, I. (1998) Development of regulatory focus: Promotion and prevention as ways of living. In J. Heckhausen & C. S. Dweck (Eds.), *Motivation and self-regulation across the life span* (pp. 78–113). New York: Cambridge University Press.

Higgins, E. T., & Sorrentino, R. M. (Eds.). (1990). *Handbook of motivation and cognition Vol. 2: Foundations of social behavior.* New York: Guilford Press.

Kahneman, D., & Miller, D. T. (1986). Norm theory: Comparing reality to its alternatives. *Psychological Review, 93*, 136–153.

Kahneman, D., & Tversky, A. (1982). The simulation heuristic In D. Kahneman, P. Slovic, & A. Tversky (Eds.), *Judgment under uncertainty: Heuristics and biases* (pp. 201–208). New York: Cambridge University Press.

Kelley, H. H. (1973). The process of causal attribution. *American Psychologist, 28*, 107–128.

Kruglanski, A. W. (1996). Motivated social cognition: Principles of the interface. In E. T. Higgins & A. W. Kruglanski (Eds.), *Social psychology: Handbook of basic principles* (pp. 493–520). New York: Guilford Press.

Kruglanski, A. W., & Webster, D. M. (1996). Motivated closing of the mind: "Seizing" and "freezing." *Psychological Review, 103*, 263–283.

Kunda, Z. (1990). The case for motivated reasoning. *Psychological Bulletin, 108*, 480–498.

Kunda, Z. (1999). *Social cognition: Making sense of people.* Cambridge, MA: MIT Press.

Lerner, J. S., & Tetlock, P. E. (1999). Accounting for the effects of accountability. *Psychological Bulletin, 125*, 255–275.

Lewin, K. (1935). *A dynamic theory of personality.* New York: McGraw-Hill.

Liberman, N., Molden, D. C., Idson, L. C., & Higgins, E. T. (2001). Promotion and prevention focus on alternative hypotheses: Implications for attributional functions. *Journal of Personality and Social Psychology, 80*, 5–18.

Lynch, J. G., & Cohen, J. L. (1978). The use of subjective expected utility theory as an aid to understanding variables that influence helping behavior. *Journal of Personality and Social Psychology, 36*, 1138–1151.

Mayseless, O., & Kruglanski, A. W. (1987). What makes you so sure? Effects of epistemic motivations on judgmental confidence. *Organizational Behavior and Human Decision Processes, 39*, 162–183.

Mikulincer, M., Kedem, P., & Paz, D. (1990). The impact of trait anxiety and situational stress on the categorization of natural objects. *Anxiety Research, 2*, 85–101.

Miller, D. T., Ross, M. (1975). Self-serving biases in the attribution of causality: Fact or fiction? *Psychological Bulletin, 82*, 213–225.

Molden, D. C., & Higgins, E. T. (2001). *Categorization under uncertainty: Regulatory focus and type of uncertainty as moderators.* Manuscript under review, Columbia University.

Morris, M. W., & Larrick, R. P. (1995). When one cause casts doubt on another: A normative analysis of discounting in causal attribution. *Psychological Review, 102,* 331–355.

Nisbett, R. E., & Ross, L. (1980). *Human inference: Strategies and shortcomings of social judgment.* Englewood Cliffs, NJ: Prentice Hall.

Roese, N. J. (1997). Counterfactual thinking. *Psychological Bulletin, 121,* 133–148.

Roese, N. J., Hur, T., & Pennington, G. L. (1999). Counterfactual thinking and regulatory focus: Implications for action versus inaction and sufficiency versus necessity. *Journal of Personality and Social Psychology, 77,* 1109–1120.

Santioso, R., Kunda, Z., & Fong, G. T. (1990). Motivated recruitment of autobiographical memories. *Journal of Personality and Social Psychology, 59,* 229–241.

Schaller, M. (1992). In-group favoritism and statistical reasoning in social inference: Implications for formation and maintenance of group stereotypes. *Journal of Personality and Social Psychology, 63,* 61–74.

Seta, J. J., McElroy, T., & Seta, C. E. (2001). To do or not to do: Desirability and consistency mediate judgments of regret. *Journal of Personality and Social Psychology, 80,* 861–870.

Shah, J., & Higgins, E. T. (1997). Expectancy X value effects: Regulatory focus as a determinant of magnitude and direction. *Journal of Personality and Social Psychology, 73,* 447–458.

Sorrentino, R. M., & Higgins, E. T. (Eds.). (1986a). *Handbook of motivation and cognition: Foundations of social behavior.* New York: Guilford Press.

Sorrentino, R. M., & Higgins, E. T. (1986b). Motivation and cognition: Warming up to synergism. In R. M. Sorrentino & E. T. Higgins (Eds.) *Handbook of motivation and cognition: Foundations of social behavior.* New York: Guilford Press.

Sorrentino, R. M., & Higgins, E. T. (Eds.). (1996). *Handbook of motivation and cognition, Vol. 3: The interpersonal context.* New York: Guilford Press.

Srull, T. K., & Wyer, R. S. (1986). The role of chronic and temporary goals in social information processing. In R. M. Sorrentino & E. T. Higgins (Eds.), *Handbook of motivation and cognition: Foundations of social behavior.* New York: Guilford Press.

Stangor, C., & McMillan, D. (1992). Memory for expectancy-congruent and expectancy-incongruent information: A review of the social and social developmental literatures. *Psychological Bulletin, 111,* 42–61.

Steele, C. M. (1988). The psychology of self-affirmation: Sustaining the integrity of the self. In L. Berkowitz (Ed.), *Advances in experimental social psychology* (Vol. 21, pp. 261–302). San Diego, CA: Academic Press.

Tanner, W. P., Jr., & Swets, J. A. (1954). A decision-making theory of visual detection. *Psychological Review, 61,* 401–409.

Tetlock, P. E., & Levi, A. (1982). Attribution bias: On the inconclusiveness of the cognition-motivation debate. *Journal of Experimental Social Psychology, 18,* 68–88.

Thompson, E. P., Roman, R. J., Moskowitz, G. B., Chaiken, S., & Bargh, J. A. (1994). Systematic processing and the debasing of covert primacy effects in impression formation: Unshackling the motivated perceiver from constraints of accessibility. *Journal of Personality and Social Psychology, 66,* 474–489.

Trope, Y., & Liberman, A. (1996). Social hypothesis testing: Cognitive and motivational mechanisms. In E. T. Higgins & A. W. Kruglanski (Eds.), *Social psychology: Handbook of basic principles* (pp. 239–270). New York: Guilford Press.

Webster, D. M. (1993). Motivated augmentation and reduction of the over-attribution bias. *Journal of Personality and Social Psychology, 65,* 261–271.

Wilson, T. D., & Schooler, J. W. (1991) Thinking too much: Introspection can reduce the quality of preferences and decisions. *Journal of Personality and Social Psychology, 60,* 181–192.

Wing-hong Lam, T., & Chiu, C. Y. (2002). The motivational function of regulatory focus in creativity. *Journal of Creative Behavior. 36,* 138–150.

Woodworth, R. S. (1899) Accuracy of voluntary movements. *Psychological Review, 3,* 1–101.

Wyer, R. S., Bodenhausen, G. V., & Srull, T. K (1984). The cognitive representation of persons and groups and its effect on recall and recognition memory. *Journal of Experimental Social Psychology, 20,* 445–469.

Wyer, R. S., & Gordon, S. E. (1982). The recall of information about persons and groups. *Journal of Experimental Social Psychology, 18,* 128–164.

Wyer, R. S., Srull, T. K., & Gordon, S. E. (1984). The effects of predicting a person's behavior on subsequent trait judgments. *Journal of Experimental Social Psychology, 20,* 29–46.

Wyer, R. S., Srull, T. K., Gordon, S. E., & Hartwick, J. (1982). Effects of processing objectives on the recall of prose material. *Journal of Personality and Social Psychology, 43,* 674–688.

ACKNOWLEDGMENT

The research reported in this article was supported by Grant 39429 from the National Institute of Mental Health to E. Tory Higgins.

11

The Effects of Power on Those who Possess It: How Social Structure can Affect Social Cognition

Deborah A. Greenspan
Stanford University

Dacher J. Keltner
University of California, Berkeley

Cameron Anderson
Northwestern University

INTRODUCTION

Research on social cognition is typically concerned with how the minds of individuals perceive, encode, recall, and judge the behavior of social targets. Recently this literature has been touched by invigorated interest in the social and interpersonal contexts in which social cognitions occur (e.g., Levine, Resnick, & Higgins, 1993; Resnick, Levine, & Teasley, 1991; Thompson, Le-

237

vine, & Messick, 1999). Building on classic work by Asch (1951), Festinger (1954), McGuire (1969), and Zajonc (1960; 1965), among others, psychologists who care about the social and sociological determinants of behavior have begun to investigate how social systems such as culture (Markus & Kitayama, 1991; Morris and Peng, 1994), demography (McGuire & Padawer-Singer, 1976, Steele & Aronson, 1995), democracy (Keltner & Robinson, 1996; Nemeth, 1986; Gruenfeld, 1995; Gruenfeld & Preston, 2000), hierarchy (Bargh, Raymond, Pryor, & Strack, 1995; Fiske, 1993; Jost & Banaji, 1994; Keltner, Gruenfeld, & Anderson, in press), accountability (Tetlock, 1992), and interpersonal relationships (Staudinger & Baltes,1996; Wegner, Erber, & Raymond, 1991) affect basic cognitive processes.

Bob Wyer was, as usual, a pioneer in this branch of social cognition research. After having what would easily count as a successful career developing a seminal and purely individual paradigm for the study of person memory, Wyer began to look outside the head and into the world of the social perceiver (Wyer, Lambert, Budesheim, & Gruenfeld, 1992). Wyer's work on how social cognition is affected by conversations (Wyer, Budesheim, & Lambert, 1990; Wyer & Gruenfeld, 1995a; 1995b; Wyer, Swan, & Gruenfeld, 1995), communication norms (Gruenfeld & Wyer, 1992; Wyer, Budesheim, Lambert & Swan, 1994), political affiliations (Waenke & Wyer, 1996), and close relationships (Gaelick, Bodenhausen, & Wyer, 1985) illuminated and directed the field toward a number of important aspects of social context.

Wyer's very direct influence on at least one of us is evident in the focus of this chapter, which highlights the effects of power on social cognition and behavior. In earlier work, Keltner, Gruenfeld, and Anderson (in press) proposed that power activates the general tendency to approach rather than inhibit, leading to automatic rather than controlled responses. Here, we elaborate the social cognitive consequences of possessing power and the implications of those consequences for social behavior.

To do this, we integrate evidence from our own research with evidence from a number of other psychological domains. We begin by situating our theory within the literature on power, which emphasizes its origins (Emerson, 1962), forms (French & Raven, 1959), and effects (Fiske, 1993; Kipnis, 1972; Sachdev & Bourhis, 1991). Next, we present our theory in the form of three propositions about how power affects cognitive control mechanisms, social perception, and motor activity. Finally, we present the empirical evidence on which these propositions are based, test some preliminary hypotheses, and speculate about the implications of our findings for behavior in specific contexts.

PREVIOUS APPROACHES TO THE STUDY OF POWER

The notion that power corrupts is a widely held tenet of conventional wisdom. History provides many vivid examples of corruption in the powerful, and current events concur: individuals with disproportionate control over others' fates seem unusually susceptible to forces of greed and depravity. Perhaps this is not surprising. Power, by definition, reduces dependence on other people, which might explain why power appears to reduce concern for the social consequences of one's actions. However, the fact that power also leads to increased responsibility for others' outcomes presents a paradox: The actions of the powerful *matter more*, in terms of their social consequences, than the actions of those with less power, yet the powerful seem to *care less* about the social consequences of their actions.

The concept of power has been defined in many ways and conceived at many levels of analysis (for reviews see Kipnis, 1976; Lee-Chai & Bargh, 2001; Ng, 1980). Power is applied to individuals (French & Raven, 1959; Winter, 1973), members of interacting dyads (Mannix & Neale, 1993; Thibaut & Kelley, 1959), factions and coalitions within small groups (Festinger, Schachter, & Back, 1950; French & Snyder, 1959, Komorita, 1984; Murnighan, 1978) and groups that compete for resources in organizations (Mannix, 1993; Kaarbo, 1996; Pfeffer & Salancik, 1974), and communities (Green, Wong, & Strolovitch, 1996; Keltner & Robinson, 1996; 1997).

In the psychological literature, power is traditionally defined as the ability to control outcomes without social interference. Some definitions emphasize control over one's own outcomes (Weber, 1947), while others emphasize control over the outcomes and actions of others (Blau, 1964; Thibaut & Kelley, 1959). Operationally, however, power is often defined in terms of resource dependence; more precisely, in terms of its absence (Emerson, 1962; Thibaut & Kelley, 1959). Other operationalizations define power in terms of organizational roles (e.g., supervisor vs. subordinate, Kipnis & Cosentino, 1969). Empirical definitions of power emphasize resource distributions, which qualify as both a structural determinant of power (e.g., Murnighan, 1978) and an outcome measure (e.g., Sachdev & Bourhis, 1991). Such approaches can be tautological in that they define power in terms of its consequences. They also assume, implicitly, that structural determinants of power lead automatically to the performance of control acts, without consideration of the role of intervening mechanisms.

In contrast, our approach distinguishes among the structural determinants of power (e.g., social hierarchy, organizational roles, resource control), the subjective experience of power (e.g., feelings of control, responsibility, superiority), and the formal exercise of power (e.g., the performance of control acts). In our review, we draw on previous traditions by defining the ability to provide rewards and punishments as a critical antecedent to the sense of power. We expand on prior work by emphasizing the sense of power and its psychological effects, which mediate the link between one's ability to control outcomes and the effects of that ability on one's social behavior. This definition applies to individuals and to groups, and distinguishes among the objective and the subjective aspects of power. Whereas power is often treated as a categorical variable that is dispositional and generalizable across situations, we assume that the determinants, experience and exercise of power vary within people and across situations.

OVERVIEW OF THE THEORY

Our theory specifies how the psychological reactions of powerholders to the experience of power affect their subsequent social behaviors. Figure 11.1 displays the proposed sequence of events. The sequence begins at the top of the figure with "origins of power" (A), and ends at the bottom with "social behavior" (D).

Power Differences are a Consequence of Social Organization (A→B)

In social systems, resources and work are distributed across individuals, which creates dependence relations and opportunities for interpersonal control (Emerson, 1962). An individual or group that controls access to desired resources holds power over those who desire access. Control over desired resources creates opportunities to reward and punish others. Thus those with power can control others' actions as well as their outcomes. We assume that for power to be experienced, it must be recognized in the context of a particular episode. This experience can be derived from the possession of status, expertise, and charisma, as well as from formal authority (French & Raven, 1959). However, the decision to exercise power depends on the perceived presence or absence of social and physical constraints. Consistent with this argument, the ability to control others does not always lead to the experience or exercise of power (Wrong, 1979).

The Experience of Power is Disinhibiting (B→C)

We begin with the premise that human behavior reflects a dynamic tension in the relative activity of behavioral approach and inhibition systems (Carver & White, 1994; Gray, 1994; Higgins, 1999). Whereas the behavioral approach system involves positive affect, attention to rewards, and goal-directed behavior, the behavioral inhibition system is characterized by avoidance-related affect (e.g., anxiety, fear) heightened concern regarding social threat and avoidant behavior. Under conditions of interdependence, humans must balance the motivation to approach desired outcomes with the motivation to maintain social relationships (James, 1890). These motivations lead to inhibition, which brings behavior under conscious control (Carver & Scheier, 1981; Wicklund, 1975). In contrast, the experience of power includes awareness that one can act at will without social interference or serious social consequences (Weber, 1947). When social constraints are not evident, responses are more automatic than controlled (Wegner & Bargh, 1998). Thus, power is a force of disinhibition: it deactivates mechanisms of self-regulation and behavioral control, and increases reliance on pre-existing cognitive representations, as well as heuristics, "habits-of-mind," and other "dominant" response routines.

Disinhibition Affects Social Behavior in the Powerful (C→D)

Social perception. Power shifts attention away from social determinants of behavior toward personal, dispositional determinants, which include automatic, top-down cognitive responses. This means that power will affect the motivation for social information processing, as well as how social targets are perceived (Fiske & Taylor, 1991). Because of their reduced concern with social consequences, individuals with power will be less aware of others and what they are doing than those with less power (Chance, 1967; Ellyson & Dovidio, 1985; Gruenfeld & Fan, 1998). The powerful will also be less accurate in their judgments and appraisals of others (Fiske, 1993), and more likely to misperceive others' interests and positions than those with less power (Keltner & Robinson, 1996; 1997). This occurs not only because of inattention, but because the powerful perceive others through a lens of self-interest. When social targets are attended to, they will be perceived in terms of the qualities that make them useful to the perceiver, rather than qualities that enable them to be understood.

Motor response. By activating the behavioral approach system, increasing reliance on automatic responses and reducing concern for the social consequences of those responses, power short-circuits deliberative consideration of response choices. Powerful actors think of, rather than about, acting. Whereas consideration of response alternatives inhibits action (James, 1890; Tetlock, 1992), single-minded thought of a particular action facilitates its performance. Thus power restores a direct link between impulse and action (Kipnis, 1972). Actors with power will act more, with greater magnitude, and in ways that are more idiosyncratic and socially inappropriate than actors with less power (Galinsky, Gruenfeld, & Magee, 2002).

EVIDENCE FOR THE THEORY

Power is Disinhibiting (B→C)

The theoretical basis of this proposition is that power activates the behavioral approach system, reducing both the motivation and capacity for self regulation. Since automatic responses precede control responses in time, they are actually overridden or suppressed by attempts at self control (Neely, 1977; Posner & Snyder, 1975). Inhibitory responses require considerable effort, so they only occur when both motivation and capacity are sufficient. Thus when either the motivation or capacity to self-regulate is insufficient (e.g., under conditions of power), behavior recedes from conscious control. We refer to the release of control mechanisms and restoration of automatic responses as "disinhibition."

As noted earlier, there is surprisingly little systematic research on psychological reactions to power in those who possess it. The literature on self control is no exception. In their recent review of this literature, Wegner & Bargh (1998) did not discuss the effects of power at all. However, they review a number of established findings and principles that provide indirect support for our contention.

The proposition that power is disinhibiting can be justified on two grounds. First, since power reduces dependence on others, it is likely to reduce concern for the social consequences of one's actions and the perceived need to self regulate (Chance, 1967; Erber & Fiske, 1984; Keltner & Robinson, 1996; 1997). This is consistent with Jastrow's (1906) principle of utility, which suggests that attentional resources are allocated first to responses that require careful monitoring and control, and that routine modes of responding recede from conscious awareness to free cognitive resources for this purpose. It is also consistent with Taylor's (1998; Fiske & Taylor, 1991) notion of people as motivated tacticians who attend carefully to stimuli that are most relevant for personal goal attainment, while delegating less relevant stimuli to automatic, non-conscious processing. From this perspective, power not only reduces social constraint per se, it might also reduce awareness of constraints that do exist by making them seem unimportant. Thus people with power are disinhibited because they feel free to behave as they wish.

In addition to this purely motivational rationale, it can be argued that power reduces the cognitive capacity for self-regulation. Since powerholders typically have greater responsibility than those without power, their focus on the tasks for which they are responsible might overwhelm their ability to attend to more peripheral social stimuli (Fiske, 1993). Control processes require greater effort than automatic ones (Shiffrin, 1988), and since cognitive resources are limited, only the most important tasks are subject to conscious regulation. It is therefore possible that by increasing cognitive load, power inadvertently disinhibits behaviors that are not central to the completion of critical tasks.

To test the proposition that power is disinhibiting, we looked for evidence of a relationship between power and two direct psychological correlates of disinhibition. According to our definition, disinhibition corresponds with limited consideration of response alternatives. This suggests that power should be associated with low levels of cognitive deliberation (H1). Our definition also implies a strong correspondence between internal psychological states and social behavior. Therefore we predict that power is associated with high correlations between behavior on the one hand, and personality and emotion on the other (H2).

Power is Associated with Low Levels of Deliberation

Galinsky, Gruenfeld and Magee (2002) examined this hypothesis using a procedure developed to distinguish implemental from deliberative mind-sets (Gollwitzer, Heckhausen, & Steller, 1990). They asked participants to recall a specific time in which they either had power over someone or in which someone else had power over them. Afterward, participants were shown an incomplete fairy tale about a king who was called into battle and faced leaving his beloved daughter, the princess, behind. They were asked to complete the story by writing three sentences at the end. Participants' responses were content-analyzed by counting the number of active- and passive-verb phrases, which correspond to implemental and deliberative thinking, respectively. Consistent with predictions, subjects in the high-power condition used more implemental verb phrases than deliberative, and the opposite was true for those in the low-power condition.

Similar findings have been observed in research on cognitive complexity. Cognitive complexity corresponds to a style of reasoning that involves careful consideration of response options and their respective consequences (Suedfeld, Tetlock, & Streufert, 1992). Whereas high levels of complexity reflect recognition of trade-offs among response choices, low levels of complexity reflect use of a single evaluative dimension to distinguish good and bad alternatives. Studies of reasoning by individuals and groups show that in the absence of concern about the social consequences of one's actions, complexity is generally low, relative to conditions in which social consequences matter. For example, Tetlock and his colleagues have established that decision makers who are not held accountable for the content and quality of their decisions exhibit lower levels of cognitive complexity than those who make the same judgments and believe they will have to justify their actions (for reviews see Tetlock, 1992; Lerner & Tetlock, 1999).

A recent study of U.S. Supreme Court justices supports this conclusion (Gruenfeld & Kim, 2002). We examined the relationship between justices' power and their complexity levels by comparing opinions endorsed by coalitions of different sizes. In the Supreme Court, like other democratic decision groups that use a "majority wins" rule, the power of a coalition corresponds directly to its size (Davis, 1973; Jost, 1998). All opinions in our sample were single-authored, but each opinion was written on behalf of a coalition of other justices who collectively endorsed it. We assumed, therefore, that the power of an opinion's author corresponded to the size of the endorsing coalition. Consistent with Hypothesis 1, the relationship between power and justices' complexity levels was generally negative: complexity decreases as power increases. It is interesting to note, however, that this effect was significant only for the authors of majority opinions. In the authors of minority opinions, the relationship between coalition size and complexity was unexpectedly non-systematic.

This finding is consistent with earlier research showing that the authors of majority opinions are less cognitively complex when the group is unanimous, and their actions unconstrained, than when they encounter resistance in the form of a vocal minority (Gruenfeld, 1995; see also Janis, 1972; Janis & Mann, 1991; Nemeth, 1986). In fact, an experiment designed to test this explanation directly showed that when subjects were assigned to majorities in unanimous or non-unanimous decision groups, and all groups considered the same case, their complexity actually decreased in response to unanimous conditions (Gruenfeld, Thomas-Hunt, & Kim, 1998). This was true for both their public statements and their private, anonymous responses.

Perhaps the most direct evidence for the negative relationship between power and cognitive complexity was found by Woike (1994), who showed in a study of person perception that individuals with a dominance orientation formed impressions of a target that were less cognitively complex than individuals with a communal orientation. Specifically, dominance-motivated subjects exhibited more cognitive differentiation, whereas communally-motivated subjects exhibited more cognitive integration in their impressions. Woike argued that cognitive differentiation corresponded with the perceiver's desire to maintain psychological distance (i.e., separation) from the target. In contrast, cognitive integration corresponded with the perceiver's desire to connect with the target and consider his or her point of view. In one experiment, male subjects who exhibited "agentic" motives in their descriptions of a recently experienced event described a social target with lower levels of cognitive integration than female subjects who exhibited "communal" motives. An agentic orientation was defined as the motivation to have impact and control others, whereas communal orientation was defined as the motivation to be connected and intimate with others. In a second experiment, subjects who were high in power motivation exhibited lower levels of integration than those who were high in intimacy motivation, regardless of gender.

In sum, these findings demonstrate that power is associated with low levels of cognitive complexity. They support our contention that power disinhibits by reducing careful thought about the potential consequences of one's responses, and by limiting consideration of available response alternatives.

Power is Associated with High Correlations
Between Psychological States and Behavior

If power disinhibits by releasing control mechanisms and increasing reliance on automatic responding, the actions of those with power should correspond more closely to their internal psychological states than to social norms or other external standards for guiding behavior. Moreover, this correspondence should be greater in high-power than low-power individuals.

Two studies have tested this hypothesis. One study examined the effects of power on the relationships among personality, emotion, and behavior in interactions between pairs of fraternity members (Keltner, Young, Heerey, Oemig, & Monarch, 1998). The pairs were composed of high status "active" members, who were chosen based on their leadership within the fraternity, and newly admitted "pledge" members. Subjects in the study completed a questionnaire designed to measure neuroticism, and later, engaged in a "teasing" exercise in which they were instructed to generate a nickname for their partner and to explain its meaning. Consistent with predictions, the neuroticism indices of "active" members who had been in the fraternity for at least two years reliably predicted both their reports of negative emotion ($r = .45, p < .05$ for negative emotion), and their physical expressions of positive emotion ($r = -.48, p < .05$). In contrast, the neuroticism indices of recently admitted "pledge" members did not predict either of these other measures ($rs = .13$ and $-.16$, ns). The high- and low-power fraternity members did not differ in their levels of neuroticism or experienced emotion.

Anderson & Keltner (1999) found that high-power subjects were less susceptible to emotional contagion than low-power subjects. In this experiment, pairs of undergraduates living in the same dormitory engaged in three tasks that were designed to elicit embarrassment. In each pair, one member performed an embarrassing task while the other observed. Contagion was measured by correlating the empathic emotion displayed by the observer with the emotion exhibited by the performer. When the observer was a low-status dorm member, contagion was greater than when the observer was high-status. LaFrance and Banaji (1992) also found a stronger correlation between certain kinds of emotion (e.g., anger) and behavior in men than in women. Finally, it has also been shown that males are better judges of their own physiological responses than females. To the extent that power corresponds with sex in these studies, these findings are consistent with our hypothesis.

Summary

These considerations support the proposition that automatic responses are activated by the experience of power. They provide evidence that power disinhibits by reducing self-consciousness and careful consideration of response alternatives, and restoring a direct link between internal states—such as personality and emotion—and physical behavior. As illustrated in Fig.11.1, disinhibition in response to the experience of power has important consequences for subsequent actions by the powerful. These consequences are discussed next.

Power Affects Social Behavior (B→D)

The effects of disinhibition on social behavior are manifold. We have chosen to focus on two specific types of behavior because of their importance in the field of social psychology. One is social perception; the other is motor activity. The effects of power on each type of social behavior will be discussed in turn.

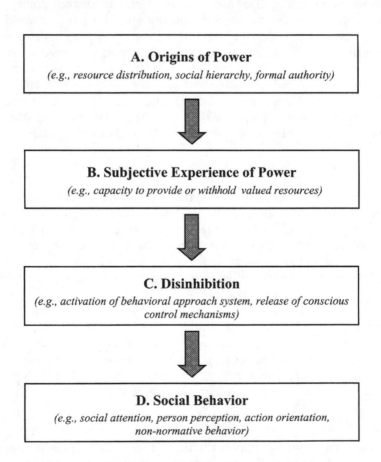

FIG. 11.1   Events underlying the effects of power on those who possess it.

Power Colors Social Perception

It has long been argued that those with power are less attentive to others than those without power. For example, Chance (1967) advanced the attention structure hypothesis, and documented in studies of social interactions among children and adults that low-status individuals look at high-status individuals, whereas high-status individuals are less inclined to look at others. Similarly, power has been operationalized as the visual dominance ratio, which indicates that when high-power individuals speak, low-power individuals listen carefully, but that when low-power individuals speak, high-power individuals are more inclined to look away (Ellyson & Dovidio, 1985).

The role of disinhibition in this process has not been previously considered, however, and it allows us to generate more specific predictions about the nature and consequences of these attentional effects. The notion that power deflects attention away from social cues, toward internal psychological cues, suggests that the *focus*, rather than *amount*, of attention is affected by power (H3). Moreover, the proposed effects of power on automaticity suggest that power should reduce attentiveness, particularly, to those aspects of social targets that are not useful or relevant to the pursuit of self interest (H4). Indeed, we hypothesize that power may in fact increase attentiveness to those characteristics of social targets that make them appear useful for satisfying personal goals (see also Overbeck & Park, 2001).

Power is Associated with Low Levels of Social Awareness

To test this hypothesis, we examined the attributions of high- and low-power subjects for group performance outcomes (Gruenfeld & Fan, 1998). Equal numbers of high-power and low-power subjects collaborated on a group production task that involved assembling a complex puzzle in as little time as possible. The high-power subjects differed from the low-power subjects in that they were given control over how the work was to be accomplished. They were also given a blueprint of the puzzle, but were not allowed to show it to the low-power subjects. After the groups had completed the task, they were given veridical feedback about their performance relative to other groups, and members were asked to individually generate an explanation for their group's performance. Members wrote their explanations on a single sheet of paper, and their responses were content-analyzed. Although there were no systematic differences between the actual contributions of high- and low-power subjects, or the length of their explanations, high-power subjects' explanations made significantly fewer references to the actions of other people than the explanations of low-power subjects. In their group-performance attributions, low-power subjects were significantly more likely to both give credit and assign blame to other people than were high-power subjects, who were more likely to discuss their own motivations and abilities, and were more likely to refer to characteristics of the task. Consistent with prior research, this result suggests that power reduces awareness of what others are doing. As a consequence, we believe, power should also reduce the accuracy of social perception. Susan Fiske's work supports this hypothesis. She found that individuals with power are more likely to use stereotypes, and less likely to use individuating information than are individuals with less power (Fiske, 1993).

Power is Associated with Misperception
of Social Targets' Interests

Keltner and his colleagues tested this hypothesis at the group level in the context of social and political conflicts. They predicted that members of majority groups, who have power because they represent the status quo, would be more likely to stereotype their opposition as extremists than members of their minority-group counterparts. In one study (Keltner & Robinson, 1996; 1997), they surveyed the attitudes and book preferences of 273 "traditionalist" and "revisionist" English professors, who differed in their inclinations to preserve or change the English curriculum in college courses. Consistent with previous work on misperception in ideological disputes, both groups overestimated the differences in their attitudes and book preferences, and the extremity of their opponent's conviction. However, traditionalists were more prone to polarize the two sides' attitudes and to underestimate the book preferences they shared with their opponents. Traditionalists, who also tended to be tenured and male, were more likely to stereotype the two camps as extremist, and they were also more likely to erroneously assume that they shared few book preferences in common with their opponents.

A second study (Ebenbach & Keltner, 1998) replicated this finding in a comparison of college students whose attitudes placed them either in the numerical majority or in the numerical minority on a variety of social issues (e.g., gun control, the death penalty). Majority members were more likely than minority members to overestimate the extremism of the average members of both sides.

Similar findings have been observed in the literature on conflict resolution. That is, high-power disputants are typically less aware of their opponents' underlying interests than are low-power disputants, who are therefore more likely to discover integrative solutions that benefit both parties (Mannix & Neale, 1993; see also Kim, 1997; Sondak & Bazerman, 1991). Mannix & Neale found that when buyers and sellers in a market simulation had unequal power, low-power subjects made final offers of higher joint gain than did high-power subjects. The authors inferred that a power disadvantage might have compelled negotiators to consider the available options and both parties' interests more carefully.

The effects of power on accuracy in social perception might likewise account for the finding that males are less accurate than females in their judgments of others' emotions, intentions, and nonverbal behaviors (Hall, 1984). Plant, Hyde, Keltner, and Devine (2000) found that male subjects, when asked to judge the nature of negative emotion displayed by an infant, were more likely to assign stereotypical emotions than female subjects. Specifically, they were more likely to label the emotion as "anger" when they thought the infant was male than when they thought the infant was female. Female subjects were more even-handed in their assessments.

A related result suggests that power may affect the tendency to take another's perspective as well. After manipulating power using the experiential priming procedure described earlier, Gruenfeld, Galinsky, and Magee (2000) asked study participants, who were alone in a room, to draw a capital "E" on their foreheads with a nontoxic wash-off Crayola marker. This task was initially developed to study perspective-taking (Hass, 1984). Consistent with our expectations, the majority of subjects in the high-power condition displayed their disregard for others' perspectives by drawing the "E" so that it was illegible (i.e., backward) to any observer but legible (i.e., forward) to themselves. In contrast, subjects in the low-power condition were more likely to draw the "E" so that others could read it but it was illegible (i.e., backward) from their own perspective.

Summary and Implications

These findings demonstrate that social perceivers with power are less attentive to others actions, interest, and perspectives than are those without power. While other people can be relevant to the goals of both high- and low-power perceivers, the interests and expectations of others are not equally relevant to both. Perceivers who lack social control are motivated to understand the causal relations in their environment, which leads to systematic consideration of the factors that compel others to behave as they do, including dispositional and situational influences. In contrast, understanding what motivates others is less important for perceivers who possess power, because it is less likely to have an impact on their goal attainment.

Hence, powerful perceivers are likely to engage in only superficial appraisals of social targets, such as simple categorization of acts and characterization of actors' stable characteristics (Gilbert, 1998). However, superficial appraisals are unlikely to include the more controlled, effortful process of correcting those attributions through consideration of situational determinants of targets' actions.

Powerful perceivers are more likely to be aware of the extent to which a social target provides access to desired resources (e.g., sex, status, money, nourishment) than they are to be aware of those targets' interests and expectations in a particular situation. This suggests that in addition to the well-established finding that power affects the amount of attention allocated to social perception, power should also affect the characteristics attended to. We believe that whereas low-power perceivers attend to the animate reactions of targets to specific situations—which is what makes them human—high-power perceivers attend to targets' inanimate characteristics, which leads to the perception of humans as objects. Hence an implication of our theory that has not been tested is that power leads to the objectification of social targets (H5).

Power is Associated With Action (B→D)

Perhaps the simplest prediction from our theoretical framework is that high-powered individuals are likely to exhibit disinhibited motor responses. A wealth of previously documented findings are consistent with this prediction, and numerous explanations for such effects have been proposed. But, the role of disinhibition and automatic response on motor behavior has not been tested directly. One clear implication of our theory is that behavior is disinhibited by single-minded thought of the act to be performed. Behavior is inhibited, we believe, by consideration of response alternatives and their social consequences. Although there is little empirical evidence for this argument, William James (1890) wrote about it as a conclusion from his own work:

> It is the absence of scruples, of consequences, of considerations, the extraordinary simplification of each moment's mental outlook, that gives to the explosive individual such motor energy and ease; it need not be the greater intensity of any of his passions, motives, or thoughts. (p. 538)

Based on these considerations, we predict that power affects the fluency (H6) and the magnitude of expressive behavior (H7), as well as the proclivity to engage in idiosyncratic behaviors that are typically inhibited in social situations (H8). Evidence bearing on each of these hypotheses will be presented in turn.

Power Affects Activity Level

In the psycholinguistic literature, it is well established that high-power individuals talk more, interrupt others more, are more likely to speak out of turn, and are more directive of others' verbal contributions than low-power individuals (DePaulo & Friedman, 1998). Similarly, research on small groups has documented that high-power group members tend to be more actively and physically engaged in group projects, whereas low-power members are often observed to be passive and withdrawn; that is, less physically active (Moreland & Levine, 1989).

In a direct test of this hypothesis, Galinsky et al. (2002) showed that power creates an action-orientation in the powerholder. Participants in high-power conditions were more likely to take a "hit" in a simulated game of blackjack, to remove an annoying stimulus when it was unclear whether doing so was permitted, to give and take large amounts in a social dilemma, and to project an action-orientation on to the protagonist in a fairy tale, relative to low-power and control conditions.

Power Affects the Magnitude of Physical Gesture

High-status individuals adopt less inhibited postures than those with low status: They tend to position themselves asymmetrically, taking up as much space as possible, whereas low-status individuals tend to hold themselves more rigidly, and to minimize the amount of space they occupy (Ellyson & Dovidio, 1985). The study of fraternity members described earlier also supports this hypothesis (Keltner et al., 1998). In that study, high-power members' smiles were more intense than those of low-power members, in response to the same joke.

Power Affects the Proclivity to Perform
Idiosyncratic, Socially Inappropriate Acts

Ward and Keltner (cited in Keltner et al., in press) have shown support for this prediction in studies of table manners and sexual behavior. In one study, groups of either three females or three males engaged in a series of group discussion tasks. One individual in each group was chosen at random to evaluate the performance of the other two, and to assign points at the end of the experiment based on their performance that would be used in a lottery when the experiment was finished. This individual was thereby given power over the other two subjects. After subjects had spent more than 30 minutes discussing a long list of social issues, the experimenter arrived with a plate of five cookies, ostensibly to refresh the three participants. Consistent with predictions, subjects in the high-power condition were more likely to take a second cookie than those in the low-power condition, and this was especially true for female subjects. Content analysis of video tapes showed that high-power subjects were also more likely to chew with their mouths open, and to get crumbs on their faces and on the table. In addition, the eating behavior of male subjects was generally less inhibited than that of female subjects.

Prior research has shown a similar relationship between power and sexual activity. For example, the simple priming of power-related concepts can make sexual concepts more accessible, at least in those with a propensity for harassment (Bargh et al., 1995), suggesting that power can disinhibit sexual responses. Moreover, the incidence of rape is highest in cultures that emphasize male dominance over females, where it is common to use sexual threat as a means of social control. The effect of manipulated power on sexual behavior was recently assessed in a study of flirtation (Ward, Gonzaga, & Keltner, cited in Keltner et al., in press). In this experiment, female–male dyads were told that they would engage in a series of creativity tasks. In one condition, the female was given power over the male using the performance-evaluation manipulation described in the previous study, and in a second condition the male was given power over the female. In a third condition, the two participants had equal power. Subjects in the high-power condition flirted in a more disinhibited fashion than those in a low-power condition, and this was true for both males and females.

Studies of physical aggression show a similar pattern. For example, the incidence of hate crimes against disliked minority groups is greatest when the power of the majority is greatest (Green, Abelson, & Garnett, 1996; Green, Wong, & Strolovitch, 1996). As the power distance between groups approaches equilibrium, however, the incidence of hate crime drops off. It is interesting to note that discrimination and feelings of dislike toward such groups do not necessarily dissipate in such settings; rather, they are expressed in more passive (i.e., less physically overt) ways (Sears, 1988).

Summary

These findings suggest that power disinhibits motor responses in a number of important ways: By restoring a direct link between internal psychological states and the acts that satisfy them, power increases activity level, the magnitude of physical gesture, and the tendency to perform idiosyncratic and socially inappropriate behaviors.

Moderating factors (A→C, D, E)

As noted earlier, the ability to control outcomes does not always lead to the enactment of outcome control. This is because power occurs in social systems that are dynamic and multi-dimensional, with respect to social relationships and psychological experience. The chain of mechanisms described so far is expected to generalize across social systems to the extent that power differences exist. However, each of the links in the causal chain is susceptible to moderation by a number of other variables that can accompany power and power differences in the context of a specific interpersonal episode. Although a full discussion of moderating factors is beyond the scope of this chapter, we note briefly, in this section, how some of these variables might limit disinhibition in response to the experience of power.

Accountability

One important variable that often accompanies structural power, particularly in organizational contexts, is personal accountability for one's actions. People who are able to control others' outcomes but know they will be held accountable for the means and consequences of their actions are more likely to consider social consequences, and take others' interests into account than those who are not accountable (Tetlock, 1992; Lerner & Tetlock, 1999). This explains why U.S. presidents exhibit greater cognitive complexity after they are elected than prior to election (Tetlock, 1981). Although U.S. presidents possess greater power than presidential candidates, presidents are more accountable to a larger and more diverse set of constituents for the consequences of their policy actions than are presidential candidates. On the basis of our argument, however, it is fair to assume that elected Presidents are more likely to perform disinhibited acts for which they believe they will not be held accountable.

It is interesting to note that this finding bears on the potential mechanisms by which power disinhibits. Whereas elected presidents are less dependent on constituents than are presidential candidates, they are also more responsible for a greater range of important outcomes. The finding that complexity increases after presidents are elected might therefore suggest that cognitive capacity, rather than motivation per se, accounts for incidents of inattention to social standards of behavior. Presumably, accountability constrains the disinhibiting effects of power because the powerful wish to avoid the social punishments those with less power can potentially invoke, such as dislike, disapproval, or disrespect. Thus people with power may attempt to control their behavior because they do not want to lose status, even if their power base is secure.

Culture

Responses to the experience of power are likely to vary across cultures as well. Culture affects many aspects of power, including the extent to which power differences are accepted and consensually reinforced (e.g., in high power-distance cultures) as opposed to being disputed, challenged, consensually diminished, and negotiated (e.g., in low power-distance cultures). High power-distance is likely to facilitate disinhibition in the powerful, as well as inhibition in the powerless. Low power-distance, in contrast, should moderate these effects by creating incentives to deviate from status-appropriate behaviors. For example, when power-distance is low and social mobility is high, low-power individuals might be more likely to challenge the existing power structure by modeling high-power behavior. In fact, it could be argued that this is a reasonable strategy for acquiring power in low power-distance cultures (e.g., Kipnis, 1972). Under these conditions, high-power individuals might try to minimize such challenges by low-power individuals by attempts to appease and pacify them.

Culture is also likely to moderate the content of automatic responding in those with power. Automatic responses are dominant responses; they are the thoughts and behaviors that are most well-learned. In individualistic cultures, automatic responses are likely to reflect the desire for personal dominance and autonomy. In collectivistic cultures, however, automatic responses might be more group-serving. For example, some collectivistic cultures teach members to value responsibility and concern for one's subordinates. Culture can also affect the kinds of behaviors that are most inhibited. Since disinhibition in the powerful is most likely to affect those actions that were previously inhibited, this suggests that disinhibition will have different effects on behavior by powerful actors in different cultures.

System Stability

Conditions that affect the maintenance of power can also moderate its psychological effects. In a democracy or a meritocracy, the powerful are vulnerable to having their power revoked or usurped. We assume that when power is negotiable, it is less likely to lead to disinhibition than when it is irrevocably bestowed. This suggests that powerholders whose legitimacy is being challenged should be less likely to disinhibit than those who legitimacy is more secure. Support for this argument was obtained in the Supreme Court research described earlier. Gruenfeld and Preston (2000) found that Supreme Court justices who overturned legal precedent were more cognitively simple in their reasoning about legal issues than those who upheld precedent and were more cognitively complex. When precedent is overturned, new powerholders are liberated from the burden of legitimation, and their new dominance is vividly affirmed. In contrast, majority members who uphold precedent are in the position of having to defend the status quo against challenges. The hate-crime research mentioned earlier is also consistent with this argument: The incidence of hate crimes against minority members is highest when the power distance between majority and minority groups is greatest; it drops off as the balance of power approaches equilibrium (Green et al., 1996).

GENERAL DISCUSSION

This paper reviews the effects of power on those who possess it. It documents our central thesis—that power is disinhibiting—and explains the psychological mechanisms underlying this effect. It also explores the implications of these mechanisms for behavior in a number of specific social contexts. We argued that the experience of power activates the behavioral approach system and, where inhibitions are already functional, deactivates cognitive control mechanisms, increases response automaticity, and restores a direct link between internal states and the acts that satisfy them. This, in turn, affects the social perceptions and motor activities of those who possess power.

It is important to note that our intention in this paper has been to discuss the cognitive aspects of a recently proposed theory, rather than to test the theory in its entirety. The fact that we find support for some of our most basic hypotheses does not imply that we have evidence for the full constellation of mechanisms we discuss. An obvious limitation in our analysis is that a number of the studies we cite as support are correlational, and are thus open to alternative interpretations.

One alternative involves the direction of causality. When studies compare samples that vary naturally in power (e.g., high- vs. low-status fraternity brothers, supervisors vs. subordinates), it is possible that observed differences in behavior are the cause of power differences, rather than the consequence. This possibility cannot be entirely dismissed, since there are studies showing that, for example, expressions of anger are perceived as conveying power, whereas expressions of sadness are perceived as conveying powerlessness (Tiedens, 2001). There are other viable theoretical alternatives to our story that we have not yet investigated systematically. For example, it is possible that individuals with power appear to be disinhibited from conventional social norms, when in fact they are simply responding to a different set of normative constraints. Moreover, when we attribute differences between men and women, majorities and minorities, and those with high and low SES to power, we may be observing the effects of factors that are confounded with power, rather than of power per se. More research is needed to assess the relative explanatory power of these alternatives; however, the data we have already accumulated from studies in which power is manipulated and participants are randomly assigned to conditions help to bolster the strength of our claim that power can have the effects we hypothesize.

Does Power Corrupt?

We introduced this inquiry by referring to the adage that power corrupts. A question we have not addressed directly, however, is whether our findings support this conclusion. What is clear, from our review, is that power reduces sensitivity to widely held social norms, and that it colors perceptions of others' interests. Power also increases the proclivity to act on internal drives, including self-interest. There is no reason to believe, however, that this should always lead to corruption. There are many situations in which counter-normative and decisive actions have prosocial benefits, while inaction in response to social pressures is irresponsible, if not immoral. Consider, for example, the phenomena of bystander apathy and pluralistic ignorance (Latane & Darley, 1970). In fact, many organizations are actively engaged in attempts to reduce conformity, and to increase initiative, among employees who are too often excessive in their deference to even dysfunctional cultural and political norms.

Our analysis suggests that power increases the performance of individuals' dominant responses: Those that are most well-learned and easiest to access. In this sense, power makes people more true to themselves. Thus the normative consequences of disinhibition in the powerful depend largely on the deepest instincts of those individuals who acquire power. Individuals who are highly competitive, instrumental, and distrustful will become more so, but tendencies toward cooperation and altruism will also be amplified in the powerful. In sum, the normative effects of power on behavior might depend more on the disposition of the powerholder than on the situation he or she faces.

REFERENCES

Anderson, C., & Keltner, D. J. (1999). *Self-rated power, dominance and approach behaviors.* Unpublished manuscript.

Asch, S. E. (1951). Effects of group pressure upon the modification and distortion of judgments. In H. Guetzkow (Ed.), *Groups, leadership, and men* (pp. 177–190). Pittsburgh, PA: Carnegie Press.

Bargh, J., Raymond, P., Pryor, J. B., & Strack, F. (1995). Attractiveness of the underling: An automatic power-sex association and its consequences for sexual harassment and aggression. *Journal of Personality and Social Psychology, 68,* 768–781.

Blau, P. (1964). *Exchange and power in social life.* New York: Wiley.

Carver, C. S., & Scheier, M. F. (1981). *Attention and self-regulation: A control-theory approach to human behavior.* New York: Springer-Verlag.

Carver, C. S., & White, T. L. (1994). Behavioral inhibition, behavioral activation, and affective responses to impending reward and punishment: The BIS/BAS Scales. *Journal of Personality and Social Psychology, 67,* 319–333.

Chance, M. (1967). Attention structure as the basis of primate rank orders. *Man, 2,* 503–518.

Davis, J. H. (1973). Group decision and social interaction: A theory of social decision schemes. *Psychological Review, 80,* 97–125.

DePaulo, B. M., & Friedman, H. S. (1998). Nonverbal Communication. In D. Gilbert, S. T. Fiske, & G. Lindzey (Eds.), *Handbook of social psychology* (4th ed., Vol. 2, pp. 3–40). New York: McGraw-Hill.

Ebenbach, D. H., & Keltner, D. (1998). Power, emotion and judgmental accuracy in social conflict: Motivating the cognitive miser. *Basic and Applied Social Psychology, 20,* 7–21.

Ellyson, S. L., & Dovidio, J. F. (Eds.). (1985). *Power, dominance, and nonverbal behavior.* New York: Springer-Verlag.

Emerson, R. M. (1962). Power-dependence relations. *American Sociological Review, 27,* 31–41.

Erber, R., & Fiske, S. T. (1984). Outcome dependency and attention to inconsistent information. *Journal of Personality and Social Psychology, 47,* 709–726.

Festinger, L. (1954). A theory of social comparison processes. *Human Relations, 7,* 117–140.

Festinger, L., Schachter, S., & Back, K. (1950). *Social pressures in informal groups.* New York: Harper.

Fiske, S. T. (1993). Controlling other people: The impact of power on stereotyping. *American Psychologist, 48,* 621–628.

Fiske, S. T., & Taylor, S. (1991). *Social cognition* (2nd ed.). New York: McGraw-Hill.

French, J. R. P., Jr., & Snyder, R. (1959). Leadership and interpersonal power. In D. Cartwright (Ed.), *Studies in social power* (pp. 118–149). Oxford, England.

French, J. R. P., Jr., & Raven, B. H. (1959). The bases of social power. In D. Cartwright (Ed.), *Studies in social power* (pp. 150–167). Ann Arbor, MI: University of Michigan Press.

Galinsky, A., Gruenfeld, D. H., & Magee, J. (2002). *From power to action.* Unpublished manuscript.

Gaelick, L., Bodenhausen, G., & Wyer, R. S., Jr. (1985). Emotional communication in close relationships. *Journal of Personality and Social Psychology, 49,* 1246–1265.

Gilbert, D. T. (1998). Ordinary personology. In D. Gilbert, S. T. Fiske, & G. Lindzey (Eds.), *Handbook of social psychology* (4th ed., Vol. 2, pp. 89–150). New York: McGraw-Hill.

Gollwitzer, P. M., Heckhausen, H., & Steller, B. (1990). Deliberative and implemental mind-sets: Cognitive tuning toward congruous thoughts and information. *Journal of Personality and Social Psychology, 59,* 1119–1127.

Gray, J. A. (1994). Three fundamental emotion systems. In P. Ekman & R. J. Davidson (Eds.), *The nature of emotion: Fundamental questions* (pp. 243–247). New York: Oxford University Press.

Green, D. P., Abelson, R. P., & Garnett, M. (1996). The distinctive views of hate-crime perpetrators and white supremacists. In D. A. Prentice & D. T. Miller (Eds.), *Cultural divides: Understanding and overcoming group conflict.* New York: Russell Sage Foundation.

Green, D. P., Wong, J., & Strolovitch, D. (1996). *The effects of demographic change on hate crime.* Working paper no. 96-06. Institution for Social and Policy Studies, Yale University.

Gruenfeld, D. H. (1995). Status, ideology and integrative complexity on the U.S. Supreme Court: Rethinking the politics of political decision making. *Journal of Personality and Social Psychology, 68,* 5–20.

Gruenfeld, D. H., & Fan, E. T. (1998). *Power and performance attributions.* Unpublished manuscript.

Gruenfeld, D. H., Galinsky, A., & Magee, J. (2000). *Power and objectification.* Unpublished manuscript.

Gruenfeld, D. H., & Kim, P. H. (2002). *Relative power among the powerful: Effects on styles of reasoning.* Working paper, Stanford University.

Gruenfeld, D. H., & Preston, J. (2000). Upending the status quo: Cognitive complexity in Supreme Court justices who overturn legal precedent. *Personality and Social Psychology Bulletin, 26,* 1013–1022.

Gruenfeld, D. H., Thomas-Hunt, M., & Kim, P. H. (1998). Cognitive flexibility, communication strategy, and integrative complexity in groups: Public versus private reactions to majority and minority status. *Journal of Experimental Social Psychology, 34,* 202–226.

Gruenfeld, D. H., & Wyer, R. S. Jr. (1992). The semantics and pragmatics of social influence: How affirmations and denials affect beliefs in referent propositions. *Journal of Personality and Social Psychology, 62,* 38–49.

Hall, J. A. (1984). *Nonverbal sex differences.* Baltimore: Johns Hopkins University Press.

Hass, G.R. (1984). Perspective taking and self awareness: Drawing an E on your forehead. *Journal of Personality and Social Psychology, 46,* 788–798.

Higgins, E. T. (1999). Promotion and prevention as motivational duality: Implications for evaluative processes. In S. Chaiken & Y. Trope (Eds.), *Dual-process theories in social psychology* (pp. 503–525). New York: Guilford Press.

James, W. (1890). *Principles of psychology.* New York: Holt.

Janis, I., & Mann, L. (1991). Cognitive complexity in international decision making. In P. Suedfeld & P. E. Tetlock (Eds.), *Psychology and social policy* (pp. 33–49). New York: Hemisphere.

Janis, I. L. (1972). *Victims of groupthink.* Boston: Houghton-Mifflin.

Jastrow, J. (1906). *The subconscious.* Boston: Houghton-Mifflin.

Jost, J. T. (1998). Fairness norms and the potential for mutual agreements involving majority and minority groups. To appear in M. A. Neale, E. A. Mannix, & R. Wageman (Eds.), *Research on Managing Groups and Teams: Context* (Vol. 2). Greenwich, CT: JAI Press.

Jost, J. T., & Banaji, M. R. (1994). The role of stereotyping in system-justification and the production of false consciousness. *British Journal of Social Psychology, 33,* 1–27.

Kaarbo, J. (1996). Power and influence in foreign policy decision making: The role of junior coalition partners in German and Israeli Foreign Policy. *International Studies Quarterly, 40,* 501–530.

Keltner, D. J., Gruenfeld, D. H., & Anderson, C. (in press). Power, approach and inhibition. *Psychological Review.*

Keltner, D., & Robinson, R. J. (1996). Extremism, power, and the imagined basis of social conflict. *Current Directions in Psychological Science, 5,* 101–105.

Keltner, D., & Robinson, R. J. (1997). Defending the status quo: Power and bias in social conflict. *Personality and Social Psychology Bulletin, 23,* 1066–1077.

Keltner, D. J., Young, R. C., Heerey, E. A., Oemig, C., & Monarch, N. D. (1998). Teasing in hierarchical and intimate relations. *Journal of Personality and Social Psychology, 75,* 1231–1247.

Kim, P. H. (1997). Strategic timing in group negotiations: The implications of forced entry and forced exit or negotiators with unequal power. *Organization Behavior and Human Decision Processes, 71,* 263–286.

Kipnis, D. (1972). Does power corrupt? *Journal of Personality and Social Psychology, 24,* 33–41.

Kipnis, D. (1976). *The powerholders.* Oxford, England: University of Chicago Press.

Kipnis, D., & Cosentino, D. (1969). Use of leadership powers in industry. *Journal of Applied Psychology, 53*(6), 460–466.

Komorita, S. S. (1984). Coalition bargaining. In L. Berkowitz (Ed.), *Advances in experimental social psychology* (Vol. 18, pp. 183–245). Orlando: FL: Academic Press.

LaFrance, M., & Banaji, M. (1992). Towards a reconsideration of the gender-emotion relationship. In M. S. Clark (Ed.), *Emotion and social behavior: Review of personality and social psychology* (Vol. 14). Newbury Park, CA: Sage.

Latane, B., & Darley, J. M. (1970). *The unresponsive bystander: Why doesn't he help?* New York: Appleton-Century-Crofts.

Lee-Chai, A. Y., & Bargh, J. A. (2001). *The use and abuse of power: Multiple perspectives on the causes of corruption.* Philadelphia: Psychology Press/Taylor & Francis.

Lerner, J. S., & Tetlock, P. E. (1999). Accounting for the effects of accountability. *Psychology Bulletin, 125*(2), 255–275.

Levine, J. M., Resnick, L. B., & Higgins, E. T. (1993). Social Foundations of Cognition. *Annual Review of Psychology, 44*, 585–612.

Mannix, E. A., & Neale, M. A. (1993). Power imbalance and the pattern of exchange in dyadic negotiation. *Group Decision and Negotiation, 2*, 119–133.

Mannix, E. A. (1993). Organizations as resource dilemmas: The effects of power balance on coalition formation in small groups. *Organizational Behavior and Human Decision Processes, 55*, 1–22.

Markus, H. R., & Kitayama, S. (1991). Culture and the self: Implications for cognition, emotion and motivation. *Psychological Review, 98*, 224–253.

Moreland, R. L., & Levine, J. M. (1989). Newcomers and oldtimers in small groups. In P. Paulus (Ed.), *Psychology of group influence* (2nd ed., pp. 143–186). Hillsdale, NJ: Lawrence Erlbaum Associates.

McGuire, W. J. (1969). The nature of attitudes and attitude change. In G. Lindzey & E. Aronson (Eds.), *The Handbook of Social Psychology, 3*, 136–324.

McGuire, W. J., & Padawer-Singer, A. (1976). Trait salience in the spontaneous self concept. *Journal of Personality and Social Psychology, 33*(6), 743–754.

Morris, M. W., & Peng. K. (1994). Culture and cause: American and Chinese attributions for social and physical events. *Journal of Personality and Social Psychology, 67*, 949–971.

Murnighan, J. K. (1978). Models of faction formation: Game theoretic, social psychological, and political perspectives. *Psychological Bulletin, 85*, 113–153.

Neely, J. H. (1977). Semantic priming and retrieval from lexical memory: Roles of inhibitionless spreading activation and limited-capacity attention. *Journal of Experimental Psychology: General, 106*, 226–254.

Nemeth, C. J. (1986). Differential contributions of majority and minority influence. *Psychological Review, 93*, 23–32.

Ng, S. H. (1980). *The social psychology of power.* San Diego, CA: Academic Press.

Overbeck, J. R., & Park, B. (2001). When power does not corrupt: superior individuation processes among powerful perceivers. *Journal of Personality and Social Psychology, 81* (4), 549–565.

Pfeffer, J., & Salancik, G. R. (1974). Organizational decision making as a political process: The case of a university budget. *Administrative Science Quarterly, 19*(2), 135–151.

Plant, A., Hyde, J. S., Keltner, D., & Devine, P. D. (2000). The gender stereotyping of emotions. *Psychology of Women Quarterly, 24*, 80–91.

Posner, M. I., & Snyder, C. R. R. (1975). Attention and cognitive control. In R. L. Solso (Ed.), *Information processing and cognition: The Loyola symposium* (pp. 55–85). Hillsdale, NJ: Lawrence Erlbaum Associates.

Resnick, L. B., Levine, J. M., & Teasley, S. D. (1991). *Perspectives on socially shared cognition.* Washington, DC: APA.

Sachdev, I., & Bourhis, R. Y. (1991). Power and status differentials in minority and majority group relations. *European Journal of Social Psychology, 21*(1), 1–24.

Sears, D. O. (1988). Symbolic racism. In P. Katz & D. A. Taylor (Eds.), *Eliminating racism: Profiles in controversy* (pp. 53–84). New York: Plenum.

Shiffrin, R. M. (1988). Attention. In R. C. Atkinson, R. T., Herrnstein, G. Lindzey, & R. D. Luce (Eds.), *Steven's handbook of experimental psychology* (2nd ed., Vol. 2, pp. 739–811). New York: Wiley.

Sondak, H., & Bazerman, M. (1991). Power balance and the rationality of outcomes in matching markets. *Organizational Behavior and Human Decision Processes, 50,* 1–23.

Staudinger, U. M., & Baltes, P. B. (1996). Interactive minds: A facilitative setting for wisdom-related performance? *Journal of Personality and Social Psychology, 71,* 746–762.

Steele, C. M., & Aronson, J. (1995). Stereotype threat and the intellectual test performance of African Americans. *Journal of Personality and Social Psychology, 69,* 797–811.

Suedfeld, P., Tetlock, P. E., & Streufert, S. (1992). Conceptual/integrative complexity. In C. Smith (Ed.), *Motivation and personality: Handbook of thematic content analysis* (pp. 401–418). Cambridge, MA: Cambridge University Press.

Taylor, S. E. (1998). The social being in social psychology. In D. Gilbert, S. T. Fiske, & G. Lindzey (Eds.), *Handbook of social psychology* (4th ed., Vol. 2, pp. 58–95). New York: McGraw-Hill.

Tetlock, P. E. (1981). Pre to postelection shifts in presidential rhetoric: Cognitive adjustment or impression management. *Journal of Personality and Social Psychology, 41,* 207–213.

Tetlock, P. E. (1992). The impact of accountability on judgment and choice: Toward a social contingency model. In M. P. Zanna (Ed.), *Advances in experimental social psychology* (Vol. 25, pp. 331–376). New York: Academic Press.

Thibaut, J. W., & Kelley, H. H. (1959). *The social psychology of groups.* New York: Wiley.

Thompson, L. L., Levine, J. M., & Messick, D. M. (1999). *Shared cognition in organizations: The management of knowledge.* Mahwah, NJ: Lawrence Erlbaum Associates.

Tiedens, L. A. (2001). Anger and advancement versus sadness and subjugation: The effect of negative emotion expressions on status conferral. *Journal of Personality and Social Psychology, 80,* 86–94.

Waenke, M., & Wyer, R. S., Jr. (1996). Individual differences in person memory: The role of sociopolitical ideology and in-group versus out-group membership in responses to socially relevant behavior. *Personality and Social Psychology Bulletin, 22,* 742–754.

Weber, M. (1947). *The theory of social and economic organization.* New York: Free Press.

Wegner, D. M., & Bargh, J. A. (1998). Control and automaticity in social life. In D. Gilbert, S. T. Fiske, & G. Lindzey (Eds.), *Handbook of social psychology* (4th ed., Vol. 2, pp. 446–496). New York: McGraw-Hill.

Wegner, D., Erber, R., & Raymond, P. (1991). Transactive memory in close relationships. *Journal of Personality and Social Psychology, 61,* 923–939.

Wicklund, R. (1975). Objective self awareness. In L. Berkowitz (Ed.), *Advances in experimental social psychology* (Vol. 8). New York: Academic Press.

Winter, D. G. (1973). *The power motive.* New York: Free Press.

Woike, B. A. (1994). The use of differentiation and integration processes: Empirical studies of "separate" and "connected" ways of thinking. *Journal of Personality and Social Psychology, 67,* 142–150.

Wrong, D. H. (1979). Some problems in defining social power. *American Journal of Sociology, 73,* 673–681.

Wyer, R. S., Jr., Budesheim, T. L., & Lambert, A. J. (1990). Cognitive representation of conversations about persons. *Journal of Personality and Social Psychology, 58,* 218–238.

Wyer, R. S., Jr., Budesheim, T. L., Lambert, A. J., & Swan, S. (1994). Person memory and judgment: Pragmatic influences on impressions formed in a social context. *Journal of Personality and Social Psychology, 66,* 254–267.

Wyer, R. S., Jr., & Gruenfeld, D. H. (1995a). Information processing in social contexts: Implications for social memory and judgment. In M. Zanna (Ed.), *Advances in experimental social psychology* (v. 27, pp. 49–91). San Diego, CA: Academic Press.

Wyer, R. S., Jr., & Gruenfeld, D. H. (1995b). Information processing in interpersonal communication. In D. E. Hewes (Ed.), *The cognitive bases of interpersonal communication.* Hillsdale, NJ: Lawrence Erlbaum Associates.

Wyer, R. S., Jr., Lambert, A. J., Budesheim, T. L., & Gruenfeld, D. H. (1992). Theory and research on person impression formation: A look to the future. In L. Martin & A. Tesser (Eds.), *The construction of social judgment.* Hillsdale, NJ: Lawrence Erlbaum Associates.

Wyer, R. S., Jr., Swan, S., & Gruenfeld, D. H. (1995). Impression formation in informal conversations. *Social Cognition, 13,* 243–272.

Zajonc, R. B. (1960). The process of cognitive tuning and communication. *Journal of Abnormal Social Psychology, 61,* 159–167.

Zajonc, R. B. (1965). Social facilitation. *Science, 149,* 269–274.

12

Value Conflicts in Intergroup Perception: A Social Cognitive Perspective

Natalie A. Wyer
Free University of Amsterdam

Nature smiles at the union of freedom and equality in our utopias. For freedom and equality are sworn and everlasting enemies, and when one prevails the other dies.

Will Durant, philosopher

All men may be created equal, but as a culture we often behave according to the principle of "survival of the fittest." Philosophers have viewed the ideals of egalitarianism and individualism, equality and equity, as pitted against each other since Aristotle first described two distinct systems of social justice. The first of these systems was based on the notion that humanity alone was enough to warrant an equal share in life. The second maintained that individual contributions and merits were important in distributing proportional outcomes to members of society.

Equality and equity form the basis of two fundamental value systems in Western societies. So ingrained are these values in our culture that most Americans express support for both ideals, despite their apparent inconsistencies (Lipset, 1963; Lipset & Schneider, 1978). Indeed, the national

263

mood has historically swung between these two core value orientations. One need only reflect on our most recent past to notice a marked change from a period of passionate concern for equality in the 1960s and early 1970s to one marked by greater concern for individual achievement and upward mobility in the 1980s.

Yet whether the country as a whole leans toward either the individualistic or the egalitarian ideal, both values are endorsed simultaneously by many Americans (Katz, Wackenhut, & Hass, 1986). Which value carries greater weight in guiding interpersonal and intergroup behavior may vary across people as well as within an individual, over time and across situations as the two values compete for influence.

Predicting if and when human behavior will be governed by either of these two conflicting values is no simple matter. In this chapter, I consider the cognitive structures and processes that underlie this problem, and provide some initial evidence for a social cognitive model of the role these conflicting values play in intergroup perception.

THE ROLE OF VALUES
IN INTERGROUP PERCEPTION

Since Allport's (1954) and Rokeach's (1960, 1968a) treatments of the subject, we have known that values play a key role in how people evaluate others. Rokeach's belief congruence model made explicit the idea that we react positively or negatively to others based on whether they conform to or violate values that are important to us. This tendency to evaluate others based on their adherence to cherished values extends to groups as well. For instance, Biernat, Vescio, Theno, and Crandall (1996) found that the perception that out-group members violate cherished in-group values led to more negative evaluations of the out-group (see also Insko, Nacoste, & Moe, 1983).

Indeed, many contemporary theories of racial prejudice are based in part on Rokeach's (1968a) belief congruence hypothesis. Though these theories vary somewhat in their depiction of how egalitarian and individualistic values relate to racial attitudes, the picture that emerges from the collection of theoretical perspectives is fairly consistent (Gaertner & Dovidio, 1986; Katz et al, 1986; Kinder & Sears, 1981; McConahay & Hough, 1976). Specifically, endorsing egalitarian values gives rise to relatively positive or sympathetic attitudes towards disadvantaged minority groups. In contrast, the endorsement of individualistic attitudes results in more negative or disrespectful feelings towards the same groups.

Moskowitz and his colleagues (Moskowitz, Gollwitzer, Wasel, & Schaal, 1999; see also Moskowitz, 2001; Moskowitz, Salomon, & Taylor, 2000) have suggested that values influence not only intergroup attitudes but also stereotypes. In their work on chronic egalitarianism, Moskowitz et al. have been able to identify individuals who have chronically accessible egalitarian goals, and have demonstrated that gender stereotypes are not automatically activated for those individuals. This finding suggests that stereotype activation is prevented by the presence of chronically accessible goals that are inconsistent with the stereotype.

Thus the existing body of work on values and intergroup relations suggests that values play an important role in how minority groups are perceived. However, the cognitive structures and processes underlying the influence of various values, some of which are in direct conflict with each other, have been largely ignored (with the notable exception of the aforementioned work by Moskowitz et al, 1999, 2000; Moskowitz, 2001).

CONFLICTING COGNITIONS: A BRIEF SOCIAL PSYCHOLOGICAL HISTORY

The problem of conflicting beliefs is, of course, not unique to the study of values. It is almost a truism in social psychology that people strive to maintain consistency among their beliefs, attitudes, and behaviors. Though the role of consistency motives can be found at least as far back as psychodynamic theory, it was not until the 1950s that cognitive consistency became a central theme in social psychological research. For example, Heider's (1946) balance theory emphasized the importance of having consistent relations among one's beliefs, with the consequence that inconsistencies should result in an unpleasant state of imbalance that the individual should be motivated to resolve—primarily through changing one or more of the inconsistent beliefs.

The original balance theory has been extended in several different directions—perhaps most famously toward the development of cognitive dissonance (Festinger, 1957) and self-perception (Bem, 1972) theories. Consistency theories were extended in a second, quite distinct direction by McGuire (1960a, 1960b) and later Wyer (1973, 1974; Wyer & Goldberg, 1970; Wyer & Hartwick, 1980, 1984)) in their work on logical reasoning. McGuire detailed a model of how beliefs are constructed as a function of logical, syllogistic, reasoning. That is, McGuire (1960a, 1960b) described a person's belief in a given proposition A as based on his or her belief in one or more supporting propositions (e.g., B). For example, if one is asked to judge the validity of the proposition, "If America continues to rely on foreign oil, the U.S. military presence in the Middle East will increase," one may consider the validity of supporting propositions (e.g., "If America continues to rely on foreign oil, it will become increasingly involved in resolving disputes between oil-rich countries," and "When America becomes involved in resolving international disputes, it increases its military presence in affected nations"). Thus according to McGuire's model, people use a process of logical inference to construct their beliefs.

Wyer (1973, 1974; Wyer & Goldberg, 1970) elaborated on the McGuire (1960a, 1960b) model by incorporating conditional probabilities. Wyer (1973) developed a weighted averaging model to describe how beliefs are constructed, which improved the predictive validity and generality of McGuire's original model. Wyer and his colleagues went several steps further, however, in developing the now-familiar "bin model" (Wyer & Hartwick, 1980), which provided an account for how inconsistent beliefs could be represented simultaneously in memory.

With the bin model, Wyer and his colleagues (Wyer & Hartwick, 1980, 1984; for a review see Wyer & Srull, 1989) demonstrated the crucial role of belief accessibility in determining whether relationships among beliefs were logically consistent, thus conforming to the probabilogical model. For example, Henninger and Wyer (1976) reported the important finding that the consistency among different beliefs depends on their relationship being accessible at the time they are reported. If the relationship between two beliefs is not salient at the time of judgment, people are likely to base their judgments on disparate sources of information, resulting in apparent inconsistencies.

Wyer's insight regarding the role of belief accessibility in determining the logical relations among beliefs extended the applicability of the original probabilogical model enormously. Accordingly, the utility of the model for understanding how people maintain consistency among their beliefs was greatly increased. The notion that discrepancies among *accessible* beliefs elicit motivation to resolve inconsistencies has received a great deal of attention over the past 30 years.

BEYOND LOGIC: VALUES IN CONFLICT

In the years that followed Wyer's original work on belief consistency, attention shifted away from beliefs about hypothetical propositions to beliefs about other people. Indeed, the study of inconsistency resolution in the impression formation process became something of a cottage industry throughout the 1970s and 80s. And although different models were developed to describe how inconsistency resolution takes place (Wyer & Srull, 1989; Hamilton, Driscoll, & Worth, 1989; Klein & Loftus, 1990), the picture that emerged was quite consistent with early cognitive consistency theories. Specifically, person perceivers seem to have little tolerance for inconsistency in their beliefs about other people. As a consequence, perceivers employ various strategies to resolve inconsistencies when they arise.

Given human beings' motive to maintain coherent, consistent impressions of their own and others' personalities, it stands to reason that people should strive for consistency in other, more abstract, social beliefs as well. Individuals do not define themselves and others merely by the collection of personality traits that they possess, but by their values, attitudes, and goals. Given the complex nature of these beliefs, it is hardly surprising that people experience conflicts among competing values and goals. In recent years, a number of researchers have delved into these and related questions.

The value pluralism model, developed by Tetlock and colleagues (Tetlock, 1986, 1989; Tetlock, Peterson, & Lerner, 1996) is, to date, the most comprehensive theoretical perspective on value inconsistency. According to the value pluralism model, the perception of inconsistencies among one's core values produces psychological discomfort. In order to reduce that discomfort, individuals resort to a number of strategies to resolve the conflict between different values. Whenever possible, a simple "bolstering and denial" strategy will be used, whereby the stronger value is favored over the weaker value. When such simple strategies are insufficient, individuals may resort to more complex methods for conflict-resolution, culminating in explicit trade-off reasoning in which they consciously decide to sacrifice one value in favor of another, and call upon features of the broader social context to justify those trade-offs.

Tetlock's (1986) model has been well-supported by research on various socio-political issues, and certainly presents a reasonable framework for viewing value conflict. However, the scope of the value pluralism model is limited to conflict resolution of a conscious, deliberative variety. Whilst values (and the conflicts among them) certainly influence people at this conscious level, they also likely do so in a less deliberate, less controlled way. That is, values likely guide perceptions, judgments, and behavior through a more subtle, subconscious route. For example, Katz and Hass (1988) have suggested that activating egalitarian or individualistic values leads to a spread of activation to associated (e.g., racial) attitudes.

INFORMATION-PROCESSING PERSPECTIVES
ON CONFLICT RESOLUTION

Although the Katz and Hass (1988) model of value accessibility has not yet been adequately tested, there are parallels in Shah and Kruglanski's (2000; Shah, Kruglanski, & Friedman, in press) goal systems theory that are worth noting here. According to goal systems theory, a person's goals and the means available to achieve them are associated within a complex network in memory. In this network, various goals and means are interconnected with both excitatory and inhibitory links. To the extent that one means-goal link is activated (e.g., that means A will achieve goal X), other related links will be inhibited (e.g., that means B would also achieve goal X or that means A could also lead me to goal Y). For example, if I view running as the best way to keep fit, I will be less likely to consider that swimming could also allow me to stay in shape, or that taking a jog could be a form of entertainment.

Though Shah et al. (in press) do not explicitly consider the implications of their theory for value-attitude relations, the goals-means memory structure that they describe provides an interesting framework for considering the interrelations among values and attitudes. Consider, for example, the case of values and racial attitudes. Both egalitarian and individualistic values have implications for a perceiver's attitudes towards economically disadvantaged minority groups. However, within a goal systems theory type of framework, to the extent that one value is associated with attitudes towards the group, the implications of the second value should be inhibited.

This type of model (see Fig. 12.1) provides a more concrete specification of how egalitarian and individualistic values might influence the expression of related racial attitudes than the less defined model proposed by Katz and Hass (1988). It also allows for a less controlled, deliberative influence of values than is encompassed within Tetlock's (1986) value pluralism model. Moreover, the model presented in Figure 1 not only makes predictions about excitatory influences of activated values, but inhibitory effects as well.

A SOCIAL COGNITIVE PERSPECTIVE ON VALUE CONFLICT AND INTERGROUP PERCEPTION

The model presented in Fig. 1 describes the relationship between endorsement of two core values—egalitarianism and individualism—and intergroup attitudes and stereotypes. Individualistic values are positively associated (i.e., are connected via an excitatory link) with negative out-group attitudes and stereotypes, whereas egalitarian values are posi-

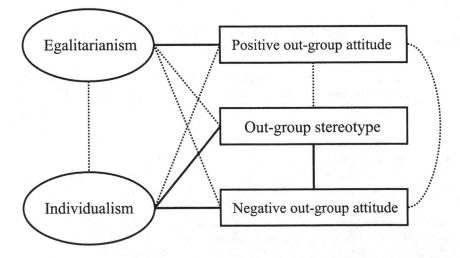

FIG. 12.1   Systems of values, out-group attitudes, and out-group stereotypes. Solid lines represent positive/excitatory associations. Broken lines represent negative/inhibitory associations.

tively associated with positive attitudes. Because the two values have opposing implications for out-group attitudes, they will be negatively associated with each other (connected via an inhibitory link). In addition, because egalitarian values are negatively associated with individualistic values, they will also be negatively associated with out-group stereotypes.

There are several implications of the model. First, it predicts that activating one of the two values will have direct consequences for both the accessibility of the other value as well as the accessibility of attitudes and stereotypes. For example, activating egalitarian values should lead to inhibition of individualistic values as well as structures associated with those values (negative attitudes and stereotypes), while simultaneously resulting in activation of positive attitudes. Thus the accessibility of egalitarian versus individualistic values should have a direct effect on the accessibility of out-group attitudes and stereotypes.

THE EFFECT OF VALUE ACCESSIBILITY
ON INTERGROUP PERCEPTION

People have multiple attitudes and values stored in memory. Several lines of research suggest that it is even possible to have multiple (different) attitudes about the same attitude object stored in memory (Devine, 1989; Fazio, 1986; Smith & DeCoster, 2000; Wilson, Lindsey, & Schooler, 2000). Thus it is likely that people may have multiple values stored in memory that have conflicting implications. As suggested earlier, the relative strength and/or accessibility of these value representations may be the critical factor in predicting how intergroup perceptions and evaluations will be affected.

A crucial assumption is that values vary in their level of accessibility, and that these variations can influence judgments. We know from the past 25 years of research in social cognition that people are influenced by the mental representations that are accessible to them. This influence occurs in a number of domains. For example, accessible personality traits influence the way we interpret ambiguous behavior (Bargh & Pietramonaco, 1982; Higgins, Rholes, & Jones, 1977; Srull & Wyer, 1979). Accessible attitudes make us more likely to behave in ways consistent with those attitudes (Fazio, Powell, & Williams, 1989). Finally, accessible stereotypes make us more likely to judge others in stereotypic ways (Devine, 1989). It is likely, then, that accessible values also influence us in a number of ways.

Research in social cognition has revealed that higher levels of accessibility can result from at least two sources. First, values (or any other construct) can become more accessible as the result of frequent activation. The more frequently a person thinks about a particular value, the more accessible that value will become. For example, someone who often thinks about the importance of equality and uses those beliefs on a regular basis will have more accessible egalitarian values than someone who rarely thinks about equality. Ultimately, a person's most important, or most frequently activated, values will become chronically accessible (see Bargh, 1997, for a review) so that they enjoy a more or less constant state of heightened accessibility.

Values can also become temporarily more accessible. When a value has been recently activated, it will be more accessible for some period of time following the activation (Bargh, 1997). For example, reading a news story about racial discrimination might activate egalitarian values. Those values would then remain accessible for a short period of time after reading the story.

Regardless of the source of accessibility, once an egalitarian or individualistic value has been activated, it should have direct consequences for related constructs. Following the model shown in Fig. 12.1, a number of specific predictions can be made about the effects of value activation on the accessibility of out-group attitudes and out-group stereotypes. First, however, a couple of preliminary steps must be taken to establish the plausibility of the model.

Values as Representations

Implicit in the model shown in Fig. 12.1 is the assumption that values are represented as cognitive structures that can vary in their mental accessibility. If we are to make this assumption, we must first consider what that representation might look like. While research that directly addresses the question of how values are represented in memory has been scarce, we can start to think about the problem by considering how other, related constructs are represented in memory. Fortunately, when it comes to one closely related construct—the attitude—there has been ample attention paid to the question of representation.

Though there are varying accounts of attitude representation (e.g., Pratkanis and Greenwald, 1989; Zanna & Rempel, 1986), the most prominent among these has been one proposed by Fazio and his colleagues (Fazio, 1986, 1989, 1995; Fazio, Chen, McDonel, & Sherman, 1982; Fazio, Powell, & Herr, 1983; Fazio, Sanbonmatsu, Powell, & Kardes, 1986; Fazio & Williams, 1986; Powell & Fazio, 1984). Fazio has suggested that attitudes are represented as links, or associations, between an attitude object and the perceiver's evaluation of that object. The strength of an attitude is determined by the frequency with which the object-evaluation link becomes activated. Given sufficient frequency, an attitude may become automatically activated whenever the attitude object is encountered (Fazio et al., 1986; see also Bargh, Chaiken, Govender, & Pratto, 1992).

Fazio's (1986) model is useful when thinking about how values might be represented in memory. Attitudes and values are commonly thought of as two types of beliefs that differ in terms of their level of abstractness and their centrality in the individual's belief system (Rokeach, 1968a, 1968b). If attitudes are represented in memory as associations between objects (e.g., flowers) and evaluations (e.g., good), then values may be represented in a similar manner.

Like attitudes, values are typically thought of as beliefs. However, distinct from attitudes, values are more abstract, and are more closely tied to the self-concept (Schwartz & Bilsky, 1987, 1990). These differences should be reflected in the nature of the value representation. For example, like attitudes, values may be represented as associations between an object and an evaluation. However, since values are more abstract than attitudes, the object should also be more abstract (e.g., freedom or equality). And since values are more central to the self-concept, the evaluation may not be simply positive or negative, but may involve a moral connotation. This would allow values to function as guidelines or goals that would have direct implications for the self. In other words, rather than being represented as object-evaluation links (as Fazio, 1986, argues that attitudes are represented), values may be represented as abstract concept-obligation links (see Fig. 12.2).

For example, values may be represented as associations between the content of values (e.g., world peace or kindness) and thoughts such as "ought" or "should." That is, beyond favorably evaluating world peace or kindness (in which case one would simply have positive attitudes toward those objects), one might attach to such abstract concepts certain ideas that connote a sense of obligation to think or behave consistently with those concepts.

As with attitudes, values may become stronger through frequent activation of the concept-obligation link. As the number of times that an individual makes the judgment that he or she should act or think in ways consistent

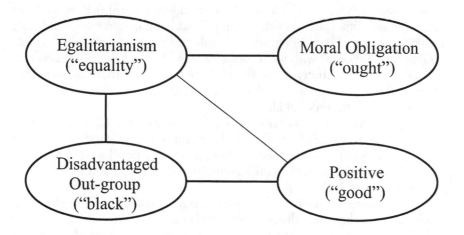

FIG. 12.2   Structure of value and attitude representations.

with an abstract concept (world peace, kindness) increases, the stronger the association between the concept and the obligation will become. The stronger the association becomes, the greater the accessibility of the value. Furthermore, when the association has been recently activated, the value may become temporarily more accessible (Bargh, 1989, 1997; Bargh & Chartrand, 2000; Fazio, 1986, 1989, 1995; Fazio et al., 1982, 1983, 1986; Fazio & Williams, 1986; Powell & Fazio, 1984).

Chronic Differences in Value Accessibility

I have suggested that value representations are structurally similar to attitude representations. That is, values may also be represented as associations involving particular value concepts and an evaluation of that concept. Unlike attitudes, the evaluative side of the association may be more than a simple valence judgment (i.e., good or bad). Indeed, endorsement of a value does not simply reflect the perceived desirability of the value's content; it also reflects a sense of moral obligation.

In an initial study designed to test this model of value representation, I compared two types of measures of egalitarian and individualistic values. The first involved traditional questionnaire measures of the extent to which people endorse egalitarian and individualistic values. The second measure was a reaction time task based on Fazio et al.'s (1986) paradigm. This measure was developed to assess the strength of association between the content of the two values and conceptions of "ought" and "should," which may reflect the extent to which people mentally represent those values.

Individuals who hold egalitarian values may store certain words (e.g., fairness, help, equality) in memory as goals for behavior or outcomes—in other words, behaviors in which egalitarian individuals think they ought to engage or outcomes that they think they should obtain. On the other hand, individuals who hold individualistic values may associate ideas about "ought" and "should" with words consistent with that value (e.g., deserve, earn, hardworking). Individuals who endorse both egalitarian and individualistic value orientations would then be likely to associate "ought" and "should" with both types of ideas.

In a preliminary session of the study, participants completed a number of questionnaire measures, including the humanitarian-egalitarian (HE) scale and the protestant ethic (PE) scale. These two scales, developed by Katz and Hass (1988), measure explicit endorsement of egalitarian and individualistic values respectively.

In a subsequent session, a subliminal priming paradigm was employed to determine whether individuals who overtly endorse egalitarian and/or individualistic values also have mental associations between words that are representative of those values and words such as "ought" and "should." When participants are subliminally (i.e., subconsciously) primed with a word that is related to a given construct, that construct should become activated. Because of associations in memory, words or ideas that are consistent with that construct should also become somewhat activated. Participants should therefore be faster to make judgments about those related words than they would be had they not been primed.

Participants engaged in a lexical decision task in which they made judgments about a series of words. That is, participants viewed (on a computer) a series of letter strings (which included both actual words and non-words), and were asked to decide whether each of the letter strings was or was not a word. Six types of target letter strings were presented: (1) individualism-related words such as "deserve" and "hardworking," (2) egalitarian-related words such as "equality" and "help," (3) positive words such as "happy" and "puppy," (4) negative words such as "death" and "torture," (5) neutral words such as "kitchen" and "bread," and (6) non-words such as "grollip" and "hastorp." The amount of time required to respond to each target was measured and recorded by the computer.

Before each target was presented, participants were subliminally presented with one of four types of primes. Participants were primed with value-suggestive words such as "ought" and "should," which should activate constructs that are consistent with those words (i.e., participants' values). A number of different control primes were also used. First, in order to rule out the possibility that the value primes were actually activating some other construct (e.g., attitudes) rather than values, non-value-suggestive words such as "good" and "want" were also used as primes. In addition, neutral words such as "house" and "food" as well as non-word letter strings such as "xxxxx" and "bbbbb" were used to provide baseline estimates of how long it took participants to respond to each target word in the absence of a related or semantic prime.

By examining the amount of time required to respond to individualistic and egalitarian targets following a value-related prime compared to other types of primes, it is possible to estimate the relative strength of association between the prime and the target. The strength of association can be considered a measure of how strongly the value is represented in memory. Individuals with strong individualistic values should show facilitation in their latencies to respond to individualistic words following "should" and "ought" primes. Likewise, individuals who hold strong egalitarian values should show facilitation for egalitarian words following those primes.

This experiment yielded two important findings. The first finding generated by this experiment was that explicit measures of egalitarian and individualistic values were also significantly correlated (p's < .01) with responses on the implicit measure of values used in this experiment (see Tables 12.1 and 12.2). This finding begins to establish the validity of this re-

TABLE 12.1

Mean Facilitation Scores (in ms) for Egalitarian and Individualistic
Target Words as a Function of Level of Egalitarianism.

Level of egalitarianism	Facilitation of egalitarian targets	Facilitation of individualistic targets
Low	−12.86	31.07
Moderate	9.20	7.92
High	53.69	6.19

TABLE 12.2

Mean Facilitation Scores (in ms) for Egalitarian and Individualistic
Target Words as a Function of Level of Individualism.

Level of individualism	Facilitation of egalitarian targets	Facilitation of individualistic targets
Low	2.35	−34.02
Moderate	28.12	23.92
High	18.27	43.98

sponse time paradigm for determining what values are represented in memory. Furthermore, these results support the hypothesis that values are represented as mental associations between the abstract content of values (e.g., equality or independence) and ideas of moral obligation.

Second, the extent to which positive primes facilitated or inhibited egalitarian or individualistic targets was not predicted by participants' explicit endorsement of egalitarian or individualistic values. This finding is consistent with the proposition that the mental representation of values is distinct from that of attitudes. If values were merely generalized attitudes (e.g., Eagly and Chaiken, 1993), one would expect that positive (e.g., "good") primes would facilitate value judgments as much or more than moral obligation (e.g., "should") primes for people who endorse the value. This was not the case—indeed, the extent to which positive primes facilitated responses to egalitarian and individualistic targets was unrelated to participants' endorsement of those values. Thus, consistent with the proposed model, values apparently involve notions of morality rather than simple evaluation.

There was one aspect of the relationship between the implicit and explicit measures that was unexpected (though not necessarily inconsistent with the hypotheses). That is, the results of the analysis in which participants were divided into groups based on their responses to the questionnaire measures of egalitarianism and individualism reflected a pattern of slight inhibition in responding to targets that reflected values that were not endorsed. That is, participants who were classified as low in egalitarianism responded more slowly to egalitarian words following value primes than following control primes. The parallel pattern was observed among participants who were identified as low in individualism.

Although inhibition was not specifically predicted (and the magnitude of these inhibition effects was not significantly different from 0), these findings are actually consistent with other research that has demonstrated that activating a mental representation may lead to inhibited responses to information that is inconsistent with the content of that representation. For example, Dijksterhuis and van Knippenberg (1996) reported that stereotype activation led not only to a facilitation of responses to stereotype-consistent information, but also to an inhibition of responses to stereotype-inconsistent information. Furthermore, many cognitive psychologists have argued, and found evidence to support, the possibility that activating a particular idea may lead to an automatic inhibition of competing ideas (e.g., Logan, 1980; Milner, 1957; Neely, 1977; Posner, 1978; Shallice, 1972).

Similar findings have also been reported in the social psychological literature (e.g., Macrae, Bodenhausen, & Milne, 1995; Sedikides, 1990). For example, Macrae et al. (1995) presented participants with a target person who could be categorized as either a female or as Asian. By depicting the target person in different contexts (e.g., putting on make-up versus eating rice), they were able to activate different categorizations. For example, when shown the Asian woman eating rice, participants' Asian category was activated. Interestingly, not only was the female category not activated for participants in this condition, it was actually inhibited. Thus it appears that when two categories were in competition, the activation of one was accompanied by inhibition of the other.

In the current research, inhibition may be understood by considering that participants' value systems were activated by the presentation of the value-related primes. Thus their responses to any information consistent with that value system should have been facilitated. In contrast, information that was value-relevant, yet inconsistent with their personal value systems, would likely have been inhibited. Participants in this experiment who disagreed with the content of a particular value were therefore inhibited in their responses to that value when primed with value-related words.

Thus the inhibition effects that were found in this experiment may have been due to an incompatibility between the information that had been activated (i.e., the participants' value systems) and the information to which participants were required to respond (i.e., the egalitarian or individualistic target word). If so, then inducing participants to disagree with a value may lead to similar levels of inhibition when they are asked to respond to information related to that value. This possibility was further investigated in a second study.

Priming Values

The results of the initial study provided evidence that egalitarian and individualistic values are represented in memory as associations between the content of those values and ideas of moral obligation (i.e., what one should or ought to do). In that experiment, individual differences in participants' endorsement of egalitarian and individualistic values predicted the strength of those associations.

Given the premise that both values are represented in memory for many people, it should be possible to manipulate the relative accessibility of those representations. This hypothesis was first tested in an experiment by Katz and Hass (1988). In that experiment, participants first completed either a scale measure of egalitarianism or a scale measure of individualism, and then completed measures of their racial attitudes. Katz and Hass argued that the initial scale that participants completed served to prime, or activate, the corresponding value. That is, if participants had completed a scale of egalitarianism, then egalitarian values should have been activated. Likewise, if they had completed a scale of individualism, then individualistic values should have been activated. In fact, Katz and Hass found support for their prediction that priming participants with egalitarianism led them to express more positive attitudes towards Black Americans, whereas priming them with individualism resulted in their expressing more negative racial attitudes.

However, there are a number of aspects of Katz and Hass' (1988) experiment that cast doubt on the conclusion that differences in expressed racial attitudes were actually caused by the activation of participants' mental representations of egalitarian and individualistic values. As is the case with many explicit measures, the racial attitude scales used by Katz and Hass were vulnerable to demand characteristics. Specifically, having just completed a questionnaire that contained such items as "One should be kind to all people" and "There should be equality for everyone—because we are all human beings," participants may have felt compelled to espouse favorable attitudes toward Black Americans, not because their egalitarian values had been activated but rather because they wanted to respond in a manner consistent with their responses on the first questionnaire. Consequently, it is unclear whether the observed differences in racial attitudes were actually due to an increase in the cognitive accessibility of egalitarian or individualistic values. Indeed, Katz and Hass (1988) did not obtain any independent evidence that representations of egalitarian and individualistic values had been activated as the result of participants' completing the corresponding scales.

The above discussion does not rule out the possibility that values can be activated via priming manipulations. However, as of yet, there have not been any experiments that have directly tested that possibility. As discussed earlier in this chapter, the notion that racial attitudes are associated with values such as egalitarianism and individualism is central to many theories of prejudice (e.g., Gaertner & Dovidio, 1986; Katz et al., 1986; Kinder & Sears, 1981; Rokeach, 1960). One implication of such an idea is that the activation of one's values may result in changes in their attitudes. Thus it becomes important to demonstrate, first, that value representations can become more or less accessible (or activated) due to changes in the environment (e.g., priming).

Therefore, in a second experiment, I tested the hypothesis that value representations can be activated in memory. Participants in this experiment engaged in two tasks. First, they were exposed to a priming manipulation. Specifically, participants were presented with a statement that reflected either egalitarian ("All people are created equal; therefore, they should be treated equally") or individualistic ("People should get what they deserve; therefore, people who work hard should be rewarded") values. They were instructed to spend 10 minutes writing an essay that either supported the statement or opposed it. Following the priming task, they completed the lexical decision task that was used in the first study.

Based on the reasoning outlined above, a number of predictions were made regarding facilitation/inhibition during the lexical decision task. In particular, a similar pattern of facilitation and inhibition was expected to occur in this experiment as occurred in the first study. However, in this experiment, these differences are expected to occur as a function of the priming manipulation, rather than as a function of individual differences in value endorsement. Thus participants in the pro-egalitarian prime condition were expected to experience facilitation for egalitarian target words following value primes. In contrast, participants in the anti-egalitarian prime condition should show inhibition in their responses to those targets. Likewise, participants in the pro-individualism prime condition should show facilitation in their responses to individualistic target words following value primes, whereas those in the anti-individualism prime condition were expected to show inhibition on those trials.

A further prediction, derived from the model shown in Fig. 12.1, is that activating one value should actually inhibit the other. Egalitarian and individualistic values are depicted as negatively associated within the value system. Thus participants primed with pro-egalitarian values should show inhibition in responding to individualistic targets. Likewise, participants primed with pro-individualistic values should show inhibition in their responses to egalitarian targets.

The results of this experiment supported the hypothesis that values can, in fact, be automatically activated. Participants in this experiment who were primed with pro- and anti-egalitarianism demonstrated similar patterns of facilitation and inhibition in responding to egalitarian words, as did participants in the first experiment who did and did not endorse egalitarian values. Likewise, participants in this study, who were primed with pro- and anti-individualism, showed similar patterns of facilitation and inhibition in responding to individualistic words, as did participants in the first experiment who did and did not endorse individualistic values (see Table 12.3).

These findings indicate that individual differences in the extent to which people endorse egalitarian and individualistic values may be roughly simulated by experimentally manipulating the accessibility of those values. This suggests that the accessibility of egalitarian versus individualistic values is likely to vary across time, given different situational cues that make either of the values more salient than the other.

The value-priming manipulation resulted in the target value becoming more accessible, but also in the other value becoming inhibited. This finding, while diverging from the results of the first experiment, is consistent with the model presented in Fig. 12.1, which was inspired in part by Shah et al.'s (in press) goal systems theory. Why did cross-value inhibition occur in this study but not in the first experiment? Let us return for a moment to the original goal systems theory. According to that theory, the stronger the association between one set of means and a particular goal, the greater the likelihood that other potential means will be inhibited. Extending this reasoning

TABLE 12.3

Mean Facilitation Scores (in ms) for Egalitarian and Individualistic Target Words Following Egalitarian Primes as a Function of Level of Primed Position.

Prime	Facilitation of egalitarian targets	Facilitation of individualistic targets
Pro-egalitarian	36.04	−17.78
Anti-egalitarian	19.44	56.39
Pro-individualism	−19.52	39.79
Anti-individualism	36.69	−48.33

to the present study, one possibility is that the priming manipulation made salient a particular solution to the problem of distributing economic resources. If egalitarian means are made salient as a way of achieving the goal of fairness, other alternative means (e.g., individualism) should be inhibited. In the first experiment, chronic levels of value accessibility were measured outside of a particular context (e.g., the distribution of resources), thus no inhibition should have occurred.

Testing for the Effects of Value Accessibility on Intergroup Perception

Given that value accessibility can be effectively manipulated, it is now possible to investigate the effects of activating values on attitudes and stereotypes of different groups. Because many theories (Gaertner & Dovidio, 1986; Katz et al., 1986; Kinder & Sears, 1981) posit an association between values and racial attitudes, one clear prediction is that activating one's values ought to have a direct effect on the accessibility of one's racial attitudes. Thus for a person who stores representations of both egalitarian and individualistic values (and therefore both positive and negative racial attitudes), activating one of these values but not the other may have a direct influence on such attitudes.

Based on the model presented in Fig. 12.1, activating individualistic values should have two distinct effects. First, priming individualism should lead to negative racial attitudes becoming more accessible. Second, priming individualism should result in activation of racial stereotypes. Likewise, activating egalitarian values should also have two specific effects. First, priming egalitarianism should lead to positive racial attitudes becoming more accessible. Second, priming egalitarianism should result in inhibition of racial stereotypes (see also Moskowitz et al., 1999).

I conducted a third experiment to directly test the effects of value activation on the accessibility of racial attitudes and stereotypes. In this experiment, participants were first primed with egalitarian or individualistic values, and then presented with implicit (response time) measures of their attitudes and stereotypes, which should eliminate the possibility of demand characteristics.

Thus participants in this experiment engaged in two tasks. The first task involved a priming manipulation, in which participants wrote essays in support of egalitarianism or individualism. They then went on to complete a response time measure that was designed to assess attitude and stereotype accessibility.

The response time measure was conceptually similar to measures used in previous research to assess racial attitudes and stereotypes (e.g., Dovidio, Evans, & Tyler, 1986). Specifically, participants were subliminally primed with racial category words (e.g., Blacks, African), positive words (e.g., good, like), negative words (e.g., hate, bad), and non-words. Following each prime, participants were required to make an evaluative (i.e., positive or negative) judgment about a target word. The target words varied in both their valence (positive or negative) and their stereotypicality (stereotypic or neutral).

By comparing the amount of time required by participants to respond to each of these types of targets following racial category primes and following non-word control primes, it is possible to obtain a measure of attitude accessibility. That is, if positive racial attitudes have been activated, then participants should experience facilitation for responses to positive target words following racial category primes. Likewise, if negative racial attitudes have been activated, participants should experience facilitation for negative target words following racial category primes.

Similarly, stereotype accessibility can be measured by comparing participants' response latencies for stereotypic target words following racial category primes to those following non-word primes. That is, if participants' stereotypes are accessible, then they should be faster to respond to stereotypic target words when they have been subliminally primed with a racial category label than when they have been primed with a control stimulus.

Following from the model in Fig. 12.1, a number of predictions were generated regarding participants' patterns of facilitation and inhibition on the reaction time measure. First, effects of the priming manipulation on racial attitude accessibility were expected. Specifically, participants who were primed with egalitarian values should be facilitated in their responses to positive targets (and inhibited in their responses to negative targets) following racial category primes. In contrast, participants who were primed with individualistic values should be facilitated in their responses to negative targets (and inhibited in their responses to positive targets) following racial primes.

A second prediction was that the priming manipulation would impact the accessibility of traditional racial stereotypes. In particular, based on Fig. 1 (as well as work by Moskowitz et al., 1999), participants who were primed with individualistic values were expected to experience facilitation in their responses to stereotypic target words following racial category primes. In contrast, participants who were primed with egalitarian values should show inhibition in their responses to those same stereotypic targets.

The results provided partial support for these predictions. As seen in Table 12.4, participants in the individualistic prime condition showed facilitation for both stereotypic and non-stereotypic negative targets, suggesting that general negative attitudes were activated for these participants. However, they also showed facilitation for the positive stereotypic targets, suggesting activation of general stereotypes. Only the positive non-stereotypic targets were inhibited for participants in the individualistic prime condition, suggesting that positive racial attitudes were somewhat inhibited (as long as they did not coincide with the stereotype).

Participants who were primed with egalitarianism showed a quite different pattern of responses. Although responses to non-stereotypic and positive targets were wholly unaffected, these participants showed significant inhibition in responding to negative stereotypic targets. This pattern suggests that priming egalitarianism led to inhibition of the negative aspects (but not the positive aspects) of racial stereotypes (see Table 12.4).

Thus while many theories of values and racial prejudice imply that activating egalitarian versus individualistic values ought to impact the accessibility of positive versus negative attitudes towards Blacks, the results of this experiment paint a more limited picture. Though priming individualistic values did appear to activate negative racial attitudes, the egalitarian value prime had no consistent effect on either positive or negative racial attitudes.

However, evidence was found to support the hypothesis that values and racial stereotypes are associated in memory. Participants who were primed with individualistic values experienced facilitation in responding to words that were associated with the Black stereotype after they had been presented with a subliminal racial prime. In contrast, participants who were primed with egalitarian values experienced inhibition in responding to negative stereotype trials.

The use of an evaluation task rather than a lexical decision task (as used in the first two experiments) is a shift in methodology that warrants some discussion, particularly in light of recent work by Wittenbrink, Judd, and Park (2001). Wittenbrink et al. have demonstrated that the nature of the judgment (e.g., conceptual or evaluative) made in a response time (lexical decision or evaluation) task creates a particular context in which stimuli are processed. Specifically, Wittenbrink et al. found that an evaluative judgment context produces a pattern of generalized prejudice in which out-group primes facilitate negative judgments and in-group primes facilitate positive judgments. In contrast, a conceptual judgment context produces a more specific stereotypic prejudice pattern

TABLE 12.4

Mean Facilitation/Inhibition Scores (in ms) Following Racial Category Prime as a Function of Primed Value and Target Word Valence X Stereotypicality.

	Stereotypic		Non-Stereotypic	
Prime	Positive	Negative	Positive	Negative
Egalitarian	–17.1	–57.5	–6.3	14.7
Individualistic	68.8	85.5	–34.0	34.7

in which the in-group/positive and out-group/negative trials are facilitated only when the targets are stereotype-relevant. In light of Wittenbrink et al.'s (2001) results, it may seem surprising that target stereotypicality had an effect on speed of evaluative judgments in the present study. The apparent inconsistency between the present results and the findings reported by Wittenbrink et al. will need further investigation in order to be resolved. One possibility is that the initial priming task encouraged participants to view the second evaluation task in more conceptual terms. That is, perhaps focusing on an important value led participants to process the words in the evaluation task for meaning as well as for valence, hence the combination of valence and stereotypicality effects for individualism-primed participants.

Egalitarianism and Racial Attitudes

One of the unexpected findings from the third experiment was that activating egalitarian values did not influence the accessibility of positive racial attitudes. This finding is in contrast to prior research (e.g., Katz & Hass, 1988), which suggested that egalitarianism is related to positive attitudes towards Blacks. However, whereas the prior findings rest on correlational evidence, this study constitutes the first experimental work to investigate the impact of priming egalitarianism on implicit measures of attitude accessibility.

The possibility that egalitarianism is not directly associated with positive racial attitudes raises a number of interesting questions. First and foremost, it would seem to necessitate the development of a new explanation for the correlations between the two that have been repeatedly found. One possibility, of course, is that egalitarianism is correlated with positive racial attitudes because of their joint relationship with some third variable (e.g., liberalism, the rejection of racial stereotypes, etc.).

However, it may also be useful to reconsider what egalitarian values ought to dictate when it comes to racial attitudes. Egalitarianism is defined by its emphasis on equality—egalitarian beliefs should dictate equal treatment of all groups. Thus the finding that priming egalitarianism does not increase the accessibility of positive attitudes towards one particular group should perhaps not come as a surprise. Possessing positive attitudes towards any specific group would indicate the same lack of equality as possessing negative attitudes. As the results of the third study suggest, egalitarianism may play a different role in determining racial attitudes than has previously been suggested. For example, egalitarianism may be more closely related to a tendency to avoid using superficial characteristics (such as race) in forming evaluations than to a tendency to form globally positive evaluations.

Reflections on the Basis of Value-Attitude and Value-Stereotype Associations

One question worth raising concerns the origin of value-attitude and value-stereotype associations. Two possibilities seem plausible, both of which can be considered in the context of past research on cognitive consistency (Heider, 1946; McGuire, 1960a, 1960b; Wyer, 1973, 1974). The first explanation is that attitudes and stereotypes may develop as a function of people's values. That is, people evaluate others based on whether or not they conform to or violate important values (e.g,. Rokeach, 1961). This hypothesis can be extended to apply to stereotypes—that is, that people develop social stereotypes based on attributes that indicate conformity or violation of important values. By developing value-congruent attitudes and stereotype-relevant beliefs, perceivers maintain consistency among their beliefs.

However, there is a second possibility that is worth considering. Perhaps values are not the basis for developing racial attitudes and stereotypes. Rather, perhaps they are the basis for justifying those attitudes and stereotypes. Given that most individuals prefer to view themselves as righteous and fair, acknowledging that they have negative attitudes and stereotypes about out-groups may create an unpleasant state of inconsistency. In order to restore consistency, people may call upon higher-order beliefs (e.g., values) in order to reinforce their view that their out-group attitudes and stereotypes are justified (for similar arguments, see Kristiansen & Zanna, 1988). This sort of rationalization or justification process might result in associations between individualistic values and negative racial attitudes. The fact that people may be less likely to feel compelled to justify positive racial attitudes is also consistent with the finding that egalitarianism and positive racial attitudes are not associated in memory.

A justification process can also account for the relationship between values and racial stereotypes. That is, values may also be used to justify or discredit racial stereotypes. For example, drawing on individualistic values may help to justify stereotypic notions that Blacks are lazy, while considering egalitarian values may reinforce the belief that differences among races are due to situational factors. Furthermore, theories such as social identity theory (Tajfel, 1981; Tajfel & Turner, 1979) and, more recently, system justification theory (Jost & Banaji, 1994; Jost & Stangor, 1997; Yzerbyt, Rocher, & Schadron, 1997) can be extended to generate the hypothesis that negative stereotypes become associated with values through a justification or rationalization process. That is, people are motivated to perceive out-groups in a negative light. As a result, they will tend to impute negative qualities onto the out-group, including characteristics that imply violations of important values (e.g., individualism). Likewise, rationalization or justification processes may lead unprejudiced individuals to associate their rejection of racial stereotypes with egalitarian values. That is, people may use egalitarian values to bolster, or reinforce, their non-stereotypic beliefs (Abelson, 1959, 1968).

The results of the three experiments reported here do not speak to how associations between values, attitudes, and stereotypes are formed, but both possibilities offered here fit well within existing theories of cognitive consistency.

CONCLUSION

The drive to maintain consistency in our beliefs is a powerful one. Though social cognitive approaches have addressed inconsistency resolution in the domains of person impressions and attitudes, it has thus far neglected the issue of inconsistencies among personal values. The research here represents only an initial step toward a better understanding of how values are represented in memory and how they exert influence on out-group attitudes and stereotypes.

Though only preliminary evidence, the data discussed here suggest that motives for cognitive consistency do extend to the realm of values. Further, models of how inconsistencies among other types of beliefs can be represented in memory seem to be well-suited to describing the nature of value representations. Early work growing out of Wyer's (Wyer & Hartwick, 1980, 1984) "bin model" and later work on goal inconsistencies (Shah et al, in press) point to the important role that accessibility plays in resolving conflicts among different beliefs. Thus it may well turn out that the conflict between our convictions that "all men are created equal" and that "only the fittest shall survive" will continue to influence our perceptions in apparently inconsistent ways, depending on the belief that we are reminded of at a particular moment in time.

REFERENCES

Abelson, R. P. (1959). Modes of resolution in belief dilemmas. *Journal of Conflict Resolution, 3,* 343–352.

Abelson, R. P. (1968). Psychological implication. In R. P. Abelson, E. Aronson, W. J. McGuire, T. M. Newcomb, M. J. Rosenberg, & P. H. Tannenbaum (Eds.), *Theories of cognitive consistency: A sourcebook* (pp. 112–139). Chicago: Rand McNally.

Allport, G. W. (1954). *The nature of prejudice.* Cambridge, MA: Addison-Wesley.

Bargh, J. A. (1989). Conditional automaticity: Varieties of automatic influence in social perception and cognition. In J. S. Uleman & J. A. Bargh (Eds.), *Unintended thought* (pp. 1–51). New York: Guilford Press.

Bargh, J. A. (1997). The automaticity of everyday life. In R. S. Wyer, Jr. (Ed.), *Advances in social cognition* (Vol. 10, pp. 1–62). Mahwah, NJ: Lawrence Erlbaum Associates.

Bargh, J. A., Chaiken, S., Govender, R., & Pratto, F. (1992). The generality of the automatic attitude activation effect. *Journal of Personality and Social Psychology, 62,* 893–912.

Bargh, J. A., & Chartrand, T. L. (2000). The mind in the middle: A practical guide to priming and automaticity research. In H. T. Reis & C. M. Judd (Eds.) Handbook of research methods in social and personality psychology (pp. 253–285). New York: Cambridge University Press.

Bargh, J. A., & Pietromonaco, P. (1982). Automatic information processing and social perception: The influence of trait information presented outside of conscious awareness on impression formation. Journal of Personality and Social Psychology, 43, 437–449.

Bem, D. J. (1972). Self-perception theory. In L. Berkowitz (Ed.), Advances in experimental social psychology (Vol. 6, pp. 1–62). San Diego, CA: Academic Press.

Biernat, M., Vescio, T. K., Theno, S. A., & Crandall, C. S. (1996). Values and prejudice: Toward understanding the impact of American values on outgroup attitudes. In C. Seligman, J. M. Olson, & M. P. Zanna, (Eds.), The psychology of values: The Ontario symposium (Vol. 8, pp. 153–189). Mahwah, NJ: Lawrence Erlbaum Associates.

Devine, P. G. (1989). Stereotypes and prejudice: Their automatic and controlled components. Journal of Personality and Social Psychology, 56, 5–18.

Dijksterhuis, A., & van Knippenberg, A. (1996). The knife that cuts both ways: Facilitated and inhibited access to traits as a result of stereotype activation. Journal of Experimental Social Psychology, 32, 271–288.

Dovidio, J. F., Evans, N., & Tyler, R. B. (1986). Racial stereotypes: The contents of their cognitive representations. Journal of Experimental Social Psychology, 22, 22–37.

Eagly, A. H., & Chaiken, S. (1993). The psychology of attitudes. Orlando, FL: Harcourt-Brace.

Fazio, R. H. (1986). How do attitudes guide behavior? In R. M. Sorrentino & E. T. Higgins (Eds.), Handbook of motivation and cognition: Foundations of social behavior (pp. 204–243). New York: Guilford Press.

Fazio, R. H. (1989). On the power and functionality of attitudes: The role of attitude accessibility. In A. R. Pratkanis, S. J. Breckler, & A. G. Greenwald (Eds.), Attitude structure and function (pp. 153–179). Hillsdale, NJ: Lawrence Erlbaum Associates.

Fazio, R. H. (1995). Attitudes as object evaluation associations: Determinants, consequences, and correlates of attitude accessibility. In R. E. Petty & J. A. Krosnick (Eds.), Attitude strength: Antecedents and consequences. Ohio State University series on attitudes and persuasion (Vol. 4, pp. 247–282). Hillsdale, NJ: Lawrence Erlbaum Associates.

Fazio, R. H., Chen, J., McDonel, E. C., & Sherman, S. J. (1982). Attitude accessibility, attitude behavior consistency, and the strength of the object evaluation association. Journal of Experimental Social Psychology, 18, 339–357.

Fazio, R. H., Powell, M. C., & Herr, P. M. (1983). Toward a process model of the attitude behavior relation: Accessing one's attitude upon mere observation of the attitude object. Journal of Personality and Social Psychology, 44, 723–735.

Fazio, R. H., Powell, M. C., & Williams, C. J. (1989). The role of attitude accessibility in the attitude to behavior process. Journal of Consumer Research, 16, 280–288.

Fazio, R. H., Sanbonmatsu, D. M., Powell, M. C., & Kardes, F. R. (1986). On the automatic activation of attitudes. *Journal of Personality and Social Psychology, 50,* 229–238.

Fazio, R. H., & Williams, C. J. (1986). Attitude accessibility as a moderator of the attitude perception and attitude behavior relations: An investigation of the 1984 presidential election. *Journal of Personality and Social Psychology, 51,* 505–514.

Festinger, L. (1957). *A theory of cognitive dissonance.* Evanston, IL: Row, Peterson.

Gaertner, S. L., & Dovidio, J. F. (1986). The aversive form of racism. In J. F. Dovidio & S. L. Gaertner (Eds.), *Prejudice, discrimination, and racism* (pp. 61–89). New York: Academic Press.

Hamilton, D. L., Driscoll, D. M., & Worth, L. T. (1989) Cognitive organization of impressions: Effects of incongruency in complex representations. *Journal of Personality and Social Psychology, 57,* 925–939.

Heider, F. (1946). Attitudes and cognitive organization. *Journal of Psychology, 21,* 107–112.

Henninger, M., & Wyer, R. S. (1976). The recognition and elimination of inconsistencies among syllogistically related beliefs: Some new light on the Socratic effect. *Journal of Personality and Social Psychology, 34,* 680–693.

Higgins, E. T., Rholes, W. S., & Jones, C. R. (1977). Category accessibility and impression formation. *Journal of Experimental Social Psychology, 13,* 141–154.

Insko, C. A., Nacoste, R. W., & Moe, J. L. (1983). Belief congruence and racial discrimination: Review of the evidence and critical evaluation. *European Journal of Social Psychology, 13,* 153–174.

Jost, J. T., & Banaji, M. R. (1994). The role of stereotyping in system justification and the production of false consciousness. *British Journal of Social Psychology, 33,* 1–27.

Jost, J. T., & Stangor, C. (1997). Commentary: Individual, group, and system levels of analysis and their relevance for stereotyping and intergroup relations. In R. Spears, P. J. Oakes, N. Ellemers, & S. A. Haslam (Eds.), *The social psychology of stereotyping and group life* (pp. 336–358). Oxford, UK: Blackwell.

Katz, I., & Hass, R. G. (1988). Racial ambivalence and American value conflict: Correlational and priming studies of dual cognitive structures. *Journal of Personality and Social Psychology, 55,* 893–905.

Katz, I., Wackenhut, J., & Hass, R. G. (1986). In S. L. Gaertner & J. F. Dovidio (Eds.), *Prejudice, Discrimination, and Racism* (pp. 35–59). New York: Harcourt Brace.

Kinder, D. R., & Sears, D. O. (1981). Prejudice and politics: Symbolic racism versus racial threats to the good life. *Journal of Personality and Social Psychology, 40,* 414–431.

Klein, S. B., & Loftus, J. (1990). Rethinking the role of organization in person memory: An independent trace storage model. *Journal of Personality and Social Psychology, 59,* 400–410.

Kristiansen, C. M., & Zanna, M. P. (1988). Justifying attitudes by appealing to values: A functional perspective. *British Journal of Social Psychology, 27,* 247–256.

Lipset, S. M. (1963). *The first new Nation; The United States in historical and comparative perspective.* New York: Basic Books.

Lipset, S. M., & Schneider, W. (1978). The Bakke case: How would it be decided at the bar of public opinion? *Public Opinion, 1,* 38–44.

Logan, G. D. (1980). Attention and automaticity in Stroop and priming tasks: Theory and data. *Cognitive Psychology, 12,* 523–553.

Macrae, C. N., Bodenhausen, G. V., & Milne, A. B. (1995). The dissection of selection in person perception: Inhibitory processes in social stereotyping. *Journal of Personality and Social Psychology, 69,* 397–407.

McConahay, J. B., & Hough, J. C. Jr. (1976). Symbolic racism. *Journal of Social Issues, 32,* 23–45.

McGuire, W. J. (1960a). Cognitive consistency and attitude change. *Journal of Abnormal and Social Psychology, 60,* 345–353.

McGuire, W. J. (1960b). A syllogistic analysis of cognitive relationships. In C. I. Hovland & M. J. Rosenberg (Eds.), *Attitude organization and change: An analysis of consistency among attitude components* (pp. 65–111). New Haven, CT: Yale University Press.

Milner, P. M. (1957). The cell assembly: Mark II. *Psychological Review, 64,* 242–252.

Moskowitz, G. B. (2001). Preconscious control and compensatory cognition. In G. B. Moskowitz (Ed.), *Cognitive social psychology: The Princeton Symposium on the Legacy and Future of Social Cognition* (pp. 333–358). Mahwah, NJ: Lawrence Erlbaum Associates.

Moskowitz, G. B., Gollwitzer, P. M., Wasel, W., & Schaal, B. (1999). Preconscious control of stereotype activation through chronic egalitarian goals. *Journal of Personality and Social Psychology, 77,* 167–184.

Moskowitz, G. B., Salomon, A. R., & Taylor, C. M. (2000). Preconsciously controlling stereotyping: Implicitly activated egalitarian goals prevent the activation of stereotypes. *Social Cognition, 18,* 151–177.

Neely, J. H. (1977). Semantic priming and retrieval from lexical memory: Roles of inhibitionless spreading activation and limited capacity attention. *Journal of Experimental Psychology: General, 106,* 226–254.

Posner, M. I. (1978). *Chromometric explorations of the mind.* Hillsdale, NJ: Lawrence Erlbaum Associates.

Powell, M. C., & Fazio, R. H. (1984). Attitude accessibility as a function of repeated attitudinal expression. *Personality and Social Psychology Bulletin, 10,* 139–148.

Pratkanis, A. R., & Greenwald, A. G. (1989). A sociocognitive model of attitude structure and function. In L. Berkowitz (Ed.), *Advances in experimental social psychology* (Vol. 22, pp. 245–285). San Diego, CA: Academic Press.

Rokeach, M. (1960). *The open and closed mind.* New York: Basic Books.

Rokeach, M. (1961). Belief versus race as determinants of social distance: Comment on Triandis' paper. *Journal of Abnormal and Social Psychology, 62,* 187–188.

Rokeach, M. (1968a). *Beliefs, attitudes, and values: A theory of organization and change.* San Francisco: Jossey Bass.

Rokeach, M. (1968b). A theory of organization and change within value attitude systems. *Journal of Social Issues, 24,* 13–33.

Schwartz, S. H., & Bilsky, W. (1987). Toward a universal psychological structure o f human values. *Journal of Personality and Social Psychology, 53,* 550–562.

Schwartz, S. H., & Bilsky, W. (1990). Toward a theory of the universal content and structure of values: Extensions and cross-cultural replications. *Journal of Personality and Social Psychology, 58,* 878–891.

Sedikides, C. (1990). Effects of fortuitously activated constructs versus activated communication goals on person impressions. *Journal of Personality and Social Psychology, 58,* 397–408.

Shah, J. Y., & Kruglanski, A. W. (2000). Aspects of goal networks: Implications for self-regulation. In M. Boekaerts & P. R. Pintrich (Eds.), *Handbook of self-regulation* (pp. 85–110). San Diego, CA: Academic Press.

Shah, J. Y., Kruglanski, A. W., & Friedman, R. (in press). Goal systems theory: Integrating the cognitive and motivational aspects of self-regulation. To appear in J. Olson & M. Zanna (Eds.), *The Ontario Symposium on Personality and Social Psychology.* Mahwah, NJ: Lawrence Erlbaum Associates.

Shallice, T. (1972). Dual functions of consciousness. *Psychological Review, 79,* 383–393.

Smith, E. R., & DeCoster, J. (2000). Dual-process models in social and cognitive psychology: Conceptual integration and links to underlying memory systems. *Personality and Social Psychology Review, 4,* 108–131.

Srull, T. K., & Wyer, R. S., Jr. (1979). The role of category accessibility in the interpretation of information about persons: Some determinants and implications. *Journal of Personality and Social Psychology, 37,* 1660–1672.

Tajfel, H. (1981). Social stereotypes and social groups. In J. C. Turner & H. Giles (Eds.), *Intergroup Behavior.* Oxford, UK: Basil Blackwell.

Tajfel, H., & Turner, J. C. (1979). An integrative theory of intergroup conflict. In W. G. Austin & S. Worchel (Eds.), *The social psychology of intergroup relations* (pp. 33–47). Monterey, CA: Brooks/Cole.

Tetlock, P. E. (1989). Structure and function in political belief systems. In A. R. Pratkanis & S. J. Breckler, (Eds.), *Attitude structure and function. The third Ohio State University volume on attitudes and persuasion* (pp. 129–151). Hillsdale, NJ: Lawrence Erlbaum Associates.

Tetlock, P. E., Peterson, R. S., & Lerner, J. S. (1996). Revising the value pluralism model: Incorporating social content and context postulates. In C. Seligman & J. M. Olson (Eds.), *The psychology of values: The Ontario symposium* (Vol. 8, pp. 25–51). Mahwah, NJ: Lawrence Erlbaum Associates.

Tetlock, P. E. (1986). A value pluralism model of ideological reasoning. *Journal of Personality and Social Psychology, 50,* 819–827.

Wilson, T. D., Lindsey, S., & Schooler, T. Y. (2000). A model of dual attitudes. *Psychological Review, 107,* 101–126.

Wittenbrink, B., Judd, C. M., & Park, B. (2001). Evaluative versus conceptual judgments in automatic stereotyping and prejudice. *Journal of Experimental Social Psychology, 37,* 244–252.

Wyer, R. S., Jr. (1973). Category ratings as "subjective expected values": Implications for attitude formation and change. *Psychological Review, 80,* 446–467.

Wyer, R. S., Jr. (1974). *Cognitive organization and change: An information-processing approach.* Hillsdale, NJ: Lawrence Erlbaum Associates.

Wyer, R. S., Jr., & Goldberg, L. (1970). A probabilistic analysis of the relationships among beliefs and attitudes. *Psychological Review, 77,* 100–120.

Wyer, R. S., Jr., & Hartwick, J. (1980). The role of information retrieval and conditional inference processes in belief formation and change. In L. Berkowitz (Ed.), *Advances in experimental social psychology* (Vol. 13, pp. 241–284). San Diego, CA: Academic Press.

Wyer, R. S., Jr., & Hartwick, J. (1984). The recall and use of belief statements as bases for judgments: Some determinants and implications. *Journal of Experimental Social Psychology, 20,* 65–85.

Wyer, R. S., Jr., & Srull, T. K. (1989). *Memory and cognition in its social context.* Hillsdale, NJ: Lawrence Erlbaum Associates.

Yzerbyt, V., Rocher, S., & Schadron, G. (1997). Stereotypes as explanations: A subjective essentialistic view of group perception. In R. Spears, P. J. Oakes, N. Ellemers, & S. A. Haslam (Eds.), *The social psychology of stereotyping and group life* (pp. 20–50). Oxford, UK: Blackwell.

Zanna, M. P., & Rempel, J. K. (1986). Attitudes: A new look at an old concept. In D. Bar Tal & A. W. Kruglanski (Eds.), *The social psychology of knowledge* (pp. 315–334). Cambridge, UK: Cambridge University Press.

Author Index

A

Aarts, H., 56, *72*
Abelson, R. P., 21, *22*, 170, *176*, *177*, 252, 257, 284, *284*
Abrahams, D., 115, *129*
Abrams, D., 145, *152*
Ajzen, I., 190, *205*
Allport, F. H., 189, *205*
Allport, G. W., 135, *150*, 157, *176*, 184, 187, 202, *205*, 264, *284*
Ambady, N., 145, 146, *153*
Andersen, S. M., 110, *124*, *125*
Anderson, C., 245, 251, 252, *256*, *258*
Anderson, C. A., 161, *176*, *179*
Anderson, M. C., 41, 42, *46*
Anderson, N. H., 26, *46*, 156, *176*
Arbib, M., 70, *74*
Arbuckle, T., 110, *126*
Aronson, J., 238, *260*
Aronson, V., 115, *129*
Asch, S. E., 26, 36, *46*, 110, *124*, 156, *176*, 182, 185, 187, 201, 203, *205*, 238, *256*
Atkinson, J. W., 164, *178*
Austin, G. A., 220, *231*
Ayduk, O. N., 219, *233*

B

Back, K., 239, *257*
Baddeley, A., 100, *124*
Baltes, P. B., 238, *260*
Banaji, M. R., 104, *126*, 170, *176*, *177*, 238, 245, *258*, *259*, 283, *286*
Bardach, L., 36, *46*

Bargh, J. A., 30, 38, 44, *46*, 54, 62, 67, 70, 71, 72, *73*, *74*, 102, 110, *124*, *126*, *130*, 132, *150*, 195, *205*, 213, *235*, 238, 239, 241, 242, 251, *256*, *259*, *261*, 269, 270, 272, *284*, *285*
Barnes, B. D., 149, *150*
Baron, R. S., 185, 186, 190, 192 ,194, 195, *205*
Barsalou, L. W., 166, *176*
Bassili, J. N., 99, 101, 115, 116, 119, *124*, *125*, 218, *231*
Baumeister, R. F., 146, *150*, 164, *176*
Bazerman, M., 248, *260*
Begg, I. M., 198, *207*
Belli, R. F., 56, 57, 58, *77*
Bem, D. J., 212, *231*, 265, *285*
Berelson, B., 15, *23*
Bergman, A., 149, *150*
Berkowitz, L., 98, *125*
Berscheid, E., 110, 113, *126*
Bessenoff, G. R., 31, 32, *49*
Biernat, M., 137, 145, *150*, 264, *285*
Biller, B., 55, *76*
Bilsky, W., 271, *288*
Birrell, B., 202, *208*
Bjork, E. L., 41, *46*
Bjork, R. A., 41, *46*
Blanchard, F. A., 187, *206*
Blank, A., 105, *127*
Blascovich, J., 164, *176*
Blau, P., 239, *256*
Bless, H., 53, 54, 55–57, 60, 61, 62–65, 67, 71, 72, *73*, *75*, 76, 81, 88, 89, *93*, *94*
Bobo, L., 191, *208*
Bobrow, D. G., 31, *46*
Bodenhausen, G. V., 51, 54, 64, *73*, 134–136, 139–141, 143, 144, 146–148, *150–153*, 156, 157, *176*, *180*, 182,

291

Weber, R., 27, 36, *46*
Weber, S. J., 111, *129*
Webster, D. M., 86, 93, 212, 213, *233, 235*
Wegener, D. T., 17, *24,* 105, 118, 120, *128, 129*
Wegner, D., 238, *261*
Wegner, D. M., 102, *130,* 241, 242, *261*
Welbourne, J. L., 159, *180*
Wetherell, M. S., 142, 148, *154,* 164, *180*
Wheeler, L., 110, *127*
White, J. D., 27, *50*
White, R. W., 164, 168, *180*
White, T. L., 240, *256*
Whitney, P., 111, *130*
Wicklund, R. A., 86, *95,* 204, *208,* 240, *261*
Wieczorkowska, G., 160–163, 173, 174, *178*
Williams, C. J., 194, 195, 198, *206,* 269, 270, 272, *286*
Wilson, D., 81, *94*
Wilson, T. D., 81, *95,* 213, *235,* 269, *288*
Wing-hong Lam, T., 220, *235*
Winkielman, P., 53, 56–58, 68, 69, 71, *74–77*
Winter, D. G., 239, *261*
Winter, L., 99, 111, 115, *130*
Wittenbrink, B., 198, *209,* 281, 282, *289*
Woike, B. A., 244, *261*
Wong, J., 239, 252, *257*
Wong, K. F. E., 81, *95*
Woodworth, R. S., 18, *24,* 225, *235*
Worth, L. T., 43, *47,* 266, *286*
Wrong, D. H., 240, *261*
Wundt, W., 134, *154*

Wyer, N. A., 164, *176*
Wyer, R. S., 17, 21, *24,* 26–29, 33, 34, 41, 45, *48–50,* 51–54, 56, 65–68, 71, *73, 76, 77,* 79, 80, 90, *94, 95,* 103, 106, 107, 110, 111, 120, 122, *127–130,* 132, 133, 136, 137, *153,* 154, 156–159, 164, *176, 177, 180,* 182, 183, 188, 190, 194, 202, 206, *208, 209,* 212, 213, 231, *234, 235,.*238, *257, 258, 260, 261,* 265, 266, 269, 283, 284, *286, 288, 289*

Y

Yee, P., 187, *206*
Young, R. C., 245, 251, *258*
Yzerbyt, V. Y., 159, 170, *179, 180,* 283, *289*

Z

Zadny, J., 27, *50*
Zajonc, R. B., 68, *77,* 115, 118, *127, 130,* 185, 189, 194, *209,* 238, *261*
Zanna, M. P., 270, 283, *287, 289*
Zarate, M. A., 157, *179*
Zebrowitz, L. A., 113, *128, 130*
Zingmark, B., 111, *130*

Subject Index

A

Accessibility, 51–72, 79–92, 122, 132–133, 143, 266, 269–284, *see also* Availability heuristic
Accessibility experiences, 53–61
   diagnosticity of accessibility experiences, 57–58
Accountability, 188–189, 252–253
Anchoring, 80–92
Anxiety and social perception, 191–195, 198
Assimilation effects, 53, 62–66, 80–88
Associative processing, 119–120, *see also* Person memory model
Attention, 27
Attitude change, 10–11, 13–20
Attitudes, 10–11, 168, 270–272
Attribution, 99, 222, *see also* Spontaneity of social impressions
Automaticity, 69–70, 102, 245–246
   automatic behavior, 69–70
Availability heuristic, 34, 56, *see also* Accessibility

B

Bystander inaction, 132, 255

C

Categorization, 62–66, 222–223
Cognitive complexity, 243–244
Cognitive consistency, 17–20, 26, 146, 265–266
Cognitive efficiency, 26–27, 31, 202
Cognitive load, 38–40, 43, 106, 201–203
Confidence in social judgment, 121–122

Contrast effects, 53, 62–66, 88–92
Controlled processing, 198–201
Conversational norms, 65, 90–92
Correction processes, 120–121, 203
Counterfactual thinking, 223–227

D

Depersonalization, 144
Dual-process models, 104–105

E

Ease of retrieval, *see* Accessibility experiences
Egalitarianism, 191, 263–265, 268–284, *see also* Values
Encoding processes, 27
   encoding flexibility model, 31–32
Entitativity, 158–176
Exemplars, effects on judgment, 62–65
Expectancies, 25–45 *see also* Stereotypes
   incongruency effect, 28–44, 121, 156–157, 182
Expectancy-value models, 217–218

F

Face processing, *see* Impression formation
False consensus effect, 188
Fluency of processing, 53, 68–70, *see also* Accessibility experiences

G

Goals and information processing, 137, 142–144, 213–214, 267–268
Group perception, 155–176